A Practical Introduction to Econometric Methods

A Practical Introduction to Econometric Methods: Classical and Modern

Patrick K. Watson

and

Sonja S. Teelucksingh

The University of the West Indies Press
Barbados • Jamaica • Trinidad and Tobago

University of the West Indies Press
1A Aqueduct Flats Mona
Kingston 7 Jamaica

06 05 04 03 02 5 4 3 2 1

CATALOGUING IN PUBLICATION DATA

Watson, Patrick K.
A practical introduction to econometric methods: classical and modern / Patrick K. Watson and Sonja S. Teelucksingh
p. cm.
Includes bibliographical references.
ISBN: 976-640-122-5

1. Econometrics. I. Teelucksingh, Sonja S. II. Title.

HB139.W37 2002 330.028 dc-21

Cover design by Robert Harris.

Book design by Roy Barnhill.

Contents

Foreword

A course in econometrics forms an integral part of every economics student's degree program. Since its formal development in the 1930s the field has expanded so significantly that we can probably make a distinction between "classical" and "modern" econometrics. The vast quantity of theory and techniques for handling time series, cross-sectional and panel data makes it difficult for the teacher of econometrics to select a range of topics suitable for students at the undergraduate level. Indeed, a course in econometrics taken in the 1970s is significantly different from one taken today. In addition, the development of computer programmes has opened up the field to the use of "sophisticated" techniques of estimation, testing and simulation. Students of econometrics therefore need to be guided through the range of techniques that have developed over the years.

This text on a *Practical Introduction to Econometrics Methods: Classical and Modern* by Patrick Watson and Sonja Teelucksingh provides undergraduate students with a selected survey of econometric techniques used by economists today. The text focuses on time series econometrics by developing standard econometric techniques in the first half of the presentation and then presenting recent developments in the field in the second half. Both static and dynamic econometric techniques are covered in the text.

A very useful aspect of the text is the use of data from Caribbean countries to illustrate the application of the various techniques. This approach makes the text lively and highly relevant to students and researchers who are unaware of some of the techniques. With the wide availability of econometric software packages such as EViews, PCGive and MicroFIT, readers may try their hands at some of the exercises provided in the text. It is, however, very important that readers understand the underlying principles which guide the use of the range of diagnostic testing procedures produced by these econometric programs. It is quite easy to enter data into a computer program, press a few keys and get a computer printout. The correct use and interpretation of the various techniques and testing procedures are vital to good econometric practice. The good blend of theory and application given in this text should be useful to applied economists and students. The authors provide a list of references that readers can consult for further in-depth analysis.

This text is therefore useful to the advanced undergraduate student in economics and related disciplines. Economists who have not kept up with recent developments in econometrics should find the last six chapters very useful. Graduate students who are not specializing in econometrics will find that the text is a good starting point for a course in quantitative methods.

Andrew S. Downes
Professor of Economics and University Director
Sir Arthur Lewis Institute of Social and Economic Studies
The University of the West Indies
Cave Hill, Barbados

Preface

This book grew out of 20 years of teaching courses in econometrics at the University of the West Indies and the application of econometric methods to Caribbean economic problems. It is aimed principally at final year undergraduate students of economics or those at the graduate level doing econometrics for the first time. Practising economists, especially those who are unfamiliar with the modern techniques, will also find this text very useful due to its great emphasis on practical applications to the underlying theoretical concepts. A prerequisite to an understanding of the content is a course in the elements of statistical theory and method, such as exists for most undergraduate economics degree programmes. Some basic knowledge of matrix algebra will also be assumed, and some of it is covered in the body of the text. All the main theoretical concepts are illustrated with the use of the EViews econometric software.

Chapters 1 to 8 cover the classical material and this is structured in such a way that it can be delivered in one semester. The rest of the book (chapters 9 to 15) covers the modern material and may also be delivered in one semester. It is also possible to design a one-semester course that covers the essential elements of both classical and modern econometrics and this may be suitable to graduate students who are doing econometrics for the first time. One suggested programme is chapters 1, 2, 4, 5, 6, 12, 14 and 15.

This book has two objectives. The first, and more important of the two, is to prepare students to do applied econometric work. It is largely for this reason that almost every theoretical concept introduced is illustrated using actual data and a very popular, easy-to-use econometric package: EViews. The data used are stored in an EXCEL file called WT_DATA.XLS which is available on request from either of the authors or, preferably, from the website www.uwi.tt/fss/econ. It is advisable to work through all of the illustrations and the practical questions that follow each chapter.

Notwithstanding the emphasis on application, the book is based solidly on econometric theory. Indeed, it is the second objective of this book to anchor the student in theory so that he or she may proceed, using the elements acquired here as a base, to do a more advanced graduate-type programme in econometric theory and practice with some ease.

The main inspiration for this book was the many students who, over the years, endured the delivery of courses in econometrics at the St Augustine campus of the University of the West Indies. During that time computing power grew in size and became more accessible. The days of the cards and the mainframe and the trudging over to the University Computer Centre are over, giving way to the laptop, the desktop and modern packages like EViews. But the joy of teaching and indeed learning from these students remains the same. To these unwitting participants in this exercise, we express our deepest gratitude. As always, we owe a great debt to our respective families, who stood by us in the many trying months dedicated to the production of this book, from the moment it was conceived right up to its realization.

Patrick K. Watson (pkwatson@fss.uwi.tt)
Sonja S. Teelucksingh (ssteelucksingh@fss.uwi.tt)
St Augustine
Trinidad and Tobago

Introduction

What Is This Thing Called Econometrics?

INTRODUCTION

Econometrics is about measurement in economics. It is not the only area of study in economics concerned with measurement but it is probably the best known. It has been used, directly and indirectly, to answer questions like: "What is the value of the marginal propensity to consume (mpc) of the residents of Tobago?" It can also be used to test hypotheses about the Tobago mpc: is it greater than 90%? Is it greater than the mpc of Trinidad? It can be used to forecast economic variables or to answer burning policy questions like: "How much does the government need to invest in order for unemployment to be reduced to 6.5%?" and so on. A study of econometrics promises a lot, but does it deliver the goods as promised?

Unfortunately, the use of econometrics is no guarantee that questions like those just asked will be answered satisfactorily. The first caution is that, if the tools of the trade are employed incorrectly, then the answers given to economic questions will reflect this basic inadequacy. Second, there are 101 problems associated less with the methods than with the economic data to which they are applied, so that great caution should always be used in interpreting the results obtained.

To a large extent, this book is concerned with these two problems: it is concerned first with introducing the student to econometric methods, with letting him or her know the great promise that they hold. At the same time, it is concerned with putting the student on guard against the many pitfalls that can (and often do) result from misapplication of these methods or from a misunderstanding of their inherent limitations.

CLASSICAL AND MODERN ECONOMETRICS

The term "econometrics" was coined in the 1930s when the Econometrics Society was founded. The society included such visionaries as Ragnar Frisch and Jan Tinbergen (both Nobel Laureates). At that time it was defined as almost anything requiring the application of mathematical and statistical methods to economic analysis. The fundamental tool was then, and remains even to today, regression analysis.

But even from the outset, the discipline had its detractors, not the least of whom was another visionary, John Maynard Keynes (1939). He, and others, pointed to the serious weaknesses in economic data that might (and indeed did) lead to tremendous abuse. It is possible to explain the entire history of the discipline as one of responding to concerns raised by such illustrious individuals, resulting in the elaboration of more and more sophisticated methods. By the 1950s and 1960s, a body of knowledge had become firmly established due principally to the work of the Cowles Commission (to which Frisch and Tinbergen contributed, as well as other Nobel Laureates like Koopmans, Haavelmo and others). It is this body of knowledge that fills the pages of the earlier editions of classic textbooks, such as Johnston and Dinardo (1997), Kmenta (1986) and others and is what will be described as classical econometrics. This will be the (principal) preoccupation of Part I of this work.

Classical econometrics was subject to a lot of abuse – see Watson (1987) for some Caribbean examples. Such abuse brought the discipline into disrepute and many of the sceptics, agnostics and avowed nonbelievers tore it to shreds. In particular, there was the widespread assertion that the methods could be used to provide any interpretation of economic reality that the economist wanted to justify. This was a highly unsatisfactory situation.

Many econometricians began the work of "making things right", and perhaps the leading lights in this "fightback" were those working at the London School of Economics and Political Science (the LSE) ably led by Dennis Sargan. In a seminal article, Davidson, Hendry, Sbra and Yeo (1978) introduced the principal features of the general-to-specific methodology to the world. The matters raised in this paper were espoused in other publications, including the very readable one by Hendry (1980), and were followed up by other research that eventually led to the development of the concept of cointegration, which has had an indelible effect on the discipline. The seminal paper on cointegration is Engle and Granger (1987).

Econometrics has gone through a veritable revolution with these advances and, to some extent, the critics have been silenced – at least temporarily. It is these most recent developments that will be treated in Part II of this work under the rubric of "Modern Econometrics".

In the final analysis, classical and modern econometrics are not in competition with each other. Rather, modern econometrics must be seen as an outgrowth of the classical methods, which still remain fundamentally valid. From this point of view alone, a study of classical econometrics remains a necessary exercise and, at the very least, is an indispensable introduction to a proper study of the modern methods.

EXERCISES

1. Explain the meaning of the word "econometrics".
2. Draw up a list of some economic issues to which you might wish to apply econometric methods. Discuss with your class instructor the feasibility of doing so.
3. Are the objectives of "modern econometrics" different from those of "classical econometrics"?

Part I

Classical

CHAPTER 1

The General Linear Regression Model

MODELS IN ECONOMICS AND ECONOMETRICS

Economics is about models and these models are usually expressed in very general terms. Econometric methods provide a way to obtain more precise expressions of such models. What does "more precise" mean? It means giving numerical values to concepts like the marginal propensity to consume, the multiplier and so on. It means putting numerical values into the model so that it may be used to make numerical forecasts of key economic variables that may be used by a policy maker. In order to do these things, the economist must confront the theory with data, a task that itself is plagued with difficulties. But one thing at a time!

There are some very useful papers on econometric models (the term used for economic models when they are confronted with data using econometric methods) which explain to the uninitiated the use and potential of such models. See, for example, Suits (1962) and Sowey (1985). Below is a sketch of a model that will be used throughout this book to illustrate the many methods that will be discussed. It is essentially a Keynesian-type open economy model that shows, among other things, the interaction of the multiplier and the accelerator.

Consumption function:

$$C_p = f_1(Y, i, \ldots) \quad \textbf{(1.1)}$$

Import function:

$$M = f_2(Y, p_m, p_d, \ldots) \quad \textbf{(1.2)}$$

Investment function:

$$I = f_3(Y, i, \ldots) \quad \textbf{(1.3)}$$

Income-expenditure identity:

$$Y = C_p + C_g + I + X - M \quad \textbf{(1.4)}$$

where

C_p = private consumption expenditure
C_g = government consumption expenditure
I = investment
M = imports
X = exports
Y = income
i = rate of interest
p_d = domestic price level
p_m = import price level

The application of econometric methods may typically result in an econometric model that looks like the following:

$$C_p = -2143.6 + 0.663Y + 4107.9i$$

$$I = -2816.7 + 0.364Y - 11385i$$

$$M = -1188.6 + 0.378Y - 688.7(p_m/p_d)$$

$$Y = C_p + C_g + I + X - M$$

This is also an example of a *classical* econometric model. Such models are the subject of chapters 1 to 8 of this book. At a glance, certain economic conclusions may be drawn, provided that these results are reliable (and econometric techniques allow us to determine this). It can be seen, for instance, that the mpc is estimated as 0.663. This value is somewhat low and should not be accepted unconditionally. The marginal propensity to invest is 0.364 while the marginal propensity to import is 0.378. It can also be seen that investment is negatively related to interest rates (this is predicted by standard theory), whereas consumption seems to be positively related to interest rates (this is *not* predicted by standard theory and should be the subject of further investigation). Are there any other queries or comments that can be made about this model?

If the investigator is satisfied with this model, he or she can use it to forecast values of C_p, I, M and Y (the *endogenous* variables) for given values of the other variables in the model (the *exogenous* variables). This forecast is obtained by solving the model using mathematical routines that are usually part of the econometric software like EViews.

This model has more than one equation and, in the literature, is described as a *multiple* or *simultaneous equation model*. Frequently, an investigator may be interested only in one of the equations, such as, for instance, the consumption function on which so many studies have been conducted. It is quite possible to study an equation individually (and without reference to any other) provided that certain constraints are verified, in which case it is referred to as a *single equation model*. In the first section of this book, the econometrics of single equation models will be developed in some detail and will serve as an introduction to the study of the econometrics of simultaneous equation models.

This is a very simple model which should only be used for illustrative purposes. In particular, it is *highly aggregated.* What does this mean? Take for instance the import function. It is the total import bill that is being modelled. Surely, the functional form will differ depending on the category of imports being considered so that, for instance, there should be a separate equation for the imports of capital goods as opposed to the imports of consumer goods. These and other questions must be resolved in reality but, for purposes of this book, they will not be considered any further. However, notwithstanding this oversimplification, there are still two thorny problems to be resolved before standard econometric methods can be applied to this model. They concern, first, the data to be used in order to determine specific values of economic constructs like the propensity to import (as well as the related problem of how to obtain the data). Second, they concern the specific form to be given to the functions f_1, f_2 and f_3 which, as they stand, are too general to be of use.

DATA AND ECONOMETRIC MODELS

An econometric model based on the structure like the one outlined in equations (1.1) to (1.4) may be used to explain income formation in a country over a period in time. In order to apply econometric methods to this case, the investigator must first obtain *time series* for all the variables in the model covering the same time period. Suppose he or she is able to do so and collects observations for n consecutive time periods on each variable. Then the model above is more appropriately rewritten as:

Consumption function:

$$C_{pt} = f_1(Y_t, i_t, \ldots) \qquad \textbf{(1.5)}$$

Import function:

$$M_t = f_2(Y_t, p_{mt}, p_{dt}, \ldots) \qquad \textbf{(1.6)}$$

Investment function:

$$I_t = f_3(Y_t, i_t, \ldots) \qquad \textbf{(1.7)}$$

Income-expenditure identity:

$$Y_t = C_{pt} + C_{gt} + I_t + X_t - M_t \qquad \textbf{(1.8)}$$

where a variable time subscript t has been introduced to distinguish the various time periods. Suppose, for instance, annual data are available from 1975 to 1995. Then t = 1 indicates that the observation in question pertains to 1975, t = 2 refers to 1976, and so on until t = 21 which will refer to 1995. In this illustration, n = 21. If instead it were quarterly data from 1975 to 1995, then t = 1 would refer to the first quarter of 1975, t = 2 to the second quarter of 1975, and so on right up to t = 84 for the last quarter of 1995.

The application of econometric methods to time series is widespread and the naming of some well-known econometric software packages (computer programs) such as Time Series Processor (TSP), MicroTSP and Regression Analysis for Time Series (RATS) bears testimony to this. But it is not the only possible application. The model defined by equations (1.1) to (1.4) may also be used to explain national income formation in a group or *cross section* of countries, for instance the fourteen CARICOM countries, at the same point in time. The use of the subscript t remains valid, only this time t = 1 stands for the *one* observation made on country number 1, t = 2 that made on country number 2 right up to t = 14 for the fourteenth country.[1] In this case, of course, n = 14, but cross sectional studies, which are frequently employed for microeconomic studies, are usually based on the use of survey data and involve considerably more observations.

Economic data, whether based on time series or cross sectional data, are unreliable. This point was most clearly stated very early in the history of the discipline by Morgenstern (1950) and has been the subject of numerous works ever since. See, for instance, Griliches (1985), who points out that it is this very deficiency that justifies the existence of econometrics as a special branch of study in the first place. In the final analysis, we must make do with what we have and stop blaming our own shortcomings on measurement errors and so on. Hendry (1980) sums up this position: "Economic data are notoriously unreliable … and in an important sense econometrics is little more than an attempted solution to our acute shortage of decent data." In particular, there is no obvious relationship at most times between the measured variable and the concept it is supposed to be measuring, which comes back to haunt the economist in his or her application of econometric methods. Take for instance the consumption function above. What measure of income among the many that exist (say, in the national accounts) should be used? What about permanent income? A measure of that does not even exist!

Problems like these arise because the data to be used are frequently "manufactured" by non-econometricians and for end uses quite different from econometric analysis. Unless the economist is prepared to conduct a survey for every study contemplated (a well nigh impossible task anyway), he or she has to be accommodating and at best take steps to massage the data into something that resembles the underlying economic concept or work with what is given. This is not very encouraging but it is the reality.

SPECIFYING THE MODEL

To obtain numerical results like those shown above, classical econometric methods cannot be applied directly to equations (1.1) to (1.4).[2] They need to be more specifically

[1] It is also possible to combine time series and cross sectional data into so-called *panel* or *longitudinal* data. In recent times, this has been increasing in popularity. The econometric problems associated with this kind of application, however, will not be dealt with in this book.

[2] Equation (1.4) is an identity that holds all the time. Everything is already known about this equation and econometric methods are not applied to it.

formulated. Unfortunately, these methods can only be applied to linear models.[3] What does this mean? The following is an example of a linear import function:

$$M_t = \beta_1 + \beta_2 Y_t + \beta_3 p_{mt}/p_{dt} \quad \textbf{(1.9)}$$

Linearity in this context refers more specifically to linearity in the coefficients, i.e. β_1, β_2 and β_3, and not in the variables. For example, standard econometric methods are just as easily applied to the following model because it is linear in the coefficients (although it is clearly not linear in the variables M, Y and p_m/p_d):

$$\ln M_t = \beta_1 + \beta_2 \ln Y_t + \beta_3 \ln\left(p_{mt}/p_{dt}\right) \quad \textbf{(1.10)}$$

The principal task of econometrics is the determination and evaluation of numerical values for the β coefficients. Evaluation revolves mainly around the question of the statistical adequacy of the numerical results obtained, to determine, for instance, whether these results are statistically acceptable and, if so, whether they imply rejection or non-rejection of the underlying economic theory. A model, once accepted, may be used to make numerical predictions about economic behaviour like: "If the price of oil rises to $25 per barrel, unemployment in Trinidad and Tobago will fall to 7%" and other similar predictions.

It is important to understand, at this point of initial model specification, that the final formulation may differ from this initial one. In the post-estimation stages, models are subject to various diagnostic checks and tests that may lead us to possible revisions and improved specifications. However, in the pre-estimation stage, we rely primarily on our *a priori* economic reasoning, which is usually firmly rooted in economic theory. This is not to say that the final model will always support the existing economic hypotheses; indeed, it may be in total contradiction, and may even lead to a new contribution to economic theory. But the economics, as we know it, must be responsible for the *initial* formulation, and should guide us in our anticipation of the results. Whether such expectations are realized, and the steps we must then take to handle seemingly contradictory results, is an issue to be dealt with later.

INTRODUCING THE ERROR TERM

Let us look once again at the import function defined in equation (1.9). A specification like this one, we might argue, is not at odds with standard economic theory, provided that "autonomous" imports (β_1) is positive and the marginal propensity to import (β_2) is constant and is also a positive fraction. We may also anticipate that, the more foreign prices (p_m) rise relative to domestic prices (p_d), the smaller will be the import bill, i.e. β_3 will be negative.

However, it would be very unrealistic to expect that, for every possible observation (i.e. for every value of the time index t), the left-hand side of the equation would

[3] Methods exist for applications to nonlinear models but these are fairly advanced and beyond the scope of this book.

be equal to the right-hand side. What we are more likely to have, for any given value of t is either:

$$M_t \geq \beta_1 + \beta_2 Y_t + \beta_3 p_{mt}/p_{dt}$$

or

$$M_t \leq \beta_1 + \beta_2 Y_t + \beta_3 p_{mt}/p_{dt}$$

so that, for each specific observation, there will be some discrepancy between the two sides. If this discrepancy is equal to u_t for the *t*th observation, then the following will be true:

$$M_t = \beta_1 + \beta_2 Y_t + \beta_3 p_{mt}/p_{dt} + u_t \quad \textbf{(1.11)}$$

The introduction of the "error" term, u_t, assures the equality of both sides of the equation.

DESIRABLE PROPERTIES OF THE ERROR TERM

To be economically meaningful, the error term u_t cannot simply be a "slack" variable to assure the equality of both sides of an equation such as (1.11). The specification of the equation is based on the premise that the variables Y_t and p_{mt}/p_{dt} account for the bulk of the explanation of M_t. Moreover, the effect of the income and the relative price variables on import behaviour is *systematic* in that we can predict how the consumer will respond to them. The error term, on the other hand, acts almost as a residual nuisance item whose influence is purely *random* (rather than systematic) in that we cannot predict how it is going to affect import behaviour.

We may also imagine that the error term represents the sum total of all variables affecting import behaviour other than income and relative prices but each of these excluded variables is too small to have a major effect in its own right. The individual contributions to M_t of these "latent variables" ought, for a sufficiently large number of observations, to cancel each other out. In other words, it seems reasonable to suppose that its values may be positive or negative with equal probability. Mathematically, we require that:

$$E(u_t) = 0$$

This is in fact a fundamental property of a purely random variable. But the term "purely random" implies more than that. It implies as well that, on the average, no one observation would have an unduly larger or smaller influence than any other. In mathematical terms, this requires that the variance of u_t be constant across observations, i.e.

$$Var(u_t) = E(u_t^2) = \sigma^2$$

Finally, to be purely random, the influence of a given value u_t should not carry over to another observation. Mathematically, this requires that the possible realizations of u should be uncorrelated or:

$$\mathrm{Cov}(u_t, u_s) = E(u_t u_s) = 0, s \neq t$$

A purely random variable having these three properties is referred to in the literature as *white noise*.

THE GENERAL LINEAR REGRESSION MODEL

Consider the equation:

$$\begin{aligned} & y_t = \beta_1 x_{1t} + \beta_2 x_{2t} + \beta_3 x_{3t} + \ldots + \beta_k x_{kt} + u_t \\ & k = 1, 2, \ldots, t = 1, 2, \ldots, n \\ & u_t \sim \mathrm{iid}(0, \sigma^2) \end{aligned} \qquad \textbf{(1.12)}$$

This is a general representation of models such as equation (1.11) above. This becomes obvious if we put $y_t = M_t$, $x_{1t} = 1$ for all t, $x_{2t} = Y_t$, $x_{3t} = (p_{mt}/p_{dt})$ and $k = 3$. The variable y is the *endogenous* variable which, because u is random, is also itself a random variable. It is explained by the *exogenous* variables $x_1, x_2, \ldots, x_k$ and u is the white noise error term. As above, the model is linear in the β coefficients.

The general problem of regression analysis is to use the n observations on the endogenous and exogenous variables to obtain numerical values for the β coefficients which, hopefully, will be used as estimates of the true (but unknown) values.

Let us see how this system appears for each of the n observations:

$$\begin{array}{ll} t=1 & y_1 = \beta_1 x_{11} + \beta_2 x_{21} + \beta_3 x_{31} + \ldots + \beta_k x_{k1} + u_1 \\ t=2 & y_2 = \beta_1 x_{12} + \beta_2 x_{22} + \beta_3 x_{32} + \ldots + \beta_k x_{k2} + u_2 \\ & \ldots\ldots \\ t=n & y_n = \beta_1 x_{1n} + \beta_2 x_{2n} + \beta_3 x_{3n} + \ldots + \beta_k x_{kn} + u_n \end{array}$$

This system may be written compactly in matrix notation as:[4]

$$\mathbf{y} = \mathbf{X}\boldsymbol{\beta} + \mathbf{u} \qquad \textbf{(1.13)}$$

[4] A considerable amount of the mathematical analysis in this book is done through the medium of matrix algebra. Most of the elements of matrix algebra required to make sense of the analysis is covered in Kmenta (1986), pages 738 to 749. A fuller treatment is found in Hadley (1961).

where

$$\mathbf{y}=\begin{pmatrix} y_1 \\ y_2 \\ \vdots \\ y_n \end{pmatrix}, \mathbf{X}=\begin{bmatrix} x_{11} & x_{21} & \cdots & x_{k1} \\ x_{12} & x_{22} & \cdots & x_{k2} \\ \vdots & \vdots & \vdots & \vdots \\ x_{1n} & x_{2n} & \cdots & x_{kn} \end{bmatrix}, \boldsymbol{\beta}=\begin{pmatrix} \beta_1 \\ \beta_2 \\ \vdots \\ \beta_k \end{pmatrix}, \mathbf{u}=\begin{pmatrix} u_1 \\ u_2 \\ \vdots \\ u_n \end{pmatrix}$$

ORDINARY LEAST SQUARES

What criterion must we apply to obtain estimators of the β coefficients or, equivalently, the β coefficient vector? It seems intuitively plausible that, whatever the criterion used, it should be based on some notion of minimization of the errors, u_1, u_2, ..., u_n in equation (1.12). After all, these represent aberrations from the substantive economic theory that the systematic part of equation (1.12) is attempting to model. But what do we mean by minimization of errors?

The most widely used criterion is the *least squares* criterion. It requires that the β coefficients be chosen so that:

$$S(\boldsymbol{\beta})=\sum_{t=1}^{n}\mathbf{u}_t^2=\mathbf{u}'\mathbf{u} \qquad \textbf{(1.14)}$$

be minimized. This is a standard quadratic function that can be adequately handled by the tools of differential calculus. Let us do this now.

Since $\mathbf{u} = \mathbf{y} - \mathbf{X}\beta$, then:

$$S(\boldsymbol{\beta})=\mathbf{u}'\mathbf{u}=(\mathbf{y}-\mathbf{X}\boldsymbol{\beta})'(\mathbf{y}-\mathbf{X}\boldsymbol{\beta})=\mathbf{y}'\mathbf{y}-\mathbf{y}'\mathbf{X}\boldsymbol{\beta}-\boldsymbol{\beta}'\mathbf{X}'\mathbf{y}+\boldsymbol{\beta}'\mathbf{X}'\mathbf{X}\boldsymbol{\beta}$$

Since $\mathbf{y}'\mathbf{X}\boldsymbol{\beta} = \boldsymbol{\beta}'\mathbf{X}'\mathbf{y}$, it follows that:

$$S(\boldsymbol{\beta})=\mathbf{y}'\mathbf{y}-2\boldsymbol{\beta}'\mathbf{X}'\mathbf{y}+\boldsymbol{\beta}'\mathbf{X}'\mathbf{X}\boldsymbol{\beta}$$

It is easily shown that:

$$\frac{\partial S(\boldsymbol{\beta})}{\partial \boldsymbol{\beta}}=2\mathbf{X}'\mathbf{X}\boldsymbol{\beta}-2\mathbf{X}'\mathbf{y} \qquad \textbf{(1.15)}$$

Setting this expression equal to zero gives us the well-known *normal equations*:

$$\mathbf{X}'\mathbf{X}\hat{\boldsymbol{\beta}}=\mathbf{X}'\mathbf{y} \qquad \textbf{(1.16)}$$

where $\hat{\boldsymbol{\beta}}$ is the value of $\boldsymbol{\beta}$ for which equation (1.15) is equal to zero. Provided that the $(n \times k)$ matrix $\mathbf{X}$ is of full rank k, then $\mathbf{X}'\mathbf{X}$ will be nonsingular (it admits an inverse) and equation (1.16) can be solved for $\hat{\boldsymbol{\beta}}$ to give:

$$\hat{\boldsymbol{\beta}} = (\mathbf{X}'\mathbf{X})^{-1}\mathbf{X}'\mathbf{y} = \begin{pmatrix} \hat{\beta}_1 \\ \hat{\beta}_2 \\ \vdots \\ \hat{\beta}_k \end{pmatrix} \tag{1.17}$$

which is the *ordinary least squares* (OLS) estimator.[5] Notice that, because it is a function of a random vector **y**, it is itself also a random vector and the elements $\hat{\beta}_i$, i = 1, 2, …, k are all random variables.

Special Case: k = 2 and x_{1t} = 1 for all t

Many introductory textbooks in statistics and econometrics give pride of place to this special case in which the general linear regression model becomes:

$$y_t = \beta_1 + \beta_2 x_{2t} + u_t \tag{1.18}$$

The matrices corresponding to equation (1.13) become:

$$\mathbf{y} = \begin{pmatrix} y_1 \\ y_2 \\ \vdots \\ y_n \end{pmatrix}, \mathbf{X} = \begin{pmatrix} 1 & x_{21} \\ 1 & x_{22} \\ \vdots & \vdots \\ 1 & x_{2n} \end{pmatrix}, \boldsymbol{\beta} = \begin{pmatrix} \beta_1 \\ \beta_2 \end{pmatrix}, \mathbf{u} = \begin{pmatrix} u_1 \\ u_2 \\ \vdots \\ u_n \end{pmatrix}$$

The normal equations (1.16) in this case are:

$$\begin{pmatrix} n & \sum_{t=1}^{n} x_{2t} \\ \sum_{t=1}^{n} x_{2t} & \sum_{t=1}^{n} x_{2t}^2 \end{pmatrix} \begin{pmatrix} \hat{\beta}_1 \\ \hat{\beta}_2 \end{pmatrix} = \begin{pmatrix} \sum_{t=1}^{n} y_t \\ \sum_{t=1}^{n} x_{2t} y_t \end{pmatrix} \tag{1.19}$$

[5] OLS is possible only if the rank of $\mathbf{X}'\mathbf{X}$ is equal to k. This implies that the rank of $\mathbf{X}$ must also be equal to k and, since the rank of a matrix cannot exceed the lower of the number of its rows or columns, it follows immediately that the application of OLS requires that $n \geq k$. Put another way, OLS estimation is possible if and only if there are more observations than coefficients to be estimated. In this book, it will *always* be assumed that $n \geq k$.

which, upon further simplification, gives us:

$$n\hat{\beta}_1 + \hat{\beta}_2 \sum_{t=1}^{n} x_{2t} = \sum_{t=1}^{n} y_t$$
$$\hat{\beta}_1 \sum_{t=1}^{n} x_{2t} + \hat{\beta}_2 \sum_{t=1}^{n} x_{2t}^2 = \sum_{t=1}^{n} x_{2t} y_t \qquad \textbf{(1.20)}$$

As an exercise, show that this system can be further simplified to yield:

$$\hat{\beta}_1 = \bar{y} - \hat{\beta}_2 \bar{x}_2$$
$$\hat{\beta}_2 = \frac{\sum_{t=1}^{n} x_{2t} y_t - n\bar{x}_2 \bar{y}}{\sum_{t=1}^{n} x_{2t}^2 - n\bar{x}_2^2} \qquad \textbf{(1.21)}$$

which are the well-known expressions found in introductory statistics textbooks.

NUMERICAL CALCULATION

Manual application of the formula shown in equation (1.17) is not at all recommended, especially for $k > 2$. In the first place such application is lengthy and tedious and, even for small sample sizes, is almost certain to result in error. Second, modern econometric practice requires the calculation of values other than the β coefficients. Finally, we now have the computational capability at our fingertips: for instance, this book was typed on a computer that weighs less than 2 kilograms but which has the capacity to run econometric software like EViews, AREMOS, MicroFIT, PC TSP, PC GIVE and many more. In fact, many of these are installed on the same computer and they all have the capacity to do such calculations (and even more complicated ones) in the proverbial twinkling of an eye. More than this, such calculations will be done accurately, over and over again. No such guarantee can be given by any human being, no matter how adept he or she is with figures.

It is for this reason that manual computation is not being encouraged in this book. Rather, emphasis will be put on the meaning and usefulness of the numerical values obtained through use of an econometric software package, EViews. The emphasis on the use of the computer to carry out calculations does not at all imply that we are not going to be interested in expressions like equation (1.17). In fact, there is perhaps no way other than through mathematical analysis of such "formulae" to establish the properties of the estimators and so determine their strengths and weaknesses. We will return to this subject later in this chapter.

In the meantime, we will use EViews to calculate numerical values for the β coefficients in equation (1.11):

$$M_t = \beta_1 + \beta_2 Y_t + \beta_3 p_{mt}/p_{dt} + u_t$$

EXHIBIT 1.1
Equation: $M_t = \beta_1 + \beta_2 Y_t + \beta_3 p_{mt}/p_{dt} + u_t$
Output obtained from fitting equation in EViews

```
==============================================================
LS // Dependent Variable is IMPORTS
Date: 07/22/99   Time: 11:34
Sample: 1967 1991
Included observations: 25
==============================================================
     Variable      Coefficient Std. Error  T-Statistic   Prob.
==============================================================
        C          -1188.641   696.9314   -1.705535    0.1022
      INCOME        0.377639   0.029737    12.69930    0.0000
      RATIO        -688.6762   155.8371   -4.419206    0.0002
==============================================================
R-squared             0.942446   Mean dependent var    3556.082
Adjusted R-squared    0.937214   S.D. dependent var    1531.723
S.E. of regression    383.8059   Akaike info criter    12.01244
Sum squared resid     3240753.   Schwarz criterion     12.15871
Log likelihood       -182.6290   F-statistic           180.1255
Durbin-Watson stat    1.665317   Prob(F-statistic)     0.000000
==============================================================
```

The data to be used are time series for Trinidad and Tobago for the period 1967 to 1991 and these are given (with other variables) in Appendix 1.2, as well as in an EXCEL workbook called WT_DATA.XLS. When using a package like EViews, you should avoid giving variables simplistic one-letter names like "M" (for import expenditure and so on). At the same time, the names cannot be too long, if only because EViews does not allow names that are excessively long. We have chosen IMPORTS for M, INCOME for Y and RATIO for (p_m/p_d).[6] Exhibit 1.1 shows the output that was obtained from EViews.

Much of Part I of this book will be devoted to explaining the theoretical underpinnings and practical importance of (most of) the statistical output shown in Exhibit 1.1 but, for the moment, we are interested principally in the output that shows the numerical values of the β coefficients.

The output shows, first of all, the method of estimation (LS standing for ordinary least squares) and the name of the dependent (endogenous) variable, IMPORTS (M). It also shows the date and time the calculations were performed as well as the sample period (here, 1967 to 1991) and the number of observations (25).

Under the "Variable" column are displayed the independent (exogenous) variables: C (for the constant term), INCOME (Y) and RATIO (p_{mt}/p_{dt}). Under the "Coefficient" column are displayed the estimates of the coefficients of the corresponding variables under the "Variable" column. Our estimated equation may therefore be written as (notice that the error term is left out):

$$M_t = -1188.64 + 0.378\, Y_t - 688.7\, p_{mt}/p_{dt} \qquad \textbf{(1.22)}$$

[6] There is no need to input the variable RATIO directly as it can be calculated as (p_m/p_d) within EViews. It is even possible in EViews v. 2.0 and higher, to declare (p_m/p_d) as a variable in its own right.

The rest of the output shown, as we will eventually see, allows us to carry out a fairly detailed analysis of this result. For the moment, however, let us concentrate on what it is saying to us as *economists* (this, after all, is the principal reason for doing econometrics in the first place).

The marginal propensity to import is equal to 0.378 or, put another way, for every extra dollar earned, Trinidadians spend about 38 cents on imported goods and services. Furthermore, for every unit increase in the ratio of foreign to local prices, they will spend \$688.7 million dollars less on imported goods and services. Perhaps a more useful way to put this is to consider the *percentage* change in this ratio and not the actual change so that, for every 1% increase in the ratio (i.e. one hundredth of the unit increase), Trinidadians will spend about \$6.9 million dollars less on imported goods and services.

The interpretation of the constant term requires great care and consideration. First, it does not lead to the outright rejection of the results obtained because this negative value appears at odds with economic theory or even with common sense. On the other hand, it certainly *does not* mean that Trinidadians will spend negative \$1188.64 million on imports if income and relative prices are equal to zero. Strictly speaking, we cannot tell what will happen when these variables are zero because such values are not *within the experience* of the model (i.e. no values of the exogenous variables equal to or even close to zero were used to obtain the estimates shown). The mathematical expression shown in equation (1.22) remains valid, including the value of the constant term, but only for values that are within the experience of the model, or close enough to this experience.

FORECASTING WITH ECONOMETRIC MODELS

Models like the one we have just estimated may be used for forecasting. In fact, this is one of the most important practical applications to which models like these are put.

Consider a simple problem: we want to know what imports in 1992 will be, probably with a view to taking measures to deal with a possible foreign exchange shortage. A preliminary report informs us that income in 1992 (at constant prices) will be \$17,000 million while the import and domestic price indices will be, respectively, 180 and 160. Then imports of goods and services in 1992 are forecasted as:

$$M_{1992} = -1188.64 + 0.378(17{,}000) - 688.7(180/160) = 4462.57$$

This means that, according to this model, Trinidadians will spend just under \$4500 million on imports in 1992.

There are certain limitations to using econometric models like this one for making forecasts. First, the future values of the right-hand side (exogenous) variables must be known. In actual fact, they must be forecasted outside of the model so that the final forecast of the endogenous variable is really *conditional* upon these values. Second, the coefficient values used (and indeed the future values of the exogenous variables) are estimates and subject to error. Strictly speaking, then, we should carry out the calculation shown for a range of values of the coefficients (and exogenous variables) to see, in particular, how sensitive our forecast is to (minor) changes in the coefficient (exogenous variable) values. Finally, we should ensure that, whatever the values of the exogenous variables used, they must be within, or close to those within, the experience of the model (which is the case here).

THE GAUSS–MARKOV THEOREM ON LEAST SQUARES

The white noise error term introduced above has the following properties:

$$E(u_t) = 0 \qquad all\ t \qquad (\text{Property 1})$$
$$E(u_t^2) = \sigma^2 \qquad all\ t \qquad (\text{Property 2})$$
$$E(u_t u_s) = 0 \qquad s \neq t \qquad (\text{Property 3})$$

Each one of these properties has a simple yet meaningful interpretation. Property 1 implies that the error term can influence import behaviour in either direction – positive or negative – and is prone neither to be more negative than positive or vice versa. Furthermore, the positive and negative effects tend, in the long run, to cancel each other so that, on the average, $M_t = \beta_1 + \beta_2 Y_t + \beta_3 p_{mt}/p_{dt}$, as the original specification would have it.

Property 2, the *homoscedastic* property, implies that no one realization of the error term is observation specific: it is subject to the same range of variation as any other realization, whatever the observation. Property 3, which is to be taken in conjunction with property 2, states that the observations are not correlated with each other. This simply means that the error affecting the current observation is influenced neither by the errors that have come before nor those that will occur after. This is referred to as the absence of *autocorrelation* or *serial correlation* among the errors.[7]

When the general linear regression model is expressed in matrix notation, as in equation (1.13), properties 1 to 3 are expressed compactly as:

$$E(\mathbf{u}) = \mathbf{0} \qquad (A_1)$$
$$\text{Cov}(\mathbf{u}) = E(\mathbf{u}\mathbf{u}') = \sigma^2\, \mathbf{I}_n \qquad (A_2)$$

where $\mathbf{0}$ is an $(n \times 1)$ null vector (all n elements are equal to 0) and $\mathbf{I}_n$ the $(n \times n)$ identity matrix. Refer to Appendix 1.1 for a justification and explanation of these items.

A third assumption (A_3) is also required:

$$\mathbf{X} \text{ is fixed (nonstochastic)} (A_3)$$

This assumption harks back to the underlying statistical methods for which least squares methods were developed in the first place. In the specific case of equation (1.13), it means that if the data to be used in this model were obtainable from experiments and that we were able to replicate these experiments, then the **X** values would remain constant from one experiment to the next and, if **y** were to vary at all, it would be because of variation in the error term **u**.

Under these three assumptions, it will now be proven that:

---

[7] White noise variables are often said to be identically and independently distributed with zero mean and constant variance σ^2. In the case of u_t this may be written in compact notation as $u_t \sim \text{iid}(0, \sigma^2)$.

1. $E(\hat{\boldsymbol{\beta}}) = \boldsymbol{\beta}$ i.e. $\hat{\boldsymbol{\beta}}$ is an unbiased estimator of $\boldsymbol{\beta}$
2. $Cov(\hat{\boldsymbol{\beta}}) = \sigma^2(\mathbf{X'X})^{-1}$
3. For any other unbiased estimator of $\boldsymbol{\beta}$, to be denoted $\tilde{\boldsymbol{\beta}}$, which is also linear in $\mathbf{y}$, then $Cov(\tilde{\boldsymbol{\beta}}) = Cov(\hat{\boldsymbol{\beta}}) + \mathbf{P}$, where $\mathbf{P}$ is a positive semidefinite matrix.[8]

This is the Gauss–Markov theorem, perhaps the most important result in classical econometric theory. Part (1) of this theorem implies that $E(\hat{\beta}_i) = \beta_i$, where $\hat{\beta}_i$ is the OLS estimator of the *i*th coefficient, β_i. Part (2) implies that the variance of $\hat{\beta}_i$, to be denoted $var(\hat{\beta}_i)$, is the *i*th diagonal element of the matrix $\sigma^2(\mathbf{X'X})^{-1}$ and part (3) implies that $\hat{\beta}_i$ has the smallest variance in the class of all unbiased estimators of β_i which are also linear in the observations $\mathbf{y}$. On the basis of the Gauss–Markov theorem, the OLS estimator is often described as the best linear unbiased estimator (BLUE): it is *best* because it has the smallest variance, it is obviously *linear* in $\mathbf{y}$, and it is also *unbiased*.

Proof of Part (1) of the Theorem

We know that $\hat{\boldsymbol{\beta}} = (\mathbf{X'X})^{-1}\mathbf{X'y}$. Replacing $\mathbf{y}$ by its value gives us:

$$\hat{\boldsymbol{\beta}} = (\mathbf{X'X})^{-1}\mathbf{X'}(\mathbf{X}\boldsymbol{\beta} + \mathbf{u}) = \boldsymbol{\beta} + (\mathbf{X'X})^{-1}\mathbf{X'u} \qquad \textbf{(1.23)}$$

so that:

$$E(\hat{\boldsymbol{\beta}}) = \boldsymbol{\beta} + (\mathbf{X'X})^{-1}\mathbf{X'}E(\mathbf{u})$$

since $\mathbf{X}$ is fixed. Furthermore, since by A_1, $E(\mathbf{u}) = \mathbf{0}$, then $E(\hat{\boldsymbol{\beta}}) = \boldsymbol{\beta}$, which proves the first part of the theorem.

Proof of Part (2) of the Theorem

By definition, $Cov(\hat{\boldsymbol{\beta}}) = E\{[\hat{\boldsymbol{\beta}} - E(\hat{\boldsymbol{\beta}})][\hat{\boldsymbol{\beta}} - E(\hat{\boldsymbol{\beta}})]'\}$. Since $E(\hat{\boldsymbol{\beta}}) = \boldsymbol{\beta}$, this becomes:

$$\mathbf{Cov(\hat{\boldsymbol{\beta}}) = E\{[\hat{\boldsymbol{\beta}} - \boldsymbol{\beta}][\hat{\boldsymbol{\beta}} - \boldsymbol{\beta}]'\}}$$

By equation (1.23) above, $\hat{\boldsymbol{\beta}} - \boldsymbol{\beta} = (\mathbf{X'X})^{-1}\mathbf{X'u}$ so that:

$$\begin{aligned} Cov(\hat{\boldsymbol{\beta}}) &= E\left[(\mathbf{X'X})^{-1}\mathbf{X'u}\right]\left[(\mathbf{X'X})^{-1}\mathbf{X'u}\right]' \\ &= E\left[(\mathbf{X'X})^{-1}\mathbf{X'uu'X}(\mathbf{X'X})^{-1}\right] \\ &= \left[(\mathbf{X'X})^{-1}\mathbf{X'}E(\mathbf{uu'})\mathbf{X}(\mathbf{X'X})^{-1}\right] \end{aligned}$$

[8] In matrix algebra, a positive semidefinite matrix corresponds, in scalar algebra, to a number that is greater than or equal to zero. In stricter terms, a matrix $\mathbf{A}$ is said to be positive semidefinite if there exists a vector $\mathbf{x}$ such that the quadratic form $\mathbf{x'Ax} \geq 0$, for all $\mathbf{x}$.

since **X** is fixed. Since, by A_2, $E(\mathbf{uu}') = \sigma^2 \mathbf{I}_n$, this simplifies to:

$$\text{Cov}(\hat{\boldsymbol{\beta}}) = \sigma^2\left[(\mathbf{X}'\mathbf{X})^{-1}\mathbf{X}'\mathbf{X}(\mathbf{X}'\mathbf{X})^{-1}\right]$$

$$= \sigma^2(\mathbf{X}'\mathbf{X})^{-1}$$

which proves part (2) of the theorem.

Proof of Part (3) of the Theorem

Let $\tilde{\boldsymbol{\beta}}$ be an unbiased estimator of $\boldsymbol{\beta}$ (i.e. $E(\tilde{\boldsymbol{\beta}}) = \boldsymbol{\beta}$) which is also linear in **y** and can therefore be written $\tilde{\boldsymbol{\beta}} = \mathbf{Ay}$, where **A** is some known matrix. Without loss of generality, we can let $\mathbf{A} = (\mathbf{X}'\mathbf{X})^{-1}\mathbf{X}' + \mathbf{L}$, where **L** is any nonstochastic matrix, and so:

$$\tilde{\boldsymbol{\beta}} = \left[(\mathbf{X}'\mathbf{X})^{-1}\mathbf{X}' + \mathbf{L}\right]\mathbf{y}$$

By simple algebraic manipulation, we deduce that:

$$\tilde{\boldsymbol{\beta}} = \left[(\mathbf{X}'\mathbf{X})^{-1}\mathbf{X}' + \mathbf{L}\right](\mathbf{X}\boldsymbol{\beta} + \mathbf{u}) = \boldsymbol{\beta} + (\mathbf{X}'\mathbf{X})^{-1}\mathbf{X}'\mathbf{u} + \mathbf{LX}\boldsymbol{\beta} + \mathbf{Lu}$$

By assumption, $E(\tilde{\boldsymbol{\beta}}) = \boldsymbol{\beta}$ and the clear implication of this is $\mathbf{LX} = \mathbf{0}$. Consequently:

$$\tilde{\boldsymbol{\beta}} = \boldsymbol{\beta} + \left[(\mathbf{X}'\mathbf{X})^{-1}\mathbf{X}' + \mathbf{L}\right]\mathbf{u}$$

and

$$\tilde{\boldsymbol{\beta}} - \boldsymbol{\beta} = \left[(\mathbf{X}'\mathbf{X})^{-1}\mathbf{X}' + \mathbf{L}\right]\mathbf{u}$$

By definition, $\text{Cov}(\tilde{\boldsymbol{\beta}}) = E\{[\tilde{\boldsymbol{\beta}} - \boldsymbol{\beta}][\tilde{\boldsymbol{\beta}} - \boldsymbol{\beta}]'\}$ which, given the above, yields:

$$\text{Cov}(\tilde{\boldsymbol{\beta}}) = E\left\{\left[(\mathbf{X}'\mathbf{X})^{-1}\mathbf{X}' + \mathbf{L}\right]\mathbf{u}\right\}\left\{\left[(\mathbf{X}'\mathbf{X})^{-1}\mathbf{X}' + \mathbf{L}\right]\mathbf{u}\right\}'$$

$$= E\left[(\mathbf{X}'\mathbf{X})^{-1}\mathbf{X}' + \mathbf{L}\right]\mathbf{uu}'\left[(\mathbf{X}'\mathbf{X})^{-1}\mathbf{X}' + \mathbf{L}\right]'$$

$$= E\left[(\mathbf{X}'\mathbf{X})^{-1}\mathbf{X}'\mathbf{uu}'\mathbf{X}(\mathbf{X}'\mathbf{X})^{-1} + (\mathbf{X}'\mathbf{X})^{-1}\mathbf{X}'\mathbf{uu}'\mathbf{L}' + \mathbf{Luu}'\mathbf{X}(\mathbf{X}'\mathbf{X})^{-1} + \mathbf{Luu}'\mathbf{L}'\right]$$

$$= (\mathbf{X}'\mathbf{X})^{-1}\mathbf{X}'\mathbf{X}E(\mathbf{uu}')(\mathbf{X}'\mathbf{X})^{-1} + (\mathbf{X}'\mathbf{X})^{-1}\mathbf{X}'E(\mathbf{uu}')\mathbf{L}' + \mathbf{L}E(\mathbf{uu}')\mathbf{X}(\mathbf{X}'\mathbf{X})^{-1}$$

$$+ \mathbf{L}E(\mathbf{uu}')\mathbf{L}'$$

given that **X** and **L** are nonstochastic. Since, by A_2, $E(\mathbf{uu}') = \sigma^2 \mathbf{I}_n$, this reduces to:

$$\text{Cov}(\tilde{\boldsymbol{\beta}}) = \sigma^2\left[(\mathbf{X}'\mathbf{X})^{-1}\mathbf{X}'\mathbf{X}(\mathbf{X}'\mathbf{X})^{-1} + (\mathbf{X}'\mathbf{X})^{-1}\mathbf{X}'\mathbf{L}' + \mathbf{LX}(\mathbf{X}'\mathbf{X})^{-1} + \mathbf{LL}'\right]$$

and, since $\mathbf{LX} = \mathbf{0}$, this reduces further to:

$$\text{Cov}\left(\tilde{\boldsymbol{\beta}}\right) = \sigma^2\left[(\mathbf{X}'\mathbf{X})^{-1} + \mathbf{LL}'\right]$$

that is:

$$\text{Cov}\left(\tilde{\boldsymbol{\beta}}\right) = \text{Cov}\left(\hat{\boldsymbol{\beta}}\right) + \sigma^2\,\mathbf{LL}'$$

$\sigma^2\mathbf{LL}'$ is clearly a positive semidefinite matrix and part (3) of the theorem is proven.

UNDERSTANDING THE LESSONS OF THE GAUSS–MARKOV THEOREM

The use of the word "best" to describe the OLS estimator can and frequently does result in some abuse in practice. First, OLS is best in the sense of the Gauss–Markov theorem only if assumptions A_1 to A_3 are verified. We will see in the coming chapters that there are likely to be many situations in practice where this may not be so. Second, even if we have no good reason to doubt the validity of the assumptions, there are many practitioners who do not seem to understand that the best may sometimes not be good enough.

EXERCISES

1. From your knowledge of economics, how would you proceed to obtain econometric models of the following:
   - Demand and supply functions for a popular soft drink
   - A production function for methanol
   - The demand for money in a Caribbean country
2. Try and identify the sources of the data to be used in the models mentioned in exercise 1. If the data do not exist, what would you propose to do?
3. Consider the model:

$$y_{1t} = \beta_1 + \beta_2 x_{2t} + \beta_3 x_{3t} + u_t$$

   a) Explain the terms that enter into this equation.
   b) Put this equation in the form $\mathbf{y} = \mathbf{X}\boldsymbol{\beta} + \mathbf{u}$ showing clearly the elements of the matrices $\mathbf{y}$, $\mathbf{X}$, $\boldsymbol{\beta}$ and $\mathbf{u}$.
   c) State clearly the usual assumptions about $\mathbf{X}$ and $\mathbf{u}$.
   d) Formally derive the ordinary least squares (OLS) estimator of $\boldsymbol{\beta}$.
   e) Show that the OLS estimator of $\boldsymbol{\beta}$ is unbiased and determine its covariance matrix.
   f) State and prove the Gauss–Markov theorem.

4. You wish to examine the following savings function for the island of Dominica:

$$S_d = \alpha_0 + \alpha_1 Y + \alpha_2 S_f + \alpha_3 i_r + u$$

where S_d is the level of domestic savings, Y is a measure of national income, S_f the level of foreign savings inflows, i_r a measure of the real rate of interest and u the usual disturbance term.

a) How would you justify, *a priori*, the choice of the function used? What do the coefficients mean and what do you expect their values to be?

b) Use the data provided below (found also in WT_DATA.XLS) to obtain an estimated savings function for Dominica using constant price values for the variables (hint: you may use the consumer price index to deflate the nominal values).

c) Do the estimated coefficients satisfy your *a priori* expectations?

d) Can you explain what the estimated values mean to an intelligent lay person?

Data for Dominica

Year	GDSD EC$ m	YMPD EC$ m	CPI84D	FSD EC$ m	RINTD (%)
1980	–31.430	159.570	0.795	112.600	–21.25
1981	–18.210	178.790	0.900	78.900	–7.33
1982	5.000	194.500	0.940	55.100	1.53
1983	18.700	215.800	0.978	41.900	1.59
1984	9.900	242.600	1.000	79.500	3.47
1985	13.500	266.200	1.021	62.300	3.57
1986	51.600	302.600	1.052	15.900	1.91
1987	46.700	339.300	1.102	32.700	–0.05
1988	59.200	393.200	1.127	61.400	2.50
1989	33.800	422.700	1.198	136.900	–1.46
1990	70.300	451.500	1.228	113.900	2.68

GDSD = Gross domestic savings
YMPD = Gross domestic product at market prices
CPI84D = Consumer price index, 1984 = 1.0
FSD = Inflows of foreign savings
RINTD = Real 12 month deposit rate of interest

Source: Caribbean Development Bank, Bridgetown, Barbados.

APPENDIX 1.1: MOMENTS OF FIRST AND SECOND ORDER OF RANDOM VARIABLES AND RANDOM VECTORS

Random Variables

You may remember from your study of elementary statistical methods that the expression "the mean of a random variable X is equal to μ_x" is frequently written as E(X) = μ_x. By definition, the variance of X is written as:

$$\text{var}(X) = E[X - E(X)]^2 = E(X - \mu_x)^2$$

and this is frequently written as σ_x^2.

Letting R represent the real number line, then the following expressions are easily verifiable:

$$E(aX) = a\,\mu_x, a \in R$$

$$E(a + bX) = a + b\mu_x, a, b \in R$$

$$\text{Var}(aX) = a^2\sigma_x^2, a \in R$$

$$\text{Var}(a \pm bX) = b^2\sigma_x^2, a, b \in R$$

Let Y be another random variable with mean μ_y and variance σ_y^2. It is also possible to define the covariance between X and Y as:

$$\text{Cov}(X, Y) = E\left[(X - \mu_x)(Y - \mu_y)\right] = \sigma_{xy}$$

By definition, the coefficient of correlation between X and Y is defined as:

$$\rho_{xy} = \frac{\sigma_{xy}}{\sigma_x \sigma_y}$$

If X and Y are independent, then σ_{xy} and, consequently, ρ_{xy} are equal to zero. The converse, however, is not true.

The following are easily verifiable:

$$E(aX + bY) = a\mu_x + b\mu_y, a, b \in R$$

$$\text{Var}(X \pm Y) = \sigma_x^2 + \sigma_y^2 \pm 2\sigma_{xy}$$

If X and Y are independent, then, obviously:

$$\text{Var}(X \pm Y) = \sigma_x^2 + \sigma_y^2$$

Random Matrices and Vectors

The mean of a variable[9] is often called a moment of first order (of order 1) while the variance and covariance are called moments of second order (or order 2).

Suppose we have a matrix **X** of random variables:

$$\mathbf{X} = \begin{bmatrix} X_{11} & X_{12} & \cdots & X_{1n} \\ X_{21} & X_{22} & \cdots & X_{2n} \\ \vdots & \vdots & \vdots & \vdots \\ X_{m1} & X_{m2} & \cdots & X_{mn} \end{bmatrix}$$

then, by definition:

$$E(\mathbf{X}) = \begin{bmatrix} E(X_{11}) & E(X_{12}) & \cdots & E(X_{1n}) \\ E(X_{21}) & E(X_{22}) & \cdots & E(X_{2n}) \\ \vdots & \vdots & \vdots & \vdots \\ E(X_{m1}) & E(X_{m2}) & \cdots & E(X_{mn}) \end{bmatrix}$$

that is, the expected value of a random matrix is comprised of the expected values of the corresponding random variables.

The special case where **X** consists of only one column (i.e. it is a column vector) is of special interest to us. Consider a random vector **X** whose elements are $X_1, X_2, \ldots, X_n$ and define $E(X_i) = \mu_i$. Define $E(\mathbf{X}) = \boldsymbol{\mu}$, then:

$$E(\mathbf{X}) = \boldsymbol{\mu} = \begin{bmatrix} \mu_1 \\ \mu_2 \\ \vdots \\ \mu_n \end{bmatrix}$$

Define $\text{var}(X_i) = \sigma_i^2$, and $\text{Cov}(X_i, X_j) = \sigma_{ij}$, $i \neq j$. Consider the following "covariance table" showing the moments of second order of the n random variables:

	X_1	X_2	....	X_n
X_1	σ_1^2	σ_{12}	....	σ_{1n}
X_2	σ_{21}	σ_2^2	....	σ_{2n}
$\vdots$	$\vdots$	$\vdots$	$\vdots$	$\vdots$
X_n	σ_{n1}	σ_{n2}	....	σ_n^2

The tableau clearly shows, in an ordered way, the variances (along the principal diagonal) and the covariances (the nondiagonal elements). This tableau is defined as

[9] Strictly speaking, we should talk about the mean and variance of a *distribution* of a random variable, and not of the random variable itself.

the variance-covariance matrix and sometimes more simply as the covariance or dispersion matrix of the random vector **X**. It is easy to show (and it is left to you as an exercise) that:

$$\text{Cov}(\mathbf{X}) = [\mathbf{X} - \text{E}(\mathbf{X})][\mathbf{X} - \text{E}(\mathbf{X})]'$$

The following results are easy to demonstrate:

$$\text{Cov}(\lambda \mathbf{X}) = \lambda^2 \text{ Cov}(\mathbf{X}), \lambda \in \text{R}$$

If **A** is an (m × n) matrix, then:

$$\text{Cov}(\mathbf{AX}) = \mathbf{A} \text{ Cov}(\mathbf{X}) \mathbf{A}'$$

Application to the General Linear Regression Model

In the general linear regression model $\mathbf{y} = \mathbf{X}\boldsymbol{\beta} + \mathbf{u}$, where **u** is defined as in the body of chapter 1, it is very easy to show that $\text{E}(\mathbf{u}) = 0$ and $\text{Cov}(\mathbf{u}) = \text{E}(\mathbf{uu}') = \sigma^2\mathbf{I}_n$. Prove this as an exercise.

APPENDIX 1.2: TIME SERIES DATA FOR TRINIDAD AND TOBAGO 1967–1991

Year	C_p	C_g	I	X	M	Y	p_m	p_d	r_D	r_L
1967	6259.16	1101.98	1077.77	3724.03	1174.25	10988.7	37.32	14.23	3.59	5.48
1968	6088.04	1182.67	1247.01	4245.81	1201.76	11561.8	42.10	15.44	2.30	–0.92
1969	6517.46	1258.64	993.15	4500.96	1392.73	11877.5	43.85	15.80	2.90	5.57
1970	6214.3	1443.54	1504.77	4745.31	1610.74	12297.2	42.52	16.23	2.82	4.91
1971	6409.67	1584.06	2360.55	4054.1	1983.26	12425.1	42.77	16.80	2.09	3.74
1972	6475.92	1813.33	2078.71	4705.49	1930.11	13143.3	49.89	18.36	–0.12	–2.23
1973	6370.35	1853	1875.12	5238.07	1975.5	13361	49.80	21.07	0.80	–4.88
1974	6394.34	1809.97	2707.88	5159.09	2201.51	13869.8	61.30	25.69	–3.63	–10.52
1975	6561.83	2331.04	3281.82	4647.44	2747.36	14074.8	67.90	30.11	–5.85	–7.62
1976	7045.34	2514.59	3755.91	5120.62	3460.18	14976.3	70.65	33.17	–6.28	–2.19
1977	8713.1	2384.83	3878.06	4846.57	3480.17	16342.4	79.86	37.08	–5.31	–3.18
1978	9374.93	2674.61	4964.69	4879.64	3914.55	17979.3	86.62	40.85	–5.33	–1.52
1979	10124.5	3357.72	5122.95	5244.15	5222.85	18626.5	83.20	46.90	–4.89	–4.19
1980	10664	3554.72	6281.45	5659.95	5598.19	20561.9	103.76	55.09	–5.82	–5.49
1981	12319	3824.5	4907.1	5223.2	4794.2	21479.6	124.14	62.99	–5.58	–2.70
1982	13531.8	4305.2	5036.3	5022.8	5598.6	22297.5	144.14	70.18	–5.86	0.08
1983	12101.3	3740.2	4887.1	4801.1	5531.6	19998.1	137.50	82.00	–5.84	–4.57
1984	10080.2	4045.9	4336.5	5559.4	5174.2	18847.8	121.42	92.81	–5.88	–0.39
1985	9824.4	4109.3	3390.9	5882.8	5136.2	18071.2	100.00	100.00	–5.30	4.41
1986	10265.5	4007.8	2968.6	5804.2	5567.8	17478.3	125.13	107.69	–4.62	4.82
1987	8901.3	3974.8	2363.7	5546	4104.9	16680.9	136.65	119.29	–5.09	0.66
1988	8475.9	3651.6	1558.2	6115.1	3773.4	16027.4	156.07	128.54	–4.05	4.40
1989	8099.1	3614.3	1844.6	5912	3575.1	15894.9	178.41	143.13	–4.48	1.93
1990	7667.9	3916.6	1660	6534.3	3644.4	16134.4	168.09	159.00	–4.74	1.61
1991	7999.8	3876.3	2159.7	6709.5	4108.5	16636.8	179.82	165.12	–3.43	8.70

C_p = Private consumption expenditure, constant (1985) prices, TT$ million
C_g = Government consumption expenditure, constant (1985) prices, TT$ million
I = Investment, constant (1985) prices, TT$ million
M = Imports, constant (1985) prices, TT$ million
X = Exports, constant (1985) prices, TT$ million
Y = Income, constant (1985) prices, TT$ million
r_D = Real deposit rate of interest (in percentages)
r_L = Real loan rate of interest (in percentages)
p_d = Domestic price index (1985 = 100)
p_m = Import price index (1985 = 100)

CHAPTER 2

Evaluating the Ordinary Least Squares (OLS) Regression Fit

SOME PRELIMINARY REMARKS

In chapter 1, we considered the general linear regression model:

$$y_t = \beta_1 x_{1t} + \beta_2 x_{2t} + \beta_3 x_{3t} + \ldots + \beta_k x_{kt} + u_t$$

which, in matrix notation, became:

$$\mathbf{y} = \mathbf{X}\boldsymbol{\beta} + \mathbf{u}$$

We also established the OLS estimator as:

$$\hat{\boldsymbol{\beta}} = (\mathbf{X}'\mathbf{X})^{-1}\mathbf{X}'\mathbf{y} = \begin{pmatrix} \hat{\beta}_1 \\ \hat{\beta}_2 \\ \vdots \\ \hat{\beta}_k \end{pmatrix}$$

We define the *fitted model* as:

$$\hat{y}_t = \hat{\beta}_1 x_{1t} + \hat{\beta}_2 x_{2t} + \ldots + \hat{\beta}_k x_{kt}, t = 1, 2, \ldots, n$$

or, in matrix notation:

$$\hat{\mathbf{y}} = \mathbf{X}\hat{\boldsymbol{\beta}}$$

Let us also define the *OLS residuals* as $\hat{u}_t = y_t - \hat{y}_t$ or, in matrix notation:

$$\hat{\mathbf{u}} = \begin{pmatrix} \hat{u}_1 \\ \hat{u}_2 \\ \vdots \\ \hat{u}_n \end{pmatrix} = \mathbf{y} - \hat{\mathbf{y}}$$

Rearranging, we obtain:

$$\mathbf{y} = \hat{\mathbf{y}} + \hat{\mathbf{u}}$$

or

$$\mathbf{y} = \mathbf{X}\hat{\boldsymbol{\beta}} + \hat{\mathbf{u}}$$

It is also an interesting result that $\mathbf{X}'\hat{\mathbf{u}} = \mathbf{0}$ since

$$\mathbf{X}'\hat{\mathbf{u}} = \mathbf{X}'\left(\mathbf{y} - \mathbf{X}\hat{\boldsymbol{\beta}}\right) = \mathbf{X}'\mathbf{y} - \mathbf{X}'\mathbf{X}\hat{\boldsymbol{\beta}} = \mathbf{0}$$

(from the normal equations in chapter 1). An interesting consequence of this is, *if there is a constant term in the model* (as there often is), then:

$$\sum_{t=1}^{n} \hat{u}_t = 0$$

Prove this as an exercise.

THE COEFFICIENT OF DETERMINATION AND THE ADJUSTED COEFFICIENT OF DETERMINATION

Perhaps the most widely used measure of goodness-of-fit of a regression is the coefficient of determination (also commonly called the coefficient of multiple correlation) or its closely related counterpart, the *adjusted* coefficient of determination. The (almost) universal notation R^2 is used for the former while $\overline{R}^2$ is used for the latter. Let us derive these measures.

The goodness-of-fit of the fitted values $\hat{y}_t$, t = 1, 2, ..., n must clearly be judged on the basis of how close they are to the actual (observed) values y_t, t = 1, 2, ..., n. It can be shown that, if the general linear regression model contains a constant term,[1] then

$$\overline{y} = \frac{\sum_{t=1}^{n} y_t}{n} = \frac{\sum_{t=1}^{n} \hat{y}_t}{n}$$

That is, the average value of the observed y values ($\overline{y}$) is also the average of the fitted values. Therefore, if the regression fit is a reasonably good one, we can expect that the

[1] From now on, unless it is specifically stated otherwise, the general linear regression model will be assumed to contain a constant term which, without loss of generality, may be taken to be the first exogenous variable, x_{1t}.

two following values will not differ too much from each other and that the ratio of both of them should be close to unity:

$$TSS = \sum_{t=1}^{n} (y_t - \bar{y})^2$$

$$ESS = \sum_{t=1}^{n} (\hat{y}_t - \bar{y})^2$$

The notation TSS stands for "total sum of squares" while the notation ESS stands for "explained sum of squares". It can also be shown that they have the following relationship with each other:

$$\sum_{t=1}^{n} (y_t - \bar{y})^2 = \sum_{t=1}^{n} (\hat{y}_t - \bar{y})^2 + \sum_{t=1}^{n} \hat{u}_t^2$$

where the last term is clearly the sum of squared OLS residuals or the residual sum of squares (RSS). ESS and RSS are clearly bounded from above by TSS and bounded from below by zero, since all the terms in this expression are necessarily positive or zero. ESS and TSS would be identical in value if (and only if) RSS = 0, which implies that $\hat{u}_t = 0$ for all values of t which, in turn, implies that $y_t = \hat{y}_t$ for all values of t. The more y_t differs in value from $\hat{y}_t$, the smaller ESS becomes relative to TSS and the larger RSS becomes relative to TSS. In the limit, if RSS = TSS, then ESS = 0. Put another way, the better the fit, the closer is the ratio ESS/TSS to unity and the worse the fit, the closer is the ratio to zero. This ratio defines the coefficient of determination, i.e.

$$R^2 = \frac{ESS}{TSS} = \frac{\sum_{t=1}^{n} (\hat{y}_t - \bar{y})^2}{\sum_{t=1}^{n} (y_t - \bar{y})^2}$$

By construction, $0 \leq R^2 \leq 1$. A perfect fit is attained for $R^2 = 1$ and the worst possible fit (which is no fit at all) is obtained when $R^2 = 0$. The [0, 1] interval is the goodness-of-fit scale: the closer R^2 is to 1 the better the fit, and the closer it is to 0 the worse the fit.

In the numerical computation shown under Exhibit 1.1 in chapter 1, the value of R^2 is clearly shown as:

R-squared 0.942446

This means that just over 94% of the variation in the dependent variable (IMPORTS) is explained by the regression, which indicates an eminently good fit.

There is one serious shortcoming in the use of R^2 as a measure of goodness-of-fit: the addition of more and more explanatory variables, whatever their economic significance, never will result in a decrease in value of ESS and consequently of R^2 and is more likely to result in a rise in these values. An investigator wishing to maximize the value of R^2 need simply include in the regression more and more variables, whatever the economic justification for doing so. It is for this reason that an alternative measure was developed that does not share that weakness. It is defined as:

$$\bar{R}^2 = 1 - \frac{\dfrac{\sum_{t=1}^{n} \hat{u}_t^2}{n-k}}{\dfrac{\sum_{t=1}^{n} (y_t - \bar{y})^2}{n-1}} = 1 - (1 - R^2)\frac{(n-1)}{n-k}$$

Notice that, as the number (k) of explanatory variables increases, $\bar{R}^2$ will increase only if the increase in R^2 more than compensates for the fall in the value of $(n - k)$. Otherwise, it will fall.

The capacity of $\bar{R}^2$ to rise or fall when new variables are added to the explanatory variable list is the feature that endears it to applied economists and, in modern practice, it is more widely used as a measure of goodness-of-fit than R^2. Referring once again to the numerical computations shown under Exhibit 1.1 in chapter 1, this value is also calculated and displayed as:

Adjusted R-squared 0.937214

Using this measure, the conclusion is that just below 94% of the variation in IMPORTS is explained by the regression, which makes it a very good fit.

CONFIDENCE INTERVALS FOR COEFFICIENTS

The application of OLS yielded us *point estimates* of the β coefficients. Statistical theory teaches us that *interval estimates* are probably more useful because they allow us to consider a range of possible values within which the true parameter value may be located and, furthermore, we may associate a measurable confidence level with this range. There is also a more practical reason for considering a range of values rather than one single value: the use of econometric models for forecasting and policy analysis should not be too sensitive to minor modifications in the coefficient values used and the interval identified is a useful range over which we may vary the values if only to establish that the forecasts and policy prescriptions are not radically altered as a consequence.

The determination of interval estimates for a coefficient requires knowledge about the probability distribution of the estimated coefficients. For large sample sizes, the problem to some extent is solved for us by an appeal to the famous central limit theorem, which would tell us that:

$$\frac{\hat{\beta}_i - \beta_i}{SE(\hat{\beta}_i)} \sim N(0,1)$$

where $SE(\hat{\beta}_i)$ is the standard error of $\hat{\beta}_i$ which is equal to the square root of the *i*th diagonal element of $\sigma^2(\mathbf{X'X})^{-1}$.

However, in many econometric studies, especially those involving time series analysis, samples are usually quite small. The problem, therefore, must be solved by introducing distributional assumptions up front and, at the very best, attempting to validate such assumptions afterwards. It is usual to assume that the error vector **u** is normally distributed and, more specifically:

$$\mathbf{u} \sim N(\mathbf{0}, \sigma^2 \mathbf{I}_n) \qquad (A_4)$$

It follows immediately from this assumption that $\hat{\boldsymbol{\beta}}$ is also normally distributed since, as was shown in the previous chapter:

$$\hat{\boldsymbol{\beta}} = \boldsymbol{\beta} + (\mathbf{X'X})^{-1}\mathbf{X'u}$$

More specifically:

$$\hat{\boldsymbol{\beta}} \sim N(\boldsymbol{\beta}, \sigma^2(\mathbf{X'X})^{-1})$$

In particular:

$$\hat{\beta}_i \sim N(\beta_i, \text{var}(\hat{\beta}_i))$$

where $\text{var}(\hat{\beta}_i)$ is the *i*th diagonal element of $\sigma^2(\mathbf{X'X})^{-1}$. Let v_{ii}^2 be the *i*th diagonal element of $(\mathbf{X'X})^{-1}$. Then:

$$\text{var}(\hat{\beta}_i) = \sigma^2 v_{ii}^2$$

and

$$SE(\hat{\beta}_i) = \sqrt{\sigma^2 v_{ii}^2}$$

A standard result of statistical theory is:

$$\frac{\hat{\beta}_i - \beta_i}{\sqrt{\sigma^2 v_{ii}^2}} \sim N(0,1)$$

The 100(1 – α)% confidence interval, 0 < α < 1, is therefore easily determined as:[2]

$$\left[\hat{\beta}_i \pm z_{\alpha/2} \cdot \sqrt{\sigma^2 v_{ii}^2}\right]$$

where $z_{\alpha/2}$ is defined from the normal distribution as:

$$\Pr\left(-z_{\alpha/2} \leq \frac{\hat{\beta}_i - \beta_i}{\sqrt{\sigma^2 v_{ii}^2}} \leq z_{\alpha/2}\right) = 100(1-\alpha)\%$$

There is one important limitation in applying this result: σ^2 is unknown and it must therefore be estimated from the data.

It can be shown that:

$$s^2 = \frac{\hat{\mathbf{u}}'\hat{\mathbf{u}}}{n-k}$$

is an unbiased estimator of σ^2. Moreover, it can also be shown that:

$$\frac{\hat{\mathbf{u}}'\hat{\mathbf{u}}}{\sigma^2} \sim \chi^2_{n-k}$$

It can also be shown that $Z = \hat{\beta}_i - \beta_i / \sqrt{\sigma^2 v_{ii}^2}$ is independent of $C^2 = \hat{\mathbf{u}}'\hat{\mathbf{u}}/\sigma^2 = (n-k)\, s^2/\sigma^2$ and it therefore follows that:

$$\frac{\dfrac{Z}{\sqrt{C^2}}}{\sqrt{n-k}} = \frac{\hat{\beta}_i - \hat{\beta}_i}{\sqrt{s^2 v_{ii}^2}} \sim t_{n-k}$$

where t_{n-k} indicates the Student (T) distribution with n – k degrees of freedom. Note, too, that $\sqrt{s^2 v_{ii}^2}$ is the *estimated* standard error of $\hat{\beta}_i$. The 100(1 – α)% confidence interval is now based on the Student distribution and is easily calculated as:

$$\left[\hat{\beta}_i \pm t_{\alpha/2} \cdot \sqrt{s^2 v_{ii}^2}\right]$$

where $t_{\alpha/2}$ is defined from the Student distribution as:

$$\Pr\left(-t_{\alpha/2} \leq \frac{\hat{\beta}_i - \hat{\beta}}{\sqrt{s^2 v_{ii}^2}} \leq t_{\alpha/2}\right) = 100(1-\alpha)\%$$

[2] α is usually 0.01, 0.05 or 0.10.

for (n – k) degrees of freedom. Note that s^2 can be calculated from the EViews output either as the square of the "S.E. of regression", i.e. $383.8059^2 = 147307$ or as the "Sum squared resid" divided by (n – k) or 3240753/22 = 147307.

Consider the import function that was estimated in the previous chapter:

$$M_t = \beta_1 + \beta_2 Y_t + \beta_3 p_{mt}/p_{dt} + u_t$$

The relevant part of the output from EViews is:

Variable	Coefficient	Std. Error	T-Statistic	Prob.
C	-1188.641	696.9314	-1.705535	0.1022
INCOME	0.377639	0.029737	12.69930	0.0000
RATIO	-688.6762	155.8371	-4.419206	0.0002

Here, β_2 is estimated as 0.377639 and its estimated standard error is calculated as 0.029737. The 95% confidence interval for β_2 is therefore:

$$[0.377639 - (2.074)(0.029737), 0.377639 + (2.074)(0.029737)] = [0.3160, 0.4393]$$

where 2.074 is the value of $t_{0.025}$ read from the tables of the Student distribution for (25 – 3) = 22 degrees of freedom. If the exercise were to be repeated over and over again, β_2 would lie in the calculated interval 95% of the time.

The 90% confidence interval would be:

$$[0.377639 - (1.717)(0.029737),\ 0.377639 + (1.717)(0.029737)] = [0.3266,\ 0.4287]$$

where $t_{0.05} = 1.717$ for 22 degrees of freedom. For large samples,[3] the Student distribution may be approximated by the standard normal distribution. In this case, to construct the 95% confidence interval, the value of $t_{0.025}$ can be read from the normal distribution as 1.960 (approximately 2) and for the 90% interval, the value of $t_{0.05}$ is 1.645.

SIGNIFICANCE TESTS OF COEFFICIENTS

To some extent, when an economist includes a particular variable among the exogenous variable list, he or she is not always certain that this variable can be used to explain the dependent or endogenous variable. In the import function, for instance, it is a matter for empirical verification that either the income variable or the relative price variable truly helps to explain imports. Suppose one of them, income, for example, was wrongly included, then we would expect that $\beta_2 = 0$. Testing the nullity of coefficients like β_2 is one of the most important exercises in applied econometrics. We will now look at how it is done.

[3] In practice, a sample is deemed to be large enough if there are thirty or more degrees of freedom.

An intuitively appealing procedure involves looking at the problem in the framework of the confidence intervals just discussed. Consider, for instance, the 95% interval constructed for β_2 in the import function. If we believe that a strong chance exists for $\beta_2 = 0$ to be true, then clearly the value of zero should lie in this interval. After all, the true value of β_2 will lie in this interval 95 times out of 100 and, clearly, if $\beta_2 = 0$ is true, then it should be a value in this interval. Put another way, if the value zero does not belong to this interval, the chances of it being the true value of β_2 is 5% (at best!). So if zero is not in the interval, we have very good reason to reject the hypothesis that $\beta_2 = 0$. As it stands, the interval does not contain zero, and so the hypothesis is rejected.

Of course, the student may well know that there is a more formal approach to doing a test like this one and it involves the use of the "T" statistic:

$$\left(\hat{\beta}_i - \beta_i\right) / \sqrt{s^2 v_{ii}^2}$$

In formal terms, the null hypothesis:

$$H_0 : \beta_i = 0$$

is tested against the alternative hypothesis:

$$H_1 : \beta_i \neq 0$$

at the 100α% level. The test statistic in this case is $\hat{\beta}_i / \sqrt{s^2 v_{ii}^2}$, and its *absolute value* (size irrespective of sign), which is the test statistic, is compared to $t_{\alpha/2}$ (for n – k degrees of freedom) which is defined above. The null is rejected if the test statistic exceeds $t_{\alpha/2}$ and not rejected in the event that it does not.

To illustrate from the import function we have been looking at, the test statistic is calculated as 0.377639/0.029737 = 12.6993. The value of $t_{0.025}$ read from the table is 2.074 and so the null hypothesis is resoundingly rejected at the 5% level (and therefore at all higher levels, including 10%). To test at 1%, the value of $t_{0.005}$ for 22 degrees of freedom is read as 2.819 and so the null hypothesis is rejected at this level as well.

The test of the nullity of a given regression coefficient is so popular that standard econometric packages like EViews provide the value of its test statistic automatically. It is shown in Exhibit 1.1 in the previous chapter under the column headed "T-Statistic".

The advent of modern computing capabilities also allows the calculation of "p-values", which show the lowest level of significance at which a given null hypothesis would be rejected. If, for instance, a p-value is calculated as 0.073, this simply means that the corresponding null hypothesis must be rejected at levels of significance 7.3% and higher. It can therefore be rejected at 10%, but not at 5% or 1%. EViews automatically calculates the p-value associated with the test of the nullity of a given coefficient as:

$$\Pr\left(-\text{T-statistic associated with } \hat{\beta}_i \leq \frac{\hat{\beta}_i - \beta_i}{\sqrt{s^2 v_{ii}^2}} \leq \text{T-statistic associated with } \hat{\beta}_i \right) = \text{p-value}$$

using the formula of the Student distribution. This is shown under the column headed "Prob.". EViews is programmed to print this p-value to four decimal places and, for β_2, this value is given as 0.0000, which approximates a value that is very close to zero. It is calculated from the Student distribution as:

$$\Pr\left(-12.69930 \leq \frac{\hat{\beta}_2}{\sqrt{s^2 v_{22}^2}} \leq 12.69930\right) = 0.0000$$

This means that the null is rejected even at very low levels of significance and so will also be rejected at higher levels like 1%, 5% and 10%. As an exercise, carry out this test for β_1 (the constant term) and β_3 (the coefficient of RATIO).

In addition to testing for the nullity of a given coefficient, the Student distribution is also valid for any test of the null:

$$H_0 : \beta_i = \gamma$$

against one or more of the following alternative hypotheses:

$$H_1 : \beta_i \neq \gamma$$

or

$$H_1 : \beta_i < \gamma$$

or

$$H_1 : \beta_i > \gamma$$

where γ can be any real number, not necessarily zero. Suppose, for instance, we want to test the hypothesis that the marginal propensity to import is less than 40%. This is a one-tailed test and the test statistic associated with it is:

$$\frac{\hat{\beta}_2 - 0.40}{\text{S.E.}\left(\hat{\beta}_2\right)} = \frac{0.377639 - 0.40}{0.029737} = -0.752$$

The null hypothesis is rejected in favour of the alternative if this value is less than the corresponding value read from the Student distribution for 22 degrees of freedom at the chosen significance level. At the 5% level, this value is –1.725. The null hypothesis that the marginal propensity to import is 40% cannot be rejected at the 5% level of significance.

TESTING THE SIMULTANEOUS NULLITY OF THE SLOPE COEFFICIENTS

It is important to test the nullity of a given coefficient because, as economists, we want to know whether the associated variable intervenes in the explanation of the dependent variable. But it is also important to know whether an entire subset of the supposedly explanatory variables intervene significantly or not and, in the final analysis, this can include *all* the explanatory variables. In this section of the book, we will concentrate on the case of the nullity of all the slope coefficients, i.e. all except the constant term, and will leave for later consideration the case of any particular subset. The null hypothesis we are looking at is the following:

$$H_0: \beta_2 = \beta_3 = \ldots = \beta_k = 0$$

while the best way to describe the alternative hypothesis is "not H_0".

Let us look once again at the breakdown of the variation in the dependent variable:

$$\sum_{t=1}^{n} (y_t - \bar{y})^2 = \sum_{t=1}^{n} (\hat{y}_t - \bar{y})^2 + \sum_{t=1}^{n} \hat{u}_t^2$$

If the slope coefficients are zero, then we would expect that

$$ESS = \sum_{t=1}^{n} (\hat{y}_t - \bar{y})^2$$

would be equal to zero. Therefore, if ESS is not significantly different from zero, we may conclude that there is sufficient evidence to suggest that the slope coefficients are not significantly different from zero. It can be shown that, if the null hypothesis is true, then:

$$\frac{\sum_{t=1}^{n} (\hat{y}_t - \bar{y})^2}{\sigma^2} \sim \chi^2_{k-1}$$

Using this result as it stands is a bit awkward since σ^2 is unknown. However, we do know that, whether the null is true or not,

$$\frac{\sum_{t=1}^{n} \hat{u}_t^2}{\sigma^2} \sim \chi^2_{n-k}$$

It can also be shown that, when the null is true, these two Chi squares are independent of each other. It therefore follows that:

$$\frac{\sum_{t=1}^{n} (\hat{y}_t - \bar{y})^2}{\sum_{t=1}^{n} \hat{u}_t^2} \frac{n-k}{k-1} \sim F_{k-1,n-k}$$

The null hypothesis is to be rejected at a given level of significance if the calculated value of this statistic exceeds the value read from the Fischer–Snedecor Tables for the stated degrees of freedom.

For the import function that is under consideration, the null hypothesis is:

$$H_0: \beta_2 = \beta_3 = 0$$

and the test statistic is calculated as:

$$\text{F-statistic} \quad 180.1255$$

For $(k - 1) = 2$ and $(n - k) = 22$ degrees of freedom in the numerator and denominator, respectively, the value read from the table at the 5% significance level is 3.44. The null hypothesis is resoundingly rejected at this level of significance, i.e. there is insufficient evidence to allow us to conclude that the two slope coefficients are simultaneously equal to zero.

EViews also provides the p-value associated with this test and it is shown as:

$$\text{Prob}(\text{F-statistic})\ 0.000000$$

which proves that the null will be rejected at very low significance levels, including 1%, 5% and 10%.

"ECONOMIC" EVALUATION OF REGRESSION RESULTS

As economists, we develop an understanding and appreciation of economic matters that become an indispensable part of our profession. When using the tools of regression analysis, we cannot ignore our own (perhaps subjective) feelings on the phenomenon under study simply because they will be based on this understanding and appreciation that we have developed over the years.

Consider, for instance, the import function. We may have an idea about the value of the marginal propensity to import that may be in stark contrast to the value obtained from application of the regression. If this happens, we simply cannot abandon our own feelings on the matter on the pretext that "the computer says so". Clearly, we cannot ignore what the results are telling us but neither must we accept them unquestioningly.

As we advance in our study of econometrics, we will see that there are many occasions and situations (due to data inadequacies, for instance) that will further justify the need for our personal interventions. Unfortunately, this is sometimes taken to the other extreme, and many economists are not prepared to accept any result that is at odds with their own feelings. This has led to the practice of "data mining", in which economists fiddle with hundreds of regression runs on the computer, retaining and reporting only those that suit their own fancy. This is discussed at length in Charemza and Deadman (1997) and it is not a practice to be encouraged.

REPORTING REGRESSION RESULTS

Refer to the results displayed in Exhibit 1.1 of the previous chapter. This represents an item of communication between the computer and the user. The user, assumedly, will have read the corresponding manuals and will understand the "coded" messages shown. We must not, however, assume that a third party will understand this output largely because we have no right to assume that he or she is familiar with EViews. Certain conventions have been established for reporting the results shown in Exhibit 1.1 and in Exhibit 2.1 we show what we consider to be the most popular template, using as an illustration the results from Exhibit 1.1.

EXHIBIT 2.1
Proposed template for reporting regression results

$$M_t = -1188.64 + \underset{(12.70)}{0.378\, Y_t} - \underset{(4.42)}{688.7\, p_{mt}/p_{dt}}$$

$$\bar{R}^2 = 0.937 \quad DW = 1.67 \quad F = 180.1$$

The values in parentheses below the estimated slope coefficients are the corresponding t-ratios. Notice that the t-ratio associated with the constant term is not reported. This is a matter of taste and reflects the authors' view that more attention should be paid to the value of the slope coefficients unless there is some compelling reason to do otherwise.

The values of $\bar{R}^2$ and the F-statistic are clearly shown, as well as another statistic – the Durbin–Watson statistic (DW). The use of the Durbin–Watson statistic will be discussed in chapter 4.

EXERCISES

1. Consider the general linear regression model

$$\mathbf{y} = \mathbf{X}\boldsymbol{\beta} + \mathbf{u}$$

   a) Discuss the relative usefulness of the adjusted and unadjusted coefficients of determination in the evaluation of econometric models like this one.
   b) Let β_i be the *i*th element of the coefficient vector $\boldsymbol{\beta}$. Stating clearly your assumptions, formally derive a statistic based on the Student distribution for testing the hypothesis $\beta_i = \beta_{i*}$ against $\beta_i \neq \beta_{i*}$.
   c) Describe (using an illustration if you wish) the mechanism of the test for $\beta_{i*} = 0$.
   d) How would you test the hypotheses:

$$\text{(i)}\ \beta_i = \beta_j$$

$$\text{(ii)}\ \beta_i + \beta_j = 1, i \neq j$$

e) Assuming there is a constant term in the model, formally derive (using but clearly stating assumptions) a test statistic for testing the simultaneous nullity of the slope coefficients. How would you carry out this test?

2. Return to the Dominican savings function introduced in exercise 4, Chapter 1. Consider the fit again and do the following:
   - Is the fit a good one?
   - Are the coefficients significant?
   - Carry out the F test
   - Construct a 95% confidence interval for α_1.
   - Report the results using the template shown in Exhibit 2.1 of this chapter.

CHAPTER 3

Some Issues in the Application of the General Linear Regression Model

MULTICOLLINEARITY: THE PROBLEM

In the general linear regression model:

$$y_t = \beta_1 x_{1t} + \beta_2 x_{2t} + \beta_3 x_{3t} + \ldots + \beta_k x_{kt} + u_t$$

which in matrix notation becomes:

$$\mathbf{y} = \mathbf{X}\boldsymbol{\beta} + \mathbf{u}$$

it is implicitly assumed that the columns of $\mathbf{X}$ are *linearly independent* of each other. A set of vectors $\mathbf{x}_1, \mathbf{x}_2, \ldots, \mathbf{x}_k$ is said to be linearly dependent if there exists a set of scalars $\lambda_1, \lambda_2, \ldots, \lambda_k$ not all equal to zero, such that:

$$\lambda_1 \mathbf{x}_1 + \lambda_2 \mathbf{x}_2 + \ldots + \lambda_k \mathbf{x}_k = 0$$

Similarly, it is said to be linearly independent if the only case for which the above is true is when all the λs are equal to zero.

One of the most fundamental assumptions for the application of the OLS method – perhaps *the* most fundamental – is that the matrix of explanatory variables $\mathbf{X}$ is of full rank. Recall the well-known normal equation introduced in chapter 1:

$$\mathbf{X}'\mathbf{X}\hat{\boldsymbol{\beta}} = \mathbf{X}'\mathbf{y}$$

which can be solved for $\hat{\boldsymbol{\beta}}$ to give:

$$\hat{\boldsymbol{\beta}} = (\mathbf{X}'\mathbf{X})^{-1}\mathbf{X}'\mathbf{y} = \begin{bmatrix} \hat{\beta}_1 \\ \hat{\beta}_2 \\ \vdots \\ \hat{\beta}_k \end{bmatrix}$$

provided that **X′X** admits an inverse. For a square (k × k) matrix to be invertible, it must be of full rank k, which implies that **X**, too, must be of rank k.[1] The rank of a matrix is equal to the maximum number of linearly independent rows or columns and, if two or more columns of **X** are linearly dependent, then the rank of **X** would be less than k. Let us see what this implies for OLS estimation with the use of a simple illustration.

Consider the four-variable model:

$$\mathbf{y} = \beta_1 \mathbf{x}_1 + \beta_2 \mathbf{x}_2 + \beta_3 \mathbf{x}_3 + \beta_4 \mathbf{x}_4 + \mathbf{u}$$

and suppose that:

$$\mathbf{x}_2 - \lambda_3 \mathbf{x}_3 - \lambda_4 \mathbf{x}_4 = 0$$

or

$$\mathbf{x}_2 = \lambda_3 \mathbf{x}_3 + \lambda_4 \mathbf{x}_4$$

that is, there exists linear dependence. It is easily deduced that, for some real value α:

$$\begin{aligned} \beta_2 \mathbf{x}_2 &= (\beta_2 - \alpha)\mathbf{x}_2 + \alpha \mathbf{x}_2 \\ &= (\beta_2 - \alpha)\mathbf{x}_2 + \alpha(\lambda_3 \mathbf{x}_3 + \lambda_4 \mathbf{x}_4) \end{aligned}$$

and

$$\mathbf{y} = \beta_1 \mathbf{x}_1 + (\beta_2 - \alpha)\mathbf{x}_2 + (\beta_3 + \alpha\lambda_3)\mathbf{x}_3 + (\beta_4 + \alpha\lambda_4)\mathbf{x}_4 + \mathbf{u}$$

Clearly, if we obtain a structure β_1, β_2, β_3, β_4 compatible with the **y** observations, any other structure of the form β_1, $(\beta_2 - \alpha)$, $(\beta_3 + \alpha\lambda_3)$, $(\beta_4 + \alpha\lambda_4)$ is also compatible. The relation between the distribution of the stochastic term **u** and the endogenous variable **y** will be the same for an infinite number of coefficient values, depending on whatever value we wish to give to α. From a statistical point of view, these structures are equivalent, since the observations do not allow us to distinguish between them. We say that the coefficients of the model are not *identifiable*, in which case estimation is impossible. This is the case of "perfect multicollinearity".

This perfect multicollinearity outlined above is a limiting case, however; one that is rarely, if at all, encountered in practice. What is usually referred to as multicollinearity in the literature (perhaps incorrectly so) is a less extreme case of the foregoing, and should in fact be referred to as "near-multicollinearity" or "pseudo-collinearity". This is the case where there exists a strong (but not perfect) correlation

[1] It will *always* be assumed that n ≥ k (a necessary condition for the rank of **X** to be equal to k) and the problem of multicollinearity will be concerned with the case where the rank of **X** is less than k even though n ≥ k.

between any two or more of the explanatory variables in the model. The stronger this correlation is, the more chronic is the collinearity problem. This pseudo-collinearity is more the rule than the exception with economic data, especially time series data, given the inherent nature of economic magnitudes to move together over time. Hence, with respect to economic data, the question becomes more the *degree* of pseudo-collinearity in the model, rather than its presence or absence.

In the OLS estimation exercise, the economist really has two tasks: estimation of the equation and interpretation of the results. The presence of perfect multicollinearity implies that the estimation phase cannot be undertaken. The presence of pseudo-collinearity in a regression model does not prevent OLS estimation; the danger here, however, lies, in the interpretation of the output from the estimation phase. As will become more evident later, the investigator must exercise great caution when attempting to draw definitive conclusions from a model in which pseudo-collinearity is present. Let us examine some of the more dire consequences of this pseudo-collinearity which, following a time-honoured tradition, we will refer to as multicollinearity.

When two or more columns of **X** are correlated, we cannot easily distinguish the relative contributions of each variable in the explanation of **y**. If the column vectors comprising **X** are orthogonal,[2] the coefficient values obtained from OLS estimation accurately reflect the degree to which each explanatory variable in the model serves to explain the variation in the variable **y** under study. If one or more of the explanatory variables were to be subsequently eliminated from the model, the coefficient values of the remaining explanatory variables would remain unchanged. Indeed, the absolute independence of the right-hand variables in the model means that there would no longer exist the need for the estimation of a multiple regression model – the same coefficient estimates could be obtained by performing a series of simple regressions of y on each of the explanatory **X**-variables.

With the presence of multicollinearity in the model, the coefficient values obtained from OLS estimation may no longer accurately reflect the relative importance of each explanatory variable. This loss of precision may manifest itself in three ways:

1. Specific estimates may have large errors
2. These errors may be highly correlated
3. Sampling variances will tend to be very high.

For any of the above reasons, investigators may sometimes be led to drop variables from the regression. The T-tests may, for example, show them to be insignificant. But the true situation may be, not that an explanatory variable has no effect, but rather that the sample data set has not allowed us to pick up the actual effect. Multicollinearity therefore is indicative of a problem in the data being used in the regression, and does not necessarily negate the underlying economic theory. All that is occurring is that the data are rendering us ill equipped to either validate *or* invalidate the theory.

Finally, coefficient estimates tend to become, in the presence of multicollinearity, very sensitive to particular sample data sets. As a result, the addition of a few or

[2] Vectors $\mathbf{x}_i$ and $\mathbf{x}_j$ are said to be orthogonal if $\mathbf{x}_i'\mathbf{x}_j = 0,\ i \neq j$.

more observations may produce dramatic shifts in some of the coefficient values, sometimes to the extent that the signs of the estimates may actually change.

Let us consider for illustrative purposes, the following simple case:

$$\mathbf{y} = \beta_1 \mathbf{x}_1 + \beta_2 \mathbf{x}_2 + \mathbf{u}$$

where the **x** vectors contain variables measured from the mean – for example, the first element of $\mathbf{x}_1$ is $(x_{11} - \bar{x}_1)$, and a typical element $\mathbf{x}_1$ is $(x_{1t} - \bar{x}_1)$, where $\bar{x}_1 = \Sigma x_{1t}/n$.

Therefore:

$$\mathbf{X'X} = \begin{bmatrix} x_{11} - \bar{x}_1 & \cdots & \cdots & \cdots & x_{1n} - \bar{x}_1 \\ x_{21} - \bar{x}_2 & \cdots & \cdots & \cdots & x_{2n} - \bar{x}_2 \end{bmatrix} \begin{bmatrix} x_{11} - \bar{x}_1 & x_{21} - \bar{x}_2 \\ \vdots & \vdots \\ \vdots & \vdots \\ \vdots & \vdots \\ x_{1n} - \bar{x}_1 & x_{2n} - \bar{x}_2 \end{bmatrix}$$

$$= \begin{bmatrix} \sum_{t=1}^{n} (x_{1t} - \bar{x}_1)^2 & \sum_{t=1}^{n} (x_{1t} - \bar{x}_1)(x_{2t} - \bar{x}_2) \\ \sum_{t=1}^{n} (x_{1t} - \bar{x}_1)(x_{2t} - \bar{x}_2) & \sum_{t=1}^{n} (x_{2t} - \bar{x}_2)^2 \end{bmatrix}$$

We know that the coefficient of linear correlation between x_1 and x_2 is estimated by:

$$r = \frac{\sum_{t=1}^{n} (x_{1t} - \bar{x}_1)(x_{2t} - \bar{x}_2)}{\sqrt{\sum_{t=1}^{n} (x_{1t} - \bar{x}_1)^2 \sum_{t=1}^{n} (x_{2t} - \bar{x}_2)^2}}$$

and so we can write:

$$\mathbf{X'X} = \begin{bmatrix} \dfrac{\sum_{t=1}^{n} (x_{1t} - \bar{x}_1)^2}{r\sqrt{\sum_{t=1}^{n} (x_{1t} - \bar{x}_1)^2 \sum_{t=1}^{n} (x_{2t} - \bar{x}_2)^2}} & r\sqrt{\sum_{t=1}^{n} (x_{1t} - \bar{x}_1)^2 \sum_{t=1}^{n} (x_{2t} - \bar{x}_2)^2} \\ & \sum_{t=1}^{n} (x_{2t} - \bar{x}_2)^2 \end{bmatrix}$$

We know that, for any square matrix **A,** the inverse of **A** is defined as:

$$\mathbf{A}^{-1} = \frac{1}{|\mathbf{A}|} \mathbf{A}^{+}$$

where $\mathbf{A}^+$ is the matrix of co-factors and $|\mathbf{A}|$ the determinant of $\mathbf{A}$. It follows that, since:

$$|\mathbf{X}'\mathbf{X}| = \sum_{t=1}^{n}(x_{1t}-\bar{x}_1)^2 \sum_{t=1}^{n}(x_{2t}-\bar{x}_2)^2 - r^2 \sum_{t=1}^{n}(x_{1t}-\bar{x}_1)^2 \sum_{t=1}^{n}(x_{2t}-\bar{x}_2)^2$$

$$= (1-r^2)\sum_{t=1}^{n}(x_{1t}-\bar{x}_1)^2 \sum_{t=1}^{n}(x_{2t}-\bar{x}_2)^2$$

then,

$$(\mathbf{X}'\mathbf{X})^{-1} = \frac{1}{(1-r^2)\sum_{t=1}^{n}(x_{1t}-\bar{x}_1)^2 \sum_{t=1}^{n}(x_{2t}-\bar{x}_2)^2}$$

$$\begin{bmatrix} \sum_{t=1}^{n}(x_{2t}-\bar{x}_2)^2 & -r\sqrt{\sum_{t=1}^{n}(x_{1t}-\bar{x}_1)^2 \sum_{t=1}^{n}(x_{2t}-\bar{x}_2)^2} \\ -r\sqrt{\sum_{t=1}^{n}(x_{1t}-\bar{x}_1)^2 \sum_{t=1}^{n}(x_{2t}-\bar{x}_2)^2} & \sum_{t=1}^{n}(x_{1t}-\bar{x}_1)^2 \end{bmatrix}$$

If r^2 were equal to zero (as it would if the columns of the $\mathbf{X}$ matrix were orthogonal to each other), then $|\mathbf{X}'\mathbf{X}|$ would be non-zero and so the matrix $(\mathbf{X}'\mathbf{X})^{-1}$ would exist. Conversely, if the coefficient of correlation r^2 were equal to one (as it would in the presence of perfect multicollinearity or linear dependence in the $\mathbf{X}$ matrix), $|\mathbf{X}'\mathbf{X}|$ would equal zero, and hence $(\mathbf{X}'\mathbf{X})^{-1}$ would not be invertible. However, as we have already mentioned, these two extreme cases are hardly ever the reality. Instead, the real concern arises when r^2 tends to (but does not equal) the value of one. As this occurs, the elements of the matrix $(\mathbf{X}'\mathbf{X})^{-1}$ become larger and larger. If we remember, then, that:

$$\text{var}(\hat{\boldsymbol{\beta}}) = \sigma^2(\mathbf{X}'\mathbf{X})^{-1}$$

where:

$$\hat{\boldsymbol{\beta}} = \begin{bmatrix} \hat{\beta}_1 \\ \hat{\beta}_2 \end{bmatrix}$$

is the column matrix of the OLS estimators, then clearly, increasing collinearity among the explanatory variables implies corresponding increases in the variances (and so the standard errors) of their associated coefficient estimates. This means that the presence of pseudo-collinearity may lead to a non-rejection of the classic null hypothesis that the true value of the coefficient estimate is equal to zero, and so can cause the unsuspecting investigator to erroneously exclude a possibly relevant explanatory variable from further regression analysis.

MULTICOLLINEARITY: DETECTION

There will inevitably be some degree of multicollinearity in an econometric model. The foregoing discussion highlights large standard errors of the parameter estimates as an indication of its presence. However, such standard errors and their correspondingly high p-values *could* also mean that the chosen explanatory variables have little or no relevance to the explanation of the variable under study. How does one therefore decide whether it is the multicollinearity or the economic theory underlying the model that is to blame? A possible answer lies, not in an examination of the standard errors and p-values of the model alone, but rather in the study of the $R^2, \overline{R}^2$, and F-statistics as well.

Consider the following scenario. The OLS estimation of a linear regression model yields coefficient values that have associated with them extremely large standard errors and as such, very large p-values. However, the model also shows R^2 and $\overline{R}^2$ values close to one, as well as a high F-statistic with its associated p-value close to zero. What is occurring here? On the basis of the coefficient results alone, one may conclude that the coefficient estimates are not significantly different from zero, and so the model needs to be respecified. However, the F-statistic is indicating the unequivocal rejection of the null hypothesis of the simultaneous nullity of the slope coefficients. Furthermore, the "goodness-of-fit" measures are indicating that a large portion of the variation in the dependent variable is being explained by the present regression. In *this* situation, one may surmise that it is the presence of severe multicollinearity that is responsible for such contradictory results.

A further indication of severe multicollinearity in a regression model can be found in an analysis of the correlation matrix of the explanatory variables in the model. We know that the sample correlation coefficient between x_i and x_j is defined as follows:

$$r_{ij} = \frac{\sum_{t=1}^{n}\left(x_{it} - \overline{x}_i\right)\left(x_{jt} - \overline{x}_j\right)}{\sqrt{\sum_{t=1}^{n}\left(x_{it} - \overline{x}_i\right)^2}\sqrt{\sum_{t=1}^{n}\left(x_{jt} - \overline{x}_j\right)^2}}$$

In the special case where $i = j$, $r_{ii} = 1$. We can therefore define the sample *correlation matrix* for the k explanatory variables, as follows:

$$\mathbf{R} = \begin{bmatrix} r_{11}^2 & r_{12} & \cdots & \cdots & r_{1k} \\ r_{21} & r_{22}^2 & \cdots & \cdots & r_{2k} \\ \vdots & \vdots & & & \vdots \\ \vdots & \vdots & & & \vdots \\ r_{k1} & r_{k2} & \cdots & \cdots & r_{kk}^2 \end{bmatrix}$$

where the diagonal elements represent the coefficient of correlation of each variable with itself (hence equalling one), and the off-diagonal elements represent the coefficient of correlation of each variable with another. Any off-diagonal elements close to one would therefore indicate the presence of severe multicollinearity in a model. This is not to say, however, that off-diagonal values not close to unity imply the absence of multicollinearity. For herein lies the danger of this method as an indicator of multicollinearity – while there may not be a strong correlation between any *two* variables in the model as indicated by this matrix, there could exist a strong correlation between *combinations* of the explanatory variables, which this matrix cannot indicate. EViews may be used to obtain this correlation matrix.

MULTICOLLINEARITY: A SOLUTION?

Multicollinearity is a data problem that cannot easily be remedied. A widely used solution is to remove the variables that are highly collinear. If the multicollinearity is very great, this is an intuitively justifiable procedure – the same information will still to some extent be available from the remaining variables. This amounts, however, to setting the true coefficient values of the omitted variables equal to zero, and unless this is effectively true, the OLS parameter estimates will be biased, as we shall see below.

MULTICOLLINEARITY: AN ILLUSTRATION

Let us once again consider the import function that we have looked at in chapters 1 and 2. This time, however, we modify the function to include C_g (government consumption expenditure) for which there is ample theoretical justification. For example, international lending agencies, such as the International Monetary Fund (IMF), often maintain that governments should cut their spending as this inevitably leads to increased spending on imports and, eventually, balance of payments deficits. The inclusion of C_g among the explanatory variables allows us to test this theory and, should it prove to be valid, we may use the model to measure the impact of increased government spending on imports.

The model to be fitted is:

$$M_t = \beta_1 + \beta_2 Y_t + \beta_3\, p_{mt}/p_{dt} + \beta_4 C_{gt} + u_t$$

and the results obtained by the application of OLS, with G_CONS being the notation used for C_g in EViews, are shown in Exhibit 3.1.

Here β_4 (the coefficient of C_g) is not only estimated with an incorrect (minus) sign, which appears to contradict the IMF theory, but it is also highly insignificant with a p-value of over 60%. The constant term is not at all significant and β_3 is significant only at about 9%. In fact, the only convincing explanatory variable is income with a p-value of 0.0001. And yet, there is a very high R^2 (over 90%) and an F-statistic with a p-value almost equal to zero. These are all tell-tale signs of the presence of multicollinearity. Let us look at the problem a little more closely.

Dissatisfaction with the performance of the C_g variable may entice us to drop it from the relationship, leaving us with the model already estimated in chapter 1. If

EXHIBIT 3.1
OLS Regression fit of
$M_t = \beta_1 + \beta_2 Y_t + \beta_3 p_{mt}/p_{dt} + \beta_4 C_{gt} + u_t$

LS // Dependent Variable is IMPORTS
Date: 08/12/95 Time: 18:42
Sample: 1967 1991
Included observations: 25

Variable	Coefficient	Std. Error	T-Statistic	Prob.
C	-727.4020	1191.544	-0.610470	0.5481
INCOME	0.418379	0.089812	4.658357	0.0001
RATIO	-931.5592	528.4922	-1.762673	0.0925
G_CONS	-0.225711	0.468481	-0.481793	0.6349

R-squared	0.943075	Mean dependent var	3556.082
Adjusted R-squared	0.934943	S.D. dependent var	1531.723
S.E. of regression	390.6845	Akaike info criter	12.08145
Sum squared resid	3205323.	Schwarz criterion	12.27647
Log likelihood	-182.4916	F-statistic	115.9697
Durbin-Watson stat	1.727823	Prob(F-statistic)	0.000000

EXHIBIT 3.2
Correlation matrix for Y, p_m/p_d and C_g
(from EViews)

	INCOME	G_CONS	RATIO
INCOME	1.000000	0.858551	-0.566984
G_CONS	0.858551	1.000000	-0.889659
RATIO	-0.566984	-0.889659	1.000000

we look back at those results, we will see that both β_2 and β_3 are very significant while the R^2 and F-statistics are similar to those shown in Exhibit 3.1. It would appear that we did well to drop C_g from the equation. But examination of Exhibit 3.2 above reveals that C_g is highly correlated with both Y and p_m/p_d.

So multicollinearity is indeed a problem, and the importance of C_g to the explanation of imports may have been masked. We become more convinced of this when we look at the results in Exhibit 3.3.

This time it is the income variable that is dropped and the results are astonishing. Not only does C_g have the correct sign; it is now (or appears to be!) highly significant. It also appears that the "significance" of β_3 has improved considerably: it now has a p-value of 0.0092 compared to 0.0925 in Exhibit 3.1 (and at the same time confirms the IMF fears with a vengeance: for every extra dollar that the government spends,

EXHIBIT 3.3
OLS Regression fit of
$M_t = \beta_1 + \beta_3 \, p_{mt}/p_{dt} + \beta_4 \, C_{gt} + u_t$

```
=================================================================
LS // Dependent Variable is IMPORTS
Date: 08/12/95   Time: 18:44
Sample: 1967 1991
Included observations: 25
=================================================================
     Variable     Coefficient Std. Error  T-Statistic     Prob.
=================================================================
        C          -3891.503   1363.900  -2.853217     0.0092
      G_CONS        1.828956   0.219974   8.314420     0.0000
      RATIO         1138.220   398.6708   2.855036     0.0092
=================================================================
R-squared             0.884253   Mean dependent var    3556.082
Adjusted R-squared    0.873730   S.D. dependent var    1531.723
S.E. of regression    544.2900   Akaike info criter    12.71113
Sum squared resid     6517534.   Schwarz criterion     12.85740
Log likelihood       -191.3626   F-statistic           84.03447
Durbin-Watson stat    1.238556   Prob(F-statistic)     0.000000
=================================================================
```

the Trinidad and Tobago consumers spend \$1.83 on imports). Furthermore, the R^2 and F-statistics leave us in no doubt that this is a good fit.

What then do we do? It is very difficult to answer this question at this stage of our study of econometrics but at least one word of warning is in order: the conclusions about the significance of this or that variable under the conditions of multicollinearity shown here are very tenuous and great caution should be exercised in using any of the results shown. Furthermore, the process through which variables are (arbitrarily) added and dropped from an equation, as was done here, has given rise to charges of data mining.

MISSPECIFICATION

An implicit assumption underlying the optimality of the OLS estimator (in the Gauss–Markov sense) is that the general linear regression model

$$\mathbf{y} = \mathbf{X}\boldsymbol{\beta} + \mathbf{u}$$

is correctly specified. In particular, we assumed that no important explanatory variable was missing from the model and the error term **u** effectively accounted for the missing variables. But this assumption very frequently does not hold. A model may be misspecified for several reasons. The multicollinearity problem, discussed above, often forces an investigator to drop a variable that should be contained in the true specification, because this variable may be highly correlated with the others. It may sometimes be the case that the economic theory under study may itself be defective, causing the investigator to misspecify the model. Or, as is so frequent in the field of economics, the theory may involve variables that are not directly measurable, or for which data are just not readily available, such as, for example, consumer tastes in a demand function, or capital stock in a production function.

Whatever the reason for the misspecification of a model, its effect is to subsume the influence of the missing variable(s) into the disturbance term, and it can (and will) be shown that, in this case, OLS estimation is biased. Worse than that, the bias does not disappear as the sample size increases (and OLS estimation is said to be inconsistent).

It is possible, however, to show the effect of the absence of an important explanatory variable.[3] Consider the following "true" model:

$$y_t = \beta_1 x_{1t} + \beta_2 x_{2t} + u_t$$

The economist, however, wrongly specifies that:

$$y_t = \beta_1 x_{1t} + v_t$$

and this misspecified model is fitted by OLS to yield the following:

$$\hat{\beta}_1 = (\mathbf{X}'\mathbf{X})^{-1}\mathbf{X}'\mathbf{y}$$

where

$$(\mathbf{X}'\mathbf{X})^{-1} = \left[\begin{pmatrix} x_{11} & x_{12} & \cdots & \cdots & x_{1n} \end{pmatrix} \begin{pmatrix} x_{11} \\ x_{12} \\ \vdots \\ \vdots \\ x_{1n} \end{pmatrix} \right]^{-1} = \left(\sum_{t=1}^{n} x_{1t}^2 \right)^{-1} = \frac{1}{\sum_{t=1}^{n} x_{1t}^2}$$

and

$$(\mathbf{X}'\mathbf{y}) = \begin{pmatrix} x_{11} & x_{12} & \cdots & \cdots & x_{1n} \end{pmatrix} \begin{pmatrix} y_1 \\ y_2 \\ \vdots \\ \vdots \\ y_n \end{pmatrix} = \sum_{t=1}^{n} (x_{1t} y_y)$$

Therefore:

$$\hat{\beta}_1 = (\mathbf{X}'\mathbf{X})^{-1}\mathbf{X}'\mathbf{y} = \frac{\sum_{t=1}^{n} (x_{1t} y_t)}{\sum_{t=1}^{n} x_{1t}^2}$$

[3] In Part II of this book, tests for this and other kinds of model misspecification will be studied.

We can show the biased nature of this OLS estimator in the following manner – replace y_t in this expression by its value:

$$\hat{\beta}_1 = \frac{\sum_{t=1}^{n} x_{1t}(\beta_1 x_{1t} + \beta_2 x_{2t} + u_t)}{\sum_{t=1}^{n} x_{1t}^2}$$

$$= \frac{\beta_1 \sum_{t=1}^{n} x_{1t}^2 + \beta_2 \sum_{t=1}^{n} x_{1t} x_{2t} + \sum_{t=1}^{n} x_{1t} u_t}{\sum_{t=1}^{n} x_{1t}^2}$$

$$= \beta_1 + \beta_2 \frac{\sum_{t=1}^{n} x_{1t} x_{2t}}{\sum_{t=1}^{n} x_{1t}^2} + \frac{\sum_{t=1}^{n} x_{1t} u_t}{\sum_{t=1}^{n} x_{1t}^2}$$

Therefore:

$$E(\hat{\beta}_1) = \beta_1 + \beta_2 \frac{\sum_{t=1}^{n} x_{1t} x_{2t}}{\sum_{t=1}^{n} x_{1t}^2} + 0 \neq \beta_1$$

implying that $E(\hat{\beta}_1)$ differs from β_1 by the amount

$$\left(\beta_2 \frac{\sum_{t=1}^{n} x_{1t} x_{2t}}{\sum_{t=1}^{n} x_{1t}^2} \right)$$

which is a measure of the bias. The bias can be given a very natural interpretation; if we were to run a regression

$$x_{1t} = \alpha x_{2t} + \varepsilon_t$$

then the OLS estimator of the coefficient of x_{2t} would be calculated as follows:

$$\hat{\alpha} = \frac{\sum_{t=1}^{n} x_{1t}x_{2t}}{\sum_{t=1}^{n} x_{1t}^2}$$

The bias is proportional to the coefficient of linear regression of the missing variable x_2 on the present variable x_1 and the unknown β_2 is the proportionality factor. The OLS estimator $\hat{\beta}_1$ would be unbiased if $\hat{\alpha}$ were equal to zero, which would happen if and only if the variables x_1 and x_2 were *orthogonal*. Such an occurrence is highly unlikely. Once x_1 and x_2 are in some way correlated, as they usually would be, then we run the risk of misspecification by running the regression without one or other of these variables.

It is easy to generalize to the k-variable case where more than one relevant variable may be omitted from the model. Suppose the "true" model contains k variables while the fitted model contains $k_1 < k$ (i.e. $k - k_1$ variables are omitted). The true model can be represented by:

$$\mathbf{y} = \mathbf{X}_1\boldsymbol{\beta}_1 + \mathbf{X}_2\boldsymbol{\beta}_2 + \mathbf{u} = (\mathbf{X}_1\mathbf{X}_2)\begin{pmatrix}\boldsymbol{\beta}_1 \\ \boldsymbol{\beta}_2\end{pmatrix} + \mathbf{u} = \mathbf{X}\boldsymbol{\beta} + \mathbf{u}$$

while the fitted model is:

$$\mathbf{y} = \mathbf{X}_1\boldsymbol{\beta}_1 + \mathbf{v}$$

where $\mathbf{X}_1$ is the $(n \times k_1)$ matrix of included variables and $\mathbf{X}_2$ the $(n \times k_2)$ matrix of excluded variables $(k_2 = k - k_1)$. OLS estimation yields:

$$\hat{\boldsymbol{\beta}}_1 = (\mathbf{X}_1'\mathbf{X}_1)^{-1}\mathbf{X}_1'\mathbf{y}$$

Replacing $\mathbf{y}$ by its value gives:

$$\hat{\boldsymbol{\beta}}_1 = (\mathbf{X}_1'\mathbf{X}_1)^{-1}\mathbf{X}_1'(\mathbf{X}_1\boldsymbol{\beta}_1 + \mathbf{X}_2\boldsymbol{\beta}_2 + \mathbf{u}) = \boldsymbol{\beta}_1 + (\mathbf{X}_1'\mathbf{X}_1)^{-1}\mathbf{X}_1'\mathbf{X}_2\boldsymbol{\beta}_2 + (\mathbf{X}_1'\mathbf{X}_1)^{-1}\mathbf{X}_1'\mathbf{u}$$

Since the $\mathbf{X}$ matrices are fixed and $E(\mathbf{u}) = 0$, then, clearly:

$$E(\hat{\boldsymbol{\beta}}_1) = \boldsymbol{\beta}_1 + (\mathbf{X}_1'\mathbf{X}_1)^{-1}\mathbf{X}_1'\mathbf{X}_2\boldsymbol{\beta}_2$$

so that $\hat{\boldsymbol{\beta}}_1$ is a biased estimator of $\boldsymbol{\beta}_1$ unless the omitted and excluded variables are orthogonal to each other, a possibility that we can safely rule out when dealing with economic data.

We have considered a specification error due to the absence of relevant explanatory variables, and we have seen that this leads to bias in our coefficient estimates.

There exist, however, other forms of misspecification, such as the inclusion of irrelevant explanatory variables, errors in the functional form of the regression equation, and the misspecification of the error term. What is interesting to note is that the inclusion of irrelevant variables does not introduce statistical bias in the parameter estimates. Thus, if the researcher is in doubt about the relevance of a regressor, it is preferable to include it in the function, provided that the sample is large enough (to ensure adequate degrees of freedom), and provided that data are available on the variable whose relevance is uncertain on *a priori* expectations. But beware! For we increase the risk of multicollinearity by so doing. Furthermore, we risk complicating the economic interpretation of the model. In any event, the inclusion of a host of possibly irrelevant variables so that OLS estimation gives us useful results is, practically, very unrealistic, given the small sample sizes that are characteristic of economic data. We risk obtaining unreliable estimates due to the loss of precious degrees of freedom.

DUMMY VARIABLES

In many economic models, it is sometimes necessary to introduce exogenous variables that are not directly measurable. Quite often, this variable is of a "yes/no" character, as is illustrated in the following example. Suppose we undertake a cross sectional analysis to investigate the sales of theatre seats, and we thought that the level of education of the potential customers was an appropriate explanatory variable. We may then introduce a variable that will take a value of either 0 or 1 at each sample point – 1 if the individual in question has a university degree, and 0 if not. This is an example of a "dummy variable". A dummy variable is used in instances where the researcher believes that an explanatory variable exercises a discrete rather than continuous influence on the dependent variable. As such, the dummy variable acts as a proxy for this explanatory variable, where the value 1 indicates the presence of an attribute and the value 0 indicates its absence.

Let us pursue the above illustration further. Imagine that an economist proposes to examine the model

$$c_t = \alpha_1 + \alpha_2 y_t + \alpha_3 z_t + u_t$$

where c_t represents sales of theatre seats, y_t represents personal disposable income and z_t is the dummy variable of the model, taking on the value 1 if the individual has a university degree, and 0 if not.

We can now obtain OLS estimates of the coefficients, but how do we interpret them? Notice first of all that:

$$E(c_t/\text{no degree}) = \alpha_1 + \alpha_2 y_t$$

and

$$E(c_t/\text{degree}) = (\alpha_1 + \alpha_3) + \alpha_2 y_t$$

The underlying expectation is that, for some given income level, people with university degrees are greater theatre-goers than those without, and that the difference in behaviour is accounted for by a larger value of the intercept term. The marginal propensity to purchase theatre tickets is estimated by the coefficient of y_t and is identical in both cases. The coefficient of the dummy variable z_t, α_3, therefore represents the difference in the level of autonomous purchases of the two categories of customers.

We could, of course, have carried out separate regressions, one including those with university degrees and one including those without, but this would have resulted in imprecise OLS estimators due to the loss of degrees of freedom, given the small sample sizes peculiar to economic data.

Apart from its discrete properties, a dummy variable in a regression model is a variable like any other and, as such, may be evaluated by standard significance tests. If the T-statistics and corresponding p-values indicate that the coefficient estimate α_3 is not significantly different from zero, then the conclusion is that the level of education has no significant effect on theatre-going. The testing of the null hypothesis that $\alpha_3 = 0$, therefore, is tantamount to testing the hypothesis that there is no significant difference in theatre-going between the two categories of customers.

The same problem could have been tackled using *two* dummy variables. Our model could have been written:

$$c_t = \beta_1 z_{1t} + \beta_2 z_{2t} + \beta_3 y_t + \varepsilon_t$$

where

$$z_{1t} = 0 \text{ if no degree, and 1 if degree}$$

and

$$z_{2t} = 1 \text{ if no degree, and 0 if degree}$$

Notice that:

$$E\left(c_t/\text{degree}\right) = \beta_1 + \beta_3 y_t$$

and

$$E\left(c_t/\text{no degree}\right) = \beta_2 + \beta_3 y_t$$

Careful interpretation must be given. This time, the difference in the level of autonomous consumption, represented by α_3 in the previous model, is now given by $(\beta_1 - \beta_2)$. Note also the absence of a constant term in the present model. If we put in such a term, then we cannot use the two dummy variables to represent the two different education levels, but only one. In the first place, a second dummy variable would add no further information to the model. Second, and more important, the introduction of a constant term in this model would put us in the *dummy variable trap*. Suppose we wished to fit the following model:

$$c_t = \beta_0 + \beta_1 z_{1t} + \beta_2 z_{2t} + \beta_3 y_t + u_t$$

This model could be put in matrix notation as follows:

$$\mathbf{C} = \mathbf{X}\boldsymbol{\beta} + \mathbf{u}$$

where

$$\mathbf{C} = \begin{bmatrix} c_1 \\ c_2 \\ \vdots \\ \vdots \\ c_n \end{bmatrix}; \mathbf{X} = \begin{bmatrix} 1 & z_{11} & z_{21} & y_1 \\ 1 & z_{12} & z_{22} & y_2 \\ \vdots & \vdots & \vdots & \vdots \\ \vdots & \vdots & \vdots & \vdots \\ 1 & z_{1n} & z_{2n} & y_n \end{bmatrix}; \boldsymbol{\beta} = \begin{bmatrix} \beta_0 \\ \beta_1 \\ \beta_2 \\ \beta_3 \end{bmatrix}; \text{ and } \mathbf{u} = \begin{bmatrix} u_1 \\ u_2 \\ \vdots \\ \vdots \\ u_n \end{bmatrix}$$

The two dummy variables in the model are used to represent whether the individual in question has a university degree or does not. These are clearly two independent events, and so at any particular sample point, it is easy to see that

$$z_{1t} + z_{2t} = 1$$

However, the inclusion of a constant term in the model means that our matrix of explanatory variables **X** contains a column of 1s. Therefore, the **X** matrix in this model is characterized by perfect collinearity. Recall from the preceding discussion that this implies that the matrix (**X′X**) cannot be inverted, and so OLS cannot be applied. This is the dummy variable trap.

The dummy variable technique may be extended to cover more than two characteristics provided they are all mutually exclusive. Extending the previous illustration, for example, we can fit a model:

$$c_t = \gamma_0 + \gamma_1 z_{1t} + \gamma_2 z_{2t} + \gamma_3 y_t + u_t$$

where:
z_{1t} = 1 if the individual has A levels but no university degree, and 0 if not, and
z_{2t} = 1 if the individual has a university degree, 0 if not

Notice that:

$$E(c_t/\text{A levels but no degree}) = (\gamma_0 + \gamma_1) + \gamma_3 y_t$$
$$E(c_t/\text{degree}) = (\gamma_0 + \gamma_2) + \gamma_3 y_t$$
$$E(c_t/\text{neither A levels nor degree}) = \gamma_0 + \gamma_3 y_t$$

In general, in an N-way classification, we must introduce only (N – 1) dummy variables, if we wish to retain a constant term in the model.

Dummy variables are frequently applied to time series problems as well. The classic illustration of the application of the dummy variable technique is given in the case of the Keynesian aggregate consumption function, distinguishing between consumption in wartime and in peacetime. Suppose our data set spans both periods. The model that assumes no difference in wartime or peacetime is given by:

$$c_t = \beta_0 + \beta_1 y_t + \varepsilon_t$$

If we assume that there is a shift in autonomous consumption at wartime (which we may expect on *a priori* grounds to be a downward one, due to the war effort), then the appropriate dummy becomes: $z_t = 1$ during the wartime, and $z_{2t} = 0$ during peacetime.

Our model therefore becomes:

$$c_t = \beta_0 + \beta_1 y_t + \beta_2 z_t + \varepsilon_t$$

where β_2 will represent the shift in autonomous consumption during the wartime. If β_2 is not significantly different from zero, then we may conclude that wartime has no significant effect on aggregate consumption.

The preceding examples illustrate the use of dummy variables to capture changes in the intercept terms. We can also use dummy variables to capture changes in the slope coefficients. Suppose that in the above Keynesian consumption function, we think that the wartime state of affairs will affect, not autonomous consumption levels, but rather the marginal propensity to consume. We will therefore introduce a dummy variable in the following manner:

$$c_t = \beta_0 + \beta_1 y_t + \beta_2 (z_t y_t) + \varepsilon_t$$

where

$$E(c_t/\text{wartime}) = \beta_0 + (\beta_1 + \beta_2) y_t,$$

and

$$E(c_t/\text{peacetime}) = \beta_0 + \beta_1 y_t$$

We can, of course, go one step further, and introduce a dummy variable that affects both the intercept and the slope terms, as in the following model:

$$c_t = \phi_0 + \phi_1 y_t + \phi_2 d_t + \phi_3 (d_t y_t) + \varepsilon_t$$

where d_t is our wartime/peacetime dummy variable, introduced in a manner under the hypothesis that a state of war will affect both autonomous consumption and the marginal propensity to consume.

In econometrics, the use of dummy variables is generally preferred to the estimation of separate regressions. While the latter does enable the *direct* estimation of the relevant coefficients, there remains the problem of the size of the sample, which may not be large enough to yield reliable estimators. Incorporating dummy variables into a regression enables degrees of freedom to be saved, and the investigator is still able (albeit in an indirect fashion) to obtain relevant coefficient estimates. Of course, once introduced into a regression model, a dummy variable becomes a *bona fide* variable like any other, and so will impact on the specification of the system as well as on the degrees of freedom.

ILLUSTRATION INVOLVING A DUMMY VARIABLE

We turn once again to the import function and include a dummy variable that is equal to 1 during the "boom" years (1974 to 1981) and 0 otherwise. The results obtained are displayed in Exhibit 3.4.

The dummy variable has the expected sign but is very insignificant. The overall results are not much different from those shown under Exhibit 1.1, which makes it safe to conclude that, according to these results, the boom period had no appreciable effect on the importing habits of the Trinidad and Tobago consumers.

EXHIBIT 3.4

OLS Regression fit of

$M_t = \beta_1 + \beta_2 Y_t + \beta_3 p_{mt}/p_{dt} + \beta_4 C_{gt} + \beta_5 DUMMY + u_t$

```
=============================================================
LS // Dependent Variable is IMPORTS
Date: 08/12/95   Time: 21:51
Sample: 1967 1991
Included observations: 25
=============================================================
     Variable     Coefficient Std. Error  T-Statistic    Prob.
=============================================================
        C          -1054.538   781.2754  -1.349764      0.1915
      INCOME        0.371343   0.033939   10.94148      0.0000
      RATIO        -718.9875   175.0262  -4.107886      0.0005
      DUMMY         78.90306   191.2359   0.412596      0.6841
=============================================================
R-squared             0.942909   Mean dependent var    3556.082
Adjusted R-squared    0.934753   S.D. dependent var    1531.723
S.E. of regression    391.2552   Akaike info criter    12.08437
Sum squared resid     3214693.   Schwarz criterion     12.27939
Log likelihood       -182.5280   F-statistic           115.6113
Durbin-Watson stat    1.693665   Prob(F-statistic)     0.000000
=============================================================
```

EXERCISES

1. What is meant by the term "multicollinearity"?
2. What are the principal consequences of multicollinearity for ordinary least squares (OLS) regression?
3. Look again at the savings function for Dominica which is the subject of exercise 4, chapter 1. Can you find any evidence of multicollinearity? Use the correlation matrix of the explanatory variables as part of your argument.
4. In explaining consumer behaviour, an economist fitted the model

$$C_t = \beta_0 + \beta_1 W_t + \beta_2 P_t + u_t \qquad \textbf{(1)}$$

when he knew the correct model to be

$$C_t = \beta_0 + \beta_1 W_t + \beta_2 P_t + \beta_3 A_t + u_t \qquad \textbf{(2)}$$

where C = consumption, W = wage income, P = non-wage urban income and A = non-wage rural income.

a) Why did he deliberately misspecify his model?

b) Show that the OLS estimation of (1) yields biased estimators if (2) is the true model.

5. What is a dummy variable?
6. Discuss situations where you are likely to introduce dummy variables into econometric analysis.
7. You are told that, following a hurricane, emergency measures were put in place in Dominica over the period 1984–1987. Incorporate a dummy variable into the Dominican savings function to evaluate the effect of these measures on national saving.
8. Consider the following consumption function model

$$C_t = \beta_1 + \beta_2 Y_t + \beta_3 Z_t + \beta_4 Y_t Z_t + \varepsilon_t \qquad \textbf{(1)}$$

where C = consumption, Y = income, Z = 1 in wartime and zero otherwise and ε is the standard error term.

a) Explain the purpose of the dummy variable in this model.

b) Two approaches are suggested for estimating the coefficients of this model: (i) estimating the coefficients of the model as it stands in equation (1) or (ii) fitting two separate regression lines of C_t on Y_t (one for peacetime years and one for wartime years) to the sample data. Carefully discuss the implications of these two approaches.

c) Given the model in equation (1), explain how and why you would test the following hypotheses:

i) The peacetime intercept is zero.

ii) There is no difference between the peacetime and wartime intercepts.

iii) There is no difference between the peacetime and wartime slopes.

CHAPTER 4

Generalized Least Squares, Heteroscedasticity and Autocorrelation

GENERALIZED LEAST SQUARES

In chapter 1, we considered the general linear regression model:

$$\mathbf{y} = \mathbf{X}\boldsymbol{\beta} + \mathbf{u}$$

We introduced three assumptions ($A_1 - A_3$):

1. $E(\mathbf{u}) = \mathbf{0}$, and
2. $Cov(\mathbf{u}) = E(\mathbf{uu'}) = \sigma^2\mathbf{I}_n$
3. $\mathbf{X}$ is fixed

where $\mathbf{0}$ is an $(n \times 1)$ null vector, and $\mathbf{I}_n$ is the $(n \times n)$ identity matrix.

Let us investigate the second assumption further. Cov($\mathbf{u}$) represents the variance-covariance matrix of the vector of errors $\mathbf{u}$. By definition, therefore, its diagonal elements represent the variances of the individual errors u_t, $t = 1, 2, \ldots, n$ while its off-diagonal elements represent the covariances, i.e.

$$var(u_t) = \sigma^2, \forall t$$

and

$$cov(u_t, u_s) = 0, t \neq s$$

The third assumption therefore embodies two properties of the error term – that of *homoscedasticity* and the *absence of autocorrelation*.

Suppose that, in the generalized linear regression model, $\mathbf{X}$ is fixed and E($\mathbf{u}$) = $\mathbf{0}$. But let us now assume that:

$$cov(\mathbf{u}) = \sigma^2\mathbf{V}$$

where $\mathbf{V}$ is a known, symmetric, positive definite matrix.

What is the significance of **V**? **V** may be, but is not constrained to be, the identity matrix $\mathbf{I}_n$, which itself is symmetric and positive definite. This means that the diagonal elements of the variance-covariance matrix of the **u** are no longer necessarily equal to some constant value, and the off-diagonal elements are no longer necessarily equal to zero. In other words, the disturbances may be heteroscedastic and/or autocorrelated. If they are heteroscedastic, then:

$$\mathrm{var}(u_t) = \sigma_t^2 \neq \sigma^2, t = 1, \ldots, n$$

If they are autocorrelated, then:

$$E(u_t, u_s) = \sigma_{t,s} \neq 0$$

Note that the fact that **V** is positive definite implies the following:

1. All variances are positive, that is, $\sigma_t^2 > 0, \forall t$
2. There is no perfect correlation between any two error terms

Needless to say, both heteroscedasticity and autocorrelation can occur at the same time. The presence of either one, however, is enough to violate the second assumption listed above. If we know the precise nature of the heteroscedasticity and/or the autocorrelation, we can construct the **V** matrix. Once we have done so, the estimation of our model becomes possible, not by the method of ordinary least squares (OLS), which, as we shall see, now loses some of its most valuable properties. We must use instead the method of *generalized least squares*.

Let us concentrate on the general linear regression model where the second assumption becomes Cov (**u**) = σ^2**V**. Because **V** is a positive definite matrix, there exists a non-singular matrix **P** such that:

$$\mathbf{V} = \mathbf{PP'}$$

It follows that:

$$\mathbf{P}^{-1}\mathbf{V}\,\mathbf{P'}^{-1} = \mathbf{I}$$

and

$$\mathbf{V}^{-1} = \mathbf{P'}^{-1}\,\mathbf{P}^{-1}$$

We can transform the original model by premultiplication by $\mathbf{P}^{-1}$ to obtain:

$$\mathbf{P}^{-1}\mathbf{y} = \mathbf{P}^{-1}\mathbf{X}\boldsymbol{\beta} + \mathbf{P}^{-1}\mathbf{u}$$

which can be rewritten as:

$$\mathbf{y}* = \mathbf{X}*\boldsymbol{\beta} + \mathbf{u}* \qquad \textbf{(4.1)}$$

Any unbiased estimator of $\boldsymbol{\beta}$ in the original model is also an unbiased estimator of $\boldsymbol{\beta}$ in model (4.1).

Notice that:

$$E(\mathbf{u}*) = E\left(\mathbf{P}^{-1}\mathbf{u}\right) = \mathbf{P}^{-1}E(\mathbf{u}) = 0$$

and

$$\begin{aligned}
\operatorname{cov}(\mathbf{u}*) &= \operatorname{cov}\left(\mathbf{P}^{-1}\mathbf{u}\right) = \mathbf{P}^{-1}\operatorname{cov}(\mathbf{u})\mathbf{P}'^{-1} \\
&= \mathbf{P}^{-1}\sigma^2\mathbf{V}\mathbf{P}'^{-1} \\
&= \sigma^2\mathbf{P}^{-1}\mathbf{V}\mathbf{P}'^{-1} \\
&= \sigma^2\mathbf{P}^{-1}\mathbf{P}\mathbf{P}'\mathbf{P}'^{-1} \\
&= \sigma^2\left(\mathbf{P}^{-1}\mathbf{P}\right)\left(\mathbf{P}^{-1}\mathbf{P}\right)' \\
&= \sigma^2\mathbf{I}
\end{aligned}$$

The transformed model, therefore, has the following properties:

1. $E(\mathbf{u}*) = \mathbf{0}$
2. $\operatorname{Cov}(\mathbf{u}*) = \sigma^2\mathbf{I}$
3. $\mathbf{X}*$ is fixed

These are the properties of the standard linear regression model and so we can apply OLS to the transformed model to obtain the best linear unbiased estimators. The estimators so obtained are by definition the generalized least squares (GLS) estimators. Applying OLS to the transformed model, we obtain:

$$\begin{aligned}
\tilde{\boldsymbol{\beta}} &= (\mathbf{X}*'\mathbf{X}*)^{-1}\mathbf{X}*'\mathbf{y}* \\
&= \left[\left(\mathbf{P}^{-1}\mathbf{X}\right)'\left(\mathbf{P}^{-1}\mathbf{X}\right)\right]^{-1}\left(\mathbf{P}^{-1}\mathbf{X}\right)'\left(\mathbf{P}^{-1}\mathbf{y}\right) \\
&= \left(\mathbf{X}'\mathbf{P}'^{-1}\mathbf{P}^{-1}\mathbf{X}\right)^{-1}\mathbf{X}'\mathbf{P}'^{-1}\mathbf{P}^{-1}\mathbf{y} \\
&= \left(\mathbf{X}'\mathbf{V}^{-1}\mathbf{X}\right)^{-1}\mathbf{X}'\mathbf{V}^{-1}\mathbf{y}
\end{aligned}$$

which is the OLS estimator of the transformed model and, by definition, the GLS estimator of the original model.

PROPERTIES OF THE GENERALIZED LEAST SQUARES ESTIMATOR

1. $E(\tilde{\boldsymbol{\beta}}) = \boldsymbol{\beta}$, i.e. $\tilde{\boldsymbol{\beta}}$ is *an unbiased estimator*

Proof

Since $\tilde{\boldsymbol{\beta}} = (\mathbf{X'V^{-1}X})^{-1}\mathbf{X'V^{-1}y}$, then, replacing $\mathbf{y}$ by its value yields:

$$\tilde{\boldsymbol{\beta}} = (\mathbf{X'V^{-1}X})^{-1}\mathbf{X'V^{-1}}(\mathbf{X}\boldsymbol{\beta} + \mathbf{u})$$

$$= \boldsymbol{\beta} + (\mathbf{X'V^{-1}X})^{-1}\mathbf{X'V^{-1}u}$$

Since both $\mathbf{X}$ and $\mathbf{V}$ are nonstochastic:

$$E(\tilde{\boldsymbol{\beta}}) = E\left[\boldsymbol{\beta} + (\mathbf{X'V^{-1}X})^{-1}\mathbf{X'V^{-1}u}\right]$$

$$= \boldsymbol{\beta} + (\mathbf{X'V^{-1}X})^{-1}\mathbf{X'V^{-1}}E(\mathbf{u})$$

$$= \boldsymbol{\beta} \qquad\qquad \text{Q.E.D.}$$

2. $\text{Cov}(\tilde{\boldsymbol{\beta}}) = \sigma^2(\mathbf{X'V^{-1}X})^{-1}$

Proof

By definition:

$$\text{Cov}(\tilde{\boldsymbol{\beta}}) = E\left[\tilde{\boldsymbol{\beta}} - E(\tilde{\boldsymbol{\beta}})\right]\left[\tilde{\boldsymbol{\beta}} - E(\tilde{\boldsymbol{\beta}})\right]'$$

Since $E(\tilde{\boldsymbol{\beta}}) = \boldsymbol{\beta}$:

$$\text{Cov}(\tilde{\boldsymbol{\beta}}) = E\left[(\tilde{\boldsymbol{\beta}} - \boldsymbol{\beta})(\tilde{\boldsymbol{\beta}} - \boldsymbol{\beta})'\right]$$

But from above:

$$\tilde{\boldsymbol{\beta}} = \boldsymbol{\beta} + (\mathbf{X'V^{-1}X})^{-1}\mathbf{X'V^{-1}u}$$

or

$$\tilde{\boldsymbol{\beta}} - \boldsymbol{\beta} = (\mathbf{X'V^{-1}X})^{-1}\mathbf{X'V^{-1}u}$$

Therefore:

$$\text{Cov}(\tilde{\boldsymbol{\beta}}) = \text{E}\left\{\left[(\mathbf{X'V^{-1}X})^{-1}\mathbf{X'V^{-1}u}\right]\left[(\mathbf{X'V^{-1}X})^{-1}\mathbf{X'V^{-1}u}\right]'\right\}$$

$$= \text{E}\left\{(\mathbf{X'V^{-1}X})^{-1}\mathbf{X'V^{-1}uu'V^{-1}X}(\mathbf{X'V^{-1}X})^{-1}\right\}$$

$$= (\mathbf{X'V^{-1}X})^{-1}\mathbf{X'V^{-1}}\text{E}(\mathbf{uu'})\mathbf{V^{-1}X}(\mathbf{X'V^{-1}X})^{-1}$$

$$= (\mathbf{X'V^{-1}X})^{-1}\mathbf{X'V^{-1}}\sigma^2\mathbf{VV^{-1}X}(\mathbf{X'V^{-1}X})^{-1}$$

$$= \sigma^2(\mathbf{X'V^{-1}X})^{-1}\mathbf{X'V^{-1}VV^{-1}X}(\mathbf{X'V^{-1}X})^{-1}$$

$$= \sigma^2(\mathbf{X'V^{-1}X})^{-1}\mathbf{X'IV^{-1}X}(\mathbf{X'V^{-1}X})^{-1}$$

$$= \sigma^2(\mathbf{X'V^{-1}X})^{-1}(\mathbf{X'V^{-1}X})(\mathbf{X'V^{-1}X})^{-1}$$

$$= \sigma^2(\mathbf{X'V^{-1}X})^{-1} \qquad \text{Q.E.D.}$$

3. $\tilde{\boldsymbol{\beta}}$ is the best linear unbiased estimator (BLUE) of $\boldsymbol{\beta}$ when cov($\mathbf{u}$) = σ^2V.
   We leave this as an exercise for you to do!

CONSEQUENCES OF USING ORDINARY LEAST SQUARES WHEN u ~ (0, σ^2V)

Let us first of all investigate the property of unbiasedness. Does the application of OLS still yield unbiased estimators under the new set of assumptions? Recall that:

$$\hat{\boldsymbol{\beta}} = (\mathbf{X'X})^{-1}\mathbf{X'y}$$

Replacing $\mathbf{y}$ by its true value, we obtain:

$$\hat{\boldsymbol{\beta}} = (\mathbf{X'X})^{-1}\mathbf{X'}(\mathbf{X}\boldsymbol{\beta} + \mathbf{u})$$

$$= \boldsymbol{\beta} + (\mathbf{X'X})^{-1}\mathbf{X'u}$$

Therefore:

$$\text{E}(\hat{\boldsymbol{\beta}}) = \text{E}\left[\boldsymbol{\beta} + (\mathbf{X'X})^{-1}\mathbf{X'u}\right]$$

$$= \boldsymbol{\beta} + (\mathbf{X'X})^{-1}\mathbf{X'}\text{E}(\mathbf{u})$$

$$= \boldsymbol{\beta}$$

Hence, notwithstanding the change in the second assumption, OLS estimation remains unbiased.

What about the covariance matrix of $\tilde{\boldsymbol{\beta}}$? In chapter 1, we saw that, in a model characterized by the initial three assumptions A_1 to A_3:

$$\mathrm{Cov}\left(\hat{\boldsymbol{\beta}}\right) = \sigma^2 (\mathbf{X'X})^{-1}$$

With the change in the second assumption, however:

$$\begin{aligned}
\mathrm{Cov}\left(\hat{\boldsymbol{\beta}}\right) &= \mathrm{E}\left\{\left[\hat{\boldsymbol{\beta}} - \mathrm{E}\left(\hat{\boldsymbol{\beta}}\right)\right]\left[\hat{\boldsymbol{\beta}} - \mathrm{E}\left(\hat{\boldsymbol{\beta}}\right)\right]'\right\} \\
&= \mathrm{E}\left\{\left[\hat{\boldsymbol{\beta}} - \boldsymbol{\beta}\right]\left[\hat{\boldsymbol{\beta}} - \boldsymbol{\beta}\right]'\right\} \\
&= \mathrm{E}\left\{\left[(\mathbf{X'X})^{-1}\mathbf{X'u}\right]\left[(\mathbf{X'X})^{-1}\mathbf{X'u}\right]'\right\} \\
&= \mathrm{E}\left\{(\mathbf{X'X})^{-1}\mathbf{X'uu'X}(\mathbf{X'X})^{-1}\right\} \\
&= (\mathbf{X'X})^{-1}\mathbf{X'}\mathrm{E}(\mathbf{uu'})\mathbf{X}(\mathbf{X'X})^{-1} \\
&= (\mathbf{X'X})^{-1}\mathbf{X'}\left(\sigma^2\mathbf{V}\right)\mathbf{X}(\mathbf{X'X})^{-1} \\
&= \sigma^2(\mathbf{X'X})^{-1}\mathbf{X'VX}(\mathbf{X'X})^{-1} \\
&\neq \sigma^2(\mathbf{X'X})^{-1} \text{ unless } \mathbf{V} = \mathbf{I}.
\end{aligned}$$

The consequences of using OLS when GLS is applicable are therefore very serious. OLS, while still linear and unbiased, is no longer the *best* estimator in the sense of having the minimum variance. Furthermore, if a model were to be estimated by OLS using routine econometric packages such as EViews, the standard statistics accompanying the regression results (such as the standard errors of the parameter estimates, the T-ratios and accompanying p-values, and the F-statistic) would be, at the least, unreliable measures by which to judge the model. This is due to the fact that such statistics are calculated on the assumption that:

$$\mathrm{Cov}\left(\hat{\boldsymbol{\beta}}\right) = \sigma^2 (\mathbf{X'X})^{-1}$$

However, as we saw above, when the second assumption is changed, we obtain:

$$\mathrm{Cov}\left(\hat{\boldsymbol{\beta}}\right) = \sigma^2(\mathbf{X'X})^{-1}\mathbf{X'VX}(\mathbf{X'X})^{-1} \neq \sigma^2(\mathbf{X'X})^{-1}, \text{ unless } \mathbf{V} = \mathbf{I}.$$

Hence, the statistical results so generated are incorrect, and should not be used when the third assumption is changed and there exists heteroscedasticity and/or autocorrelation in the regression model.

A related problem is that, in both expressions for Cov($\tilde{\boldsymbol{\beta}}$), σ^2 remains unknown. Traditionally, σ^2 would be estimated by:

$$s^2 = \frac{\left(\mathbf{y} - \mathbf{X}\hat{\boldsymbol{\beta}}\right)'\left(\mathbf{y} - \mathbf{X}\hat{\boldsymbol{\beta}}\right)}{n-k} = \frac{\hat{\mathbf{u}}'\hat{\mathbf{u}}}{n-k}$$

However, it can be shown that s^2 is now a biased estimator of σ^2 (this shall not be proven). The corresponding unbiased estimator is:

$$\tilde{s}^2 = \frac{\left(\mathbf{y} - \mathbf{X}\tilde{\boldsymbol{\beta}}\right)'\mathbf{V}^{-1}\left(\mathbf{y} - \mathbf{X}\tilde{\boldsymbol{\beta}}\right)}{n-k}$$

where $\tilde{\boldsymbol{\beta}}$ is the GLS estimator.

Therefore, for best results, GLS estimation should be used, with $\tilde{s}^2$ being used as an estimator for σ^2.

GLS ESTIMATION: A PRACTICAL SOLUTION?

Clearly, GLS estimation only becomes a feasible alternative to OLS estimation if the **V** matrix is known but this is usually not the case. If it were possible to obtain a consistent[1] estimator of **V**, then we could obtain what is known as the *feasible GLS estimator*, defined as:

$$\tilde{\tilde{\boldsymbol{\beta}}} = \left(\mathbf{X}'\hat{\mathbf{V}}^{-1}\mathbf{X}\right)^{-1}\mathbf{X}'\hat{\mathbf{V}}^{-1}\mathbf{y}$$

where $\hat{\mathbf{V}}$ is a consistent estimator. The calculation of the GLS estimator requires, however, the inversion of $\hat{\mathbf{V}}$. This presents a further problem. The **V** matrix is of order $n \times n$, where n is the number of observations. There are, therefore, n^2 elements in this matrix. Computationally, this is a burdensome exercise and is usually avoided.

AD HOC PROCEDURES FOR THE IDENTIFICATION OF HETEROSCEDASTICITY AND AUTOCORRELATION

Both heteroscedasticity and autocorrelation are problems associated with the error terms of the regression model. Clearly, then, the initial and most basic step that should be taken is an examination of the residual plots of the model. OLS estimation of our

[1] The meaning of the term "consistent" is defined in a later chapter.

general linear regression model acts as a *filter*, separating the signal ($\beta_1 x_{1t} + \beta_2 x_{2t} + ... + \beta_k x_{kt}$) from the *noise* ($u_t$).

If u_t were really white noise (i.e. it is homoscedastic and not autocorrelated), its plot against time would exhibit some specific patterns. More specifically, it would exhibit a "well-behaved" pattern, coming back to a well-defined mean on a regular basis.[2]

However, such "visual" inspections are of limited value and should, wherever possible, be accompanied by more rigorous testing procedures. Let us now examine the problems of heteroscedasticity and autocorrelation in more detail. It is important to note, however, that, while it is clear that both heteroscedasticity and autocorrelation can occur at the same time, the following discussion will, for the purposes of simplicity, emphasize each problem separately.

Heteroscedasticity: Some Further Considerations

The assumption of homoscedasticity is implausible in many econometric modelling exercises. In cross sectional studies in particular, it seems excessive to suppose that error terms will be homoscedastic. This has been confirmed empirically. Consider, for example, the Keynesian consumption function:

$$C_t = \alpha + \beta Y_t + u_t, \quad t = 1, 2, \ldots, n$$

Imagine that there are n households in our sample, forming a cross section of a society and so embracing both low-income and high-income households. On *a priori* grounds, we would expect that higher-income families will show much less variability in their consumption patterns than lower-income families – if their incomes were to fall, more likely than not they would maintain present living standards by using up savings. Therefore, we would expect that the variances of the error terms associated with higher-income families would be much smaller than those associated with lower income families.

Consequently:

$$\mathrm{Var}(u_t) \neq \sigma^2$$

Heteroscedasticity: Testing for its Presence

The Goldfeld–Quandt Test

In general, it is not unusual for the disturbance term to be in correlation with one or more of the explanatory variables in the model. Goldfeld and Quandt (1965) propose a test for the special case where:

$$\mathrm{var}(u_t) = \sigma^2 x_{jt}^2$$

[2] In modern econometric methodology, we say that white noise is characterized by *stationarity*, or the *absence of unit roots* – concepts that will be discussed in some detail in Part II of this book.

that is, the variances of the disturbance terms vary with the square of one of the exogenous variables in the model. Assuming away the problem of autocorrelation, our **V** matrix would look like:

$$\mathbf{V} = \begin{bmatrix} x_{j1}^2 & 0 & \cdots & \cdots & 0 \\ 0 & x_{j2}^2 & \cdots & \cdots & 0 \\ \vdots & \vdots & \ddots & & \vdots \\ \vdots & \vdots & & \ddots & \vdots \\ 0 & 0 & \cdots & \cdots & x_{jn}^2 \end{bmatrix}$$

This test aims at distinguishing between:

$\mathbf{H}_0$: the residuals are homoscedastic, with var $(u_t) = \sigma^2, \forall t$
$\mathbf{H}_1$: the residuals are heteroscedastic of the form var $(u_t) = \sigma^2 x_{jt}^2$

The testing procedure is as follows:

1. Order all observations in accordance with the size of x_j, the variable that we suspect to be correlated with the error term.
2. Divide these ranked observations into two groupings. To clearly separate them, it is suggested that we omit a certain number c of central observations from the analysis. The two groups of observations, each of size [(n–c)/2], are therefore now clearly separated, with one grouping associated with the smaller values of the responsible explanatory variable, and the other associated with the larger values.
3. We fit separate OLS regressions on the first [(n–c)/2] and the last [(n–c)/2] observations, provided as usual that:

$$\left(\frac{n-c}{n}\right) \geq k$$

The sum of squared residuals associated with each regression is defined as $\sum_{t=1}^{n} \hat{u}_{1t}^2$ and $\sum_{t=1}^{n} \hat{u}_{2t}^2$. It can be shown, under the null, that:

$$s_1 = \frac{\sum_{t=1}^{n} \hat{u}_{1t}^2}{\sigma^2} \sim \chi_v^2,\ s_2 = \frac{\sum_{t=1}^{n} \hat{u}_{2t}^2}{\sigma^2} \sim \chi_v^2$$

for v = [(n–c)/2] degrees of freedom and that s_1 and s_2 are independent of each other. Therefore, if the null were true:

$$\frac{s_2}{s_1} \sim F_{v,v}$$

and it is this property that is used to test the null hypothesis.

The test has a strong intuitive appeal: if the alternative hypothesis were true, that is, if the variances of the error term vary in proportion to the magnitude of the explanatory variable x_j, then we would expect, on *a priori* grounds, that s_2, the measure of variance associated with the larger values of x_j, would be higher than s_1. If, however, the null hypothesis represented the true state of affairs, then s_1 and s_2 would not differ significantly from one another – that is, the variances of the OLS residuals associated with each subsample would be the same, and hence be seen to be independent of the size of the explanatory variable x_j.

If the null hypothesis were true, this ratio, and hence the value of the F-statistic, would not differ significantly from one. Conversely, if the alternative hypothesis were true, and there did exist heteroscedasticity of the type indicated, then the F-statistic would differ significantly from one. The greater the magnitude of this statistic the more severe is the heteroscedasticity problem (of the specified form), and the more likely you are to reject the null hypothesis of the homoscedasticity of the error terms.

If the null is rejected, then the appropriate estimation technique is GLS, with $\mathbf{V}$ constructed as above. Note that the inversion of this matrix, previously highlighted as a possible limitation to the practical use of GLS estimation, is here a feasible suggestion, since $\mathbf{V}$ is under the assumption of the absence of autocorrelation, a diagonal matrix, whose inversion simply requires the inversion of each diagonal element of this matrix.

A significant limitation of the Goldfeld–Quandt test is the requirement that c central observations be eliminated from the sample. In the first place, the value of c is chosen arbitrarily. Second, and more important, the data constraints characteristic of econometric models would tend to make one very wary of placing further restrictions on an already limited sample space. Finally, it is unsuitable for time series data since the ordering of the data in time is ignored in carrying out the test.

The Koenker Test

This test can be applied to time series data. The null and alternative hypotheses are:

$$\mathbf{H}_0\!:\!E\left(u_t^2\right)=\sigma^2$$

$$\mathbf{H}_1\!:\!E\left(u_t^2\right)=\sigma^2+\gamma\left(\beta_1 x_{1t}+\beta_2 x_{2t}+\beta_3 x_{3t}+\ldots+\beta_k x_{kt}\right)^2$$

Clearly, if the null hypothesis were true, then the γ term in the above expression would not be significantly different from zero. The crux of the matter, therefore, is to find a way of testing the nullity of γ. Koenker (1981) proposes that OLS be run on the original model:

$$y_t=\beta_1 x_{1t}+\beta_2 x_{2t}+\beta_3 x_{3t}+\ldots+\beta_k x_{kt}+u_t$$

The squared residuals so obtained then become the dependent variable in the model:

$$\hat{u}_t^2=\alpha+\gamma\,\hat{y}_t^2$$

where $\hat{y}_t$ is the OLS fit. The parameters of this model, α and γ, can be estimated by OLS. Of course, $\hat{y}$ becomes the crucial indicator of the presence of heteroscedasticity in the model. Its significance can be judged from the routine Student and F tests outlined in chapter 1. If, on the basis of these tests, we cannot reject the null hypothesis that $\gamma = 0$, then we can conclude that the residual terms in our general linear regression model are homoscedastic. If, however, the null is rejected, then our conclusion must be that there exists heteroscedasticity, of the specified form.

Illustration of the Koenker Test for Heteroscedasticity

The great advantage of the Koenker test is that it is very simple in its conception and can be carried out in EViews doing some simple programming. Consider the import function estimated in Exhibit 1.1. Both the residuals and fitted import values are saved and the square of their values calculated and stored, respectively, as UHAT2 and IMPFIT2. The latter is regressed on the former and the results obtained are shown in Exhibit 4.1.

The coefficient of IMPFIT2 is significant at around the 6% level and we may, on the basis of such evidence, be willing to conclude that the disturbances are heteroscedastic.

EXHIBIT 4.1
Koenker test for heteroscedasticity:
OLS fit of UHAT2 = α + β IMPFIT2

```
==============================================================
LS // Dependent Variable is UHAT2
Date: 07/26/97   Time: 17:18
Sample: 1967 1991
Included observations: 25
==============================================================
     Variable      Coefficient Std. Error  T-Statistic   Prob.
==============================================================
        C            9390.723   71641.49    0.131079    0.8969
     IMPFIT2         0.008140   0.004018    2.025934    0.0545
==============================================================
R-squared             0.151430   Mean dependent var   129612.5
Adjusted R-squared    0.114535   S.D. dependent var   213277.8
S.E. of regression    200692.5   Akaike info criter   24.49568
Sum squared resid     9.26E+11   Schwarz criterion    24.59319
Log likelihood       -339.6694   F-statistic          4.104409
Durbin-Watson stat    2.634695   Prob(F-statistic)    0.054524
==============================================================
```

Other Tests for Heteroscedasticity

There are several other tests for heteroscedasticity. One of the more popular ones, due to White (1980), will be introduced in chapter 11.

Estimation in the Presence of Heteroscedasticity

The feasible generalized least squares (GLS) procedure discussed above is appropriate in the presence of heteroscedastic disturbances. The weighted least squares (WLS) estimator, which is really a special case of the GLS estimator, is another. An example of the WLS estimator is given in exercise 2 at the end of this chapter.

Autocorrelation: The Problem[3]

To say that the error term u_t of the general linear regression model is not autocorrelated is to say that the value that it assumes in any one period is completely independent of its value in any preceding period. This assumption is, as we have discussed, represented by the zero values of all off-diagonal elements in the variance-covariance matrix of **u**.

If this assumption fails to hold, that is, if the value of u_t in any one period is in some way correlated with its preceding values, then the error term is said to be autocorrelated. This means that the off-diagonal elements of the variance-covariance matrix of **u** would now be non-zero.

A special case of autocorrelation will be of great interest to us, mainly because standard tests of autocorrelation were developed on the assumption that this was the type of autocorrelation present. In the general linear regression, it is usually assumed that u_t follows a *first-order autoregressive process*, defined as:

$$u_t = \rho u_{t-1} + \varepsilon_t, |\rho| < 1$$

where ε_t is a white noise process and, in particular:

$$E(\varepsilon_t) = 0$$

$$\operatorname{var}(\varepsilon_t) = \sigma_\varepsilon^2, \forall t$$

$$E(\varepsilon_t \varepsilon_{t-s}) = 0, \text{ for } s \neq 0$$

The disturbance in period t is a linear function of the disturbance in period t – 1 plus a purely random term ε_t, which is a white noise process.

Let us calculate the moments of first and second order of u_t.

$$\begin{aligned} u_t &= \varepsilon_t + \rho u_{t-1} \\ &= \varepsilon_t + \rho(\varepsilon_{t-1} + \rho u_{t-2}) \\ &= \varepsilon_t + \rho\varepsilon_{t-1} + \rho^2 u_{t-2} \\ &= \varepsilon_t + \rho\varepsilon_{t-1} + \rho^2(\varepsilon_{t-2} + \rho u_{t-3}) \\ &= \varepsilon_t + \rho\varepsilon_{t-1} + \rho^2\varepsilon_{t-2} + \rho^3 u_{t-3} \end{aligned}$$

We can keep substituting *ad infinitum*, and we will obtain:

[3] The synonymous term "serial correlation" often appears in the literature in place of "autocorrelation".

$$u_t = \varepsilon_t + \rho\varepsilon_{t-1} + \rho^2\varepsilon_{t-2} + \rho^3\varepsilon_{t-3} + \ldots + \rho^s\varepsilon_{t-s} + \rho^{s+1}u_{t-(s+1)}$$

For sufficiently large values of s, the term $\rho^{s+1}u_{t-(s+1)}$ will tend to zero, since $|\rho| < 1$.
Therefore, we may write:

$$u_t = \varepsilon_t + \rho\varepsilon_{t-1} + \rho^2\varepsilon_{t-2} + \rho^3 u_{t-3} + \ldots + \rho^s\varepsilon_{t-s} + \ldots = \sum_{i=0}^{\infty}\rho^i\varepsilon_{t-i}$$

The expected value of u_t is found as follows:

$$E(u_t) = E\left[\sum_{i=0}^{\infty}\rho^i\varepsilon_{t-i}\right]$$

and, if and only if $\sum_{i=0}^{\infty}\rho^i < \infty$ (which is verified here since $|\rho| < 1$), then:

$$E(u_t) = 0$$

Turning now to the second-order moments, that is, $E(u_t\, u_{t+r})$, let us first determine:

$$(u_t, u_{t+r}) = (\varepsilon_t + \rho\varepsilon_{t-1} + \rho^2\varepsilon_{t-2} + \rho^3 u_{t-3} + \ldots + \rho^s\varepsilon_{t-s} + \ldots)$$
$$(\varepsilon_{t+r} + \rho\varepsilon_{t+r-1} + \rho^2\varepsilon_{t+r-2} + \ldots + \rho^i\varepsilon_{t+r-i} + \ldots)$$
$$= \rho^r\varepsilon_t^2 + \rho^{r+2}\varepsilon_{t-1}^2 + \rho^{r+4}\varepsilon_{t-2}^2 + \ldots + \rho^{r+s}\varepsilon_{t-s}^2 + \ldots + (\text{cross products})$$

where cross products are terms involving ε_t and ε_{t-r}, $r \neq 0$. With the application of the E operator, these terms would disappear since $E(\varepsilon_t\, \varepsilon_{t-s}) = 0$, for $s \neq 0$.

$$E(u_t\, u_{t+r}) = E(\rho^r\varepsilon_t^2 + \rho^{r+2}\varepsilon_{t-1}^2 + \rho^{r+4}\varepsilon_{t-2}^2 + \ldots + \rho^{r+s}\varepsilon_{t-s}^2 + \ldots + \text{ cross products})$$
$$= \rho^r E(\varepsilon_t^2) + \rho^{r+2}E(\varepsilon_{t-1}^2) + \rho^{r+4}E(\varepsilon_{t-2}^2) + \ldots + \rho^{r+s}E(\varepsilon_{t-s}^2) + \ldots$$

Since $\text{var}(\varepsilon_t) = E(\varepsilon_t^2) = \sigma_\varepsilon^2, \forall t$

$$E(u_t, u_{t+r}) = \rho^r\sigma_\varepsilon^2 + \rho^{r+2}\sigma_\varepsilon^2 + \rho^{r+4}\sigma_\varepsilon^2 + \ldots + \rho^{r+s}\sigma_\varepsilon^2 + \ldots$$
$$= \rho^r\sigma_\varepsilon^2(1 + \rho^2 + \rho^4 + \ldots + \rho^s + \ldots)$$

For $\rho < 1$, the expression in brackets sums to $[1/(1 - \rho^2)]$ so that:

$$E(u_t, u_{t+r}) = \rho^r\sigma_\varepsilon^2\left(\frac{1}{1-\rho_2}\right)$$

This expression represents the *autocovariance of order r* of u_t. For r = 0:

$$E\left(u_t^2\right) = \text{var}\left(u_t\right) = \sigma_\varepsilon^2\left(\frac{1}{1-\rho^2}\right) = \sigma^2$$

that is, the variance of the error term is homoscedastic. The autocovariance of order r, r ≠ 0, is:

$$E\left(u_t\, u_{t+r}\right) = \rho^r \sigma^2$$

When r = 1:

$$E\left(u_t\, u_{t+1}\right) = \text{cov}\left(u_t, u_{t+1}\right) = \rho\sigma^2$$

When r = 2:

$$E\left(u_t\, u_{t+2}\right) = \text{cov}\left(u_t, u_{t+2}\right) = \rho^2\sigma^2$$

and so on.

Clearly:

$$\text{cov}(\mathbf{u}) = \sigma^2 \begin{bmatrix} 1 & \rho & \rho^2 & \cdots & \cdots & \rho^{n-1} \\ \rho & 1 & \rho & \cdots & \cdots & \rho^{n-2} \\ \rho^2 & \rho & 1 & \cdots & \cdots & \rho^{n-3} \\ \vdots & \vdots & \vdots & \ddots & & \vdots \\ \vdots & \vdots & \vdots & & \ddots & \vdots \\ \rho^{n-1} & \rho^{n-2} & \rho^{n-3} & \cdots & \cdots & 1 \end{bmatrix}$$

where:

$$\sigma^2 = \sigma_\varepsilon^2\left(\frac{1}{1-\rho^2}\right)$$

and, since cov(**u**) = σ^2**V**, then:

$$\mathbf{V} = \begin{bmatrix} 1 & \rho & \rho^2 & \cdots & \cdots & \rho^{n-1} \\ \rho & 1 & \rho & \cdots & \cdots & \rho^{n-2} \\ \rho^2 & \rho & 1 & \cdots & \cdots & \rho^{n-3} \\ \vdots & \vdots & \vdots & \ddots & & \vdots \\ \vdots & \vdots & \vdots & & \ddots & \vdots \\ \rho^{n-1} & \rho^{n-2} & \rho^{n-3} & \cdots & \cdots & 1 \end{bmatrix}$$

ρ^s can be given a more concrete meaning in this model as the *autocorrelation coefficient of order s*. This is defined as:

$$\operatorname{corr}\left(u_t, u_{t-s}\right) = \frac{\operatorname{cov}\left(u_t, u_{t-s}\right)}{\sqrt{\operatorname{var}\left(u_t\right)}\sqrt{\operatorname{var}\left(u_{t-s}\right)}}$$

and it is easily shown (do it as an exercise!) that this is equal to ρ^s.

If we know the value of ρ (or can estimate it), then we can construct the **V** matrix which, theoretically, will allow us to estimate $\boldsymbol{\beta}$ by GLS. In practical terms, however, the inversion of this matrix, which is required for the application of GLS, is a complicated and cumbersome procedure, and in general is avoided. Alternative estimation procedures that yield results approximately equivalent to GLS but are computationally less burdensome are discussed later in this chapter.

Autocorrelation: Testing for its Presence Using the Durbin–Watson Statistic

The Durbin–Watson test for autocorrelation is one of the oldest and arguably still the most widely used test for autocorrelation. In fact, all standard OLS packages automatically calculate the value of the Durbin–Watson (DW) statistic on which the test is based. To its credit, this statistic is easy to calculate and the corresponding test is valid in small samples.

The DW statistic is calculated as:

$$DW = \frac{\sum_{t=2}^{n}\left(\hat{u}_t - \hat{u}_{t-1}\right)^2}{\sum_{t=1}^{n}\left(\hat{u}_t - \bar{\hat{u}}_t\right)^2}$$

If, as is usually the case, there is a constant term in the model, then $\bar{\hat{u}}_t = 0$. The DW statistic then reduces to:

$$DW = \frac{\sum_{t=2}^{n}\left(\hat{u}_t - \hat{u}_{t-1}\right)^2}{\sum_{t=1}^{n}\hat{u}_t^2}$$

Durbin and Watson (1951, 1952) established tables of critical values for this statistic which have been since modified by Savin and White (1977). These are reproduced in most standard econometric textbooks (including this one).

The DW tables are established for testing for the existence of *positive* autocorrelation in a model that includes a constant term.[4] It can be shown (some justification will be given below) that there is no autocorrelation if DW = 2 but that there is positive autocorrelation when DW < 2. The test therefore opposes the two competing hypotheses:

$$H_0: DW = 2$$
$$H_1: DW < 2$$

The mechanism of the test is as follows: Durbin and Watson calculated upper and lower significance bounds (d_U and d_L, respectively) for different combinations of n, the number of sample points, and k′, the number of explanatory variables excluding the constant term. The value of the DW statistic is compared to these bounds and:

If DW < d_L, we conclude that there is positive autocorrelation
If DW > d_U, there is no autocorrelation.

It can also be shown that the DW statistic is symmetric about the value 2 and varies in value between 0 and 4 so that the same tables could be used to test for *negative* autocorrelation if DW > 2. We simply use the test statistic:

$$DW' = 4 - DW$$

and apply it in the same way as was done with DW for the detection of positive autocorrelation:

If DW′ < d_L, we conclude that there is negative autocorrelation
If DW′ > d_U, there is no autocorrelation.

The reader may have noticed that this is not an *exact* test in the sense that there is a range of possible values for DW for which no conclusion is possible. This is the region on the real line bounded by d_L and d_U (and by 4 – d_U and 4 – d_L). The box diagram shown in Figure 4.1 illustrates this region as well as the mechanism of the test for the various values of DW.

Notice that the DW statistic is characterized by a *gap* in its distribution. There exists a region between the significance bounds d_L and d_u (and correspondingly between 4 – d_U and 4 – d_L) over which no conclusion can be drawn. A DW whose value lies in this range, therefore, tells the researcher nothing about the presence or absence of autocorrelation. This is one of the primary limitations of this test.

There are other limitations of the test. First, the test can, strictly speaking, only tell us whether the error term is an autoregressive process of order 1, or AR(1) as it is often called in the literature, or whether it is not an AR(1). There exist, however,

[4] Farebrother (1980) has established tables of critical values for the Durbin–Watson statistic when the model does not include a constant term.

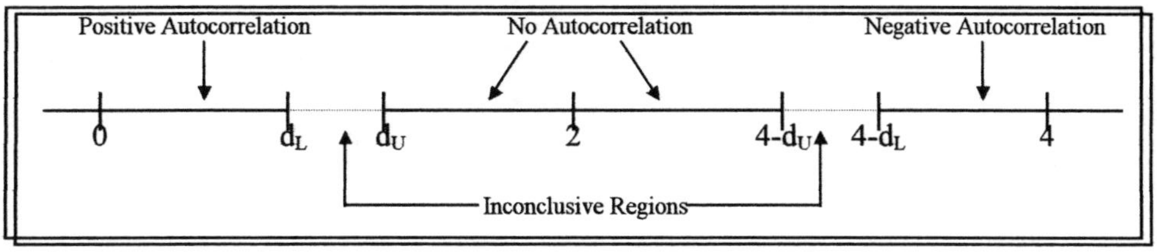

FIGURE 4.1
Box Diagram Illustrating the Mechanism of the Durbin–Watson Test

many other possible forms of autocorrelation, which, if present, can have similarly serious consequences. Hence a DW statistic close to 2 indicates, not the absence of autocorrelation in a model, but rather the absence of autocorrelation of an AR(1) form. However, as we will see in Part II of this book, it is frequently possible to approximate these various forms of autocorrelation as an AR(1) so that, intuitively, the DW test will have some power in detecting them.

Some Justification for the Mechanism of the Durbin–Watson Test

We have seen that:

$$DW = \frac{\sum_{t=2}^{n}\left(\hat{u}_t - \hat{u}_{t-1}\right)^2}{\sum_{t=1}^{n}\hat{u}_t^2}$$

Expanding, we get:

$$DW = \frac{\sum_{t=2}^{n}\hat{u}_t^2 + \hat{u}_{t-1}^2 - 2\hat{u}_t\hat{u}_{t-1}}{\sum_{t=1}^{n}\hat{u}_t^2}$$

$$= \frac{\sum_{t=2}^{n}\hat{u}_t^2}{\sum_{t=1}^{n}\hat{u}_t^2} + \frac{\sum_{t=2}^{n}\hat{u}_{t-1}^2}{\sum_{t=1}^{n}\hat{u}_t^2} - \frac{2\sum_{t=2}^{n}\hat{u}_t\hat{u}_{t-1}}{\sum_{t=1}^{n}\hat{u}_t^2}$$

In large samples:

$$\sum_{t=2}^{n}\hat{u}_t^2 \cong \sum_{t=2}^{n}\hat{u}_{t-1}^2 \cong \sum_{t=1}^{n}\hat{u}_t^2$$

Therefore, we can say that:

$$DW = 1 + 1 - \frac{2\sum \hat{u}_t \hat{u}_{t-1}}{\sum \hat{u}_t^2}$$

However, in the model:

$$\hat{u}_t = \rho \hat{u}_{t-1} + \varepsilon_t$$

our OLS estimate of ρ would be:

$$\hat{\rho} = \frac{\sum \hat{u}_t \hat{u}_{t-1}}{\sum \hat{u}_{t-1}^2} \cong \frac{\sum \hat{u}_t \hat{u}_{t-1}}{\sum \hat{u}_t^2}$$

Evidently, for large n:

$$DW \cong 2 - 2\hat{\rho}$$

$$\Rightarrow DW \cong 2(1 - \hat{\rho})$$

The consequences of this are as follows. Recall that ρ represents the autocorrelation coefficient between the residual terms. As $\hat{\rho}$ tends to –1, that is, should the error terms be characterized by *perfect negative autocorrelation*, the DW statistic would tend to a value of 4. Similarly, as $\hat{\rho}$ tends to +1, that is, should there exist *perfect positive autocorrelation* of the error terms, the DW statistic would tend to a value of 0. Finally, as $\hat{\rho}$ tends to 0, implying that there exists no autocorrelation of the defined type in the model, the DW statistic would tend to 2 in value.

It can be shown, in fact, that as $\hat{\rho}$ varies between –1 and +1, the DW statistic varies between 4 and 0, and is symmetric about 2. Thus, intuitively, the test of the hypothesis that ρ = 0 in the model:

$$\hat{u}_t = \rho \hat{u}_{t-1} + \varepsilon_t$$

is roughly equivalent to the test that DW = 2.

An Illustration of the Durbin–Watson Test for Autocorrelation

Let us examine the private consumption function for Trinidad and Tobago that was introduced in an earlier chapter. Regression results are shown in Exhibit 4.2 for the following specification (P_CONS is the notation used in EViews for private consumption expenditure):

$$C_{pt} = \beta_1 + \beta_2 Y_t + u_t$$

EXHIBIT 4.2
Equation: $C_t = \beta_1 + \beta_2 Y_t + u_t$
Output obtained from fitting equation in EViews

```
==================================================================
LS // Dependent Variable is P_CONS
Date: 08/30/95   Time: 12:20
Sample: 1967 1991
Included observations: 25
==================================================================
     Variable     Coefficient Std. Error  T-Statistic    Prob.
==================================================================
         C          -1960.845   648.5700  -3.023336     0.0060
      INCOME         0.651093   0.039624   16.43176     0.0000
==================================================================
R-squared              0.921502   Mean dependent var     8499.164
Adjusted R-squared     0.918090   S.D. dependent var     2169.299
S.E. of regression     620.8536   Akaike info criter     12.93881
Sum squared resid      8865561.   Schwarz criterion      13.03632
Log likelihood        -195.2086   F-statistic            270.0028
Durbin-Watson stat     0.847030   Prob(F-statistic)      0.000000
==================================================================
```

The DW statistic is calculated as 0.847030. For 25 observations and one regressor (not counting the constant term), the 5% critical values read from the tables are:

$$d_L = 1.29$$
$$d_U = 1.45$$

The null hypothesis that the error term is a white noise process is rejected in favour of the alternative that it is an autocorrelated AR(1) process. At this juncture, further statistical inference (for instance, significance tests) is not advisable, since the presence of serial correlation invalidates the assumptions on which such inference would normally be based.

Other Tests for Autocorrelation

Other tests for autocorrelation exist in the literature. One of these, due to Durbin (1970), will be introduced in chapter 5. Yet another of more general applicability, resulting from the work of Breusch (1978) and Godfrey (1978), will be introduced in chapter 11.

Estimation in the Presence of Autocorrelation

If ρ were known or could be reliably estimated, then obviously the correct procedure would be to build the **V** matrix and estimate the model by GLS. However, because of the difficulties associated with this due to the complex nature of **V**, we choose not to use GLS but to use, instead, procedures that are approximately equivalent.

The general basis for all such procedures that we are about to consider is the generalized difference equation model, which we now establish. Consider the model:

$$y_t = \beta_1 + \beta_2 x_{2t} + \beta_3 x_{3t} + \ldots + \beta_k x_{kt} + u_t \tag{4.2}$$

where:

$$u_t = \rho u_{t-1} + \varepsilon_t$$

Lagging expression (4.2) and multiplying throughout by ρ gives:

$$\rho y_{t-1} = \beta_1 \rho + \beta_2 \rho x_{2t-1} + \beta_3 \rho x_{3t-1} + \ldots + \beta_k \rho x_{kt-1} + \rho u_{t-1} \tag{4.3}$$

Subtracting expression (4.3) from (4.2):

$$y_t - \rho y_{t-1} = \beta_1(1-\rho) + \beta_2(x_{2t} - \rho x_{2t-1}) + \ldots + \beta_k(x_{kt} - \rho x_{kt-1}) + (u_t - \rho u_{t-1})$$

which is the generalized difference equation model. We may also write it as:

$$Y_t = \beta_1(1-\rho) + \beta_2 X_{2t} + \beta_3 X_{3t} + \ldots + \beta_k X_{kt} + \varepsilon_t \tag{4.4}$$

If ρ were known, or could be estimated, then OLS could be applied to equation (4.4) to obtain BLU estimators of the β coefficients, since the residual terms ε_t are by definition a white noise process. This procedure avoids the inversion of the **V** matrix; but we lose one observation in the process.

Unfortunately, ρ is never known and it must be estimated. The following two procedures result in the simultaneous estimation of ρ and the β coefficients.

The Cochrane–Orcutt Procedure

This is an iterative technique by which we get progressively better values for ρ. It is ideal for electronic computation and is certainly too burdensome to be done manually.

Step 1—The first step in this procedure is to fit model (4.2) by OLS, and in so doing, obtain the estimated residual terms $\hat{u}_t$ This is the *entry* or *start-up* point – it is never again repeated throughout the procedure.

Step 2—Having obtained estimates of our residual terms, we then perform the following regression by OLS:

$$\hat{u}_t = \rho \hat{u}_{t-1} + \varepsilon_t$$

and so derive an estimate for ρ.

Step 3—Our estimate $\hat{\rho}$ is then substituted for ρ in the model (4.4) to obtain:

$$y_t - \hat{\rho} y_{t-1} = \beta_1(1-\hat{\rho}) + \beta_2(x_{2t} - \hat{\rho} x_{2t-1}) + \beta_3(x_{3t} - \hat{\rho} x_{3t-1}) + \ldots + \beta_k(x_{kt} - \hat{\rho} x_{kt-1})$$
$$+ (u_t - \hat{\rho} u_{t-1})$$

We then estimate *this* model by OLS, and so obtain estimates of the β coefficients.

Step 4—The parameter estimates derived in step 3 above are then substituted into our general linear regression model (4.2) from which a new set of residual terms $\hat{\hat{u}}_t$ are derived. Note that, unlike the entry step in which the residuals were estimated through an OLS procedure, here the residuals are *calculated*.

Step 5—Run another regression:

$$\hat{\hat{u}}_t = \rho\hat{\hat{u}}_{t-1} + \varepsilon_t$$

and repeat steps 2 to 5. The procedure stops at the *r*th iteration if:

$$\left|\hat{\rho}^{r} - \hat{\rho}^{r-1}\right| < \delta$$

where δ is some small, predetermined value.

The Cochrane–Orcutt procedure is far from flawless. First, the choice of r may, because of cost and time constraints, be too low to allow convergence, and hence the researcher retains suboptimal values. Second, while the procedure is in the spirit of OLS estimation in that the idea behind it is to obtain values for ρ and β such that $\Sigma\hat{u}_t^2$ is at a minimum, the danger is that the procedure may yield a local rather than a global minimum, resulting again in suboptimal estimates.

The Hildreth–Lu Procedure

This is also an iterative procedure, once again ideal for electronic computation and very difficult to undertake manually. It is done in a grid-search manner, where ρ is allowed to progressively assume values between –1 and +1 in steps of, say, 0.1. For each value of ρ, equation (4.4) is estimated via OLS, and the procedure selects the equation with the lowest sum of squared residuals as the best.

Once the value of ρ is chosen, we can obtain a more accurate value by carrying out a more detailed grid search in the neighbourhood of the value of ρ calculated. For example, suppose that we obtain $\hat{\rho} = 0.3$. We can then examine what takes place between 0.2 and 0.4 with steps of 0.01.

Grid search procedures can be very tedious, and this is the primary drawback of this technique. It would save valuable computer time if, for example, you had *a priori* expectations about the value that ρ should assume, for example, if it is positive or negative. The danger also exists here of obtaining a local rather than a global minimum.

The EViews Procedure

Both the Cochrane–Orcutt and Hildreth–Lu procedures are special applications of the maximum likelihood approach to estimation, which will be discussed in Part II of this book. Both are also widely programmed and are available in packages like PC TSP and MicroFIT. EViews also uses a maximum likelihood approach that is an iterative Marquandt procedure (which will not be discussed here). The consumption function shown above under Exhibit 4.2 shows evidence of autocorrelation and was corrected using the EViews procedure. The results obtained are displayed in Exhibit 4.3.

EXHIBIT 4.3
Equation: $C_t = \beta_1 + \beta_2 Y_t + u_t$ corrected for autocorrelation
Output obtained from fitting equation in EViews

```
==============================================================
LS // Dependent Variable is P_CONS
Sample: 1968 1991
Included observations: 24 after adjusting endpoints
Convergence achieved after 3 iterations
==============================================================
     Variable     Coefficient Std. Error  T-Statistic     Prob.
==============================================================
        C           -3120.248   1423.792     -2.191505   0.0398
      INCOME         0.712948   0.082117      8.682084   0.0000
      AR(1)          0.531852   0.197864      2.687963   0.0138
==============================================================
R-squared            0.950820   Mean dependent var    8592.498
Adjusted R-squared   0.946136   S.D. dependent var    2164.074
S.E. of regression   502.2495   Akaike info criter    12.55466
Sum squared resid    5297345.   Schwarz criterion     12.70192
Log likelihood      -181.7105   F-statistic           203.0025
Durbin-Watson stat   2.146100   Prob(F-statistic)     0.000000
==============================================================
```

The Durbin–Watson statistic now has a value of 2.1461, which means that we must test for negative autocorrelation. The corresponding DW′ statistic defined above is calculated as:

$$DW' = 4 - 2.1461 = 1.8539$$

This value may be compared to the 5% critical values read from the tables for 24 observations and two estimated coefficients (including ρ, which is here estimated as 0.53 but excluding the constant term):

$$d_L = 1.19$$
$$d_U = 1.55$$

The null hypothesis of no serial correlation cannot be rejected.

AUTOCORRELATION AND MODEL SPECIFICATION: A WORD OF CAUTION

The DW statistic was designed as a test for autocorrelation; its value can, however, be used as an indication of the misspecification of the regression model. For example, suppose that the economist fits the model:

$$y_t = \beta x_t + v_t$$

but the "true" model is really:

$$y_t = \beta_1 x_{1t} + \beta_2 x_{2t} + u_t$$

This means that the error term of the fitted model, v_t, is not the intended white noise, but is instead equal to $(\beta_2 x_{2t} + u_t)$. Consequently, the OLS residuals of the fitted model would exhibit autocorrelation since most economic variables are autocorrelated.

One of the first questions, therefore, that should be asked when the Durbin–Watson test detects the presence of autocorrelation is whether the model has been correctly specified and whether or not this apparent "autocorrelation" can be corrected by adding the missing variable to the model. A further indication of a missing variable would be a low R^2 (or $\bar{R}^2$) which provides evidence that some of the variation of the dependent variable remains unaccounted for, and the impact of this variable on the model has been subsumed into the error term.[5]

Take for instance the import function that we have studied in previous chapters, but this time let us estimate the following specification:

$$M_t = \beta_1 + \beta_2 Y_t + u_t$$

This is the original specification without the variable p_m/p_d. The results of the properly specified model were shown under Exhibit 1.1 in chapter 1 where the Durbin–Watson statistic of 1.665 would indicate the absence of serial correlation. The results for the new specification are shown in Exhibit 4.4, where we see, among other things, that the errors now appear to be autocorrelated (justify this statement).

Inclusion of the missing variable gets rid of the autocorrelation (see chapter 2) but many an unwary researcher might be tempted to correct for the problem. If this is done, the results shown in Exhibit 4.5 are obtained.

The autocorrelation problem appears to have disappeared but a valuable variable is now missing. Compare these results with those shown in Exhibit 2.1. What are your conclusions?

Adherents to the so-called general-to-specific school tend to regard autocorrelation as an opportunity, not a challenge, and recommend totally against using the correction algorithms discussed above. Consider for instance the model:

$$y_t = \beta x_t + u_t \qquad \textbf{(4.5)}$$

with:

$$u_t = \rho u_{t-1} + \varepsilon_t, |\rho| < 1$$

[5] A low DW and a *high* R^2 and $\bar{R}^2$, by contrast, indicates not misspecification, but *spurious correlation* – that is, where the regression is picking up the relationship of the included variables to time, and not necessarily to each other. This concept is at the foundation of cointegration analysis, to be discussed in greater detail in Part II of this book.

EXHIBIT 4.4
Equation: $M_t = \beta_1 + \beta_2 Y_t + u_t$
Output obtained from fitting equation in EViews

```
==================================================================
LS // Dependent Variable is IMPORTS
Sample: 1967 1991
Included observations: 25
==================================================================
     Variable     Coefficient Std. Error  T-Statistic    Prob.
==================================================================
        C          -3707.823   538.7572  -6.882178     0.0000
      INCOME        0.452149   0.032915   13.73681     0.0000
==================================================================
R-squared              0.891356   Mean dependent var    3556.082
Adjusted R-squared     0.886632   S.D. dependent var    1531.723
S.E. of regression     515.7336   Akaike info criter    12.56780
Sum squared resid      6117567.   Schwarz criterion     12.66531
Log likelihood        -190.5710   F-statistic           188.7000
Durbin-Watson stat     1.121388   Prob(F-statistic)     0.000000
==================================================================
```

EXHIBIT 4.5
Equation: $M_t = \beta_1 + \beta_2 Y_t + u_t$ corrected for autocorrelation
Output obtained from fitting equation in EViews

```
==================================================================
LS // Dependent Variable is IMPORTS
Sample: 1968 1991
Included observations: 24 after adjusting endpoints
Convergence achieved after 6 iterations
==================================================================
     Variable     Coefficient Std. Error  T-Statistic    Prob.
==================================================================
        C          -3037.188   1052.530  -2.885607     0.0088
      INCOME        0.412648   0.062546   6.597559     0.0000
      AR(1)         0.489191   0.192967   2.535099     0.0193
==================================================================
R-squared              0.903323   Mean dependent var    3655.325
Adjusted R-squared     0.894116   S.D. dependent var    1480.286
S.E. of regression     481.6829   Akaike info criter    12.47104
Sum squared resid      4872387.   Schwarz criterion     12.61830
Log likelihood        -180.7070   F-statistic           98.10927
Durbin-Watson stat     1.788356   Prob(F-statistic)     0.000000
==================================================================
```

Equation (4.5) may be rewritten as:

$$y_t = \beta x_t + \rho y_{t-1} - \rho\beta x_{t-1} + \varepsilon_t$$

or as:

$$y_t - \rho y_{t-1} = \beta(x_t - \rho x_{t-1}) + \varepsilon_t$$

Note that the "generalized" difference form of the endogenous variable, $(y_t - \rho y_{t-1})$, is explained by a similar form of the exogenous variable, $(x_t - \rho x_{t-1})$. When this happens, the model is said to contain a "common factor". The model may be estimated in the form:

$$y_t = \beta x_t + \rho y_{t-1} + \gamma x_{t-1} + \varepsilon_t$$

under the nonlinear restriction that $\gamma = -\rho\beta$. This restriction is usually referred to as the common factor restriction. Clearly, however, a simpler approach, if the restriction is valid, is to estimate the simple regression model (4.5) allowing for first-order autocorrelation. "If the restriction is rejected," write Charemza and Deadman (1997), "then evidence of autocorrelation in the simple static equation reflects 'misspecified dynamics' in that the variables x_{t-1} and y_{t-1} have been erroneously omitted from this equation." For more detailed discussion on this common factor analysis, see the very readable articles by Hendry and Mizon (1978), Mizon (1995) or the relevant discussion of the issue in Charemza and Deadman (1997), chapter 4. Dynamic models are introduced in chapter 5.

EXERCISES

1. Consider the general linear regression model:

$$\mathbf{y} = \mathbf{X}\boldsymbol{\beta} + \mathbf{u}$$

   a) State clearly the assumptions about **X** and **u** required for the application of generalized least squares (GLS).
   b) Show that, under these assumptions, GLS is the best estimator in the sense of Gauss–Markov.
   c) Show that, under these assumptions, the OLS estimator is still unbiased and derive an expression for its covariance matrix.
   d) What are the principal consequences of using OLS when the assumptions stated in (a) are valid?

2. a) What is meant by saying that the error term of the general linear regression model is homoscedastic?
   b) Explain, by means of appropriate examples if necessary, why the assumption of homoscedasticity is not plausible in many econometric applications.
   c) Consider the model:

$$Y_t = \beta_1 + \beta_2 X_t + u_t$$

$$E\left(u_t^2\right) = \sigma^2 X_t^2$$

   i) Use an appropriate transformation to obtain a model whose error term has a variance equal to σ^2.
   ii) Show that the generalized least squares estimator of the original equation is identical to the ordinary least squares estimator of the transformed equation. (The estimator derived in this exercise is an example of weighted least squares estimation, which was mentioned in the body of this chapter.)

   d) How would you test for heteroscedasticity?
3. In the regression model:

$$Y_t = \beta X_t + u_t \quad t = 1, 2, \ldots, n$$

   X is fixed and it is known that:

$$u_t = \rho u_{t-1} + \varepsilon_t \quad -1 < \rho < 1$$

   where ε_t is a white noise sequence.
   a) Show that the OLS estimator of β is unbiased and derive an expression of its sampling variance.
   b) Assuming that the value of ρ is known, give expressions for the GLS estimator of β and its sampling variance.
   c) Show that the Durbin–Watson statistic tends to 2 for large values of n under the null hypothesis that $\rho = 0$.
4. Once again, look at the Dominica data introduced in exercise 4, chapter 1 (also available in WT_DATA.XLS). This time, fit the model:

$$S_d = \alpha_0 + \alpha_1 S_f + \alpha_3 i_r + u$$

   a) Evaluate the results and, in particular, test for autocorrelation and heteroscedasticity (use the Koenker test).
   b) Correct for autocorrelation and comment on the results. Compare these results with those obtained from fitting the original model:

$$S_d = \alpha_0 + \alpha_1 Y + \alpha_2 S_f + \alpha_3 i_r + u$$

CHAPTER 5

Introduction to Dynamic Models

DYNAMIC MODELS

Issues of dynamic econometric modelling have dominated recent developments in the econometric literature. We will have much more to say about this in the second half of this book. In this chapter, we concentrate on the more traditional aspects of dynamic econometric modelling.

We have been considering so far the general linear regression model:

$$y_t = \beta_1 x_{1t} + \beta_2 x_{2t} + \beta_3 x_{3t} + \ldots + \beta_k x_{kt} + u_t$$

$$k = 1, 2, \ldots, t = 1, 2, \ldots, n$$

$$u_t \sim \text{iid}\left(0, \sigma^2\right)$$

In this chapter, we will limit our attention to the case where the observations on the variables are made across time, i.e. they are time series. In addition, we consider the possibility that y may also be related to past values of x, as well as to its own past values. How do such situations arise in economics?

Consider, for illustrative purposes, the relationship between investment and the rate of interest. An economist may wish to consider the following investment function:

$$I_t = \beta_0 + \beta_1 r_t + u_t$$

where I_t represents investment levels in time period t, and r_t represents the interest rates prevailing in the same time period. How plausible is such a relationship?

As we all must know, economic theory postulates the existence of *lags* in economic behaviour. What this means is that economic actors take time to respond to changes in the surrounding economic environment, and it takes further time for the effect of such responses to be felt on the economic environment. Applying this reasoning in the current context, it seems reasonable to assume that potential investors will not immediately react to changes in interest rates but will instead adopt a "wait-and-see" attitude before committing what is likely to be sizeable funds to any investment projects. Furthermore, investment projects take time to implement so that once the investor is satisfied that the interest rate fall indicates a possible trend rather than a temporary aberration, and the relevant funds are secured, it is unlikely that the investment itself will occur all at once.

A more realistic approach would be, therefore, to include among the explanatory variables possible *lagged values* of the rate of interest. The following is but one possibility:

$$I_t = \beta_0 + \beta_1 r_{t-3} + u_t$$

which explains investment levels in time period by the rates of interest that prevailed three periods ago. Suppose our data set spans the time interval 1970 to 1994. Then the model specifies that observed investment in, say, the year 1980 is a function of the interest rates of 1977. Alternatively, we may impute that the impact of 1985 interest rates on investment levels will be observable in 1988.

This illustration dealt with the presence of *lagged exogenous variables* in our regression model. We can, however, specify a model in which *lagged endogenous variables* appear among our list of explanatory variables. You may have come across, for example, a consumption function that looked as follows:

$$c_t = \beta_0 + \beta_1 c_{t-1} + \beta_2 y_t + \beta_3 r_t + u_t$$

Here, current consumption levels are explained by consumption in the previous period as well as by current income and interest rate levels. The inclusion of the lagged endogenous variable c_{t-1} could be intuitively justified by "habit persistence" in consumer behaviour.

We could also specify a model in which *both* lagged endogenous and exogenous variables appear on the right-hand side:

$$c_t = \beta_0 + \beta_1 c_{t-1} + \beta_2 y_{t-1} + \beta_3 y_{t-2} + \beta_4 r_t + u_t$$

Consumption functions, like these, are in the spirit of Friedman's permanent income hypothesis. According to this hypothesis, rational economic actors, in an attempt to smooth their consumption patterns over time, consume not on the basis of their current, and possibly transitory, income levels, but rather on the basis of their *permanent* income, which is a combination of both past and present income levels.

The presence of lagged variables among our explanatory variables, however, poses certain problems for econometric analysis. In the first place, even though economic theory tells us that a lag structure is essential if we are to capture the dynamism of the world around us, it often fails to tell us the appropriate length and structure of the lag system. Second, the lag length may be too long to allow for the efficient estimation of our model by traditional methods such as OLS. Remember, the introduction of a one-period lag results in the loss of one data point. A two-period lag causes us to lose two data points, and so on. Given the short data sets usually available for economic analysis, the introduction of lengthy lags causes loss of already scarce degrees of freedom and may result in the production of unreliable parameter estimates. Finally, given the tendency of economic variables to be autocorrelated, it is likely that the introduction of lagged right-hand-side variables, be they exogenous or endogenous, will increase the chances of multicollinearity among the explanatory variables. You will recall from chapter 3 that the presence of multicollinearity in a regression model has serious implications for the reliability of the parameter estimates. How do we deal with these drawbacks?

ALMON'S POLYNOMIAL DISTRIBUTED LAG (PDL) SCHEME

We consider here a particular, but very much used, application of the lag scheme proposed by Shirley Almon (1965). The basic philosophy underlying Almon's work is as follows. Consider the general model:

$$y_t = \alpha_0 x_t + \alpha_1 x_{t-1} + \alpha_2 x_{t-2} + \ldots + \alpha_s x_{t-s} + u_t$$

which, in matrix notation, becomes:

$$\mathbf{y} = \mathbf{X}\boldsymbol{\alpha} + \mathbf{u}$$

where:

$$\mathbf{y} = \begin{bmatrix} y_1 \\ y_2 \\ \vdots \\ \vdots \\ y_n \end{bmatrix}, \mathbf{X} = \begin{bmatrix} x_1 & x_0 & x_{-1} & \cdots & \cdots & x_{1-s} \\ x_2 & x_1 & x_0 & \cdots & \cdots & x_{2-s} \\ \vdots & \vdots & \vdots & & & \vdots \\ \vdots & \vdots & \vdots & & & \vdots \\ x_n & x_{n-1} & x_{n-2} & \cdots & \cdots & x_{n-s} \end{bmatrix}, \boldsymbol{\alpha} = \begin{bmatrix} \alpha_0 \\ \alpha_1 \\ \vdots \\ \vdots \\ \alpha_s \end{bmatrix}, \text{ and } \mathbf{u} = \begin{bmatrix} u_1 \\ u_2 \\ \vdots \\ \vdots \\ u_n \end{bmatrix}$$

We consider, for simplicity, the case where the variation in y is being explained by lagged values of only one variable x. The method may, however, easily be extended to cases involving lagged values of other variables.

Application of OLS to the above model yields:

$$\hat{\boldsymbol{\alpha}} = (\mathbf{X}'\mathbf{X})^{-1}\mathbf{X}'\mathbf{y}$$

However, the value of s in the above model, that is, the length of the lag, is assumed to be intolerably large, so that the direct estimation of the (s + 1) coefficients α_0, α_1, α_2, …, α_s may not yield reliable results. Almon proposes to reduce the parameter space to one containing (r + 1) coefficients where r is (considerably) less than s. This will result in an equivalent model of the form:

$$y_t = a_0 x_{0t} + a_1 x_{1t} + a_2 x_{2t} + \ldots + a_r x_{rt} + u_t \tag{5.2}$$

The fundamental problem is, therefore, the transformation of the original model (5.1) into (5.2). The underlying idea in Almon's analysis is that α_i may be approximated by some function of the lag length i, for instance:

$$\alpha_i = f(i)$$

This simply means that the value of the coefficient of the explanatory variable, lagged to order i, will depend in some way upon i, the length of the lag.

It is further proposed that f(i) can, in turn, be approximated by a polynomial in i of degree r like the one shown below:

$$\alpha_i = f(i) = a_0 + a_1 i + a_2 i^2 + \ldots + a_r i^r \quad \textbf{(5.3)}$$

This last step has as its justification Weierstrass's theorem, which states that *any* function can always be approximated by a polynomial of appropriate order. However, this theorem is silent on the value to be assigned to r, the order of the polynomial, and the choice of the value of r remains arbitrary. In the post-estimation stage, significance tests on the estimated a coefficients can be used to justify our choice.

By equation (5.3):

$$\begin{array}{lllllllll}
\alpha_0 = a_0 & & & & & & & & \\
\alpha_1 = a_0 & + & 1a_1 & + & 1^2 a_2 & + & \ldots & 1^r a_r \\
\alpha_2 = a_0 & + & 2a_1 & + & 2^2 a_2 & + & \ldots & 2^r a_r \\
\ldots & & \ldots & & \ldots & & \ldots & \ldots \\
\alpha_s = a_0 & + & sa_1 & + & s^2 a_2 & + & \ldots & s^r a_r
\end{array}$$

This system of equations may be represented as:

$$\begin{bmatrix} \alpha_0 \\ \alpha_1 \\ \alpha_2 \\ \vdots \\ \vdots \\ \alpha_s \end{bmatrix} = \begin{bmatrix} 1 & 0 & 0 & \ldots & \ldots & 0 \\ 1 & 1 & 1 & \ldots & \ldots & 1 \\ 1 & 2 & 2^2 & \ldots & \ldots & 2^r \\ \vdots & \vdots & \vdots & & & \vdots \\ \vdots & \vdots & \vdots & & & \vdots \\ 1 & s & s^2 & \ldots & \ldots & s^r \end{bmatrix} \begin{bmatrix} a_0 \\ a_1 \\ a_2 \\ \vdots \\ \vdots \\ a_r \end{bmatrix}$$

$$\Rightarrow \underset{(s+1,1)}{\boldsymbol{\alpha}} = \underset{(s+1,r+1)}{\mathbf{K}} \underset{(r+1,1)}{\mathbf{a}}$$

where s is the length of the lag, r is the order of the polynomial and **K** the matrix that transforms **a** into $\boldsymbol{\alpha}$.

Our original system:

$$\mathbf{y} = \mathbf{X}\boldsymbol{\alpha} + \mathbf{u}$$

may therefore be rewritten as:

$$\mathbf{y} = \mathbf{XKa} + \mathbf{u}$$

$$\Rightarrow \mathbf{y} = \mathbf{X} * \mathbf{a} + \mathbf{u}$$

Application of OLS to this transformed system yields:

$$\hat{\mathbf{a}} = (\mathbf{X}*'\mathbf{X}*)^{-1}\mathbf{X}*'\mathbf{y}$$

$$= \left[(\mathbf{XK})'\mathbf{XK}\right]^{-1}(\mathbf{XK})'\mathbf{y}$$

$$= (\mathbf{K'X'XK})^{-1}\mathbf{K'X'y}$$

The original parameter estimates are then obtained as:

$$\hat{\boldsymbol{\alpha}} = \mathrm{K}\hat{\mathbf{a}} \qquad \textbf{(5.4)}$$

It is easily established that:

$$\mathrm{E}(\hat{\boldsymbol{\alpha}}) = \mathrm{E}(\mathbf{K}\hat{\mathbf{a}}) = \mathbf{K}\mathrm{E}(\hat{\mathbf{a}}) = \mathbf{Ka} = \boldsymbol{\alpha}$$

$$\mathrm{cov}(\hat{\boldsymbol{\alpha}}) = \mathrm{cov}(\mathbf{K}\hat{\mathbf{a}}) = \mathbf{K}\ \mathrm{cov}(\hat{\mathbf{a}})\mathbf{K}' = \sigma^2\mathbf{K}(\mathbf{K'X'XK})^{-1}\mathbf{K}'$$

On the assumption that **K** is the true transformation matrix, it can be shown that the OLS estimator of the transformed model, $\hat{\mathbf{a}}$, is BLUE. This means that $\hat{\alpha}$ is also BLUE. The prerequisite for this, however, is that s and r, values of which have to be assigned before the transformed model can be estimated, *must* be of the correct orders. If not, then we run the risk of obtaining *biased* estimators.

We can carry out the routine significance tests on the a coefficients. We would be particularly interested in the significance of the estimate of the coefficient a_r. If this estimate were not significantly different from zero, then our conclusion would be that we have assigned the approximating polynomial too high an order. Conversely, should this estimate prove to be significantly different from zero, then we could feel content in the knowledge that our approximating polynomial is not an unrealistic choice.

The coefficient α_0 measures the effect of a one unit change in the current value of x on the present y value. By extension, the coefficient α_1 measures the effect on current y of a one unit change of the preceding value of x, and so on. We can say, therefore, that each coefficient, taken on its own, measures the *impact effect*, that is, the immediate effect of changes in the value of present or past x on present y. If we were to sum all the coefficient values, we obtain the combined or *dynamic* effect of the preceding *and* the present values of the explanatory variable x on the variable y under study.

Illustration of Almon's Polynomial Distributed Lag Scheme

Let us again look at the consumption function for Trinidad and Tobago that was estimated by OLS in the previous chapter. This time, it is specified as:

$$\mathrm{C}_{\mathrm{pt}} = \beta + \alpha_0\mathrm{Y}_{\mathrm{t}} + \alpha_1\mathrm{Y}_{\mathrm{t-1}} + \alpha_2\mathrm{Y}_{\mathrm{t-2}} + \ldots + \alpha_7\mathrm{Y}_{\mathrm{t-7}} + \mathrm{u}_{\mathrm{t}}$$

EXHIBIT 5.1
Equation: $C_{pt} = \beta + \alpha_0 Y_t + \alpha_1 Y_{t-1} + \alpha_2 Y_{t-2} + ... + \alpha_7 Y_{t-7} + u_t$
Output obtained from fitting equation in EViews

```
===============================================================
LS // Dependent Variable is P_CONS
Date: 08/31/95   Time: 07:34
Sample: 1974 1991
Included observations: 18 after adjusting endpoints
===============================================================
     Variable       Coefficient Std. Error  T-Statistic   Prob.
===============================================================
        C            -4268.212   883.4497  -4.831302    0.0009
      INCOME          0.386401   0.149795   2.579540    0.0297
    INCOME(-1)        0.711552   0.242087   2.939246    0.0165
    INCOME(-2)       -0.369838   0.239103  -1.546772    0.1563
    INCOME(-3)       -0.223422   0.238068  -0.938481    0.3725
    INCOME(-4)        0.414088   0.238491   1.736285    0.1165
    INCOME(-5)       -0.089753   0.236246  -0.379915    0.7128
    INCOME(-6)        0.041768   0.235457   0.177389    0.8631
    INCOME(-7)       -0.096222   0.134194 - 0.717041    0.4915
===============================================================
R-squared              0.980055   Mean dependent var    9341.344
Adjusted R-squared     0.962326   S.D. dependent var    1988.254
S.E. of regression     385.9179   Akaike info criter    12.21810
Sum squared resid      1340393.   Schwarz criterion     12.66329
Log likelihood        -126.5038   F-statistic           55.27938
Durbin-Watson stat     1.827440   Prob(F-statistic)     0.000001
===============================================================
```

Current consumption is explained by income up to 7 years (periods) ago.[1] This specification was fitted directly in EViews and the results obtained are displayed in Exhibit 5.1. Compare these results to those shown in Exhibit 5.2, obtained by fitting this same function by the Almon procedure using a third-order polynomial.

The polynomial approximation of the α coefficients in EViews is obtained as:

$$\alpha_i = f\left[i - (s^*/2)\right]$$

where s* = s if s is even and s* = s – 1 if s is odd. In the above, a_i is estimated by the coefficient attached to the "variable" PDLi+1 and the original α coefficients are estimated by applying equation (5.4) above. These are shown in the output as the coefficients corresponding to the lag lengths i = 0, 1, ..., 7. EViews also shows a graphical plot of these coefficients as well as their sum (as "Sum of Lags").

Let us begin some analysis and interpretation of these results by, first of all, comparing the results obtained by direct estimation to those obtained by application of the Almon procedure. Both show very high $\bar{R}^2$ values (about 96%) and in both

[1] Note the presence of the constant term β which changes nothing in the discussion of the previous section.

EXHIBIT 5.2

Equation: $C_{pt} = \beta + \alpha_0 Y_t + \alpha_1 Y_{t-1} + \alpha_2 Y_{t-2} + \ldots + \alpha_7 Y_{t-7} + u_t$

Fitted by Almon's PDL scheme using third-order polynomial approximation

```
==============================================================
LS // Dependent Variable is P_CONS
Date: 08/31/95   Time: 07:25
Sample: 1974 1991
Included observations: 18 after adjusting endpoints
==============================================================
     Variable      Coefficient Std. Error  T-Statistic   Prob.
==============================================================
        C           -4751.150   913.3949  -5.201638    0.0002
      PDL01         -0.054748   0.034087  -1.606121    0.1323
      PDL02          0.065757   0.048305   1.361283    0.1966
      PDL03          0.048405   0.010601   4.565969    0.0005
      PDL04         -0.018034   0.005964  -3.023578    0.0098
==============================================================
R-squared              0.967071   Mean dependent var   9341.344
Adjusted R-squared     0.956940   S.D. dependent var   1988.254
S.E. of regression     412.5825   Akaike info criter   12.27501
Sum squared resid      2212916.   Schwarz criterion    12.52233
Log likelihood        -131.0159   F-statistic          95.44860
Durbin-Watson stat     2.144822   Prob(F-statistic)    0.000000
==============================================================
Lag Distribution of INCOME   i Coefficient  Std. Error  T-Statist
==============================================================
   .            *|           0    0.67054    0.08772    7.64407
   .  *          |           1    0.15163    0.03979    3.81027
  *.             |           2   -0.05407    0.05980   -0.90412
  *.             |           3   -0.05475    0.03409   -1.60612
   .*            |           4    0.04138    0.03427    1.20757
   .  *          |           5    0.12611    0.06101    2.06707
   .  *          |           6    0.09125    0.04171    2.18758
 *  .            |           7   -0.17142    0.07840   -2.18651
==============================================================
                     Sum of Lags    0.80068    0.05320    15.0506
==============================================================
```

cases the Durbin–Watson statistic indicates an absence of autocorrelation. In Exhibit 5.3, the estimated α values are shown and compared.

First, the Almon scheme achieves significance for a greater number of coefficients, which may be a consequence of the smaller effect of multicollinearity here than in the OLS case. Second, the signs attached to each coefficient are identical in both cases but they are markedly different in values and consequently will have different policy implications. For instance, the OLS results imply that consumers will spend about 39 cents out of a \$1.00 increase in current income while, if the Almon results are accepted, they will spend about 67 cents. Finally, the "long run" effect of a \$1.00 increase in income is about 95 cents in the OLS case and only about 80 cents in the Almon case. Economic theory predicts that this value should

EXHIBIT 5.3
Equation: $C_{pt} = \beta + \alpha_0 Y_t + \alpha_1 Y_{t-1} + \alpha_2 Y_{t-2} + \ldots + \alpha_7 Y_{t-7} + u_t$
Comparison of coefficient estimates obtained by OLS and Almon's PDL scheme

Lag	OLS	Almon
0	0.386401*	0.67054*
1	0.711552*	0.15163*
2	–0.369838	–0.05407
3	–0.223422	–0.05475
4	0.414088	0.04138
5	0.089753	0.12011*
6	0.041768	0.09125*
7	–0.096222	–0.17142*
Sum of Lags	0.95408	0.80068

* Significant at 5% level or better.

be close to \$1.00, which would mean that the OLS result is more acceptable. What do you think?

THE KOYCK TRANSFORMATION

This is another very widely used transformation in applied econometric work. Consider again the model (5.1). The Koyck (1954) transformation identifies, as does the Almon scheme, an explicit form of the lag coefficients, which indicates that as the lag length increases, the explanatory variable exerts less of an impact on the current value of y. However, while Almon assumes that a polynomial of a fairly low degree can represent the lag coefficients, Koyck suggests that they undergo *geometric decay*, that is, the values of the lag coefficients decline in the pattern of a geometric progression.

The basic model assumes that s is infinitely large and:

$$\alpha_1 = f(i) = \alpha\lambda^i, \quad 0 < \lambda < 1 \quad i = 1,2,\ldots$$

Therefore, our general model above may be rewritten as follows:

$$\begin{aligned} y_t &= \alpha\lambda^0 x_t + \alpha\lambda^1 x_{t-1} + \alpha\lambda^2 x_{t-2} + \ldots + \alpha\lambda^s x_{t-s} + \ldots + u_t \\ \Rightarrow y_t &= \alpha\left[x_t + \lambda x_{t-1} + \lambda^2 x_{t-2} + \ldots + \lambda^s x_{t-s} + \ldots\right] + u_t \end{aligned} \tag{5.5}$$

Again, however, because of the seemingly infinite number of coefficients, direct estimation is not feasible. Koyck therefore proposes the following transformation.

Lagging expression (5.5), we obtain:

$$y_{t-1} = \alpha\left[x_{t-1} + \lambda x_{t-2} + \lambda^2 x_{t-3} + \ldots + \lambda^{s-1} x_{t-s} + \ldots\right] + u_{t-1} \tag{5.6}$$

Multiply both sides of equation (5.6) by λ to obtain:

$$\lambda y_{t-1} = \alpha\left[\lambda x_{t-1} + \lambda^2 xt_{-2} + \lambda^3 x_{t-3} + \ldots + \lambda^s x_{t-s} + \ldots\right] + \lambda u_{t-1} \quad \textbf{(5.7)}$$

Subtracting equation (5.7) from equation (5.5), we get:

$$\begin{aligned} y_t - \lambda y_{t-1} &= \alpha x_t + \left[u_t - \lambda u_{t-1}\right] \\ \Rightarrow y_t &= \alpha x_t + \lambda y_{t-1} + v_t \end{aligned} \quad \textbf{(5.8)}$$

This transformed model, which contains only two coefficients, can now be directly estimated by OLS.

It is important to note two things about the transformed model. First, it contains a lagged endogenous variable, and second, if the disturbance term u_t of the original model is white noise (the standard assumption) then the transformed disturbance v_t is autocorrelated.[2] These have consequences for OLS estimation. It can be shown that, when lagged values of an endogenous variable are included among our regressors, OLS estimation results in biased parameter estimates. If, in addition to the presence of a lagged endogenous variable, the disturbance terms are autocorrelated,[3] then OLS estimation becomes inconsistent as well as biased.

Of course, we may be lucky in that the transformed disturbance is itself white noise (which implies that the original disturbance is not). We have to test whether this is so or not.

In economic theory and applied econometric work, a model is very often specified as:

$$y_t = \alpha x_t + \lambda y_{t-1} + v_t$$

without any specific reference to Koyck. We must understand, however, that should our OLS estimate of λ be a positive fraction, and our OLS estimate of α be positive, then the model is equivalent to a Koyck transformation.

Illustration of the Koyck Transformation

If we apply the Koyck transformation to the consumption function studied above we will obtain a specification like the following:

$$C_{pt} = \beta_\lambda + \alpha Y_t + \lambda C_{pt-1} + u_t$$

This model was fitted using OLS and the results obtained are displayed in Exhibit 5.4.

---

[2] It is in fact a moving average process of order 1 or an MA(1). See chapter 13.

[3] We refer here to autocorrelation of *any* form, not just to the AR(1) procedure to which our discussion of autocorrelation in the preceding chapter was limited.

EXHIBIT 5.4

Equation: $C_{pt} = \beta + \alpha_0 Y_t + \alpha_1 Y_{t-1} + \alpha_2 Y_{t-2} + \ldots + \alpha_7 Y_{t-s} + \ldots + u_t$

Fitted to Koyck transformation: $C_{pt} = \beta_\lambda + \alpha Y_t + \lambda C_{pt-1} + u_t$

```
==============================================================
LS // Dependent Variable is P_CONS
Date: 08/31/95   Time: 10:26
Sample: 1968 1991
Included observations: 24 after adjusting endpoints
==============================================================
```

Variable	Coefficient	Std. Error	T-Statistic	Prob.
C	-1876.958	594.0039	-3.159841	0.0047
INCOME	0.485882	0.073228	6.635162	0.0000
P_CONS(-1)	0.300569	0.102009	2.946495	0.0077

R-squared	0.950487	Mean dependent var	8592.498
Adjusted R-squared	0.945771	S.D. dependent var	2164.074
S.E. of regression	503.9503	Akaike info criter	12.56142
Sum squared resid	5333285.	Schwarz criterion	12.70868
Log likelihood	-181.7916	F-statistic	201.5637
Durbin-Watson stat	1.473037	Prob(F-statistic)	0.000000

The $\overline{R}^2$ value (about 95%) is more than reasonable and indicates a very good fit. All coefficients carry the correct sign and, in particular, λ is a positive fraction. The short run marginal propensity to consume (mpc) is calculated at about 0.49, meaning that the Trinidadian consumer would spend immediately about half of any increase in current income. Of some concern, however, is the long run mpc, which is calculated as 0.695,[4] which, if correct, would mean that the Trinidadian public spends over time only 70 cents for every (permanent) increase of \$1.00. This not only contradicts standard economic theory but appears counterintuitive as well.

The Durbin–Watson statistic is an unreliable indicator of autocorrelation when, as happens here, there are lagged values of the endogenous variable among the regressors (we will elaborate further on this point later in the chapter). However, if it were to be applied, it would fall in the inconclusive region at the 5% level of significance. It is argued in Watson (1987) and others that this is such an unlikely occurrence that it should lead to rejection of the null hypothesis.

THE PARTIAL ADJUSTMENT MODEL

This is a very popular economic model which can be shown to be equivalent to a Koyck transformation. Consider the model:

$$y_t^* = a_0 + a_1 x_t + u_t$$

[4] This is calculated as (0.485882) ÷ (1 – 0.300509).

Here y_t^* represents some *desired* level of y in period t, which, as the equation suggests, depends on the value of some explanatory variable x in the same time period. It is not possible, however, to estimate this equation, given that the levels of y_t^* are unobservable. It becomes necessary, therefore, to postulate some behavioural pattern by which the actual, observed levels of y_t are *adjusted* to their desired levels.

The model suggests an adjustment pattern of the following form:

$$y_t - y_{t-1} = \theta\left(y_t^* - y_{t-1}\right) + u_t \quad 0 < \theta < 1 \tag{5.9}$$

where

$$u_t \sim NID\left(0, \sigma^2\right)$$

The change in the level of y from one period to the next, $(y_t - y_{t-1})$, is a fraction of the difference between the level of y in the previous period, and the desired level of y in the current period. The actual level of change, therefore, is only a fraction of the desired level of change.

It is further suggested that:

$$y_t^* = \delta x_t$$

that is, the desired levels of y in the current period are a function of some observable economic variable x in the same time period. Suppose, for example, that we were attempting to estimate a consumption function, where y_t^* represented desired levels of consumption. We could reasonably say that such desires are formed on the basis of income levels x_t, where increases in income would correspondingly lead to increases in "expected" consumption. Hence, while for purposes of estimation desired consumption is directly unobservable, we have made it *indirectly* observable on the basis of what, hopefully, is a very realistic and practical assumption.

Replacing y_t^* in expression (5.9), we obtain:

$$\begin{aligned} y_t - y_{t-1} &= \theta\left(\delta x_t - y_{t-1}\right) + u_t \\ \Rightarrow y_t - y_{t-1} &= \theta\delta x_t - \theta y_{t-1} + u_t \\ \Rightarrow y_t &= \theta\delta x_t + y_{t-1} - \theta y_{t-1} + u_t \\ \Rightarrow y_t &= \theta\delta x_t + (1-\theta) y_{t-1} + u_t \end{aligned} \tag{5.10}$$

Clearly, the partial adjustment model is a special case of the Koyck transformation, with:

$$\alpha = \theta\delta$$

and

$$\lambda = 1 - \theta$$

The difference is, however, that while the error term in expression (5.8) is autocorrelated, hence rendering OLS estimation of this model both biased and inconsistent, there is an absence of autocorrelation in the error term in expression (5.10), since we assume that u_t~NID(0, σ^2). Hence the application of OLS to *this* model would yield consistent, though biased, parameter estimates.

If the consumption function fitted in the previous section were interpreted as a partial adjustment model (and it can be), then θ is estimated as (1 – 0.300509) = 0.699. This means that the average period of adjustment is about 1.5 years.

THE ADAPTIVE EXPECTATIONS MODEL

This model postulates that the level of y in any one time period depends, not on the actual level of the explanatory variable in the same time period, but rather on its *expected* level. We can therefore write:

$$y_t = \beta x_t^* + u_t$$

where x_t^* represents these expectations, and u_t~NID(0, σ^2).

Expectations are formed on the basis of the following rule:

$$x_t^* - x_{t-1}^* = \theta\left(x_t - x_{t-1}^*\right) \quad 0 < \theta < 1 \tag{5.11}$$

The degree to which one's expectations are changed or adapted is a function of the degree to which the expectations held in the preceding period are realized. Clearly, if one's expectations are fulfilled, that is, should $x_t = x_{t-1}^*$, then there would be no need to revise such expectations, and x_t^* would be the same as x_{t-1}^*. The model, therefore, suggests that changes in expectations are a function of the accuracy of the forecast of the present period value made in the preceding period.

We can rewrite expression (5.11) as follows:

$$x_t^* - x_{t-1}^* = \theta\left(x_t - x_{t-1}^*\right)$$

$$\Rightarrow x_t^* = \theta x_t + x_{t-1}^* - \theta x_{t-1}^* \tag{5.12}$$

$$\Rightarrow x_t^* = \theta x_t + (1-\theta) x_{t-1}^*$$

Here, the current expectation of x (of its value in the next period) is a convex linear combination of its value in the current period and the expectation made about the current value in the previous period.

Replacing x_t^* with its value in the model yields:

$$y_t = \beta x_t^* + u_t$$

and we obtain:

$$
\begin{aligned}
& y_t = \beta\left[\theta x_t + (1-\theta)x^*_{t-1}\right] + u_t \\
& \Rightarrow y_t = \beta\theta x_t + \beta(1-\theta)\, x^*_{t-1} + u_t
\end{aligned}
\tag{5.13}
$$

However, on the basis of expression (5.11), we may write:

$$x^*_{t-1} = \theta x_{t-1} + (1-\theta)\, x^*_{t-2}$$

And now, replacing x^*_{t-1} with its value in expression (5.13):

$$
\begin{aligned}
& y_t = \beta\theta x_t + \beta(1-\theta)\left[\theta x_{t-1} + (1-\theta)x^*_{t-2}\right] + u_t \\
& \Rightarrow y_t = \beta\theta x_t + \beta\theta(1-\theta)x_{t-1} + \beta(1-\theta)^2\, x^*_{t-2} + u_t
\end{aligned}
$$

Now substituting in a similar fashion for x^*_{t-2}:

$$
\begin{aligned}
& y_t = \beta\theta x_t + \beta\theta(1-\theta)x_{t-1} + \beta(1-\theta)^2\left[\theta x_{t-2} + (1-\theta)\, x^*_{t-3}\right] + u_t \\
& \Rightarrow y_t = \beta\theta x_t + \beta\theta(1-\theta)x_{t-1} + \beta\theta(1-\theta)^2 x_{t-2} + \beta(1-\theta)x^*_{t-3} + u_t
\end{aligned}
$$

With continuous substitution, we will obtain:

$$
\begin{aligned}
& y_t = \beta\theta x_t = \beta\theta(1-\theta)x_{t-1} + \beta\theta(1-\theta)^2\, x_{t-2} + \ldots + \beta\theta(1-\theta)^s\, x_{t-s} + \ldots + u_t \\
& \Rightarrow y_t = \beta\theta\left[x_t + (1-\theta)x_{t-1} + (1-\theta)^2\, x_{t-2} + \ldots + (1-\theta)^s\, x_{t-s} + \ldots\right] + u_t
\end{aligned}
\tag{5.14}
$$

Note the absence of a term in x^* since this would, in the limit, tend to zero under the assumption that θ is a positive fraction.

If we lag expression (5.14), we get:

$$y_{t-1} = \beta\theta\left[x_{t-1} + (1-\theta)x_{t-2} + (1-\theta)^2\, x_{t-3} + \ldots + (1-\theta)^{s-1}\, x_{t-s} + \ldots\right] + u_{t-1} \tag{5.15}$$

Multiplying equation (5.15) throughout by the term $(1 - \theta)$ yields:

$$
\begin{aligned}
(1-\theta)y_{t-1} = {} & \beta\theta\left[(1-\theta)x_{t-1} + (1-\theta)^2\, x_{t-2} + (1-\theta)^3\, x_{t-3} + \ldots + (1-\theta)^s\, x_{t-s} + \ldots\right] \\
& + (1-\theta)u_{t-1}
\end{aligned}
\tag{5.16}
$$

Subtracting expression (5.16) from expression (5.14) gives:

$$y_t - (1-\theta)y_{t-1} = \beta\theta x_t + u_t - (1-\theta)u_{t-1}$$

$$\Rightarrow y_t = \beta\theta x_t + (1-\theta)y_{t-1} + u_t - (1-\theta)u_{t-1} \quad \textbf{(5.17)}$$

$$\Rightarrow y_t = \beta\theta x_t + (1-\theta)y_{t-1} + \omega_t$$

Clearly, this is equivalent to the Koyck transformation, with:

$$\alpha = \beta\theta$$

and

$$\lambda = (1-\theta)$$

Note, however, that OLS estimation of expression (5.17) is biased and probably inconsistent, given the presence among the explanatory variables of a lagged value of the endogenous variable and the possible autocorrelation of the disturbance term.

If the consumption function fitted in the previous section were interpreted as an adaptive expectations model (and it can be), then θ is estimated as (1 – 0.300509) = 0.699. This means that the average period of adjustment is about 1.5 years.

ERROR CORRECTION MECHANISM (ECM) MODELS

The error correction mechanism (ECM) model is extremely popular. It received its greatest impetus from the work of Davidson et al. (1978) and has since found its way into the rapidly expanding area of cointegration. It presupposes that some variable y has an equilibrium path defined by:

$$y_t^* = f(x_t)$$

In the short run, there are adjustments to deviations from the long run path which are defined by the ECM model:

$$\Delta y_t = \alpha \Delta x_t + \beta\left(y_{t-1} - y_{t-1}^*\right) + u_t$$

Consider the simple case where:

$$y_t^* = \lambda_1 + \lambda_2 x_t$$

then:

$$\Delta y_t = \alpha\Delta x_t + \beta\left(y_{t-1} - \lambda_1 - \lambda_2 x_{t-1}\right) + u_t$$

$$= -\beta\lambda_1 + \alpha\Delta x_t + \beta y_{t-1} - \beta\lambda_2 x_{t-1} + u_t \quad \textbf{(5.18)}$$

$$= \gamma + \alpha\Delta x_t + \beta y_{t-1} + \theta x_{t-1} + u_t$$

The coefficients α, β, γ and θ can be estimated by, for example, OLS. It can be shown that consistent estimators are so obtained – see Stock (1987), Engle and Granger (1987) and Holden and Perman (1994). We would expect β to be less than zero in value and to be (very) significant if the ECM model were to be applicable. What would $\beta = 0$ mean?

This model is an important input into the theory of cointegration, and estimation of its parameters by methods other than direct application of OLS to equation (5.18) will be discussed in some detail in Part II of this book.

Illustration of the Error Correction Mechanism Model

Consider once again the consumption function, where the equilibrium consumption path is defined by:

$$C^*_{pt} = \lambda_1 + \lambda_2 Y_t$$

so that the ECM model is written as:

$$\Delta C_{pt} \gamma + \alpha \Delta Y_t + \beta C_{pt-1} + \theta Y_{t-1} + u_t$$

This regression was run using EViews and the results obtained are shown in Exhibit 5.5.

EXHIBIT 5.5
ECM version of consumption function
$\Delta C_{pt} = \gamma + \alpha \Delta Y_t + \beta C_{pt-1} + \theta Y_{t-1} + u_t$

```
LS // Dependent Variable is D(P_CONS)
Date: 10/15/95   Time: 23:18
Sample: 1968 1991
Included observations: 24 after adjusting endpoints
```

Variable	Coefficient	Std. Error	T-Statistic	Prob.
C	-1651.819	630.8543	-2.618384	0.0165
D(INCOME)	0.606561	0.136858	4.432058	0.0003
P_CONS(-1)	-0.515144	0.203931	-2.526071	0.0201
INCOME(-1)	0.372198	0.131236	2.836106	0.0102

R-squared	0.713400	Mean dependent var	72.52673
Adjusted R-squared	0.670410	S.D. dependent var	875.9847
S.E. of regression	502.9020	Akaike info criter	12.59180
Sum squared resid	5058208.	Schwarz criterion	12.78814
Log likelihood	-181.1562	F-statistic	16.59458
Durbin-Watson stat	1.976866	Prob(F-statistic)	0.000012

In EViews, ΔC_{pt} and ΔY_t are shown as D(P_CONS) and D(INCOME), respectively. The β coefficient is estimated as 0.515 and it is significant. This means that just over half the deviation from the equilibrium path is made up in the following period. What are the estimated values of the λ coefficients?

AUTOREGRESSIVE DISTRIBUTED LAG (ADL) MODELS

The following is an example of an autoregressive distributed lag (ADL) model:

$$y_t = \beta_0 + \sum_{i=1}^{p} \beta_i y_{t-i} + \sum_{i=0}^{q} \alpha_i x_{t-1} + u_t$$

It is "autoregressive" because it has, among the explanatory variables, lagged values of the endogenous variable and it is a "distributed lag" model because the exogenous variable is lagged. There can be more than one exogenous variable and the values of p and q are to be determined empirically. A possible eventual specification might be:

$$y_t = \beta_0 + \beta_1 y_{t-1} + \alpha_0 x_t + \alpha_1 x_{t-1} + u_t \qquad \textbf{(5.19)}$$

This model was made popular by Davidson et al. (1978) and it can be shown that an ECM-type model can be derived from it. Indeed, from equation (5.19), we obtain:

$$y_t - y_{t-1} = \beta_0 + (\beta_1 - 1) y_{t-1} + \alpha_0 x_t + (\alpha_0 - \alpha_0 + \alpha_1) x_{t-1} + u$$

$$\Rightarrow \Delta y_t = \beta_0 + \gamma_1 y_{t-1} + \alpha_0 (x_t - x_{t-1}) + (\alpha_1 - \alpha_0) x_{t-1} + u_t \qquad \textbf{(5.20)}$$

$$= \beta_0 + \alpha_0 \Delta x_t + \gamma_1 (y_{t-1} - \theta x_{t-1}) + u_t$$

where $-\theta\gamma_1 = (\alpha_1 - \alpha_0)$. This is clearly an ECM model with an equilibrium path:

$$y_t^* = \theta x_t$$

and γ_1 is the speed of adjustment.

Equation (5.19) may be estimated directly by OLS. Suggested solutions to the estimation of equation (5.20) are given in Part II. What happens if $\gamma_1 = 0$?

Illustration of the Autoregressive Distributed Lag Model

Consider the following version of the consumption function:

$$C_{pt} = \beta_0 + \beta_1 C_{pt-1} + \alpha_0 Y_t + \alpha_1 Y_{t-1} + u_t$$

This specification was fitted using EViews and the results shown in Exhibit 5.6 were obtained.

EXHIBIT 5.6

Equation: $C_{pt} = \beta_0 + \beta_1 C_{pt-1} + \alpha_0 Y_t + \alpha_1 Y_{t-1} + u_t$

```
==============================================================
LS // Dependent Variable is P_CONS
Date: 10/16/95   Time: 00:45
Sample: 1968 1991
Included observations: 24 after adjusting endpoints
==============================================================
     Variable      Coefficient Std. Error  T-Statistic   Prob.
==============================================================
        C           -1651.819   630.8543  -2.618384    0.0165
    P_CONS(-1)       0.484856   0.203931   2.377554    0.0275
      INCOME         0.606561   0.136858   4.432058    0.0003
    INCOME(-1)      -0.234364   0.224722  -1.042902    0.3094
==============================================================
R-squared            0.953040   Mean dependent var   8592.498
Adjusted R-squared   0.945996   S.D. dependent var   2164.074
S.E. of regression   502.9020   Akaike info criter   12.59180
Sum squared resid    5058208.   Schwarz criterion    12.78814
Log likelihood      -181.1562   F-statistic          135.2992
Durbin-Watson stat   1.976866   Prob(F-statistic)    0.000000
==============================================================
```

What justification is there for dropping the lagged income variable from this regression? Redo the regression excluding the lagged income variable and compare it with the results obtained in Exhibit 5.6.

THE DURBIN TEST FOR AUTOCORRELATION IN THE PRESENCE OF LAGGED ENDOGENOUS VARIABLES

The Durbin–Watson (DW) statistic introduced in chapter 4 is an unreliable measure of autocorrelation when lagged values of the endogenous variable are present among the regressors. In fact, it is biased towards the value of 2 (this shall not be proven). For this reason, Durbin (1970) developed an alternative test (the Durbin 'h' test) to cater for the situation in which lagged endogenous variables are present. It is based on the statistic:

$$h = \hat{\rho}\sqrt{\frac{n}{1 - n\hat{v}}} \sim N(0,1)$$

where $\hat{\rho}$ is the OLS estimator of ρ in:

$$\hat{u}_t = \rho \hat{u}_{t-1} + \varepsilon_t$$

and $\hat{v}$ is the variance associated with the estimator of the coefficient associated with the lagged endogenous variable in the model. We have shown in chapter 4 that:

$$DW \cong 2(1-\hat{\rho})$$

so that $\hat{\rho}$ can be calculated as:

$$\hat{\rho} \cong 1-\frac{1}{2}DW$$

Under the null hypothesis of the absence of autocorrelation, h is asymptotically normally distributed with zero mean and unit variance. The test is also valid when the model contains lags of order higher than 1.

This testing alternative is, however, limited: it is valid only in (very) large samples, and clearly cannot be calculated for n $\hat{v} > 1$.

Illustration of the Durbin h-Test

Unfortunately, EViews does not automatically calculate h, but it supplies all the information necessary to do so. Let us look once again at the results displayed in Exhibit 5.4. Application of the h formula yields:

$$h = \left(1-\frac{1.473037}{2}\right)\sqrt{\frac{24}{1-24(0.102009)^2}} = 1.490218$$

Since h is distributed (asymptotically) as a standard normal variable, the null hypothesis of "no autocorrelation" cannot be rejected at the 5% level since the calculated h value is less than the (one-tailed test) critical value of 1.645. But strictly speaking, this test is valid in only (very) large samples, which means that we should use this result with extreme caution, especially given the fact observed above that the Durbin–Watson statistic would fall in the inconclusive region of the test.

If we accept the conclusion about the absence of autocorrelation, we can proceed to conduct tests of significance and it is interesting to note that all coefficients are highly significant.

EXERCISES

1. Consider the following investment function model:

$$I_t = a + b_0 Y_t + b_1 Y_{t-1} + b_3 Y_{t-2} + \ldots + b_s Y_{t-s} + u_t \qquad \textbf{(1)}$$

where I is investment, Y is income and u the usual disturbance term.

a) Briefly explain the economic rationale underlying a model like this one.

b) Discuss the econometric difficulty involved in direct estimation of the coefficients of this model by OLS.

c) Transform the model using the methods proposed by (i) Almon and (ii) Koyck and compare the two methods.

2. It is proposed to study the supply of loans by commercial banks for business purposes in Trinidad and Tobago using the following "adaptive expectations" model:

$$L_t = a + bD_t^* + u_t$$

$$\left(D_t^* - D_{t-1}^*\right) = \theta\left(D_t - D_{t-1}^*\right),\ 0 < \theta < 1$$

L_t = supply of loans during period t
D_t = level of bank deposits during period t
D^*_t = expected level of bank deposits for period t + 1 formed at time t.

a) Discuss the economic rationale of this model.
b) Trace the steps by which this model can be transformed into:

$$L_t = a + bD_t + c\,L_{t-1} + u_t$$

and show clearly the link between the coefficients of the original and transformed models.

c) The following results were obtained through the application of OLS to data spanning 43 quarters (measured in millions of TT$):

$$L_t = 19.4 + 0.058D_t + 0.811\,L_{t-1} + u_t$$

$$(0.032) \qquad (0.011)$$

$$R^2 = 0.995 \qquad DW = 1.87 \qquad F = 3827$$

(figures in parentheses are standard errors)
Discuss these results.

3. Discuss the partial adjustment model and the econometric difficulties associated with the estimation of its parameters.
4. Using:
   a) The Almon coefficient scheme
   b) The partial adjustment model
   fit the Dominican data to the model:

$$S_d = f(Y)$$

and evaluate the results obtained.

CHAPTER 6

The Instrumental Variable Estimator

INTRODUCTION

In chapter 5, we met for the first time cases where lagged values of the endogenous variable appeared among the regressors. This is clearly a violation of assumption A_3, introduced in chapter 1 (that the regressors are fixed or nonstochastic). This assumption was important in establishing that OLS was an unbiased estimator. We are now going to introduce the possibility of stochastic regressors among the X variables.

Throughout this book we have been using the following import function for our many illustrations:

$$M_t = \beta_1 + \beta_2 Y_t + \beta_3 p_{mt}/p_{dt} + u_t$$

but if we look at chapter 1, we will notice that this function is but one in a system of equations that includes, in particular, the identity:

$$Y_t = C_{pt} + C_{gt} + I_t + X_t - M_t \qquad \textbf{(6.1)}$$

The presence among the explanatory variables of the income variable Y in the imports equation makes a big difference. Indeed, by equation (6.1), Y is also a function of M and consequently of the disturbance term u_t and so Y is also random and, more importantly perhaps, not independent of u_t. Once again, the assumption that the matrix of explanatory variables is non-random is clearly violated here. So the presence of Y among the explanatory variables results in OLS being a biased estimating procedure.

There are many other situations in practice other than the presence of lagged endogenous variables or other variables related to the error term among the regressors which have implications for the OLS estimator. Later on in this chapter, for instance, we will study the "errors in variables" case that occurs so frequently in practice. To understand these implications fully, however, we must first understand the concept of a consistent estimator.

CONSISTENT ESTIMATORS

Consider a random variable X whose probability density function $f(\cdot|\theta)$ depends on some unknown parameter (or some vector of parameters) θ. We want to estimate θ by:

$$\hat{\theta}_n = \hat{\theta}(X_1, X_2, \ldots, X_n)$$

where $X_1, X_2, \ldots, X_n$ is a random sample of size n drawn on X. Suppose that, for small n, $\hat{\theta}_n$ had undesirable properties (for instance it could be a biased estimator) or suppose we were simply unable to establish its small sample properties. We would then have no option but to ask about its properties as n got larger. It would, in particular, seem intuitively reasonable to ask that a minimum requirement should be that the estimator $\hat{\theta}_n$ "converged" in value to the parameter θ that it is estimating. Indeed, if as the sample size increased, the estimator either diverged from the true parameter value or its relationship with the true parameter value could not be established, then such an estimator would be quite useless and it would be better to obtain an alternative one.

The notion of a *consistent* estimator is a reflection of this kind of intuitive thinking but requires convergence in a probabilistic sense rather than convergence in actual values. Consider the sequence:

$$P_n = \Pr\left(\left|\hat{\theta}_n - \theta\right| \le \varepsilon\right), n = 1, 2, \ldots,$$

where ε is some arbitrarily small value (for example $\varepsilon = 0.0001$). What does P_n measure? It measures the probability of $\hat{\theta}_n$ being more or less identical in value to θ. If this probability is small, then clearly $\hat{\theta}_n$ is not the estimator we are looking for, but if it is large and, in particular, if it is equal to 1 (its largest value) then we will be happy with the choice of such an estimator. In many instances in practice, it is difficult to determine the exact value of P_n and it is frequently simpler to determine its limiting value. Let us denote this limiting value P and define it as:

$$\lim_{n \to \infty} P_n = P$$

Then $\hat{\theta}_n$ is a *consistent* estimator of θ if $P = 1$. Intuitively, a consistent estimator of a parameter θ is one that "converges in probability" to θ or, in simpler terms, is one that is very likely to be not much different in value from θ as the sample gets larger and larger. In the limit, it is no different at all from θ for all intents and purposes. In the literature, the expression:

$$\text{plim}\,\hat{\theta}_n = \theta$$

indicates that $\hat{\theta}_n$ converges in probability to, or is a consistent estimator of, θ. The "plim" operator, as it is frequently called, has some very interesting properties, some of which we now consider.

- If k is constant, then:

$$\text{plim}\,k = k$$

- If plim $\alpha = a$ and plim $\beta = b$ then:

$$\text{plim}(\alpha * \beta) = \text{plim}\,\alpha * \text{plim}\,\beta = a * b$$

where $*$ indicates any one of the standard arithmetic operators with the caveat, of course, that if $*$ indicates division, then $b \neq 0$. This result is true even if α, β, a and b are vectors or matrices, with the proviso that they conform to the indicated operation and that division means multiplication by the inverse (if it exists). An interesting application of this result is, if **A** is a nonsingular $n \times n$ matrix, then:

$$\text{plim}\left(\mathbf{A}^{-1}\right) = \left(\text{plim}\,\mathbf{A}\right)^{-1}$$

- (Slutsky's theorem) If $g(\alpha)$ is a continuous function of α and plim $\alpha =$ a, then:

$$\text{plim}\left[g(\alpha)\right] = g(a)$$

To establish consistency, it suffices to establish that plim $\hat{\theta}_n = \theta$. It is sometimes simpler, however, to prove that the following conditions hold:

$$E\left(\hat{\theta}_n\right) = \theta$$

$$\lim_{n \to \infty} \text{var}\left(\hat{\theta}_n\right) = 0$$

Note, however, that these are sufficient and not necessary conditions of consistency.

IS OLS CONSISTENT?

In the general linear regression model studied in chapter 1, OLS is consistent under assumptions A1 to A3. Indeed, we have already established that it is unbiased and that its covariance matrix is $\sigma^2 (\mathbf{X}'\mathbf{X})^{-1}$. But:

$$\lim_{n \to \infty} \sigma^2 (\mathbf{X}'\mathbf{X})^{-1} = \lim_{n \to \infty} \frac{\sigma^2}{n}\left(\frac{\mathbf{X}'\mathbf{X}}{n}\right)^{-1} = \lim_{n \to \infty} \frac{\sigma^2}{n} \lim\left(\frac{\mathbf{X}'\mathbf{X}}{n}\right)^{-1} = 0$$

so that the OLS estimator is consistent.

But does this result hold when **X** is not fixed, as is the case for equation (6.1) above? It would indeed if the following condition holds:

$$\text{plim}\left(\frac{\mathbf{X}'\mathbf{u}}{n}\right) = 0 \quad (A_5)$$

This requires that, for each of the explanatory variables x_i

$$\text{plim}\ \frac{1}{n}\sum_{t=1}^{n} x_{it} u_t = 0$$

Does this hold for the imports equation, for instance? Since it has already been shown that Y is random because u is, then clearly we cannot assume that

$$\text{plim}\ \frac{1}{n}\sum_{t=1}^{n} Y_t u_t = 0$$

Consequently, application of OLS to this equation yields not only biased but inconsistent estimators. What then is a more appropriate estimation procedure?

THE INSTRUMENTAL VARIABLE ESTIMATOR

The introduction of "simultaneity" into the system is but one reason why OLS becomes inconsistent, but OLS applied to the general linear regression model is always inconsistent whenever, and for whatever reason

$$\text{plim}\left(\frac{\mathbf{X'u}}{n}\right) \neq 0$$

The presence of lagged values of the endogenous variable among the regressors is frequently another cause of inconsistency, as well as measurement errors (to be taken up below).

The proof of the inconsistency of OLS when

$$\text{plim}\left(\frac{\mathbf{X'u}}{n}\right) \neq 0$$

is very simple: we saw in chapter 1 that:

$$\hat{\boldsymbol{\beta}} = \boldsymbol{\beta} + (\mathbf{X'X})^{-1}\mathbf{X'u}$$

so that:

$$\text{plim}\left(\hat{\boldsymbol{\beta}}\right) = \boldsymbol{\beta} + \text{plim}\left(\frac{\mathbf{X'X}}{n}\right)^{-1}\left(\frac{\mathbf{X'u}}{n}\right) = \boldsymbol{\beta} + \text{plim}\left(\frac{\mathbf{X'X}}{n}\right)^{-1} \text{plim}\left(\frac{\mathbf{X'u}}{\mathbf{n}}\right)$$

It seems rather unreasonable to assume that:

$$\text{plim}\left(\frac{\mathbf{X'X}}{n}\right)^{-1} = 0$$

and in fact the opposite is usually explicitly assumed. The consistency of $\hat{\boldsymbol{\beta}}$ then clearly requires that:

$$\text{plim}\left(\frac{\mathbf{X'u}}{n}\right) = 0$$

If this is not the case (as we are now assuming), then OLS estimation is inconsistent.

A consistent estimator of $\boldsymbol{\beta}$ is the *instrumental variable* estimator, defined as:

$$\hat{\boldsymbol{\beta}}_{IV} = (\mathbf{Z'X})^{-1}\mathbf{Z'y}$$

where $\mathbf{Z}$ is an (n × k) matrix of "instruments" with:

$$\text{plim}\left(\frac{\mathbf{Z'u}}{n}\right) = 0$$

The proof of the consistency of $\hat{\boldsymbol{\beta}}_{IV}$ is straightforward:

$$\hat{\boldsymbol{\beta}}_{IV} = (\mathbf{Z'X})^{-1}\mathbf{Z'}(\mathbf{X}\boldsymbol{\beta} + \mathbf{u}) = \boldsymbol{\beta} + (\mathbf{Z'X})^{-1}\mathbf{Z'u}$$

so that:

$$\text{plim}\left(\hat{\boldsymbol{\beta}}_{IV}\right) = \boldsymbol{\beta} + \text{plim}\left(\frac{\mathbf{Z'X}}{n}\right)^{-1}\left(\frac{\mathbf{Z'u}}{n}\right) = \boldsymbol{\beta} + \text{plim}\left(\frac{\mathbf{Z'X}}{n}\right)^{-1}\text{plim}\left(\frac{\mathbf{Z'u}}{n}\right) = \boldsymbol{\beta}$$

The problem remains, of course, to determine the matrix $\mathbf{Z}$ in a given situation. Apart from being uncorrelated with the disturbance term the columns of $\mathbf{Z}$ must be highly correlated with the columns of $\mathbf{X}$.[1] This makes the choice easier for us but does not solve the problem entirely. Take, once again, the imports equation: the $\mathbf{X}$ matrix would look like:

$$\mathbf{X} = \begin{bmatrix} 1 & Y_1 & (p_m/p_d)_1 \\ 1 & Y_2 & (p_m/p_d)_2 \\ \vdots & \vdots & \vdots \\ 1 & Y_n & (p_m/p_d)_n \end{bmatrix}$$

The $\mathbf{Z}$ matrix need differ from the $\mathbf{X}$ matrix only by the Y column, which must be replaced because it is correlated with the error term. In a country like Trinidad and Tobago, national income is highly correlated with government current expenditure (C_{gt}) which, in the model, is uncorrelated with the error term. The $\mathbf{Z}$ matrix would look like:

$$\mathbf{Z} = \begin{bmatrix} 1 & C_{g1} & (p_m/p_d)_1 \\ 1 & C_{g2} & (p_m/p_d)_2 \\ \vdots & \vdots & \vdots \\ 1 & C_{gn} & (p_m/p_d)_n \end{bmatrix}$$

[1] This statement has to be taken on trust here but has an obvious common sense appeal.

The other two columns are not correlated with the error term and are very highly correlated with the corresponding columns of the **X** matrix: in fact, they are identical to the columns of the **X** matrix and therefore are perfectly correlated.

EViews has a procedure for carrying out instrumental variable estimation which is related to the two-stage least squares estimation method to be introduced in chapter 7. Using the import function as an example, it chooses as the instrument for Y the OLS fitted value of Y on a list of variables not related to the error term (called the "instrument list") which *must* include all such variables appearing in the equation (in this case the constant term, the ratio p_m/p_d) *as well as* at least one other such variable not included in the equation (for example C_g). The **Z** matrix in this case would look like:

$$\mathbf{Z} = \begin{bmatrix} 1 & \hat{Y}_1 & (p_m/p_d)_1 \\ 1 & \hat{Y}_2 & (p_m/p_d)_2 \\ \vdots & \vdots & \vdots \\ 1 & \hat{Y}_n & (p_m/p_d)_n \end{bmatrix}$$

where:

$$\hat{Y}_t = \hat{\alpha}_1 + \hat{\alpha}_2 \frac{p_{mt}}{p_{dt}} + \hat{\alpha}_3 C_g, \quad t = 1, 2, \ldots, n$$

where the αs are OLS estimators.

In general, if an equation contains G variables among the k regressors that are related to the error term, then the EViews instrument list must include all variables in the equation not related to the error term, plus at least G such variables that do not appear in the equation.[2]

The EViews procedure was used to fit the imports equation using as the instrument list the constant term, the ratio p_m/p_d (both of which appear in the equation) and government current expenditure, C_g (which does not appear in the equation and which, in the model, is not related to the disturbance term). The results of this exercise are displayed in Exhibit 6.1.

Notice that the "instrument list" contains the constant term (C) and RATIO (p_m/p_d) as well as G_CONS (C_g). Compare these results to those obtained by estimation with OLS in chapter 1.

THE ERRORS IN VARIABLES MODEL

In this section, we will concentrate on the problem associated with measurement errors in economic variables. That economic variables suffer from such errors is an understatement, and many of the pitfalls identified by Morgenstern (1950) remain valid up to today.

[2] The justification for this statement will be given in chapter 7.

EXHIBIT 6.1
Instrumental variable estimation of
$M_t = \beta_1 + \beta_2 Y_t + \beta_3\, p_{mt}/p_{dt} + u_t$

```
==================================================================
TSLS // Dependent Variable is IMPORTS
Date: 08/13/95   Time: 21:47
Sample: 1967 1991
Included observations: 25
Instrument list:   C G_CONS RATIO
==================================================================
     Variable        Coefficient Std. Error  T-Statistic   Prob.
==================================================================
        C             -1074.987   734.9657  -1.462636    0.1577
      INCOME           0.372419   0.031607   11.78275    0.0000
      RATIO           -704.1884   159.1260  -4.425351    0.0002
==================================================================
R-squared                0.942366   Mean dependent var   3556.082
Adjusted R-squared       0.937126   S.D. dependent var   1531.723
S.E. of regression       384.0746   Akaike info criter   12.01384
Sum squared resid        3245293.   Schwarz criterion    12.16011
F-statistic              168.7667   Durbin-Watson stat   1.653607
Prob(F-statistic)        0.000000
==================================================================
```

When fitting the model:

$$\mathbf{y} = \mathbf{X}\boldsymbol{\beta} + \mathbf{u}$$

it is vital that **y** and **X** be correctly measured. If this is the case, then the only error is contained in the disturbance term **u**. However, the nature of economic data makes this assumption very difficult to realize in practice.[3] Let us consider what happens when variables are measured with error, and what must be done when this occurs.

Suppose that, in the above model, **y** and **X** are incorrectly measured, so that we in fact observe:

$$\mathbf{y} = \tilde{\mathbf{y}} + \mathbf{y}_e$$

$$\mathbf{X} = \tilde{\mathbf{X}} + \mathbf{X}_e$$

where $\tilde{\mathbf{y}}$ and $\tilde{\mathbf{X}}$ are the correct measures. We are therefore attempting to fit a *true* model:

$$\tilde{\mathbf{y}} = \tilde{\mathbf{X}}\boldsymbol{\beta} + \mathbf{u}$$

but do not succeed in doing so because of the presence of this measurement error.

[3] See Intriligator et al. (1996) for a discussion of Friedman's permanent income theory of the consumption function, which is a specific illustration of an errors in variables model in economics.

Replacing $\tilde{\mathbf{y}}$ and $\tilde{\mathbf{X}}$ in the true model, we obtain:

$$\mathbf{y}-\mathbf{y}_e=(\mathbf{X}-\mathbf{X}_e)\boldsymbol{\beta}+\mathbf{u}$$

$$\mathbf{y}-\mathbf{y}_e=\mathbf{X}\boldsymbol{\beta}-\mathbf{X}_e\boldsymbol{\beta}+\mathbf{u}$$

$$\mathbf{y}=\mathbf{X}\boldsymbol{\beta}+\mathbf{y}_e+\mathbf{u}-\mathbf{X}_e\boldsymbol{\beta}$$

Letting $\mathbf{V} = \mathbf{y}_e + \mathbf{u}$ and $\boldsymbol{\omega} = \mathbf{V} - \mathbf{X}_e\boldsymbol{\beta}$, the last expression becomes:

$$\mathbf{y}=\mathbf{X}\boldsymbol{\beta}+\boldsymbol{\omega}$$

We therefore see that our disturbance term has changed. What are the implications of these errors for OLS estimation? It can and will be proven that, when there exists a measurement error in the variables, OLS estimation becomes inconsistent.

The OLS estimator of β in the model:

$$\mathbf{y}=\mathbf{X}\boldsymbol{\beta}+\boldsymbol{\omega}$$

is, as usual, defined as:

$$\begin{aligned}\hat{\boldsymbol{\beta}}&=(\mathbf{X}'\mathbf{X})^{-1}\mathbf{X}'\mathbf{y}\\&=(\mathbf{X}'\mathbf{X})^{-1}\mathbf{X}'(\mathbf{X}\boldsymbol{\beta}+\boldsymbol{\omega})\\&=(\mathbf{X}'\mathbf{X})^{-1}\mathbf{X}'\mathbf{X}\boldsymbol{\beta}+(\mathbf{X}'\mathbf{X})^{-1}\mathbf{X}'\boldsymbol{\omega}\\&=\boldsymbol{\beta}+(\mathbf{X}'\mathbf{X})^{-1}\mathbf{X}'\boldsymbol{\omega}\end{aligned} \tag{6.2}$$

For $\hat{\boldsymbol{\beta}}$ to be a consistent estimator, it is necessary that:

$$\text{plim}\left(\hat{\boldsymbol{\beta}}\right)=\boldsymbol{\beta}$$

that is, that $\hat{\boldsymbol{\beta}}$ converges in probability to $\boldsymbol{\beta}$.

Applying the plim operator to expression (6.2) above, we obtain:

$$\text{plim}\left(\hat{\boldsymbol{\beta}}\right)=\boldsymbol{\beta}+\text{plim}\left(\frac{1}{n}\mathbf{X}'\mathbf{X}\right)^{-1}\text{plim}\left(\frac{1}{n}\mathbf{X}'\boldsymbol{\omega}\right)$$

Under the assumption that:

$$\text{plim}\left(\frac{1}{n}\mathbf{X}'\mathbf{X}\right)^{-1}\neq 0$$

the condition for the consistency of the OLS estimator is that:

$$\text{plim}\left(\frac{1}{n}\mathbf{X}'\boldsymbol{\omega}\right)=0$$

To investigate this matter, we make the following assumptions:

1. **u**, **y** and $\mathbf{X}_e$ are pairwise uncorrelated
2. E(**V**) = E($\mathbf{y}_e$ + **u**) = 0
3. cov(**V**) = cov($\mathbf{y}_e$ + **u**) = $\sigma^2_{u+e}\mathbf{I}$

Clearly:

$$\begin{aligned}\text{plim}\left(\frac{1}{n}\mathbf{X}'\boldsymbol{\omega}\right)&=\text{plim}\left(\frac{1}{n}\mathbf{X}'\left[\mathbf{V}-\mathbf{X}_e\boldsymbol{\beta}\right]\right)\\&=\text{plim}\left(\frac{1}{n}\mathbf{X}'\mathbf{V}\right)-\text{plim}\left(\frac{1}{n}\mathbf{X}'\mathbf{X}_e\boldsymbol{\beta}\right)\end{aligned}$$

We can make the assumption here that:

$$\text{plim}\left(\frac{1}{n}\mathbf{X}'\mathbf{V}\right)=0$$

since $\mathbf{X}'\mathbf{V} = (\tilde{\mathbf{X}} + \mathbf{X}_e)'\,\mathbf{V}$, and the assumption was already made that X_e is not related to the error in y_e or in u. As such, the question of whether

$$\text{plim}\left(\frac{1}{n}\mathbf{X}'\boldsymbol{\omega}\right)=0$$

rests in whether

$$\text{plim}\left(\frac{1}{n}\mathbf{X}'\mathbf{X}_e\boldsymbol{\beta}\right)=0$$

$$\begin{aligned}\text{plim}\left(\frac{1}{n}\mathbf{X}'\mathbf{X}_e\boldsymbol{\beta}\right)&=\text{plim}\frac{1}{n}\left[\left(\tilde{\mathbf{X}}'+\mathbf{X}_e'\right)\mathbf{X}_e\boldsymbol{\beta}\right]\\&=\text{plim}\frac{1}{n}\tilde{\mathbf{X}}'\mathbf{X}_e\boldsymbol{\beta}+\text{plim}\left(\frac{1}{n}\mathbf{X}_e'\mathbf{X}_e\right)\boldsymbol{\beta}\end{aligned}$$

Even if we were to make the somewhat heroic assumption that the errors in measurement are unrelated to the true measures of the economic variable under consideration, which would, of course, imply that:

$$\text{plim}\left(\frac{1}{n}\tilde{\mathbf{X}}'\mathbf{X}_e\boldsymbol{\beta}\right)=0$$

no assumption can reasonably be made to make

$$\text{plim}\left(\frac{1}{n}\mathbf{X}_e'\mathbf{X}_e\right)\boldsymbol{\beta}=0$$

Given that $\mathbf{X}_e'\mathbf{X}_e$ is a positive semidefinite matrix, it cannot be assumed to disappear in large samples. Therefore, we find that

$$\text{plim}\left(\frac{1}{n}\mathbf{X}'\boldsymbol{\omega}\right)\neq 0$$

with the implication being that when there exist measurement errors in an econometric model, the application of OLS results in inconsistent parameter estimates. As such, alternative estimation methods may be preferred. One such alternative is to use an instrumental variables approach. If we could find a matrix **Z** of instruments uncorrelated in the limit with the disturbance term u and the measurement errors **V**, then:

$$\hat{\boldsymbol{\beta}}=(\mathbf{Z}'\mathbf{X})^{-1}\mathbf{Z}'\mathbf{y}$$

will be a consistent estimator of $\boldsymbol{\beta}$.

EXERCISES

1. Consider the model:

$$y_t=\beta\, y_{t-1}=u_t \quad -1<\beta<1$$

where:

$$u_t=\rho\, u_{t-1}+\varepsilon_t \quad -1<\rho<1$$

Show:

a) that the OLS estimator of β is inconsistent.

b) that a consistent estimator of β can be obtained by using y_{t-2} as an instrument for y_{t-1}.

2. Consider the model:

$$y_{1t} = \beta_0 + \beta_1 x_{1t} + \beta_2 y_{2t} + u_t$$

   a) What are the main consequences for OLS estimation when:
      - x_1 is measured with error.
      - y_2 is correlated in the limit with u.

   b) Stating all necessary assumptions, derive instrumental variable estimators for the β coefficients when y_2 is correlated in the limit with u and show that they are consistent. [Hint: use matrix algebra.]

3. Use the Dominican data to fit the following equation using the instrumental variable estimator with S_{d-1} and i_r in the EViews instrument list:

$$S_d = \alpha_0 + \alpha_1 Y + \alpha_2 S_{f-1} + \alpha_3 i_r + u$$

   Evaluate the results obtained.

CHAPTER 7

The Econometrics of Simultaneous Equation Systems

INTRODUCTION

In chapter 1, the model that was introduced contained several equations. Consider now a specification of each equation in the system:

$$C_{pt} = g_{11} + b_{14} Y_t + g_{12} C_{pt-1} + u_{1t} \quad \textbf{(7.1)}$$

$$M_t = g_{21} + b_{24} Y_t + g_{23} \frac{p_{mt}}{p_{dt}} + u_{2t} \quad \textbf{(7.2)}$$

$$I_t = g_{31} + g_{34} Y_{t-1} + g_{35} D_t + u_{3t} \quad \textbf{(7.3)}$$

$$Y_t = C_{pt} + C_{gt} + I_t + X_t - M_t \quad \textbf{(7.4)}$$

D is a dummy variable that is equal to 1 if the observation pertains to the "boom" years, 1974 to 1981, and it is equal to 0 if not, while u is the usual disturbance (error) term associated with each of the behavioural equations. Note that equation (7.4) is an accounting identity and so this equation holds without a disturbance term. The choice of the subscripts for the constant coefficients of the model will be justified below, but rest assured that it is purely a mater of notational convenience and nothing more.

The system defined by equations (7.1) to (7.4) is the *structural form* (SF) of the model (since it describes the economic structure of the phenomenon under study). Two categories of variables are to be distinguished: the endogenous variables C_p, M, I and Y, which are the "unknowns" of the system, and the *predetermined* variables, which combine the exogenous variables as well as the lagged endogenous variables.

What makes this system more than just a collection of "single equations" that can be estimated by OLS? The one big difference is the presence among the explanatory variables of current values of the endogenous variables. Let us look at equation (7.2), which is the import function that has been studied in previous chapters. Here, imports (M) are explained by the current value of income (Y). However, by equation (7.4), Y is also a function of M and consequently of the disturbance term u_{2t} and so Y is also random and not independent of u_{2t}. Recall from chapter 6 that this results in the inconsistency of the OLS estimator, in which case a possible estimation procedure is the instrumental variable (IV) estimator introduced in that chapter. One of the objectives of the present chapter is to introduce the *two stage least squares estimator*, which is a very special case of the IV estimator. This and other estimating procedures that yield consistent estimators within the framework of a multiple (simultaneous) equation system require knowledge of the *reduced form* (RF) of the model, which leads to the thorny mathematical problem of the *identification* of the equations in the model. Both these concepts are introduced in the next section.

IDENTIFICATION

The RF of model (7.1) to (7.4) is obtained by solving it so that the endogenous variables are written as functions of the predetermined variables and the error terms only. This is algebraically very clumsy and so we introduce a simpler system to better illustrate the concept.

Consider the two-equation econometric model:

$$C_{pt} = \alpha Y_t + u_t \tag{7.5}$$

$$Y_t = C_{pt} + I_t \tag{7.6}$$

This is another example of an SF and characterizes a very simple economy with no government and no foreign sector. The RF is obtained in the following steps. Substituting equation (7.5) into equation (7.6) we get:

$$\Rightarrow \quad Y_t = \alpha Y_t + u_t + I_t$$

$$\Rightarrow \quad Y_t - \alpha Y_t = Y_t(1-\alpha) = I_t + u_t \tag{7.7}$$

$$\Rightarrow \quad Y_t = \frac{I_t}{(1+\alpha)} + \frac{u_t}{(1+\alpha)}$$

This is the RF of the income equation. Do you recognize it?

By a similar procedure, the RF of the private consumption equation is obtained as:

$$\Rightarrow \quad C_t = \frac{\alpha I_t}{(1-\alpha)} + \frac{u_t}{(1-\alpha)} \tag{7.8}$$

These equations may be conveniently written as:

$$C_t = \pi_1 I_t + v_{1t} \tag{7.9}$$

$$Y_t = \pi_2 I_t + v_{2t} \tag{7.10}$$

where:

$$\pi_1 = \frac{\alpha}{(1-\alpha)}$$

$$\pi_2 = \frac{1}{(1-\alpha)}$$

$$v_{1t} = \frac{u_t}{(1-\alpha)} = v_{2t}$$

The coefficients in equations (7.9) and (7.10) can be consistently estimated by OLS (why?). A consistent estimator of α can then be derived as $\hat{\pi}_1/\hat{\pi}_2$ where the ^ indicates the OLS estimator.

This is a simple illustration of the *indirect least squares* (ILS) method,[1] which is applicable in only very special cases like this one where the parameter α is *exactly identified*. If equation (7.6) is modified only slightly to allow for government consumption expenditure:

$$Y_t = C_{pt} + C_{gt} + I_t \quad \textbf{(7.11)}$$

the ILS method would not now be applicable. In this case, solving the system yields the RF:

$$C_{pt} = \frac{\alpha}{1-\alpha} I_t + \frac{\alpha}{1-\alpha} C_{gt} + \frac{1}{1-\alpha} u_t = \pi_{11} I_t + \pi_{12} C_{gt} + v_{1t} \quad \textbf{(7.12)}$$

$$Y_t = \frac{I_t}{1-\alpha} + \frac{C_{gt}}{1-\alpha} + \frac{u_t}{1-\alpha} = \pi_{21} I_t + \pi_{22} C_{gt} + v_{2t} \quad \textbf{(7.13)}$$

There still is a unique solution for α:

$$\alpha = \frac{\pi_{11}}{\pi_{21}} = \frac{\pi_{12}}{\pi_{22}}$$

But when the πs in the RF are estimated by OLS, it is usually true that:

$$\frac{\hat{\pi}_{11}}{\hat{\pi}_{21}} \neq \frac{\hat{\pi}_{12}}{\hat{\pi}_{22}}$$

where ^ indicates OLS estimators of the RF parameters. But each ratio represents a consistent estimator of α – so which is/are to be chosen? This dilemma arises because

[1] It will be shown below that this is a consistent estimator.

the parameter α is *overidentified*. Clearly the ILS method is not applicable when the parameters of an equation are overidentified since it results in a choice but with no clear selection criteria. However, it is still possible to obtain a consistent estimator, and the *two stage least squares* estimator, which will be introduced shortly, yields consistent and efficient estimators in this case.[2]

There are some cases, however, when knowledge of the reduced form does not allow us to deduce a unique estimator of the SF parameters. In such a situation, the parameters of the equation are *not identifiable*. Consider the following illustration:

$$C_{pt} = \alpha_0 + \alpha_1 Y_t + u_{1t} \quad \textbf{(7.14)}$$

$$I_t = \beta_0 + \beta_1 Y_t + u_{2t} \quad \textbf{(7.15)}$$

$$Y_t = C_{pt} + I_t$$

The RF corresponding to this SF is:

$$C_{pt} = \frac{\alpha(1-\beta_1)+\alpha_1\beta_0}{1-\alpha_1-\beta_1} + \frac{(\alpha_1 u_{2t} = \beta_1 u_{1t})}{1-\alpha_1-\beta_1} = \pi_1 + v_{1t} \quad \textbf{(7.16)}$$

$$I_t = \frac{\beta_0(1-\alpha_1)+\beta_1\alpha_0}{1-\alpha_1-\beta_1} + \frac{(\beta_1 u_{1t} - \alpha_1 u_{2t})}{1-\alpha_1-\beta_1} = \pi_2 + v_{2t} \quad \textbf{(7.17)}$$

$$Y_t = \frac{(\alpha_0+\beta_0)}{1-\alpha_1-\beta_1} + \frac{(u_{1t}+u_{2t})}{1-\alpha_1-\beta_1} = \pi_3 + v_{3t} \quad \textbf{(7.18)}$$

It is impossible to obtain unique solutions for the SF parameters α_0, α_1, β_0 and β_1 given knowledge of the RF coefficients π_1, π_2 and π_3. The α and β coefficients (and by extension equations 7.14 and 7.15) are not identifiable![3]

IDENTIFIABILITY OF AN EQUATION AND RESTRICTIONS ON THE STRUCTURAL FORM

In a system of equations, an equation is *identifiable* if its parameters are either exactly identified or overidentified. In both cases, knowledge of the RF yields a unique solution for the SF parameters. An equation of the SF is not identifiable when its parameters cannot be uniquely determined from knowledge of the RF parameters. The identifiability of a system is determined equation by equation and a system as a whole is said to be not identifiable if at least one of its equations is not.

[2] It can be shown that the two stage least squares estimator is an optimal linear combination of the two consistent estimators of α shown here.

[3] It is possible for the coefficients of one or more equations in a system to be identifiable while those of other equations may not be. See below.

The identification of an equation is a mathematical problem and, by itself, does not necessarily challenge the underlying economic theory that resulted in the given specification. But a non-identified equation is a serious challenge to the economist since its parameters cannot be estimated consistently. The solution to the problem is also a mathematical one: it requires the imposition of sufficient restrictions on the structural form and, hopefully, these restrictions will make economic sense.

What does all this mean? Consider the system defined by equations (7.5) to (7.6). The system as a whole has three variables: C_p, Y and I, but equation (7.5) only has two. Put another way, the absence of I_t is a restriction on equation (7.5), and the existence of this restriction is enough to ensure the identification of the parameters of the equation (in this case, only one coefficient, α). One way to look at this is to imagine that equation (7.5) is written as:

$$C_{pt} = \alpha Y_t + \beta I_t + u_t$$

where $\beta = 0$; that is we impose the value of zero on the coefficient of β.[4] When viewed in this way, equation (7.6) has two restrictions: the coefficients of C_{pt} and I_t are both equal to one. This is a moot point since we *know* the values of these coefficients and are not in any way concerned with their estimation (why estimate them when we already know them?), but it serves to underscore the point.

Consider now the system represented by equations (7.5) and (7.11). This system has four variables: C_p, Y, C_g and I while equation (7.5) only has two. There are thus two restrictions on equation (7.5) and, apparently, these are more than are required because they result in overidentification of the equation. Once again, equation (7.5) may be written:

$$C_{pt} = \alpha Y_t + \beta I_t + \gamma C_{gt} + u_t$$

where $\beta = \gamma = 0$.

Finally, let us look at the system defined by equations (7.14), (7.15) and (7.6). There are four variables in this system: the constant term, C_p, Y and I. In equations (7.14) and (7.15), which can be written, respectively, as:

$$C_{pt} = \alpha_0 + \alpha_1 Y_t + 0.I_t + u_{1t}$$

$$I_t = \beta_0 + \beta_1 Y_t + 0.C_{pt} + u_{2t}$$

there is one restriction each. It would appear that, in this case, one restriction is not enough to ensure the identifiability of either equation. Can we extract some general rule? We can, as shown in the following section.

Conditions of Identifiability of an Equation

Let us rewrite the system of equations (7.5) and (7.6) in the following way:

[4] These *zero-type* restrictions (as they are called in the literature) are very popular in practice.

$$C_{pt} - \alpha Y_t - 0.I_t = u_t$$

$$-C_{pt} + Y_t - I_t = 0$$

or, in matrix notation:

$$\begin{pmatrix} 1 & -\alpha \\ -1 & 1 \end{pmatrix} \begin{pmatrix} C_{pt} \\ Y_t \end{pmatrix} + \begin{pmatrix} 0 \\ -1 \end{pmatrix} I_t = \begin{pmatrix} u_t \\ 0 \end{pmatrix} \quad \textbf{(7.19)}$$

which distinguishes the endogenous from the predetermined variables.

The RF is easily derived from this SF as:

$$\begin{pmatrix} C_{pt} \\ Y_t \end{pmatrix} = -\begin{pmatrix} 1 & \alpha \\ -1 & 1 \end{pmatrix}^{-1} \begin{pmatrix} 0 \\ -1 \end{pmatrix} I_t + \begin{pmatrix} 1 & \alpha \\ -1 & 1 \end{pmatrix}^{-1} \begin{pmatrix} u_t \\ 0 \end{pmatrix} \quad \textbf{(7.20)}$$

If we define:

$$\mathbf{B} = \begin{pmatrix} 1 & \alpha \\ -1 & 1 \end{pmatrix}, \mathbf{y}_t = \begin{pmatrix} C_{pt} \\ Y_t \end{pmatrix}, \mathbf{\Gamma} = \begin{pmatrix} 0 \\ -1 \end{pmatrix}, \mathbf{x}_t = I_t, \mathbf{u}_t = \begin{pmatrix} u_t \\ 0 \end{pmatrix}$$

then the SF defined by equation (7.19) is written succinctly as:

$$\mathbf{B}\mathbf{y}_t + \mathbf{\Gamma}\mathbf{x}_t = \mathbf{u}_t \quad \textbf{(7.21)}$$

and the RF as:

$$\begin{aligned} \mathbf{Y}_t &= -\mathbf{B}^{-1}\mathbf{\Gamma}\mathbf{x}_t + \mathbf{B}^{-1}\mathbf{u}_t \\ &= \mathbf{\Pi}\mathbf{x}_t + \mathbf{v}_t \end{aligned} \quad \textbf{(7.22)}$$

where $\mathbf{\Pi} = -\mathbf{B}^{-1}\,\mathbf{\Gamma}$ and $\mathbf{v}_t = \mathbf{B}^{-1}\mathbf{u}_t$.

What we notice is that the SF parameters **B** and **Γ** yield the RF parameters **Π**. The identification problem can be stated as: does knowledge of **Π** allow us to uniquely determine **B** and **Γ**? If the answer to this question is "yes", then the system is identifiable. If "no", then it is not identifiable.

Let us put this idea to use in a more general setting. Consider a system that has G current endogenous variables y_{1t}, y_{2t}, …, y_{Gt}, and K predetermined variables x_{1t}, x_{2t}, ..., x_{Kt}, t = 1, 2, ..., n. In its most general form, the system can be written, for t = 1, 2, ..., n, as:

$$\begin{array}{cccccc} \beta_{11}y_{1t} + \beta_{12}y_{2t} + & \cdots & + \beta_{1G}y_{Gt} + \gamma_{11}x_{1t} + \gamma_{12}x_{2t} + & \cdots & + \gamma_{1K}x_{Kt} = u_{1t} \\ \beta_{21}y_{1t} + \beta_{22}y_{2t} + & \cdots & + \beta_{2G}y_{Gt} + \gamma_{21}x_{1t} + \gamma_{22}x_{2t} + & \cdots & + \gamma_{2K}x_{Kt} = u_{2t} \\ \vdots & \vdots & \vdots & \vdots & \vdots \\ \vdots & \vdots & \vdots & \vdots & \vdots \\ \beta_{G1}y_{1t} + \beta_{G2}y_{2t} + & \cdots & + \beta_{GG}y_{Gt} + \gamma_{G1}x_{1t} + \gamma_{G2}x_{2t} + & \cdots & + \gamma_{GK}x_{Kt} = u_{Gt} \end{array}$$

Defining:

$$\underset{(G,G)}{\mathbf{B}} = \begin{pmatrix} \beta_{11} & \beta_{12} & \cdots & \cdots & \beta_{1G} \\ \beta_{21} & \beta_{22} & \cdots & \cdots & \beta_{2G} \\ \vdots & \vdots & \ddots & & \vdots \\ \vdots & \vdots & & \ddots & \vdots \\ \beta_{G1} & \beta_{G2} & \cdots & \cdots & \beta_{GG} \end{pmatrix}, \underset{(G,K)}{\mathbf{\Gamma}} = \begin{pmatrix} \gamma_{11} & \gamma_{12} & \cdots & \cdots & \gamma_{1K} \\ \gamma_{21} & \gamma_{22} & \cdots & \cdots & \gamma_{2K} \\ \vdots & \vdots & \vdots & \vdots & \vdots \\ \vdots & \vdots & \vdots & \vdots & \vdots \\ \gamma_{G1} & \gamma_{G2} & \cdots & \cdots & \gamma_{GK} \end{pmatrix},$$

$$\underset{(G,1)}{\mathbf{Y}_t} = \begin{pmatrix} y_{1t} \\ y_{2t} \\ \vdots \\ \vdots \\ y_{Gt} \end{pmatrix}, \mathbf{X}_t = \begin{pmatrix} x_{1t} \\ x_{2t} \\ \vdots \\ \vdots \\ x_{Kt} \end{pmatrix}, \mathbf{u}_t = \begin{pmatrix} u_{1t} \\ u_{2t} \\ \vdots \\ \vdots \\ u_{Gt} \end{pmatrix}$$

then this SF may be written compactly as:

$$\mathbf{By}_t + \mathbf{\Gamma x}_t = \mathbf{u}_t$$

and the RF obtained as above.

In the absence of further information about the **B** and **Γ** matrices, each equation in this system is *statistically* the same. For instance, OLS applied to each equation would yield identical values for the β and γ coefficients. In other words, the individual coefficients are not identifiable – unless restrictions are imposed on some of them, such as the zero-type restrictions introduced above. How many restrictions are necessary? It is best to use an illustration to answer this question.

Let us refer back to the system of four equations (7.1) to (7.4) introduced at the beginning of this chapter and let us discuss the identifiability of equation (7.1). Letting $\beta_{ij} = -b_{ij}$ and $\gamma_{ij} = -g_{ij}$, this system may be rewritten as:

$$C_{pt} + 0.M_t + 0.I_t + \beta_{14}Y_t + \gamma_{11}.1 + \gamma_{12}C_{pt-1} + 0.\frac{p_{mt}}{p_{dt}} + 0.Y_{t-1} + 0.D_t + 0.C_{gt} + 0.X_t = u_{1t}$$

$$0.C_{pt} + M_t + 0.I_t + \beta_{24}Y_t + \gamma_{21}.1 + 0.C_{pt-1} + \gamma_{23}.\frac{p_{mt}}{p_{dt}} + 0.Y_{t-1} + 0.D_t + 0.C_{gt} + 0.X_t = u_{2t}$$

$$0.C_{pt} + 0.M_t + I_t + 0.Y_t + \gamma_{31}.1 + 0.C_{pt-1} + 0.\frac{p_{mt}}{p_{dt}} + \gamma_{34}.Y_{t-1} + \gamma_{35}.Dt + 0.C_{gt} + 0.X_t = u_{3t}$$

$$-C_{pt} + M_t - I_t + Y_t + 0.1 + 0.C_{pt-1} + 0.\frac{p_{mt}}{p_{dt}} + 0.Y_{t-1} + 0.D_t + 0.C_{gt} - 0.X_t = 0$$

Note two things. First, the convention has been introduced that the coefficient of the *i*th endogenous variable in the *i*th equation is equal to one. This, strictly speaking, is not a restriction but a matter of convenience. It is equivalent to dividing throughout each equation by the coefficient of this variable so that the coefficients shown are really "scaled up" by this value. Second, when written in a form like this, the restrictions imposed on each equation appear clearly. For instance, in the consumption equation, the coefficient of M_t (β_{12}) is equal to zero. So too are the coefficients of I_t, p_{mt}/p_{dt}, Y_{t-1}, D_t, C_{gt} and X_t. There are thus seven zero-type restrictions on this equation. What about the others? This system as a whole may be written as:

$$\begin{bmatrix} 1 & 0 & 0 & \beta_{14} & \gamma_{11} & \gamma_{12} & 0 & 0 & 0 & 0 & 0 \\ 0 & 1 & 0 & \beta_{24} & \gamma_{21} & 0 & \gamma_{23} & 0 & 0 & 0 & 0 \\ 0 & 0 & 1 & 0 & \gamma_{31} & 0 & 0 & \gamma_{34} & \gamma_{35} & 0 & 0 \\ -1 & 1 & -1 & 1 & 0 & 0 & 0 & 0 & 0 & 0 & -1 \end{bmatrix} \begin{bmatrix} C_{pt} \\ M_t \\ I_t \\ Y_t \\ 1 \\ C_{pt-1} \\ \frac{p_{mt}}{p_{dt}} \\ Y_{t-1} \\ D_t \\ C_{gt} \\ X_t \end{bmatrix} = \begin{bmatrix} u_{1t} \\ u_{2t} \\ u_{3t} \\ 0 \end{bmatrix}$$

or, more succinctly, as:

$$\mathbf{A}\mathbf{z}_t = \mathbf{u}_t$$

where the matrices are obvious. It is clear that, using that notation used above:

$$\mathbf{A} = (\mathbf{B}:\boldsymbol{\Gamma}) \text{ and } \mathbf{z}_t = \begin{pmatrix} \mathbf{y}_t \\ \mathbf{x}_t \end{pmatrix}$$

The matrix **A** is frequently referred to in the literature as the matrix of detached coefficients (for obvious reasons). This matrix is central to the identification exercise. Let us define $a_1 = (1\ \ 0\ \ 0\ \ B_{14}\ \ \gamma_{11}\ \ \gamma_{12}\ \ 0\ \ 0\ \ 0\ \ 0\ \ 0)$ which is the first row of **A**.

Consider the first zero-type restriction (the one imposed on the coefficient of M_t). This restriction can be written as:

$$1_1 = \begin{pmatrix} 0 \\ 1 \\ 0 \\ 0 \\ 0 \\ 0 \\ 0 \\ 0 \\ 0 \\ 0 \\ 0 \end{pmatrix}$$

since, clearly, $a_1' 1_1 = 0$. Similarly, the other six restrictions can be written:

$$1_2 = \begin{pmatrix} 0 \\ 0 \\ 1 \\ 0 \\ 0 \\ 0 \\ 0 \\ 0 \\ 0 \\ 0 \\ 0 \end{pmatrix}, 1_3 = \begin{pmatrix} 0 \\ 0 \\ 0 \\ 0 \\ 0 \\ 0 \\ 1 \\ 0 \\ 0 \\ 0 \\ 0 \end{pmatrix}, 1_4 = \begin{pmatrix} 0 \\ 0 \\ 0 \\ 0 \\ 0 \\ 0 \\ 0 \\ 1 \\ 0 \\ 0 \\ 0 \end{pmatrix}, 1_5 = \begin{pmatrix} 0 \\ 0 \\ 0 \\ 0 \\ 0 \\ 0 \\ 0 \\ 0 \\ 1 \\ 0 \\ 0 \end{pmatrix}, 1_6 = \begin{pmatrix} 0 \\ 0 \\ 0 \\ 0 \\ 0 \\ 0 \\ 0 \\ 0 \\ 0 \\ 1 \\ 0 \end{pmatrix}, 1_7 = \begin{pmatrix} 0 \\ 0 \\ 0 \\ 0 \\ 0 \\ 0 \\ 0 \\ 0 \\ 0 \\ 0 \\ 1 \end{pmatrix}$$

In all cases, $a_1' 1_i = 0$, $i = 1, 2, ..., 7$.

Consider now the matrix **L** whose columns comprise the seven column vectors l_1 to l_7:

$$\underset{(11,7)}{\mathbf{L}} = \begin{pmatrix} 0 & 0 & 0 & 0 & 0 & 0 & 0 \\ 1 & 0 & 0 & 0 & 0 & 0 & 0 \\ 0 & 1 & 0 & 0 & 0 & 0 & 0 \\ 0 & 0 & 0 & 0 & 0 & 0 & 0 \\ 0 & 0 & 0 & 0 & 0 & 0 & 0 \\ 0 & 0 & 0 & 0 & 0 & 0 & 0 \\ 0 & 0 & 1 & 0 & 0 & 0 & 0 \\ 0 & 0 & 0 & 1 & 0 & 0 & 0 \\ 0 & 0 & 0 & 0 & 1 & 0 & 0 \\ 0 & 0 & 0 & 0 & 0 & 1 & 0 \\ 0 & 0 & 0 & 0 & 0 & 0 & 1 \end{pmatrix}$$

Consider now the matrix $\underset{(4,7)}{\mathbf{Q}} = \mathbf{AL}$. The first row of this matrix is, by construction, a row of zeros. The maximum rank of **Q** is therefore equal to 3.

Theorem (stated without proof): the rank condition of identification

The first equation of this system is identifiable if the rank of **Q** is equal to 3.

In general, **Q** will be of dimension (G,h) where G is the number of equations in the system and h the number of constraints on the equation. The *rank condition of identification*, which is a necessary and sufficient condition of identification, requires that the rank of **Q** be equal to G – 1.

Let us return to the **Q** matrix of our example. This is calculated as:

$$\mathbf{Q} = \begin{bmatrix} 0 & 0 & 0 & 0 & 0 & 0 & 0 \\ 1 & \beta_{24} & \gamma_{23} & 0 & 0 & 0 & 0 \\ 0 & 1 & 0 & \gamma_{34} & \gamma_{35} & 0 & 0 \\ 1 & -1 & 0 & 0 & 0 & 0 & -1 \end{bmatrix}$$

It is easily verified (do this as an exercise[5]) that, in this case, the rank of Q is indeed equal to 3 and the consumption equation is identifiable. Can you, as an exercise, determine the identifiability of the import and investment equations using the rank condition?

From the rank condition, we may derive the easier-to-use *order condition of identification*. It is really a rule of thumb that is obtained as follows: Q is of order (G,h). If, for identification, the rank of Q must be equal to G – 1, then it follows

[5] The rank of this matrix is either 3, 2, 1 or 0. To prove that it is 3, it suffices to find a 3 × 3 submatrix whose determinant is non-zero.

that $G > G - 1$ (which is, of course, always true) and $h \geq G - 1$. *This latter is the order condition of identification, which requires that the number of restrictions imposed on an equation be at least as great as the number of equations in the system less one.*

Note, however, that the order condition is necessary, not sufficient. If $h < G - 1$, then we conclude that the equation is not identifiable. But if $h \geq G - 1$, all we really know is that there is not sufficient information to say that the equation is not identifiable. *In practice, however, it is almost invariably true that, if $h \geq G - 1$, the equation is identifiable.*

In the first equation of the system defined by equations (7.1) to (7.4), there are seven restrictions and four equations. Since 7 is greater than $(4 - 1) = 3$, the equation is identifiable. In fact it is overidentified, which is always the case when $h > G - 1$. When $h = G - 1$, the equation is exactly identified. What conclusions can you draw about equations (7.2) and (7.3)?

ESTIMATION IN SIMULTANEOUS EQUATION MODELS

We have already met the indirect least squares (ILS) estimator, which is applicable only in cases where the parameters of an equation are exactly identified. In this section, our main concern is to introduce the *two stage least squares (2SLS) estimator* and, later on, we will show that the ILS is but a special case of the 2SLS.

Consider, once again, the SF defined by equations (7.5) and (7.11) and whose RF is shown by equations (7.12) to (7.13). We wish to estimate the coefficients of equation (7.5).[6] OLS would yield inconsistent estimators because of the presence among the explanatory variables of the current endogenous variable Y_t which, as was shown above, is correlated in the limit with the error term. The 2SLS estimator solves this problem by:

1. Replacing Y_t in equation (7.10) by $\hat{Y}_t$, the fitted value of Y_t obtained by OLS regression on the RF equation (7.13).
2. Applying OLS to the SF equation (7.10) using $\hat{Y}_t$ instead of Y_t.

The estimator obtained in this second step is appropriately termed the two stage least squares estimator, since OLS is applied twice (once to the RF equation and once to the modified SF equation). Let us look at the procedure in some more detail.

Step 1
The RF equation (7.13) appears as:

$$Y_t = \pi_{21} I_t + \pi_{22} C_{gt} + v_{2t}$$

OLS is applied to this equation in the classic manner discussed in chapter 1. Denote the OLS estimators of the π coefficients as $\hat{\pi}_{21}$ and $\hat{\pi}_{22}$ and define:

---

[6] Here, of course, there is only one coefficient to estimate.

$$\hat{Y}_t = \hat{\pi}_{21} I_t + \hat{\pi}_{22} C_{gt} \tag{7.23}$$

and:

$$\hat{v}_{2t} = Y_t - \hat{Y}_t \tag{7.24}$$

Step 2
From step 1, $Y_t = \hat{Y}_t + \hat{v}_{2t}$ so that equation (7.5) may be written as:

$$\begin{aligned} C_t &= \alpha\left(\hat{Y}_t + \hat{v}_{2t}\right) + u_t \\ &= \alpha\hat{Y}_t + \left(u_t + \alpha\hat{v}_{2t}\right) \\ &= \alpha\hat{Y}_t + \varepsilon_t \end{aligned} \tag{7.25}$$

OLS is applied to equation (7.25) in the classic manner. the OLS estimator of α so obtained is the two stage least squares estimator and is denoted $\hat{\alpha}_{2SLS}$.

Consistency of the Two Stage Least Squares Estimator

From our knowledge of the OLS estimator, we know that:

$$\begin{aligned} \hat{\alpha}_{2SLS} &= \frac{\sum C_t \hat{Y}_t}{\sum \hat{Y}_t^2} \\ &= \frac{\sum\left(\alpha\hat{Y}_t + \varepsilon_t\right)\hat{Y}_t}{\sum \hat{Y}_t^2} \\ &= \frac{\alpha\sum \hat{Y}_t^2}{\sum \hat{Y}_t^2} + \frac{\sum \hat{Y}_t\varepsilon_t}{\sum \hat{Y}_t^2} \\ &= \alpha + \frac{\sum \hat{Y}_t\varepsilon_t}{\sum \hat{Y}_t^2} \end{aligned}$$

$$\Rightarrow \operatorname{plim}\hat{\alpha}_{2SLS} = \alpha + \frac{\operatorname{plim}\frac{1}{n}\sum \hat{Y}_t\varepsilon_t}{\operatorname{plim}\frac{1}{n}\sum \hat{Y}_t^2}$$

Clearly $\hat{\alpha}_{2SLS}$ is consistent if

$$\text{plim}\frac{1}{n}\sum \hat{Y}_t\varepsilon_t = 0$$

Of course, this is not surprising since this is the precise requirement for the OLS estimator to be consistent – and the 2SLS estimator is the OLS estimator of α in equation (7.25).

Lemma

$$\text{plim}\frac{1}{n}\sum \hat{Y}_t\varepsilon_t = 0$$

Proof of Lemma

$$\text{plim}\frac{1}{n}\sum \hat{Y}_t\varepsilon_t = \text{plim}\frac{1}{n}\sum \hat{Y}_t\left(u_t + \alpha\hat{v}_{2t}\right)$$

$$= \text{plim}\frac{1}{n}\sum \hat{Y}_t u_t + \alpha\,\text{plim}\frac{1}{n}\sum \hat{Y}_t\hat{v}_{2t}$$

It is a classic result of OLS (see chapter 2) that $\sum \hat{Y}_t\hat{v}_{2t} = 0$, so:

$$\text{plim}\frac{1}{n}\sum \hat{Y}_t\varepsilon_t = \text{plim}\frac{1}{n}\sum \hat{Y}_t u_t$$

$$= \text{plim}\frac{1}{n}\sum\left(\hat{\pi}_{21}I_t + \hat{\pi}_{22}C_{gt}\right)u_t$$

$$= \hat{\pi}_{21}\text{plim}\frac{1}{n}\sum I_t u_t + \hat{\pi}_{22}\text{plim}\frac{1}{n}\sum C_{gt}u_t$$

By assumption, I and C_g are strictly exogenous and, in particular:

$$\text{plim}\frac{1}{n}\sum I_t u_t = \text{plim}\frac{1}{n}\sum C_{gt}u_t = 0$$

$$\Rightarrow \text{plim}\frac{1}{n}\sum \hat{Y}_t\varepsilon_t = 0 \quad \text{Q.E.D}$$

Corollary

$\hat{\alpha}_{2SLS}$ is a consistent estimator of α since:

$$\text{plim}\,\hat{\alpha}_{2SLS} = \alpha$$

The Two Stage Least Squares Estimator as an Instrumental Variable Estimator

Consider again the SF defined by equations (7.5) and (7.11) where we are interested in estimating α, the parameter(s) of equation (7.5). If we use $\hat{Y}_t$ as an estimator of Y_t, then the IV estimator of α can be shown to be identical to the 2SLS estimator already derived.

From chapter 6, the IV estimator would be:

$$\hat{\alpha}_{IV} = \frac{\sum C_t \hat{Y}_t}{\sum \hat{Y}_t Y_t}$$

But:

$$\sum \hat{Y}_t Y_t = \sum \hat{Y}_t \left(\hat{Y}_t + \hat{v}_{2t}\right) = \sum \hat{Y}_t^2 + \sum \hat{Y}_t \hat{v}_{2t}$$

and, since $\sum \hat{Y}_t \hat{v}_{2t} = 0$, then:

$$\sum \hat{Y}_t Y_t = \sum \hat{Y}_t^2$$

$$\Rightarrow \hat{\alpha}_{IV} = \frac{\sum C_t \hat{Y}_t}{\sum \hat{Y}_t^2} = \hat{\alpha}_{2SLS} \quad \text{Q.E.D.}$$

Equivalence of Two Stage Least Squares and Indirect Least Squares in the Case of an Exactly Identified Equation

For the SF defined by equations (7.5) and (7.6), equation (7.5) was exactly identified. The RF of this system was defined by equations (7.9) and (7.10) and the ILS estimator of α was defined by:

$$\hat{\alpha}_{ILS} = \frac{\hat{\pi}_1}{\hat{\pi}_2}$$

where $\hat{\pi}_1$ and $\hat{\pi}_2$ are OLS estimators. More specifically:

$$\hat{\pi}_1 = \frac{\sum C_t I_t}{\sum I_t^2}$$

$$\hat{\pi}_2 = \frac{\sum Y_t I_t}{\sum I_t^2}$$

so that:

$$\hat{\alpha}_{ILS} = \frac{\sum C_t I_t}{\sum Y_t I_t}$$

In this case, the 2SLS estimator of α would have been obtained as follows.

The fitted value of Y_t, $\hat{Y}_t$ is obtained from the RF as:

$$\hat{Y}_t = \hat{\pi}_2 I_t$$

The 2SLS estimator is:

$$\hat{\alpha}_{2SLS} = \frac{\sum C_t \hat{Y}_t}{\sum \hat{Y}_t^2}$$

$$= \frac{\hat{\pi}_2 \sum C_t I_t}{\hat{\pi}_2 \sum \hat{Y}_t I_t}$$

$$= \frac{\sum C_t I_t}{\sum (Y_t - \hat{v}_{2t}) I_t}$$

$$= \frac{\sum C_t I_t}{\sum Y_t I_t - \sum I_t \hat{v}_{2t}}$$

and since $\sum I_t \hat{V}_{2t} = 0$:

$$\hat{\alpha}_{2SLS} = \frac{\sum C_t I_t}{\sum Y_t I_t} = \hat{\alpha}_{ILS} \quad \text{Q.E.D}$$

Illustration of the Two Stage Least Squares Estimator

The 2SLS estimation of the consumption equation (7.1), obtained using EViews, is shown in Exhibit 7.1. You will notice the "Instrument list", which contains all the predetermined variables in the system as a whole. EViews examines the list of regressors in equation (7.1) and identifies Y_t as an endogenous variable, since it is not included in the Instrument list. In the first phase of 2SLS (the "RF" phase), the following regression is performed using OLS:

EXHIBIT 7.1
2SLS estimation of
$C_{pt} = g_{11} + b_{14}Y_t + g_{12}C_{pt-1} + u_{1t}$

```
================================================================
TSLS // Dependent Variable is P_CONS
Date: 10/17/95   Time: 09:31
Sample: 1968 1991
Included observations: 24 after adjusting endpoints
Instrument list: C P_CONS(-1) G_CONS RATIO DUMMY INCOME(-1)
        EXPORTS
================================================================
     Variable      Coefficient Std. Error  T-Statistic   Prob.
================================================================
        C            -1731.626   610.1810  -2.837889    0.0099
      INCOME          0.460703   0.076926   5.988880    0.0000
      P_CONS(-1)      0.331614   0.106126   3.124725    0.0051
================================================================
R-squared             0.950208   Mean dependent var    8592.498
Adjusted R-squared    0.945466   S.D. dependent var    2164.074
S.E. of regression    505.3669   Akaike info criter    12.56704
Sum squared resid     5363310.   Schwarz criterion     12.71429
F-statistic           196.4792   Durbin-Watson stat    1.512975
Prob(F-statistic)     0.000000
================================================================
```

$$Y_t = \pi_{11} + \pi_{12} C_{pt-1} + \pi_{13} C_{gt} + \pi_{14} \frac{p_{mt}}{p_{dt}} + \pi_{15} D_t + \pi_{16} Y_{t-1} + \pi_{17} X_t + v_{1t} \quad \textbf{(7.26)}$$

In the second phase, the following OLS regression is performed:

$$C_{pt} = g_{11} + b_{14} \hat{Y}_t + g_{12} C_{pt-1} + \upsilon_{1t} \quad \textbf{(7.27)}$$

where $\hat{Y}_t$ is the OLS fit of Y_t obtained from equation (7.26). It is the results obtained in this phase that are reported in Exhibit 7.1.

In similar fashion, EViews performs the 2SLS estimation on the import equation (7.2), obtaining the results shown in Exhibit 7.2.

The investment equation (7.3) is a peculiar one. There are no endogenous variables among its regressors and so there is no need to apply 2SLS since OLS will do. In fact, in this case, OLS and 2SLS yield identical results. Can you elaborate on this statement? The OLS estimation of equation (7.3) is shown in Exhibit 7.3.

As an exercise,

1. Comment on the results obtained
2. Fit equations (7.1) and (7.2) by OLS and compare the results obtained to the 2SLS results

EXHIBIT 7.2
2SLS estimation of
$M_t = g_{21} + b_{24}Y_t + g_{23}(p_{mt}/p_{dt}) + u_{2t}$

```
============================================================
TSLS // Dependent Variable is IMPORTS
Date: 10/17/95   Time: 09:32
Sample: 1968 1991
Included observations: 24 after adjusting endpoints
Instrument list: C P_CONS(-1) G_CONS RATIO DUMMY INCOME(-1)
        EXPORTS
============================================================
     Variable      Coefficient Std. Error  T-Statistic   Prob.
============================================================
        C            -1235.738   731.8105  -1.688604   0.1061
      INCOME          0.379946   0.031813   11.94308   0.0000
      RATIO          -684.0292   160.4902  -4.262125   0.0003
============================================================
R-squared            0.935694   Mean dependent var   3655.325
Adjusted R-squared   0.929570   S.D. dependent var   1480.286
S.E. of regression   392.8482   Akaike info criter   12.06332
Sum squared resid    3240924.   Schwarz criterion    12.21057
F-statistic          151.5560   Durbin-Watson stat   1.664664
Prob(F-statistic)    0.000000
============================================================
```

EXHIBIT 7.3
2SLS (OLS) estimation of
$I_t = g_{31} + g_{34}Y_{t-1} + g_{35} D_t + u_{3t}$

```
============================================================
LS // Dependent Variable is INV
Date: 10/17/95   Time: 09:35
Sample: 1968 1991
Included observations: 24 after adjusting endpoints
============================================================
     Variable      Coefficient Std. Error  T-Statistic   Prob.
============================================================
        C            -2528.634   688.2246  -3.674141   0.0014
      INCOME(-1)      0.316308   0.041907   7.547917   0.0000
      DUMMY           1759.333   284.1274   6.192057   0.0000
============================================================
R-squared            0.825362   Mean dependent var   3131.866
Adjusted R-squared   0.808730   S.D. dependent var   1499.113
S.E. of regression   655.6290   Akaike info criter   13.08766
Sum squared resid    9026836.   Schwarz criterion    13.23492
Log likelihood      -188.1064   F-statistic          49.62437
Durbin-Watson stat   1.327772   Prob(F-statistic)    0.000000
============================================================
```

A word of caution: the Durbin–Watson statistic and R^2 do not have the same interpretation in the case of 2SLS estimation. Also, the T-statistic is asymptotically normal – it does not have a Student distribution in small samples.

EXERCISES

1. Consider the model:

$$\text{Supply } q_t = ap_t + u_t$$

$$\text{Demand } q_t = bp_t + gr_t + v_t$$

where q and p are endogenous and r exogenous.

a) Use the order condition of identification to show that the supply equation is identifiable while the demand equation is not.
b) Derive the indirect least squares estimator of a.
c) Derive the two stage least squares (2SLS) estimator of a and show that it is identical to the ILS estimator.
d) Prove that the 2SLS estimator is consistent.
e) Given that OLS is theoretically an inconsistent estimating procedure, how do you account for its popularity in practice in the estimation of simultaneous equations systems, very often in preference to 2SLS?

2. In the following simultaneous equation model, the y values are current endogenous and the x values are exogenous variables:

$$y_{1t} = a_1 + c_1 y_{2t} + f_1 x_{1t} + g_1 x_{2t} + h_1 x_{3t} + u_{1t}$$

$$y_{2t} = a_2 + d_2 y_{3t} + f_2 x_{1t} + g_2 x_{2t} + u_{2t}$$

$$y_{3t} = a_3 + b_3 y_{1t} + c_3 y_{2t} + f_3 x_{1t} + u_{3t}$$

a) Using the order condition for identification, study the identifiability of the three equations.
b) Using the rank condition for identification, determine whether or not the second equation is identifiable.
c) Select an equation whose coefficients are identifiable and describe in detail how you would obtain consistent estimators for its coeffecients.

3. Consider the following labour market model:

$$L_t = a_0 + a_1 W_t + a_2 S_t + u_t \ldots(1)$$

$$W_t = b_0 + b_1 L_t + b_2 P_t + v_t \ldots(2)$$

where L is the number of persons employed; W is the real wages index; S is sales; and P is a measure of labour productivity. Both S and P are exogenously determined variables.
a) Obtain the reduced-form equations for L_t and W_t.
b) Discuss the identifiability of the two equations.
c) Outline a technique for estimating equation (1).
4. Consider the following model:

$$Y_{1t} = a_{11} X_{1t} + u_{1t}$$

$$Y_{2t} = b_{23} Y_{3t} + b_{21} (X_{1t} - X_{2t}) + u_{2t}$$

$$Y_{3t} = b_{31} (Y_{1t} - Y_{2t}) + b_{31} X_{1t} + u_{3t}$$

where the Xs are predetermined variables.
a) Discuss the identification of each equation in the model.
b) Suggest, with reasons, a suitable method of estimation for each equation.
5. Using the Trinidad and Tobago data provided in WT_DATA.XLS, fit the model (7.1) to (7.4) using two stage least squares.

CHAPTER 8

Simulation of Econometric Models

INTRODUCTION

An econometric model consists of one or more (simultaneous) equations that have been fitted by standard econometric methods such as OLS and 2SLS. It can be solved to determine the fitted or predicted values of its endogenous variables over the period of estimation, and these can be used to evaluate the "goodness of fit" of the model. In the single equation case, we have already met statistics such as R^2 and $\overline{R}^2$, which are based on a comparison of the actual and fitted values of the endogenous variables. In this chapter, other statistics in this spirit will be introduced which can be used to evaluate "model accuracy" in both the single and multiple equation cases.

However, a model can also be solved to produce values that lie outside of the sample period and, in chapter 1, we did precisely this in the case of the single equation model to obtain forecasts of the endogenous variable. At that time, it was pointed out that one of the inherent difficulties in forecasting with an econometric model was the necessity to have knowledge of the future values of the exogenous variables, and this problem is even more relevant in the case of multiple equation models.

The need to specify future values of exogenous variables, however, is not without some merit. Suppose, for instance, that the econometric model is being used by a state planning agency and one of the exogenous variables is "Public Investment" or some tax rate. The agency may choose to define certain policy measures that are translated into values for these exogenous variables. When the model is solved into the future using such values, the effect of the policy on the endogenous variables of the model can be observed and this will give some indication about the desirability of the (proposed) policy measures.[1]

It is largely because the effects of policy measures can be *simulated* using an econometric model (almost as in a laboratory) that the terms "model solution" and "model simulation" are used almost interchangeably in the literature.

DYNAMIC AND STATIC SIMULATION

Consider an equation such as the following:

$$C_{pt} = g_{11} + b_{14} Y_t + g_{12} C_{p,t-1} + u_{1t}$$

[1] In the literature on economic policy (e.g. Theil, 1966), the subset of exogenous variables that can be used to effect economic policy are called *policy variables* while the endogenous variables that we hope to influence by such measures are called *target variables*.

which is equation (7.1) of the previous chapter. You will notice that, in order to solve for C_{pt}, knowledge about $C_{p,t-1}$ is required. We may decide to use the actual (observed) value of $C_{p,t-1}$ or we may use instead the value that was obtained by solving the model one period ago. The former approach is referred to as *static simulation* while the latter is defined as *dynamic simulation*. In a word, dynamic simulation calculates "forecasts" for periods after the first period in the sample by using the previously forecasted values of the lagged left-hand variable, while static simulation uses actual rather than forecasted values (it can only be used when actual data are available).

Which one should we use? It would seem that, if simulation is being used to evaluate the "goodness of fit" of the model, then dynamic simulation over the sample period (or some subset of this period) would be the preferred option. After all, the model is supposed to be a representation of reality and, ideally, it should replicate reality without the "feedback" from the real world. On the other hand, if the model is being used to forecast the future, then, if the actual value is available for the lagged variable, it should be used. Unfortunately, this option may not be available if the forecast horizon is long, since the lagged future values may not have been observed at the time the forecast is to be made.

SOME USEFUL SUMMARY STATISTICS

The summary statistics to be discussed in this section are applicable both for judging the goodness-of-fit of a model over the sample period or for evaluating forecasts outside the sample period.

Root Mean Square Error

Let Y_t be the actual value of the endogenous variable and Y^s_t be the simulated value at time t. The root mean square error (RMSE) is based on the concept of the mean square error (MSE), which may be defined as:

$$MSE_1 = \frac{\sum_{t=1}^{n} (Y_t^s - Y_t)^2}{n}$$

where n is the period over which the simulation is carried out. Another possible measure of the MSE that appears in the literature is:

$$MSE_2 = \frac{\sum_{t=1}^{n} (P_t - A_t)^2}{n} = \frac{1}{n} \sum_{t=1}^{n} \left(\frac{Y_t^s - Y_t}{Y_{t-1}} \right)^2$$

where:

$$A_t = \frac{Y_t - Y_{t-1}}{Y_{t-1}}$$

is the actual growth rate of the variable Y and

$$P_t = \frac{Y_t^s - Y_{t-1}}{Y_{t-1}}$$

is the predicted growth rate. The RMSE is derived as:

$$\text{RMSE} = \sqrt{\text{MSE}_1}$$

The RMSE may be used to choose between alternative models as, based on this criterion, a model is to be preferred to another if it yields a smaller RMSE. However, great caution must be exercised in using this measure other than for comparing models, since its size will be influenced by the actual Y values. The reason for this is simple: the RMSE is bounded from below by zero but has no upper limit. A value of zero is obtained if the simulated value is exactly equal to the actual value for all t. But values close to zero need not necessarily indicate that the model is performing well since, if the Y values are typically small, then a relatively small value for the RMSE may still be a cause for concern. At the same time, if the Y values are typically large, then a relatively large value for the RMSE may not be a cause for concern.

An analogous term, the root mean square percentage error (%RMSE) is defined as:

$$\%\text{RMSE} = \sqrt{\frac{1}{n}\sum_{t=1}^{n}\left(\frac{Y_t^s - Y_t}{Y_t}\right)^2} \times 100$$

Once again, this measure is bounded from below by zero and has no upper limit, but since this measures a percentage error its value does not depend on the size of the typical Y values. For instance, a value of 10 means that, on the average, there is a 10% forecast error while a value of 25 indicates a 25% forecast error. *Ceteris paribus*, it is always better to have a lower value for %RMSE than a larger one.

Mean Absolute (or Mean Difference) Error

The mean absolute (or mean difference) error is defined as:

$$\text{MAE} = \frac{\sum_{t=1}^{n}\left|Y_t - Y_t^s\right|}{n}$$

while the analogous mean absolute percentage error is defined as:

$$\%\text{MAE} = \frac{1}{n}\sum_{t=1}^{n}\left|\frac{Y_t^2 - Y_t}{Y_t}\right| \times 100$$

The MAE and %MAE are based on the absolute values of the differences rather than on the square of the differences as was the case for the RMSE and the %RMSE. Clearly, the RMSE penalizes larger errors more stringently than does the MAE and from this point of view is the more desirable of the two. However, like the RMSE, the MAE should be used only to make comparisons between models since they both suffer from the fact that "large" and "small" values do not have a precise interpretation. In similar vein, the %MAE statistic removes this shortcoming.

The Theil Inequality Coefficient

The Theil inequality coefficient is defined as:

$$U = \frac{\sqrt{MSE_2}}{\sqrt{\frac{1}{n}\sum_{t=1}^{n} A_t^2}}$$

U is bounded from below by zero (this occurs when the simulated and actual values are identical for all t) and has no upper limit. However, unlike the RMSE and MAE measures, large values do have an immediate interpretation: U = 1 indicates a "forecast" just as accurate as one of "no change" ($Y^s_t = Y_{t-1}$, which implies that $P_t = 0$), and a value of U greater than one means that the prediction is less accurate than the simple prediction of no change. It is always desirable, therefore, to get values of U close to zero and certainly less than one.

The Theil Decomposition[2]

It can be shown that:

$$MSE_2 = (\bar{p} - \bar{a})^2 + S^2_{p-a}$$

where S^2_{p-a} is the variance of the prediction errors ($P_t - A_t$), $\bar{p}$ is the arithmetic average of P, and $\bar{a}$ is the arithmetic average of A. Clearly, a model that is forecasting perfectly will have $(\bar{p} - \bar{a})$ [and so $(\bar{p} - \bar{a})^2$] = 0, with all the error then tied up in S^2_{p-a}. We refer to the first term $(\bar{p} - \bar{a})^2$ as the bias component, which indicates the extent to which the magnitude of the MSE is the consequence of a tendency to estimate too high or too low a level of the forecast variable.

Theil (1966) shows that a further decomposition of MSE_2 is possible. If we let r denote the coefficient of correlation between A and P, we can obtain the following:

$$S^2_{p-a} = S^2_p + S^2_a - 2rS_pS_a$$

$$= (S_p - S_a)^2 + 2(1-r)S_pS_a$$

[2] The discussion that follows draws heavily from Maddala (1977).

and:

$$S_{p-a}^2 = \left(S_p - rS_a\right)^2 + \left(1 - r^2\right)S_a^2$$

where $(S_p - S_a)^2$ is the variance component, $2(1 - r)\, S_pS_a$ is the covariance component, $(S_p - rS_a)^2$ is the regression component, and $(1 - r^2)\, S^2_a$ is the disturbance component.

We can therefore decompose the MSE into either one of two sets of components – bias, variance and covariance, or bias, regression and disturbance. Corresponding to these two decompositions, Theil defines two sets of statistics:

$$U^M = \frac{(\bar{p} - \bar{a})^2}{MSE} = \text{bias proportion}$$

$$U^S = \frac{\left(S_p - S_a\right)^2}{MSE} = \text{variance proportion}$$

$$U^C = \frac{2(1 - r)S_pS_a}{MSE} = \text{covariance proportion}$$

and:

$$U^M = \frac{(\bar{p} - \bar{a})^2}{MSE} = \text{bias proportion}$$

$$U^R = \frac{\left(S_p - rS_a\right)^2}{MSE} = \text{regression proportion}$$

$$U^D = \frac{\left(1 - r^2\right)S_a^2}{MSE} = \text{disturbance proportion}$$

It is clear that $U^M + U^S + U^C = U^M + U^R + U^D = 1$.

The bias proportion U^M is an indication of systematic error, that is, it measures the extent to which the average values of the simulated and actual time series deviate from each other. Clearly we would hope for a value of U^M that is close to zero, whatever the value of the Theil U, since a large value would mean the presence of a systematic bias and so indicate the need for revision of the model (or of the forecast).

Maddala (1977) argues that, of the other two decompositions, the decomposition U^R, U^D is more meaningful than the decomposition U^S, U^C. Granger and Newbold (1973) further argue that it is hard to give any meaningful interpretation at all to U^S and U^C since, as they demonstrate, when $U^M = 0$, these two quantities can take on any values subject to the restriction that $0 \leq U^S, U^C \leq 1$, and $U^S + U^C = 1$. On the other hand, U^M and U^R tend to zero for the optimal predictor.

Notwithstanding these arguments, Pindyck and Rubinfeld (1998) argue that the variance proportion U^S indicates the ability of the model to replicate the degree of variability in the variable of interest. A large value of U^S, they insist, means that the actual series has fluctuated considerably while the simulated series has shown little fluctuation, or vice versa – clearly an undesirable occurrence and one that would also lead to a revision of the model. The covariance proportion U^C, they continue, measures the unsystematic error, that is, it represents the remaining error after deviations from actual values have been accounted for. Since there would never exist a situation where predictions are perfectly correlated with actual outcomes, the value of this component of error is, in their opinion, not a cause for concern. Given that the summation of the three measures gives a value of one, the implication is that the ideal distribution of inequality over the three proportions is $U^M = U^S = 0$ and $U^C = 1$.

Of all the summary statistics, the Theil decomposition (whichever one is used) offers the possibility of the most comprehensive analysis of model simulation and it is strongly recommended that it is used in preference to all the others. A strong case for this approach is made in Watson (1987).

Regression and Correlation Measures

An intuitively appealing measure of model or forecast accuracy is the simple coefficient of correlation between actual and simulated values. The principal shortcoming of this measure is that it does not penalize systematic linear bias. To overcome this, Mincer and Zarnowitz (1969) propose a test of predictive efficiency based on the regression of the actual on the simulated values:

$$Y_t = \alpha + \beta Y_t^S$$

The ideal situation is one in which $\alpha = 0$ and $\beta = 1$. Since the regression estimates of α and β are usually correlated, their individual t-ratios provide inappropriate tests of the efficiency hypothesis and a joint F-test is required. Artis (1988) presents examples in which the individual and joint tests are in conflict. Granger and Newbold (1986), however, are very critical of the Mincer–Zarnovitz suggestion.

SOME ILLUSTRATIONS OF THE USE OF MODEL SIMULATION

Evaluation of Goodness-of-Fit of Single Equation Systems

Let us estimate equation (7.1) by OLS. The results obtained are shown in Exhibit 8.1. The model so obtained may be stored in EViews as:

$$P\_CONS = -1876.9578 + 0.48588218 * INCOME + 0.3005688 * P\_CONS(-1)$$

and, at any time after, may be solved. It is also possible to solve it without storing it if use is made of the "FORECAST" button which is made available at the same time the output in Exhibit 8.1 is displayed. The summary results obtained from static and dynamic simulations over the estimation period (frequently called *historical* simulation) are shown in Exhibit 8.2.

The simulated value of P_CONS is, in each case, denoted P_CONSF. You will notice that EViews reports the decomposition involving U^S and U^C (and not the one

EXHIBIT 8.1
OLS fit of equation (7.1)
$C_{pt} = g_{11} + b_{14}Y_t + g_{12}C_{p,t-1} + u_{1t}$

```
=============================================================
LS // Dependent Variable is P_CONS
Date: 10/17/95   Time: 18:32
Sample: 1968 1991
Included observations: 24 after adjusting endpoints
=============================================================
     Variable     Coefficient Std. Error  T-Statistic    Prob.
=============================================================
        C          -1876.958   594.0039  -3.159841     0.0047
      INCOME        0.485882   0.073228   6.635162     0.0000
      P_CONS(-1)    0.300569   0.102009   2.946495     0.0077
=============================================================
R-squared             0.950487   Mean dependent var    8592.498
Adjusted R-squared    0.945771   S.D. dependent var    2164.074
S.E. of regression    503.9503   Akaike info criter    12.56142
Sum squared resid     5333285.   Schwarz criterion     12.70868
Log likelihood       -181.7916   F-statistic           201.5637
Durbin-Watson stat    1.473037   Prob(F-statistic)     0.000000
=============================================================
```

EXHIBIT 8.2
Summary statistics based on historical simulation of
P_CONS = –1876.9578 + 0.48588218*INCOME + 0.3005688*P_CONS(–1)
(EViews Output)

Static Simulation

```
======================================
Actual: P_CONS      Forecast: P_CONSF
Sample: 1968 1991
Include observations: 24
======================================
Root Mean Squared Error          471.4024
Mean Absolute Error              401.8138
Mean Absolute Percentage Erro 4.784469
Theil Inequality Coefficient  0.026652
      Bias Proportion            0.000000
      Variance Proportion        0.012695
      Covariance Proportion      0.987305
======================================
```

Dynamic Simulation

```
======================================
Actual: P_CONS      Forecast: P_CONSF
Sample: 1968 1991
Include observations: 24
======================================
Root Mean Squared Error          516.6254
Mean Absolute Error              453.4065
Mean Absolute Percentage Erro 5.524241
Theil Inequality Coefficient  0.029230
      Bias Proportion            0.000698
      Variance Proportion        0.009011
      Covariance Proportion      0.990291
======================================
```

involving U^R and U^D). This and the other summary statistics shown are clear indications of a good model. For instance, in the dynamic simulation case, U^M and U^S are very close to zero and U^C very close to unity which, according to Pindyck and Rubinfeld (1998), is the almost ideal result. The Theil inequality coefficient shows an average error of about 3%, which is reasonable by any standard.

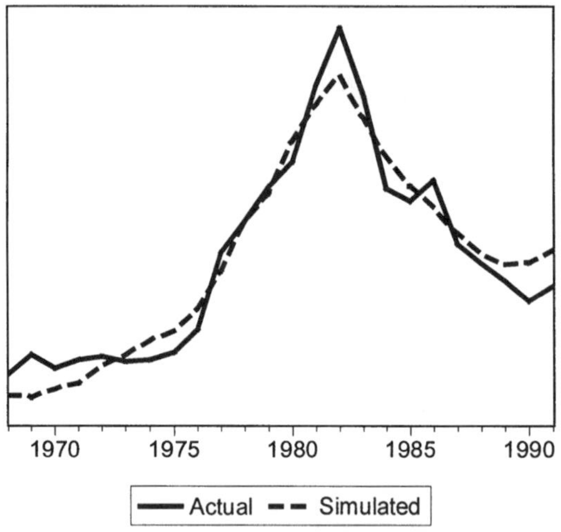

EXHIBIT 8.3
Plots of actual and simulated private consumption based on
P_CONS = –1876.9578 + 0.48588218*INCOME + 0.3005688*P_CONS(–1)
(1968–1991)

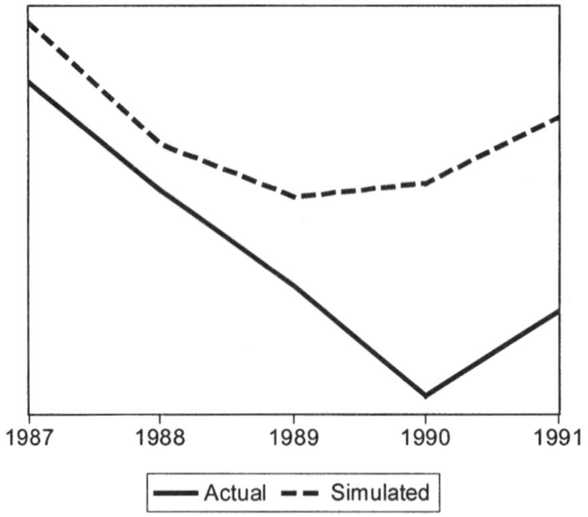

EXHIBIT 8.4
Plots of actual and simulated private consumption based on
P_CONS = –1876.9578 + 0.48588218*INCOME + 0.3005688*P_CONS(–1)
(1987–1991)

At the same time, like all summary statistics, it suffers from shortcomings like sensitivity to outliers. For this reason, it is recommended to inspect the time series plots of the actual and simulated values. This is shown in Exhibit 8.3.

The plot shows a fairly close tracking between actual and simulated values but the performance over the last few years (1987 to 1991) is a cause for concern. This becomes clearer if we take a close-up look at this shorter period, shown in Exhibit 8.4.

EXHIBIT 8.5
Actual and simulated private consumption based on P_CONS = –1876.9578 + 0.48588218*INCOME + 0.3005688*P_CONS(–1) (1987–1991)

Year	Actual	Simulated	Error	% Error
1987	8901.3	9132.5	231.2	2.60
1988	8475.9	8655.4	179.5	2.12
1989	8099.1	8447.6	348.5	4.30
1990	7667.9	8501.6	833.7	10.9
1991	7999.8	8761.9	762.1	9.53

There seems to be no obvious indication at this point that the two paths will meet and if this model is to be used for forecasting the immediate future we are likely to obtain inaccurate forecasts. But there is one consolation: the two plots seem to run (almost) parallel to each other so that, over this period the simple coefficient of correlation between actual and simulated values will be quite high (in fact, it is over 90%). If it is possible to approximate the vertical distance between the two plots, then the forecast obtained from the model can be adjusted by adding this amount to it. The actual figures shown in Exhibit 8.5 will provide some guidance.

We will lay the greatest emphasis on the last two years (1990 and 1991) where there is a forecast error of approximately 10%. If this model is used for forecasting, we can adopt a rule such as: the forecast to be used will be equal to the forecast generated by the model divided by 1.10.

Forecasting with Single Equation Systems

In this section, we will apply the *ad hoc* rule derived above. First, however, consider Exhibit 8.6, which shows the evaluation of the forecast of private consumption from 1992 to 1994 obtained from "mechanical" solution of the model. As was anticipated from the previous section, there is evidence of strong systematic bias here (but with very little variation). The graph of the actual and forecasted values shown in Exhibit 8.7 shows the details.

Exhibit 8.8 shows the adjusted forecast compared to that obtained from the model. Application of the *ad hoc* rule leads to a forecast error that is much more acceptable than the one generated by the model. This emphasizes an important point: we must never blindly accept forecasts mechanically generated from a fitted model and should seek instead to determine "add factors" which can be used to adjust these "mechanical" forecasts (in doing this we should use as well subjective economic judgment). See Klein and Young (1980).

Evaluation of Goodness-of-Fit of Multiple Equation Systems

Here we consider the system defined by equations (7.1) to (7.4) in chapter 7. Two versions of the model are considered: one estimated by OLS (model A) and the other by 2SLS (model B). The results of OLS estimation of equations (7.1) to (7.3) are shown in Exhibits 8.1, 1.1 and 7.3, respectively, and the 2SLS results are shown in chapter 7.

EXHIBIT 8.6
Comparison of actual and forecasted private consumption based on P_CONS = –1876.9578 + 0.48588218*INCOME + 0.3005688*P_CONS(–1) (1992–1994)

```
Forecast Evaluation
======================================
Actual: P_CONS     Forecast: P_CONSF
Sample: 1992 1994
Include observations: 3
======================================
Root Mean Squared Error         1146.627
Mean Absolute Error             1142.246
Mean Absolute Percentage Erro 15.37435
Theil Inequality Coefficient   0.071577
      Bias Proportion           0.992374
      Variance Proportion       0.000060
      Covariance Proportion     0.007566
======================================
```

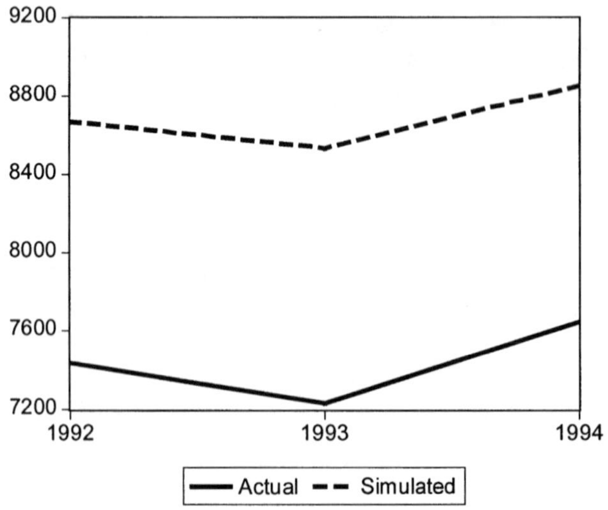

EXHIBIT 8.7
Plots of actual and forecasted private consumption based on P_CONS = –1876.9578 + 0.48588218*INCOME + 0.3005688*P_CONS(–1) (1992–1994)

EXHIBIT 8.8
Comparison of model and adjusted forecasted private consumption based on P_CONS = –1876.9578 + 0.48588218*INCOME + 0.3005688*P_CONS(–1) (1992–1994)

Year	Actual	Model Forecast	% Forecast Error	Adjusted Forecast	% Forecast Error
1992	7437.7	8670.2	16.6	7882.0	5.97
1993	7228.4	8533.4	18.1	7757.6	7.32
1994	7644.0	8851.8	15.8	8047.1	5.27

EXHIBIT 8.9
Program for model A in EViews (Equations estimated by OLS)

```
P_CONS = –1876.9578 + 0.48588218*INCOME + 0.3005688*P_CONS(–1)
IMPORTS = –1188.6408 + 0.37763924*INCOME – 688.67618*RATIO
INV = –2528.6344 + 0.31630837*INCOME(–1) + 1759.333*DUMMY
INCOME = P_CONS + G_CONS + INV +EXPORTS – IMPORTS
ASSIGN P_CONS P_CONSP IMPORTS IMPORTSP INV INVP INCOME INCOMEP
```

EXHIBIT 8.10
Program for model B in EViews (Equations estimated by 2SLS)

```
P_CONS = –1731.6262 + 0.46070333*INCOME + 0.33161351*P_CONS(–1)
IMPORTS = –1235.7383 + 0.37994557*INCOME – 684.02921*RATIO
INV = –2528.6344 + 0.31630837*INCOME(–1) + 1759.333*DUMMY
INCOME = P_CONS + G_CONS + INV +EXPORTS – IMPORTS
ASSIGN P_CONS P_CONSS IMPORTS IMPORTSS INV INVS INCOME INCOMES
```

The first step is to set up the model in EViews. Model A, which is based on OLS estimation, is set up in EViews as shown in Exhibit 8.9 and model B, which is based on 2SLS estimation, is shown in Exhibit 8.10.

The simulated values of any endogenous variable Y will be stored as YP in the case of model A and YS in the case of model B (for instance, the simulated value of P_CONS is stored as P_CONSP for model A and as P_CONSS for model B). These models are examples of linear models but EViews can solve both linear and nonlinear models (for example, those involving logarithms) by the Gauss–Seidel method. For most models it will converge rapidly and give the solution without any problems. However, it is not entirely foolproof. There are some models for which Gauss–Seidel cannot find the solution. Some types of nonlinearities and other characteristics will result in models that have no solutions or models that cannot be solved with the Gauss–Seidel method.

Gauss–Seidel works by evaluating each equation in order and then using the new value of the left-hand variable in an equation as the value of that variable when it appears in any later equation. The method is dependent on the way that you express your equations and on the order of the equations in your model. You must set up

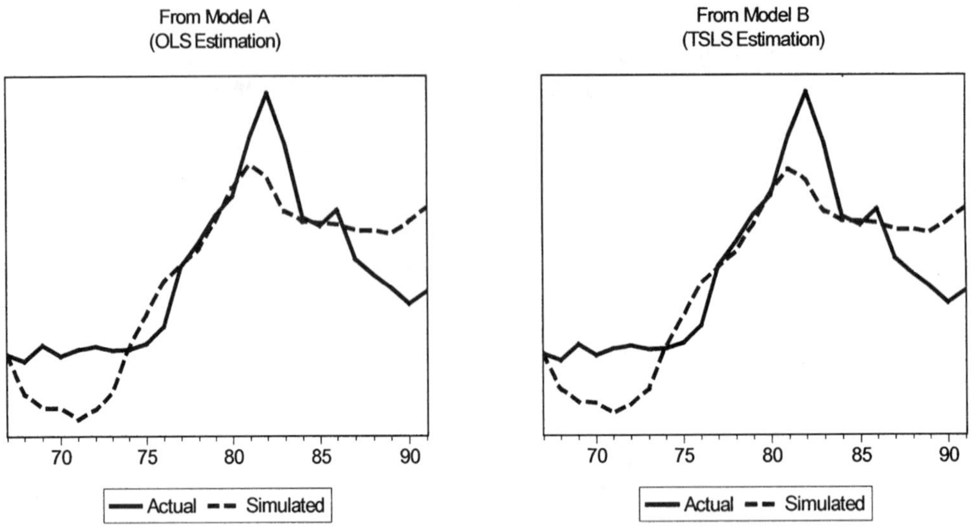

EXHIBIT 8.11
Time plots of actual and simulated private consumption expenditure

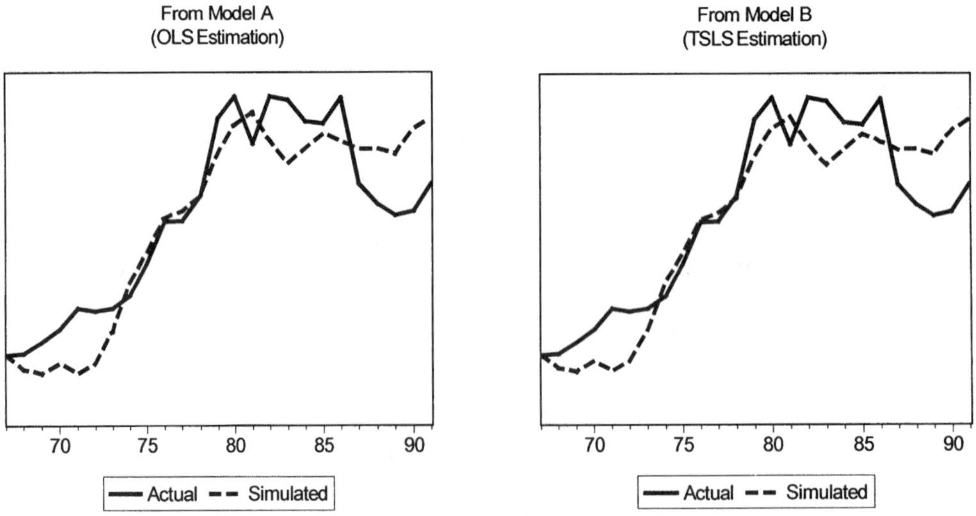

EXHIBIT 8.12
Time plots of actual and simulated imports

your equations so that each one has a different endogenous variable on the left-hand side. Sometimes you may need to rewrite identities or behavioural equations in order to put your model in this form.

EViews will reorder your equations so that ones that have no right-hand endogenous variables come first. In this way, when later equations are evaluated, the right values of at least some of their right-hand variables will be used from the start. By the same token, you should put equations early in the model if their right-hand endogenous variables are relatively unimportant.

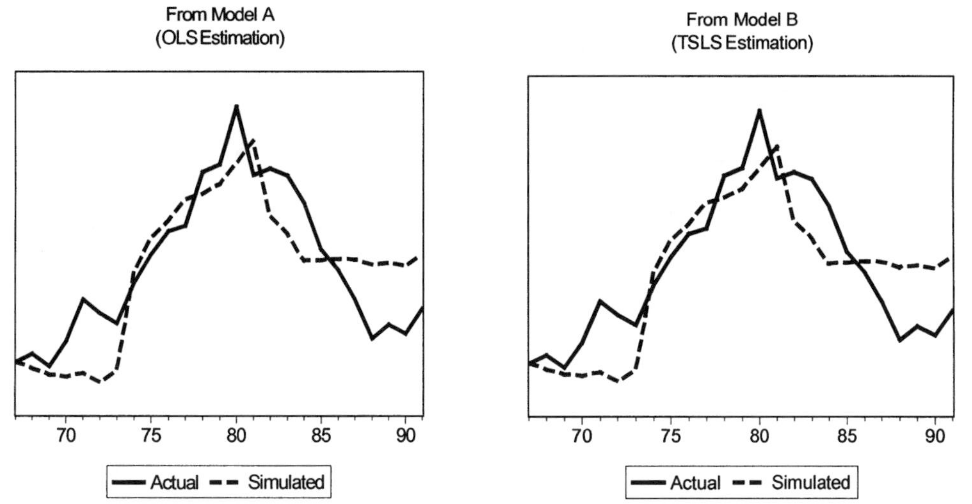

EXHIBIT 8.13
Time plots of actual and simulated investment

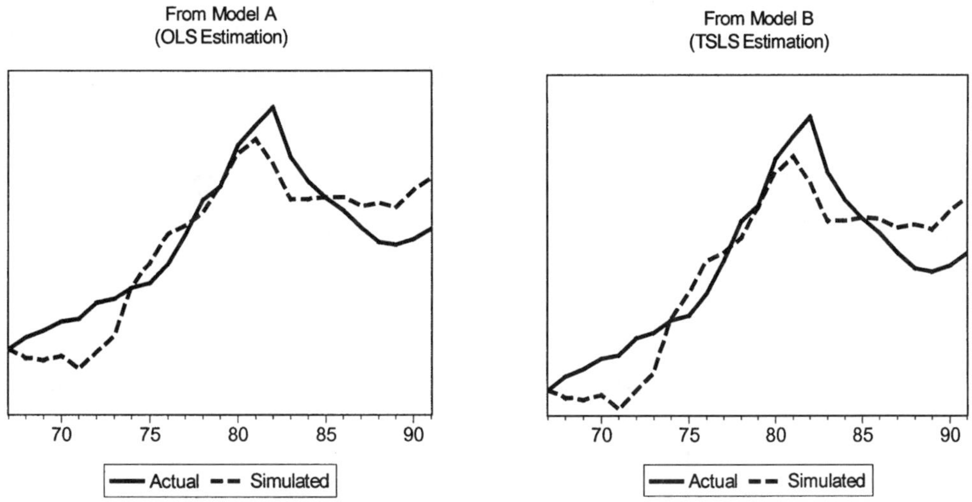

EXHIBIT 8.14
Time plots of actual and simulated national income

Consider the time plots in Exhibits 8.11 to 8.14. As with the case of the single equation model, performance seems to be inhibited by the ability of the model to properly track in the later years. In order to forecast into the future, therefore, it would be advisable to make some kind of adjustment. We will return to this point later.

Unfortunately, EViews does not provide summary statistics in the case of simulation of multiple equation systems, although the programming required to obtain them is relatively straightforward. Exhibit 8.15 shows these statistics as they were obtained from the dynamic simulation of models A and B using another package

EXHIBIT 8.15
Summary statistics based on dynamic simulation of models A and B (AREMOS output)

	Model A (OLS ESTIMATION)	Model B (2SLS ESTIMATION)
P_CONS	Theil U-statistic: 0.1473 RMSE: 1290.8994 %Mean difference: -2.0542 %RMSE: 60.7348 UM: 0.0183 UR: 0.1707 UD: 0.8110	Theil U-statistic: 0.1439 RMSE: 1260.9443 %Mean difference: -2.1520 %RMSE: 59.3254 UM: 0.0210 UR: 0.1326 UD: 0.8464
IMPORTS	Theil U-statistic: 0.1785 RMSE: 688.9488 %Mean difference: -2.0329 %RMSE: 45.9062 UM: 0.0110 UR: 0.1722 UD: 0.8168	Theil U-statistic: 0.1769 RMSE: 682.7122 %Mean difference: -2.1306 %RMSE: 45.4906 UM: 0.0123 UR: 0.1519 UD: 0.8358
INV	Theil U-statistic: 0.2639 RMSE: 896.1905 %Mean difference: -2.9818 %RMSE: 60.0191 UM: 0.0103 UR: 0.0742 UD: 0.9155	Theil U-statistic: 0.2631 RMSE: 893.3284 %Mean difference: -3.026 %RMSE: 59.8274 UM: 0.0107 UR: 0.0625 UD: 0.9269
INCOME	Theil U-statistic: 0.0888 RMSE: 1453.8802 %Mean difference: -1.2033 %RMSE: 46.3947 UM: 0.0177 UR: 0.1860 UD: 0.7963	Theil U-statistic: 0.0873 RMSE: 1429.6887 %Mean difference: -1.2414 %RMSE: 45.6228 UM: 0.0195 UR: 0.1511 UD: 0.8295

called AREMOS. AREMOS gives the Theil decomposition into U^R and U^D. You will notice, first of all, that there is remarkably little difference in the simulation performance of the two models (which is quite good in both cases) although the 2SLS seems to perform marginally better.

DYNAMIC RESPONSE (MULTIPLIER ANALYSIS) IN MULTIPLE EQUATION SYSTEMS

There are (at least) two additional requirements of estimated models like models A and B:

1. The model should be stable, in the sense that it does not explode or radically alter its behaviour because of marginal changes in the value of its coefficients and exogenous variables.
2. There is a sound and meaningful economic explanation for the response of endogenous variables to stimuli resulting from "exogenous" shocks.

Multiplier analysis is used to deal with both of these issues.

Consider some endogenous variable at time t y_{it} and an exogenous variable at time s x_{js}, $s \leq t$. Suppose there is some adjustment in x_{js} equal to ∂x_{js}. It seems legitimate to ask the question: what will be the value of the resulting change in y_{it}, or ∂y_{it}? The per unit effect of x_{js} on y_{it} is defined as the multiplier of lag (t – s):

$$m_{ij}(t-s) = \frac{\partial y_{it}}{\partial x_{js}}$$

If t = s, the resulting multiplier is referred to as the *impact* multiplier, while:

$$m_{ij} = \sum_{t=0}^{\infty} m_{ij}(t)$$

is defined as the long run multiplier. The latter measures the effect of a sustained change of x on y and, if the model is stable, it converges to a finite value.

In models of even the most moderate size, it is either extremely difficult or impossible to determine the value of these multipliers by analytical methods. It is for this reason that we resort to simulation techniques to approximate the values. How is this done?

As a first step, the model is solved to yield the simulated values (in the way that we have been doing it up to now). This step is referred to as the *base* run of the model and the values of the variable y_i shall be denoted y^b_{it}.[3] In a second step, some exogenous variable x_j is altered by an amount equal to Δx_{jt} and the model solved again. This phase is called the *simulation* run and yields values of the endogenous variable y_i denoted by y^s_{it}. A typical multiplier is approximated by:

$$\hat{m}_{ij}(t-s) = \frac{y^s_{it} - y^b_{it}}{\Delta x_{js}}$$

while the long run multiplier may be approximated by:

$$\hat{m}_{ij} = \sum_{t=1}^{n} m_{ij}(t)$$

Illustration of Dynamic Response

The variable G_CONS in model B was increased by 10% over the period 1967 to 1991. The model was then solved again over the period 1968 to 1991 and multipliers calculated on the basis of the effect of this shock on P_CONS. The various multipliers, as well as the approximate values of the long run multiplier, are shown in Exhibit 8.16.

The model is clearly stable as it converges to a new equilibrium after the shock. After 1991, the long run multiplier is approximated at 1.82 which means that, in the "long run", a sustained increase in government expenditure of \$1.00 results in an increase of \$1.82 in private consumption. The impact multiplier is 0.50 – what does this mean?

Forecasting and Policy Simulations with Multiple Equation Systems

Forecasting and policy analysis based on simulations (policy simulations) using econometric models both involve the making of projections of endogenous variables into the future on the basis of (projected) future values of exogenous variables. In both cases, specification of the exogenous variables is an expensive and time consuming exercise

[3] Alternatively, we may simply use the actual (instead of the simulated) values. This is done in Watson and Clarke (1997).

EXHIBIT 8.16
Selected multipliers based on simulation of model B

Year	Multiplier	Long run Multiplier
1968	0.50	0.50
1969	0.40	0.90
....	....	....
1988	0.13	1.95
1989	–0.02	1.93
1990	–0.14	1.79
1991	0.03	1.82

EXHIBIT 8.17
Forecast errors for model B

Year	% Error P_cons	% Error P_cons (adj)	% Error imports	% Error imports (adj)	% Error inv	% Error inv (adj)	% Error income	% Error income (adj)
1992	22.0%	–5.44%	50.4%	14.0%	95.2%	17.6%	8.64%	–17.5%
1993	34.6%	4.33%	64.0%	24.2%	119.7%	32.3%	14.2%	–14.3%
1994	33.5%	3.47%	68.4%	27.6%	92.1%	15.8%	12.5%	–16.1%

which occupies an inordinately large portion of the time of the teams involved in the exercise.

In the end, the future values of the endogenous variables obtained are conditional upon the choice of values of the exogenous variables. In addition, just as in the case of single equation models, we cannot be indifferent to the built-in biases of the estimated model and should be prepared, on the basis of "add factors", to adjust the forecasts derived from mechanical application of the model. But this is complicated by the presence of more than one equation and, in particular, the necessity to satisfy accounting identities in the model.

Illustration

In this chapter, we will not concern ourselves with practical difficulties in specifying values for the exogenous variables. We shall simply solve model B into the future using whatever values we have of the exogenous variables. In Exhibit 8.17, we display the forecasts for the period 1992 to 1994 obtained from mechanical solution, as well as from adjustments of these values based on add factors.

In this case, the adjustments result in a deterioration of the INCOME forecasts. In general, too, even the adjusted forecasts leave some room for improvement. It may be that the model itself needs further fine-tuning or greater care should be taken in determining the add factors.

EXERCISE

Term project
Discuss with your class instructor an econometric project involving (at least) the specification, estimation and validation of a simple econometric model. You must write up a report that will include:

- A clear description of the problematique
- Justification of the model chosen to quantify the problematique
- The data used in the model (together with the source of the data)
- A clear summary of the main results of the estimation and validation exercises
- Implications of the results for economic theory, policy, etc.

PART II

Modern

CHAPTER 9

Maximum Likelihood Estimation

INTRODUCTION

The maximum likelihood method of estimation is based on the idea that different populations generate different samples, and that any given sample is more likely to have come from some populations than from others. Take, for example, normal populations, which are fully characterized by a mean and a variance, and hence differ only with respect to the value of these two parameters. A given sample from a normal population may have come from a population characterized by *any* mean and *any* variance, but some populations would generate such a sample more frequently than others.

With this in mind, consider some random variable X, from which we draw a sample of size n:

$$X_1, X_2, \ldots X_n$$

Each X_i will have a distribution identical to that of X, and, since it is a random sample, X_i is independent of X_j, $i \neq j$. The probability density function (pdf) of X_i is defined as $f(x_i/\theta)$.[1] The pdf depends on some unknown parameter θ. If the distribution were normal, for example, θ would be a vector (σ^2, μ), if the distribution were binomial, θ would be p, and so on.

Consider now, the joint probability density function of $X_1, X_2, \ldots, X_n$ which we can define as:

$$L(\theta/x_1, \ldots x_n) = f(x_1/\theta) \cdot f(x_2/\theta) \ldots f(x_n/\theta)^{2}$$

Intuitively, we can say that this represents the joint probability of the sample $X_1, X_2, \ldots, X_n$ being formed. This defines the *likelihood function* of the distribution.

The likelihood function can therefore be interpreted to represent the probability of the random sample occurring. This probability is, however, unknown, because θ is unknown. We therefore want to find a way of estimating θ. How can this best be done? If the sample really had the defined distribution, then the value of θ that should be chosen is the value that gives the likelihood function the highest probability possible. Alternatively, we can say that the highest probability of the likelihood

[1] If X_i is discrete, then $f(x_i/\theta) = P(X_i = x_i/\theta)$.

[2] If the Xs are discrete, then $f(x_1/\theta) \cdot f(x_2/\theta) \ldots f(x_n/\theta) = P(X_1 = x_1, X_2 = x_2, \ldots, X_n = x_n/\theta)$.

function would be the one associated with what should be the true value of θ. It is therefore intuitively appealing to define an estimator $\hat{\theta}$ which results in L having a maximum value. This is our *maximum likelihood estimator.*

The mechanism for obtaining this estimator is straightforward in those cases where the tools of differential calculus allow us to determine a value of θ that results in a maximum value. This occurs when the function is continuous and differentiable as in the case of the normal distribution. Frequently, however, the situation is not as straightforward and we must resort to the use of fairly sophisticated numerical methods of maximization.

Let us consider a random variable X that is normally distributed. The parameters of the distribution μ and σ^2 are unknown, and so we attempt to derive their maximum likelihood estimators. Since:

$$X \sim N(\mu, \sigma^2)$$

its pdf is defined as:

$$f(x/\sigma^2, \mu) = \frac{1}{\sqrt{2\pi\sigma^2}} \exp -\frac{1}{2}\left[\frac{x-\mu}{\sigma}\right]^2$$

The likelihood function for a random sample $X_1, X_2, \ldots, X_n$ is defined as:

$$L(\theta/x_1, x_2, \ldots, x_n) = \prod_{i=1}^{n} \frac{1}{\sqrt{2\pi\sigma^2}} \exp -\frac{1}{2}\left[\frac{x_i-\mu}{\sigma}\right]^2$$

$$= \left[\frac{1}{\sqrt{2\pi\sigma^2}}\right]^n \exp -\frac{1}{2}\sum\left[\frac{x_i-\mu}{\sigma}\right]^2$$

$$= \left[(2\pi)^{-1/2}(\sigma^2)^{-1/2}\right]^n \exp -\frac{1}{2}\sum\left[\frac{x_i-\mu}{\sigma}\right]^2$$

Further simplification gives:

$$L = (2\pi)^{-n/2}(\sigma^2)^{-n/2} \exp -\frac{1}{2}\sum\left[\frac{x_i-\mu}{\sigma}\right]^2$$

The logarithmic transformation of this function is one-to-one and leaves intact the relative shape. It is also easier to handle analytically, and in fact has other useful characteristics. The logarithm of the normal likelihood function is:

$$\ln L = -\frac{n}{2}\ln 2\pi - \frac{n}{2}\ln \sigma^2 - \frac{1}{2\sigma^2}\sum(x_i-\mu)^2$$

Taking the first derivative[3] of this function with respect to μ and to σ^2, we obtain:

$$\frac{\partial \ln L}{\partial \mu} = \frac{1}{\sigma_2} \sum (x_i - \mu)$$

and:

$$\frac{\partial \ln L}{\partial \sigma^2} = -\frac{n}{2\sigma^2} + \frac{1}{2\sigma^4} \sum (x_i - \mu)^2$$

Setting these first derivatives equal to zero, and denoting by $\hat{\mu}$ and $\hat{\sigma}^2$ the solution values for μ and σ^2, respectively, we obtain:

$$\frac{1}{\hat{\sigma}^2} \sum (x_1 - \hat{\mu}) = 0$$

and:

$$-\frac{n}{2\hat{\sigma}^2} + \frac{1}{2\hat{\sigma}^4} \sum (x_i - \hat{\mu})^2 = 0$$

Solving these further yields:

$$\sum (x_i - \hat{\mu}) = 0$$

$$\Rightarrow \sum x_i - n\hat{\mu} = 0$$

$$\Rightarrow \hat{\mu} = \frac{\sum x_i}{n} = \bar{x}$$

and:

$$\frac{1}{2\hat{\sigma}^4} \sum (x_i - \hat{\mu})^2 = \frac{n}{2\hat{\sigma}^2}$$

$$\frac{2\hat{\sigma}^4}{2\hat{\sigma}^2} = \frac{\sum (x_i - \hat{\mu})^2}{n}$$

$$\Rightarrow \hat{\sigma}^2 = \frac{\sum (x_i - \hat{\mu})^2}{n}$$

[3] The first derivative of the likelihood function with respect to an unknown set of parameters is called the *efficient score* for the parameter set. Clearly, for the maximum likelihood estimator, the efficient score $S(\hat{\theta}) = 0$.

The maximum likelihood estimator of μ is therefore the arithmetic mean of the sample which, from our study of elementary statistics, we know to be an unbiased estimator. We also know that an unbiased estimator of σ^2 is:

$$s^2 = \frac{\sum (x_i - \hat{\mu})^2}{n-1}$$

Clearly, then, the MLE of σ^2 is biased although for large samples it is almost indistinguishable from s^2, an unbiased estimator.

THE CRAMER–RAO LOWER BOUND (CRLB)

Consider any unbiased estimator $\hat{\theta}$ of an unknown set of parameters θ. It can be shown that, for a scalar θ:

$$\text{var}(\hat{\theta}) \geq \frac{1}{I(\theta)} = \text{CRLB}$$

where I(θ) represents *Fisher's information quantity*, defined as:

$$I(\theta) = -E\left[\frac{\partial^2 \ln L(\theta)}{\partial \theta^2}\right]$$

If θ is a vector, the condition required is $\text{cov}(\hat{\theta}) - I^{-1}(\theta) = P$ where P is positive semidefinite, and I(θ) now represents Fisher's information matrix, defined as:

$$I(\theta) = -E\left[\frac{\partial \ln L}{\partial \theta \partial \theta'}\right]$$

What is being said here is simply that the lowest value that the variance of any unbiased estimator could have is the Cramer–Rao lower bound. In more formal terms, we can say that a sufficient condition for an unbiased estimator to be efficient is that it attains the value of the Cramer–Rao lower bound.

Consider the maximum likelihood estimator of $\hat{\mu}$, derived above as $\Sigma x_i / n = \bar{x}$, which we know to be unbiased. Let us calculate Fisher's quantity of information for μ:

$$I(\mu) = -E\left[\frac{\partial^2 \ln L(\mu, \sigma^2)}{\partial \mu^2}\right]$$

Recall that:

$$\frac{\partial \ln L}{\partial \mu} = \frac{1}{\sigma^2}\sum(x_i - \mu)$$

$$= \frac{1}{\sigma^2}\left(\sum x_i - \sum \mu\right)$$

$$= \frac{1}{\sigma^2}\sum x_i - \frac{n}{\sigma^2}\sum \mu$$

It follows that:

$$\frac{\partial^2 \ln L}{\partial \mu^2} = \frac{-n}{\sigma^2}$$

$$\Rightarrow I(\mu) = \frac{n}{\sigma^2}$$

$$\Rightarrow \frac{1}{I(\mu)} = \frac{\sigma^2}{n} = \text{CRLB}$$

It is easily shown that:

$$\text{var}(\hat{\mu}) = \frac{\sigma^2}{n}$$

and so we conclude that $\hat{\mu}$, the maximum likelihood estimator of μ, is efficient since it attains the CRLB.

It is important to note, however, that while the attainment of the CRLB is a *sufficient* condition for the efficiency of an estimator, it is not a *necessary* condition. That is to say, an estimator may be efficient *without* attaining CRLB.

PROPERTIES OF MAXIMUM LIKELIHOOD ESTIMATORS

1. If an efficient estimator exists, it is the maximum likelihood estimator.
2. The maximum likelihood estimator is always consistent, in the sense that plim $\hat{\theta} = \theta$.
3. The distribution of ($\hat{\theta} - \theta$), as the sample size increases, tends to the normal distribution with zero mean and variance $I^{-1}(\theta)$, that is:

$$\left(\hat{\theta} - \theta\right) \sim N\left(0, I^{-1}(\theta)\right)$$

This last property is equivalent to saying that $\hat{\theta}$, whatever its small sample properties, is *asymptotically efficient*. If X is distributed with a mean of μ and a variance of σ^2, the maximum likelihood estimator of μ is unbiased and asymptotically efficient while that of σ^2 is biased (see above) but still asymptotically efficient.

MAXIMUM LIKELIHOOD ESTIMATION IN THE GENERAL LINEAR REGRESSION MODEL

Remember the model:

$$y_t = \beta_1 x_{1t} + \beta_2 x_{2t} + \beta_3 x_{3t} + \ldots + \beta_k x_{kt} + u_t$$

where:

$$u_t \sim \text{NID}\left(0, \sigma^2\right)$$

The likelihood function of u_t is:

$$L\left(\sigma^2 / u_1 \ldots u_n\right) = \left[\frac{1}{2\pi\sigma^2}\right]^{\frac{n}{2}} \exp - \frac{1}{2\sigma^2} \sum u_t^2$$

Recall that:

$$\sum u_t^2 = \mathbf{u'u} = (\mathbf{y} - \mathbf{X\beta})' (\mathbf{y} - \mathbf{X\beta})$$

therefore:

$$L\left(\sigma^2 / u_1 \ldots u_n\right) = \left[\frac{1}{2\pi\sigma^2}\right]^{\frac{n}{2}} \exp - \frac{1}{2\sigma^2} (\mathbf{y} - \mathbf{X\beta})' (\mathbf{y} - \mathbf{X\beta})$$

It can be shown that:

$$L\left(\beta, \sigma^2 / y_1, y_2, \ldots, y_n\right) = L\left(\sigma^2 / u_1, u_2, \ldots u_n\right) \left|\frac{\partial u}{\partial y}\right|$$

where:

$$\frac{\partial u}{\partial y} = \begin{bmatrix} \frac{\partial u_1}{\partial y_1} & \frac{\partial u_1}{\partial y_2} & \cdots & \cdots & \frac{\partial u_1}{\partial y_n} \\ \frac{\partial u_2}{\partial y_1} & \frac{\partial u_2}{\partial y_2} & \cdots & \cdots & \frac{\partial u_2}{\partial y_n} \\ \vdots & \vdots & \ddots & & \vdots \\ \vdots & \vdots & & \ddots & \vdots \\ \frac{\partial u_n}{\partial y_1} & \frac{\partial u_n}{\partial y_2} & \cdots & \cdots & \frac{\partial u_n}{\partial y_n} \end{bmatrix}$$

In this case, this Jacobian matrix is the identity matrix and, consequently, its determinant is equal to one (we say that the Jacobian of the transformation is equal to unity). Clearly, the implication of this is that the likelihood function of u is identical to the likelihood function of y in the general linear regression model, that is:

$$L(\beta,\sigma^2/y_1,y_2,\ldots y_n)=L(\sigma^2/u_1,u_2,\ldots u_n)$$

so that:

$$L(\beta,\sigma^2/y_1,y_2,\ldots,y_n)=\left[\frac{1}{2\pi\sigma^2}\right]^{\frac{n}{2}}\exp-\frac{1}{2\sigma^2}(\mathbf{y}-\mathbf{X}\boldsymbol{\beta})'(\mathbf{y}-\mathbf{X}\boldsymbol{\beta})$$

$$\Rightarrow L(\beta,\sigma^2/y_1,y_2,\ldots,y_n)=(2\pi)^{-\frac{n}{2}}(\sigma^2)^{-\frac{n}{2}}\exp-\frac{1}{2\sigma^2}(\mathbf{y}-\mathbf{X}\boldsymbol{\beta})'(\mathbf{y}-\mathbf{X}\boldsymbol{\beta})$$

$$\ln L(\beta,\sigma^2/y_1,y_2,\ldots,y_n)=-\frac{n}{2}\ln 2\pi-\frac{n}{2}\ln\sigma^2-\frac{1}{2\sigma^2}(\mathbf{y}-\mathbf{X}\boldsymbol{\beta})'(\mathbf{y}-\mathbf{X}\boldsymbol{\beta})$$

$$=-\frac{n}{2}\ln 2\pi-\frac{n}{2}\ln\sigma^2-\frac{1}{2\sigma^2}[\mathbf{y}'\mathbf{y}-\mathbf{y}'\mathbf{X}\boldsymbol{\beta}-\boldsymbol{\beta}'\mathbf{X}'\mathbf{y}+\boldsymbol{\beta}'\mathbf{X}'\mathbf{X}\boldsymbol{\beta}]$$

Differentiating with respect to $\boldsymbol{\beta}$, we obtain:

$$\frac{\partial \ln L}{\partial \beta}=-\frac{1}{2\sigma^2}[-2\mathbf{X}'\mathbf{y}+2\mathbf{X}'\mathbf{X}\boldsymbol{\beta}]$$

Setting equal to zero and solving for $\boldsymbol{\beta}$ yields:

$$(\mathbf{X}'\mathbf{X})\hat{\boldsymbol{\beta}}=\mathbf{X}'\mathbf{y}$$

$$\Rightarrow \hat{\boldsymbol{\beta}}=(\mathbf{X}'\mathbf{X})^{-1}\mathbf{X}'\mathbf{y}$$

where $\hat{\boldsymbol{\beta}}$ is the value of $\boldsymbol{\beta}$ which is the solution of the system. It is clearly identical to the OLS estimator.

Similarly, differentiating with respect to σ^2 yields:

$$\frac{\partial \ln L}{\partial \sigma^2}=-\frac{n}{2\hat{\sigma}^2}+\frac{1}{2\hat{\sigma}^4}(\mathbf{y}-\mathbf{X}\hat{\boldsymbol{\beta}})'(\mathbf{y}-\mathbf{X}\hat{\boldsymbol{\beta}})=0$$

$$\Rightarrow \frac{1}{2\hat{\sigma}^4}(\mathbf{y}-\mathbf{X}\hat{\boldsymbol{\beta}})'(\mathbf{y}-\mathbf{X}\hat{\boldsymbol{\beta}})=\frac{n}{2\hat{\sigma}^2}$$

so that:

$$\hat{\sigma}^2=\frac{(\mathbf{y}-\mathbf{X}\hat{\boldsymbol{\beta}})'(\mathbf{y}-\mathbf{X}\hat{\boldsymbol{\beta}})}{n}=\frac{\hat{\mathbf{u}}'\hat{\mathbf{u}}'}{n}$$

Notice that, since the maximum likelihood estimator of $\boldsymbol{\beta}$ is identical to the OLS estimator, it is clearly unbiased with covariance $\sigma^2(\mathbf{X'X})^{-1}$. It is also efficient, as the following theorem shows.

Theorem

The maximum likelihood estimator of $\boldsymbol{\beta}$ is efficient.

Proof

The maximum likelihood estimator of $\boldsymbol{\beta}$ is efficient if its variance attains the CRLB. It has been proven that the maximum likelihood estimator of $\boldsymbol{\beta}$ is identical to its OLS estimator, and so we know that:

$$E\left(\hat{\boldsymbol{\beta}}\right) = \boldsymbol{\beta}$$

and:

$$\text{cov}\left(\hat{\boldsymbol{\beta}}\right) = \sigma^2 (\mathbf{X'X})^{-1}$$

We may also deduce that:

$$\frac{\partial \ln L}{\partial \beta \partial \beta'} = -\frac{1}{2\sigma^2}[-2\mathbf{X'X}] = -\frac{\mathbf{X'X}}{\sigma^2} = I(\boldsymbol{\beta})$$

and so it follows that:

$$\text{CRLB} = I^{-1}(\boldsymbol{\beta}) = \sigma^2 (\mathbf{X'X})^{-1} = \text{cov}\left(\hat{\boldsymbol{\beta}}\right)$$

The maximum likelihood estimator (which is equivalent to the OLS estimator) in the general linear regression model therefore attains the CRLB, which proves its efficiency.

The residual vector $\hat{\mathbf{u}}$ is also identical to the OLS residual vector, but the maximum likelihood estimator of σ^2 is clearly biased, since we know that an unbiased estimator is $\sigma^2 = \hat{\mathbf{u}}'\hat{\mathbf{u}}/(n-k)$. However, as the sample size increases, n and (n – k) become indistinguishable. Furthermore, the maximum likelihood estimator of σ^2, although biased, is asymptotically efficient.

EXERCISES

1. Recall the main properties of the maximum likelihood estimator.
2. Establish the second derivatives of the likelihood function of the general linear regression model and comment on it.

CHAPTER 10

The Wald, Likelihood Ratio and Lagrange Multiplier Tests

INTRODUCTION

Many of the tests that we have already met, such as the Student and F-tests, and some that we are yet to meet, are examples of at least one of the Wald, likelihood ratio (LR) or Lagrange multiplier (LM) principle testing procedures, which are now prevalent in the practice of econometrics. The fundamental concern of this discipline is the confrontation of economic theories with observable phenomena. Clearly, hypothesis testing is the primary tool of such an analysis – to be empirically validated (or invalidated, as the case may be), all theories must eventually be reduced to a testable hypothesis. The three general testing procedures are characterized by a certain symmetry where, essentially, the LM approach starts at the null hypothesis and asks whether movement towards the alternative would be an improvement. The Wald approach starts at the alternative and considers movement towards the null, and the LR method compares the two hypotheses directly on an equal basis.

A very readable introduction to this topic, on which this chapter draws heavily, is Buse (1982). A more comprehensive, though more difficult, treatment is Engle (1981).

DEFINING RESTRICTIONS ON THE PARAMETER SPACE

All three testing procedures are designed to test for *restrictions* on the parameter space. The tests of nullity of coefficients discussed in chapter 2, which are based on the Student and F-distributions, are really tests on the restriction that this or that coefficient is equal to zero. They are, as we shall see, special cases of the tests to be discussed in this chapter. But restrictions may be more general than the ones imposed in these well-known tests. For instance, consider the following consumption function:

$$C_t = \alpha Y_t + u_t$$

It is frequently asserted that $\alpha = 1$, and this "restriction" can be tested. Consider also the following Cobb–Douglas production function:

$$\ln Y_t = \alpha + \beta \ln L_t + \gamma \ln K_t + u_t$$

It is frequently claimed that $\beta + \gamma = 1$ (what does this mean?) and this "restriction" can also be tested.

In the general linear regression model:

$$\mathbf{y} = \mathbf{X}\boldsymbol{\beta} + \mathbf{u}$$

the issue is how to incorporate into our estimation procedure some prior information about a regression coefficient or coefficients, where such information can be viewed as providing certain restrictions on such coefficients. These restrictions can be of different types – some imposed by prior information about the *value* of the individual regression coefficients (as in the consumption function example), and others imposed by the *relations* among the individual regression coefficients (as in the Cobb–Douglas example). Restrictions may be linear or nonlinear.

A common way of representing a set of J linear restrictions is to write:

$$\mathbf{R}\boldsymbol{\beta} = \mathbf{r} \qquad \textbf{(10.1)}$$

where **R** is a (J × k) matrix of known constants, $\boldsymbol{\beta}$ a (k × 1) vector of the regression coefficients, and **r** a (J × 1) vector of known constants.[1] Suppose we wished to test the restriction (similar to the one associated with the Cobb–Douglas production function):

$$\beta_2 + \beta_3 = 1$$

For k = 3, this can be represented in the form of equation (10.1) as:

$$\begin{pmatrix} 0 & 1 & 1 \end{pmatrix} \begin{pmatrix} \beta_1 \\ \beta_2 \\ \beta_3 \end{pmatrix} = 1$$

where **R** is a (1 × 3) vector, $\boldsymbol{\beta}$ a (3 × 1) vector and **r** a scalar equal to 1. As yet another example, consider the following set of restrictions:

$$\beta_2 + \beta_3 = 1$$

$$\beta_2 = 0$$

$$\beta_3 = 0$$

These can be represented in the form of equation (10.1) as:

$$\begin{bmatrix} 1 & 1 & 0 \\ 0 & 1 & 0 \\ 0 & 0 & 1 \end{bmatrix} \begin{bmatrix} \beta_1 \\ \beta_2 \\ \beta_3 \end{bmatrix} = \begin{bmatrix} 1 \\ 0 \\ 0.5 \end{bmatrix}$$

[1] For mathematical reasons, it will always be assumed that $J \leq k$.

where **R** is a (3 × 3) matrix, $\boldsymbol{\beta}$ a (3 × 1) vector and **r** a (3 × 1) vector.

In chapter 2, we considered the set of (k – 1) restrictions for the general linear regression model:

$$\beta_2 = \beta_3 = \ldots = \beta_k = 0$$

which formed the basis of the familiar F-test. These restrictions can be written in the form of equation (10.1) as:

$$\begin{bmatrix} 0 & 1 & 0 & \ldots & 0 \\ 0 & 0 & 1 & \ldots & 0 \\ \vdots & \vdots & \vdots & \ddots & \vdots \\ 0 & 0 & 0 & \ldots & 1 \end{bmatrix} \begin{bmatrix} \beta_1 \\ \beta_2 \\ \vdots \\ \beta_k \end{bmatrix} = \begin{bmatrix} 0 \\ 0 \\ \vdots \\ 0 \end{bmatrix}$$

or as:

$$\begin{bmatrix} 0 & \\ 0 & \mathbf{I}_{k-1} \\ \vdots & \\ 0 & \end{bmatrix} \begin{bmatrix} \beta_1 \\ \beta_2 \\ \vdots \\ \beta_k \end{bmatrix} = \begin{bmatrix} 0 \\ 0 \\ \vdots \\ 0 \end{bmatrix}$$

Can you express the null hypothesis of the T-test in the form of equation (10.1)?

The restrictions defined in equation (10.1) will constitute the null hypothesis, while the alternative will be defined as:

$$\mathbf{R}\boldsymbol{\beta} \neq \mathbf{r}$$

Intuitively, we can compare estimation of the regression equation in which the restriction is explicitly taken into account (that is, the *restricted* parameter estimates) with the regression equation in which the restrictions are ignored (that is, the *unrestricted* parameter estimates). If the restriction were *true*, we should be indifferent to estimating it with a procedure that takes into account the restriction, since fitting it freely or fitting it as if the restriction were true should yield the same results. It is when the restriction does not hold that we would expect different results. It can be shown that, when the restrictions are explicitly taken into account, the maximum likelihood estimator of $\boldsymbol{\beta}$ is:

$$\hat{\boldsymbol{\beta}}_c = \hat{\boldsymbol{\beta}} - (\mathbf{X}'\mathbf{X})^{-1}\mathbf{R}'\left[\mathbf{R}(\mathbf{X}'\mathbf{X})^{-1}\mathbf{R}'\right]^{-1}\left(\mathbf{R}\hat{\boldsymbol{\beta}} - \mathbf{r}\right)$$

where $\hat{\boldsymbol{\beta}}$ is the unrestricted maximum likelihood estimator.

THE LIKELIHOOD RATIO TEST

The likelihood ratio test is based on the idea that if the restrictions are true, then the value of the likelihood function maximized with the restrictions imposed cannot differ too much from the value of the likelihood function maximized without the restrictions imposed. Let $L(\hat{\boldsymbol{\beta}}_c)$ be the maximum of the likelihood function taken when the restrictions are imposed, and $L(\hat{\boldsymbol{\beta}})$ be the maximum of the likelihood function when the restrictions are not imposed. If the restrictions are true, then these likelihood functions should be more or less equal, or the ratio not fundamentally different from one:

$$\frac{L(\hat{\boldsymbol{\beta}})}{L(\hat{\boldsymbol{\beta}}_c)} \approx 1$$

If the restrictions are false, then the restricted estimator $\hat{\boldsymbol{\beta}}_c$ would have the smaller likelihood. Can you suggest why this is so?

Taking the logarithm of the ratio, we obtain:

$$\ln\left[\frac{L(\hat{\boldsymbol{\beta}})}{L(\hat{\boldsymbol{\beta}}_c)}\right] = \ln L(\hat{\boldsymbol{\beta}}) - \ln L(\hat{\boldsymbol{\beta}}_c)$$

$$= -\frac{\frac{1}{2}(\mathbf{y}-\mathbf{X}\hat{\boldsymbol{\beta}})'(\mathbf{y}-\mathbf{X}\hat{\boldsymbol{\beta}})}{\sigma^2} + \frac{\frac{1}{2}(\mathbf{y}-\mathbf{X}\hat{\boldsymbol{\beta}}_c)'(\mathbf{y}-\mathbf{X}\hat{\boldsymbol{\beta}}_c)}{\sigma^2}$$

The likelihood ratio (LR) is defined by:

$$LR = \frac{-(\mathbf{y}-\mathbf{X}\hat{\boldsymbol{\beta}})'(\mathbf{y}-\mathbf{X}\hat{\boldsymbol{\beta}})+(\mathbf{y}-\mathbf{X}\hat{\boldsymbol{\beta}}_c)'(\mathbf{y}-\mathbf{X}\hat{\boldsymbol{\beta}}_c)}{\sigma^2} = \frac{\hat{\mathbf{u}}_c'\hat{\mathbf{u}}_c - \hat{\mathbf{u}}'\hat{\mathbf{u}}}{\sigma^2} = 2\ln\left[\frac{L(\hat{\boldsymbol{\beta}})}{L(\hat{\boldsymbol{\beta}}_c)}\right] \quad \textbf{(10.2)}$$

and, under the null hypothesis, it is distributed as a χ^2_J. J, you may remember, is the number of restrictions imposed.

In empirical work, σ^2 is unknown and may be estimated by:

$$s^2 = \frac{\hat{\mathbf{u}}'\hat{\mathbf{u}}}{n-k}$$

We have already established that:

$$\frac{\hat{\mathbf{u}}'\hat{\mathbf{u}}}{\sigma^2} \sim \chi^2(n-k)$$

and it can be shown to be distributed independently of LR. The following "F"-statistic can be derived:

$$LR* = \frac{\hat{\mathbf{u}}_c'\hat{\mathbf{u}}_c - \hat{\mathbf{u}}'\hat{\mathbf{u}}}{\hat{\mathbf{u}}'\hat{\mathbf{u}}}\frac{n-k}{J} \quad \textbf{(10.3)}$$

which, under the null, is distributed as $F_{J,(n-k)}$.

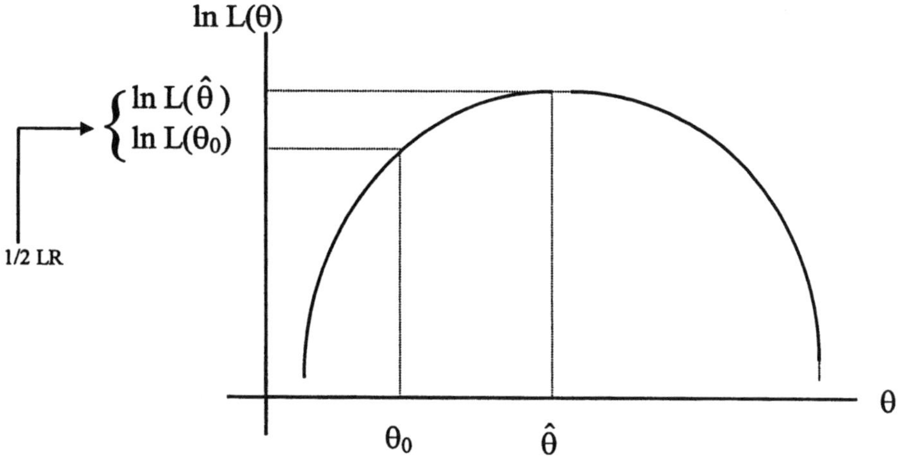

FIGURE 10.1
Illustration of the main features of the likelihood ratio test

In general, if $\hat{\boldsymbol{\theta}}$ is the unrestricted estimator of the population vector $\boldsymbol{\theta}$, and $\tilde{\boldsymbol{\theta}}$ is the restricted estimator based on J restrictions, then:

$$LR = 2\ln\left[\frac{L(\hat{\boldsymbol{\theta}})}{L(\tilde{\boldsymbol{\theta}})}\right] = 2\left[\ln L(\hat{\boldsymbol{\theta}}) - \ln L(\tilde{\boldsymbol{\theta}})\right]$$

and, under the null hypothesis (that the restrictions are true), LR is distributed asymptotically as χ^2_J, where J is the number of restrictions on the parameter space.

Consider the following simplified illustration of the LR principle taken from Buse (1982). Suppose that the vector $\boldsymbol{\theta}$ consists of only one element θ, so that the null hypothesis specifies that $\tilde{\theta} = \theta_0$, with the alternative being that $\tilde{\theta} \neq \theta_0$. Clearly, should the restriction hold true, the distance between ln L($\hat{\theta}$) and ln L(θ_0) would approach zero. Consider the plot of θ against its log likelihood ln L(θ) for a particular data set shown in Figure 10.1. Then the larger the distance between $\hat{\theta}$ and θ_0, the larger would be ½LR, and so the greater would be the evidence that the restriction does not hold true.

THE WALD TEST

This test is based on the extent to which the restrictions are violated when unrestricted rather than restricted estimators are used. The Wald statistic depends solely on the unrestricted maximum likelihood estimator. Let us use as our starting point the simplified illustration of the LR principle introduced above. Clearly, the distance ½LR depends not only on the value of $(\hat{\theta} - \theta_0)$, but also on the *curvature* of the function. Consider Figure 10.2. Here, both sets of data generate the same value of $(\hat{\theta} - \theta_0)$, but for case A, the greater curvature of the function yields a larger value of LR.

Let us denote the curvature of the log likelihood function as C ($\hat{\theta}$). Given C ($\hat{\theta}$), the larger the distance between $\hat{\theta}$ and θ_0, the further will ln L(θ_0) be from the maximum ln L ($\hat{\theta}$), and so the larger will be the distance ½LR. Conversely, for a given distance $(\hat{\theta} - \theta_0)$, the greater the curvature C ($\hat{\theta}$), the larger will be the distance ½LR.

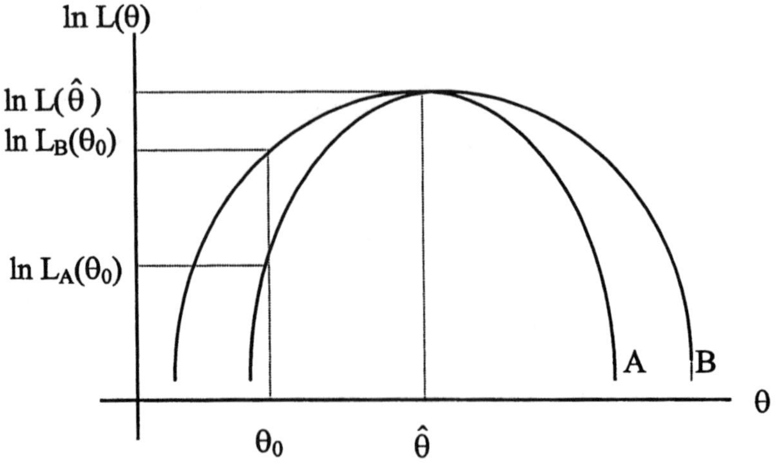

FIGURE 10.2
Illustration of the main features of the Wald test

It is these characteristics that provide the key to a diagrammatic derivation of the Wald test. Instead of considering the differences in log likelihoods as does the LR test, this test takes the intuitively appealing approach of working with the squared distance between $\hat{\theta}$ and θ_0. Large deviations of $\hat{\theta}$ from θ_0 are taken as evidence that the data do not confirm the null hypothesis. However, with our earlier observation of the curvature of the log likelihood function in mind, the squared distance $(\hat{\theta}-\theta_0)^2$ must be weighted by $C(\hat{\theta})$. A Wald statistic can now be defined, by:

$$W = \left(\hat{\theta}-\theta_0\right)^2 C\left(\hat{\theta}\right)$$

Under the null hypothesis, W is distributed as χ_1^2.

In the more general case where $\boldsymbol{\theta}$ is a vector of parameters and the restrictions on the parameter space are defined by $g(\boldsymbol{\theta}) = 0$, the Wald statistic is given by:

$$W = g'\left(\hat{\theta}\right)\left[\mathbf{G}\mathbf{I}^{-1}\left(\hat{\theta}\right)\mathbf{G}'\right]^{-1} g\left(\hat{\theta}\right)\Big]$$

where $\mathbf{I}$ is Fisher's information matrix and $\mathbf{G}$ a matrix defined by:

$$\mathbf{G} = \left[\frac{\partial g_i}{\partial \theta_q}\right], \text{where} \begin{cases} g_i = \text{the } i\text{th restriction} \\ \theta_q = \text{the } q\text{th coefficient} \end{cases}$$

$$\Rightarrow \mathbf{G} = \begin{bmatrix} \frac{\partial g_1}{\partial \theta_1} & \frac{\partial g_1}{\partial \theta_2} & \cdots & \cdots & \frac{\partial g_1}{\partial \theta_k} \\ & & \cdots & \cdots & \\ \frac{\partial g_2}{\partial \theta_1} & \frac{\partial g_2}{\partial \theta_2} & \cdots & \cdots & \frac{\partial g_2}{\partial \theta_k} \\ \vdots & \vdots & \ddots & & \vdots \\ \vdots & \vdots & & \ddots & \vdots \\ \frac{\partial g_J}{\partial \theta_1} & \frac{\partial g_J}{\partial \theta_2} & \cdots & \cdots & \frac{\partial g_J}{\partial \theta_k} \end{bmatrix}$$

Under the null hypothesis, W is distributed as χ^2_J.

In the case of the general linear regression model with the restrictions defined by equation (10.1), it is obvious that $g(\boldsymbol{\beta}) = \mathbf{R}\boldsymbol{\beta} - \mathbf{r}$ and $\mathbf{G} = \mathbf{R}$. In addition, it has already been shown that $I^{-1}(\hat{\boldsymbol{\beta}}) = \sigma^2(\mathbf{X'X})^{-1}$. The Wald statistic is therefore defined in this instance by:

$$W = \left(\mathbf{R}\hat{\boldsymbol{\beta}} - \mathbf{r}\right)' \left[\sigma^2 \mathbf{R}(\mathbf{X'X})^{-1}\mathbf{R}'\right]^{-1} \left(\mathbf{R}\hat{\boldsymbol{\beta}} - \mathbf{r}\right)$$

It is easily shown that this expression reduces to (do it as an exercise):

$$W = \frac{\hat{\mathbf{u}}_c'\hat{\mathbf{u}}_c - \hat{\mathbf{u}}'\hat{\mathbf{u}}}{\sigma^2}$$

which is identical to LR as defined in equation (10.2) above. Once again, since σ^2 is usually unknown, it must be estimated by s^2 and the following "F"-statistic can be used:

$$W* = \frac{\hat{\mathbf{u}}_c'\hat{\mathbf{u}}_c - \hat{\mathbf{u}}'\hat{\mathbf{u}}}{\hat{\mathbf{u}}'\hat{\mathbf{u}}} \frac{n-k}{J}$$

This is identical to equation (10.3) above.

THE LAGRANGE MULTIPLIER TEST

As with the Wald test, the LM test also involves the curvature of the log likelihood function, but the basic idea behind the test focuses on the characteristics of the log likelihood when the restrictions of the null hypothesis are imposed. If the null is true, then the restricted maximum likelihood estimates will be near the unrestricted estimates. Since the unrestricted estimator maximizes the log likelihood, it satisfies the equation $S(\hat{\boldsymbol{\theta}}) = 0$, where:

$$S(\boldsymbol{\theta}) = \frac{\partial \ln L}{\partial \boldsymbol{\theta}}$$

One can therefore obtain a measure of the failure of the restricted estimates to reach the maximum (which is evidence against the null hypothesis) by evaluating the extent of the departure of $S(\tilde{\boldsymbol{\theta}})$ from zero (with $\tilde{\boldsymbol{\theta}}$ representing the restricted estimates).

Once again, consider Buse's simplified one parameter case. The above discussion suggests $[S(\theta_0)]^2$ as a test statistic. However, again, the curvature of the function must be taken into account, as two data sets can generate the same slope, with one having θ_0 closer to the maximum of the log likelihood. Consider Figures 10.3 and 10.4. Here, data set A has a greater curvature at θ_0 and would therefore generate a *smaller* value of the test statistic $[S(\theta_0)]^2$, since θ_0 is nearer to the maximum point of curve A at which $S(\theta_0) = 0$.

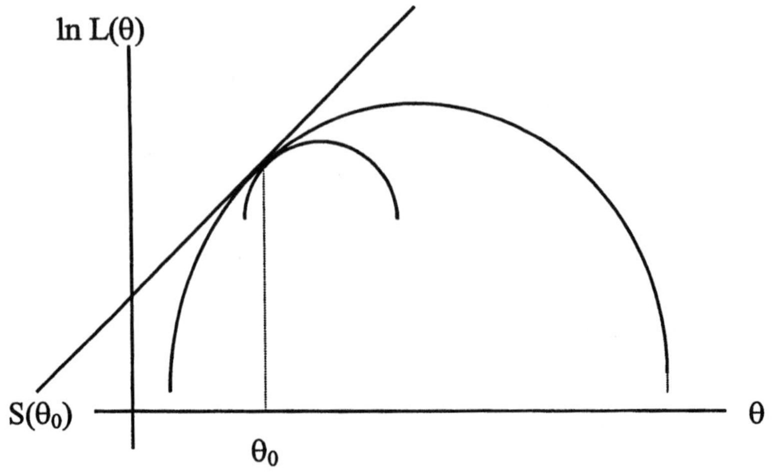

FIGURE 10.3
Illustration of the main features of the Lagrange multiplier test (I)

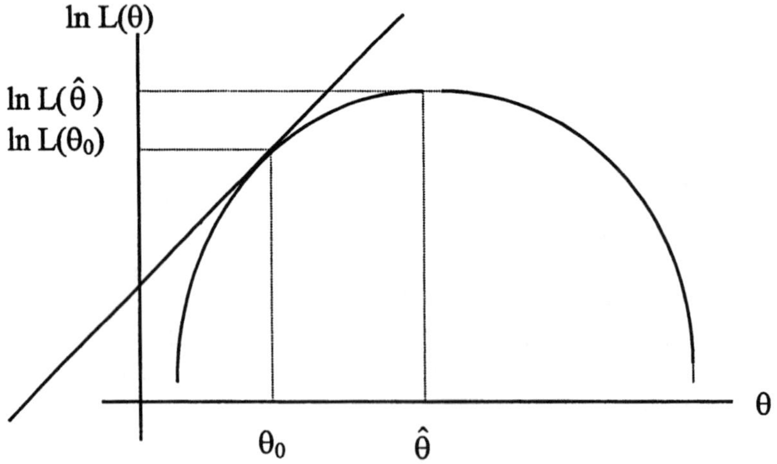

FIGURE 10.4
Illustration of the main features of the Lagrange multiplier test (II)

To get around this difficulty, we again weight by the curvature, this time in the neighbourhood of the restricted estimator. Here, however, the greater the curvature, the closer θ_0 will be to the maximum, and so the greater the likelihood of the non-rejection of the null hypothesis. This is opposed to the prior discussions, where a greater curvature meant a greater distance between the log likelihoods and so the greater the likelihood of the rejection of the null hypothesis. We therefore weight, not by the curvature $C(\theta_0)$, but rather by its inverse $C(\theta_0)^{-1}$, so that the greater the curvature, the smaller will be the value of the test statistic generated. Therefore:

$$LM = \left[S(\theta_0)\right]^2 C(\theta_0)^{-1}$$

LM is distributed under the null as χ_1^2. In the more general case where $\boldsymbol{\theta}$ is a vector of parameters, the LM statistic is defined as:

$$\text{LM} = \text{S}'(\tilde{\boldsymbol{\theta}})\text{I}^{-1}(\tilde{\boldsymbol{\theta}})\text{S}(\tilde{\boldsymbol{\theta}})$$

where $\tilde{\boldsymbol{\theta}}$ is the restricted estimator, I is Fisher's information matrix, and $\text{S}(\tilde{\boldsymbol{\theta}})$ the $k \times 1$ score matrix, defined by:

$$\text{S}(\tilde{\boldsymbol{\theta}}) = \frac{\partial \ln \text{L}(\tilde{\boldsymbol{\theta}})}{\partial \tilde{\boldsymbol{\theta}}}$$

Under the null, LM is distributed as χ_J^2. The LM test is generally not easy to compute, and we normally use a transformation of the formula proposed by Breusch and Pagan (1980).[2]

In the case of the general linear regression model with the restrictions defined by equation (10.1), it can be shown that this expression reduces to:

$$\text{LM} = \frac{\hat{\mathbf{u}}_c'\hat{\mathbf{u}}_c - \hat{\mathbf{u}}'\hat{\mathbf{u}}}{\sigma^2}$$

which is identical to LR and W as derived above. Once again, since σ^2 is usually unknown, it must be estimated by s^2 and the following "F"-statistic can be used:

$$\text{LM}* = \frac{\hat{\mathbf{u}}_c'\hat{\mathbf{u}}_c - \hat{\mathbf{u}}'\hat{\mathbf{u}}}{\hat{\mathbf{u}}'\hat{\mathbf{u}}} \frac{n-k}{J}$$

Illustration: Test of Parameter Redundancy

Consider the following model of import demand:

$$M_t = \alpha_0 + \alpha_1 M_{t-1} + \alpha_2 M_{t-2} + \beta_1 Y_{t-1} + \beta_2 Y_{t-2} + u_t$$

This is an example of an autoregressive distributed lag (ADL) model, which we met in chapter 5. Such models are widely employed in the famous Hendry general-to-specific framework. The general idea is to start with an ADL model like this one (perhaps with a more generous offering of lagged values) and to test for parameter redundancy or, put another way, for overparameterization of the model. Redundant variables (and, more particularly, their lagged values) are eliminated from the model as having no explanatory power. Consider, for instance, the OLS estimation of the ADL in Exhibit 10.1.

Suppose (for obvious reasons) we suspected that M_{t-2} and Y_{t-2} were redundant. We can test this hypothesis in the following formal framework:

[2] We will, in the next chapter, study an application of this transformation – the Breusch–Godfrey test for autocorrelation.

EXHIBIT 10.1
OLS estimation of
$M_t = \alpha_0 + \alpha_1 M_{t-1} + \alpha_2 M_{t-2} + \beta_1 Y_{t-1} + \beta_2 Y_{t-2} + u_t$

```
==============================================================
LS // Dependent Variable is IMPORTS
Sample(adjusted): 1969 1991
Included observations: 23 after adjusting endpoints
==============================================================
     Variable     Coefficient Std. Error  T-Statistic    Prob.
==============================================================
        C          -1897.372   1045.563   -1.814690     0.0863
   IMPORTS(-1)      0.480393   0.254800    1.885371     0.0756
   IMPORTS(-2)     -0.145141   0.221367   -0.655658     0.5203
    INCOME(-1)      0.262410   0.124466    2.108295     0.0493
    INCOME(-2)      0.009842   0.147158    0.066880     0.9474
==============================================================
R-squared               0.905288   Mean dependent var   3762.002
Adjusted R-squared      0.884241   S.D. dependent var   1416.092
S.E. of regression      481.8020   Akaike info criter   12.54473
Sum squared resid       4178397.   Schwarz criterion    12.79157
Log likelihood         -171.8999   F-statistic          43.01259
Durbin-Watson stat      1.942861   Prob(F-statistic)    0.000000
==============================================================
```

$$H_0: \alpha_2 = \beta_2 = 0$$
$$H_1: \text{Not } H_0$$

The null hypothesis is clearly a special case of the linear restrictions defined by equation (10.1) and can therefore be tested within the framework of either the LR, LM or Wald tests outlined in this chapter. Exhibit 10.2 shows the EViews output for the OLS output showing the statistics associated with the redundancy test.

The test results (on top) are accompanied by the OLS fit of the restricted model (below). In this particular case where values of the lagged endogenous variable appear among the regressors, less reliance should be placed on the use of the F-statistic, since its small sample properties are not known. The log likelihood ratio, of course, is asymptotically distributed as a $\chi^2(2)$ since there are two restrictions on the ADL model. The high p-value indicates that the null (the restriction is true) cannot be rejected. We should therefore prefer the model:

$$M_t = \alpha_0 + \alpha_1 M_{t-1} + \beta_1 Y_{t-1} + u_t$$

whose fit is shown in Exhibit 10.2. In the more general case of p restrictions, the log likelihood ratio would be asymptotically distributed as a $\chi^2(p)$.

Testing for redundant variables finds a natural application in general-to-specific modelling but it can be used in any modelling exercise where we believe that one or more of the variables might be irrelevant. Consider the import function:

EXHIBIT 10.2
Parameter redundancy test for model:
$M_t = \alpha_0 + \alpha_1 M_{t-1} + \alpha_2 M_{t-2} + \beta_1 Y_{t-1} + \beta_2 Y_{t-2} + u_t$
(H_0: $\alpha_2 = \beta_2 = 0$)

```
==============================================================
Redundant Variables: IMPORTS(-2) INCOME(-2)
==============================================================
F-statistic            0.271038    Probability          0.765645
Log likelihood ratio 0.682428      Probability          0.710907
==============================================================
Test Equation:
LS // Dependent Variable is IMPORTS
Date: 05/08/97   Time: 20:05
Sample: 1969 1991
Included observations: 23
==============================================================
     Variable      Coefficient Std. Error  T-Statistic   Prob.
==============================================================
        C           -1762.013   867.4629    -2.031225  0.0557
   IMPORTS(-1)       0.366307   0.189070     1.937413  0.0669
   INCOME(-1)        0.257808   0.090606     2.845365  0.0100
==============================================================
R-squared            0.902436   Mean dependent var    3762.002
Adjusted R-squared   0.892680   S.D. dependent var    1416.092
S.E. of regression   463.9090   Akaike info criter    12.40048
Sum squared resid    4304231.   Schwarz criterion     12.54859
Log likelihood      -172.2412   F-statistic           92.49681
Durbin-Watson stat   1.758086   Prob(F-statistic)     0.000000
==============================================================
```

$$M_t = \beta_0 + \beta_1 Y_t + \beta_2 p_{m,t-1} + \beta_3 p_{d,t-1} + u_t$$

Estimation of this equation by EViews yields the output shown in Exhibit 10.3.

In the output, I_PRICE = import prices (p_m) and D_PRICE = domestic prices (p_d). The clear insignificance of import prices and the insignificance of domestic prices at the 5% level might make us wonder if, together, both these variables are irrelevant. We can set up the competing hypotheses:

$$H_0: \beta_2 = \beta_3 = 0$$
$$H_1: \text{Not } H_0$$

The corresponding EViews output is shown in Exhibit 10.4.

In this case use of the F-statistic is permitted and indeed preferable, since its small sample properties are known, while the log likelihood ratio is only valid asymptotically (and the sample we are using is quite small). The null is rejected at 5% (but not at 1%) and we are likely to keep these two variables. On the basis of

EXHIBIT 10.3
OLS estimation of
$M_t = \beta_0 + \beta_1 Y_t + \beta_2 p_{m,t-1} + \beta_3 p_{d,t-1} + u_t$

```
==================================================================
LS // Dependent Variable is IMPORTS
Date: 05/09/97   Time: 05:04
Sample(adjusted): 1968 1991
Included observations: 24 after adjusting endpoints
==================================================================
     Variable      Coefficient Std. Error  T-Statistic   Prob.
==================================================================
           C         -3673.610   558.1258  -6.582047    0.0000
       INCOME         0.458708   0.048426   9.472370    0.0000
   I_PRICE(-1)       -1085.008   870.5124  -1.246401    0.2270
   D_PRICE(-1)        1456.099   747.2524   1.948604    0.0655
==================================================================
R-squared              0.911639  Mean dependent var   3655.325
Adjusted R-squared     0.898385  S.D. dependent var   1480.286
S.E. of regression     471.8723  Akaike info criter   12.46443
Sum squared resid      4453269.  Schwarz criterion    12.66077
Log likelihood        -179.6277  F-statistic          68.78158
Durbin-Watson stat     1.419186  Prob(F-statistic)    0.000000
==================================================================
```

the t-test (which of course is a special case of the parameter redundancy test) of the import price coefficient in the original model, we may wish to eliminate it from the estimated equation. Do this as an exercise.

Illustration: Testing Restrictions on Coefficient Values

Consider the model:

$$M_t = \beta_0 + \beta_1 Y_t + \beta_t + \beta_2 p_{m,t} + \beta_3 p_{d,t} + u_t$$

whose OLS estimation is shown in Exhibit 10.5.

Let us test the hypothesis:

$$H_0: \beta_2 + \beta_3 = 0$$

(which is a special case of the general restrictions defined by equation (10.1)) against the alternative:

$$H_1: \beta_2 + \beta_3 \neq 0$$

The corresponding EViews output is shown in Exhibit 10.6, where c(3) and c(4) refer, respectively, to the third and fourth coefficients appearing in the model (i.e. β_2 and β_3). You will notice that the two statistics shown in Exhibit 10.6 (appear to) yield more or

EXHIBIT 10.4
Parameter redundancy test for model:
$M_t = \beta_0 + \beta_1 Y_t + \beta_2 p_{m,t-1} + \beta_3 p_{d,t-1} + u_t$
(H_0: $\beta_2 = \beta_3 = 0$)

```
=================================================================
Redundant Variables: I_PRICE(-1) D_PRICE(-1)
=================================================================
F-statistic            3.717620    Probability           0.042385
Log likelihood ratio 7.586305    Probability           0.022524
=================================================================
Test Equation:
LS // Dependent Variable is IMPORTS
Date: 05/09/97   Time: 05:06
Sample: 1968 1991
Included observations: 24
=================================================================
     Variable      Coefficient Std. Error  T-Statistic   Prob.
=================================================================
         C          -3670.189   589.9229  -6.221471    0.0000
       INCOME        0.450058   0.035636   12.62946    0.0000
=================================================================
R-squared              0.878790    Mean dependent var   3655.325
Adjusted R-squared     0.873280    S.D. dependent var   1480.286
S.E. of regression     526.9477    Akaike info criter   12.61386
Sum squared resid      6108825.    Schwarz criterion    12.71203
Log likelihood        -183.4208    F-statistic          159.5032
Durbin-Watson stat     1.111290    Prob(F-statistic)    0.000000
=================================================================
```

less identical results and the obvious conclusion is that the null cannot be rejected (not by a long shot). However, from a purely theoretical perspective, it is preferable to use the F-statistic associated with this "Wald test", since in this case it is valid in small samples while the "Chi-square" statistic is asymptotically distributed as a $\chi^2(1)$. In other cases, like those where lagged endogenous variables appear among the explanatory variables, use of the Chi-square statistic is preferable.

In this illustration there is only one linear restriction. There may, however, be more than one restriction and, in this case, there may be as many as four (the number of coefficients in the model). Furthermore, the restrictions need not be linear. In the following chapter, we examine some special cases of application of the LR, Wald and LM tests.

CONCLUSION

The three tests discussed in this chapter differ in the information that they each require. The LR test requires knowledge of both the restricted and unrestricted estimates of the parameter, and is computationally the most demanding. The Wald test, in contrast, requires only the unrestricted parameter, and the LM test requires only the restricted parameter. Each is, however, a reasonable measure of the distance between H_0 and H_1,

EXHIBIT 10.5
OLS estimation of
$M_t = \beta_0 + \beta_1 Y_t + \beta_2 p_{m,t} + \beta_3 p_{d,t} + u_t$

```
=====================================================================
LS // Dependent Variable is IMPORTS
Date: 05/09/97   Time: 05:37
Sample: 1967 1991
Included observations: 25
=====================================================================
     Variable      Coefficient Std. Error  T-Statistic   Prob.
=====================================================================
        C           -3923.670   446.4954   -8.787706    0.0000
      INCOME         0.516727   0.042858    12.05666    0.0000
     I_PRICE        -2486.979   785.0966   -3.167736    0.0046
     D_PRICE         2470.723   638.5775    3.869104    0.0009
=====================================================================
R-squared             0.942161   Mean dependent var    3556.082
Adjusted R-squared    0.933898   S.D. dependent var    1531.723
S.E. of regression    393.8104   Akaike info criter    12.09739
Sum squared resid     3256820.   Schwarz criterion     12.29241
Log likelihood       -182.6908   F-statistic           114.0253
Durbin-Watson stat    2.135006   Prob(F-statistic)     0.000000
=====================================================================
```

EXHIBIT 10.6
Testing the restriction $\beta_2 + \beta_3 = 0$ in the model:
$M_t = \beta_0 + \beta_1 Y_t + \beta_2 p_{m,t} + \beta_3 p_{d,t} + u_t$

```
=======================================================
Wald Test:
Equation: Untitled
=======================================================
Null Hypothesis C(3) + C(4) = 0
=======================================================
F-statistic      0.004129     Probability      0.949374
Chi-square       0.004129     Probability      0.948766
=======================================================
```

and it is not surprising that when the log likelihood function is a smooth curve well approximated by a quadratic (as was the case in the illustrations we used), they all reduce to the same test. As the curvature of ln L departs from the quadratic shape, however, it is easily verified that the following inequality holds:

$$LM < LR < W$$

so that rejection of the null can be favoured by using the LM statistic, while non-rejection of the null can be favoured by using the W statistic.

EXERCISES

1. In the classical linear regression model, we wish to test the hypothesis $\mathbf{R\beta} = \mathbf{r}$ (H_0) against $\mathbf{R\beta} \neq \mathbf{r}$ (H_1). Discuss the use of the (a) likelihood ratio (b) Wald (c) Lagrange multiplier tests in this context. Show how these tests are related to the standard t- and F-tests of classical econometrics.
2. Using data provided in Appendix 1.2 of chapter 1
   a) Fit the model:

$$M_t = \beta_1 + \beta_2 Y_t + \beta_3 p_{mt} + \beta_4 p_{dt} + u_t$$

   Then use the Wald test to determine whether $\beta_3 = -\beta_4$ or not.
   b) Fit the model

$$C_t = \beta_1 + \beta_2 Y_t + \beta_3 C_{t-1} + \beta_4 C_{t-2} + \beta_5 Y_{t-1} + \beta_6 Y_{t-2} + u_t$$

   Then carry out the following tests:
   i) $\beta_3 = \beta_4 = \beta_5 = \beta_6 = 0$
   ii) $\beta_4 = \beta_5 = \beta_6 = 0$
   iii) $\beta_4 = \beta_5 = 0$
   c) Discuss the implications of the results obtained in (a) and (b).

CHAPTER 11

Specification (and Other) Tests of Model Authenticity

INTRODUCTION

All of the tests in this chapter are based on the Wald, Lagrange multiplier (LM) and likelihood ratio (LR) principles that were outlined in the preceding chapter. These principles establish the general framework within which we are able to test our model specification. Indeed, the application to our general linear regression model of the battery of tests that we outline is often within the spirit of the "general-to-specific" modelling approach that grew out of the London School of Economics, which we have alluded to. In the words of D.H. Hendry (1980), one of the best known proponents of this methodology, the three watchwords of the general-to-specific approach are "test, test and test".

RAMSEY'S RESET TEST FOR MISSPECIFICATION (DUE TO UNKNOWN OMITTED VARIABLES)

In chapter 3, we considered the effects of missing variables on OLS estimation of the general linear regression model. We saw that the effect of this kind of model misspecification was that the influence of the missing variable(s) was subsumed into the disturbance term, rendering OLS estimation both biased and inconsistent. It is therefore important that we try to avoid specification errors as much as possible.

Sometimes it is impossible or impractical to include all relevant variables, largely because of data limitations. As is so frequently the case with economic models, the theory may involve variables that are not directly measurable, or for which data are just not readily available, such as, for example, consumer tastes in a demand function, permanent income, or capital stock in a production function (see Griliches, 1985). In situations such as these, where the specification error cannot be avoided, the most the econometrician can do is to become aware of its presence and interpret his or her statistical results with caution.

Frequently, however, specification errors are committed because of ignorance about the true specification of the model. In such a case, we would like to be able to *test* whether we have misspecified the regression equation. Ramsey's RESET test (regression specification errors test) tests the hypothesis that no relevant explanatory variables have been omitted from the regression equation.

In the language of the previous chapter, let the true or *unrestricted* model be:

$$\mathbf{y} = \mathbf{X}_1\boldsymbol{\beta}_1 + \mathbf{X}_2\boldsymbol{\beta}_2 + \mathbf{u} \qquad \textbf{(11.1)}$$

where X_1 is a known (n × [k – J]) matrix and X_2 an unknown (n × J) matrix. Let the *restricted* model be:

$$\mathbf{y} = \mathbf{X}_1\boldsymbol{\beta}_1 + \mathbf{u} \qquad \textbf{(11.2)}$$

which is the model that is fitted by OLS. Clearly, the test for the misspecification of our fitted model would rest in the test of the significance of the nullity of the J β_2 coefficients in the unrestricted model. Our null and alternative hypotheses are therefore:

$$H_0{:}\boldsymbol{\beta}_2 = 0$$
$$H_a{:}\boldsymbol{\beta}_2 \neq 0$$

In the current context, however, the matrix $\mathbf{X}_2$ is unknown. Ramsey (1969) proposes that, since $\mathbf{X}_2$ is unknown, we *approximate* $\mathbf{X}_2\boldsymbol{\beta}_2$ by $\mathbf{Z}\boldsymbol{\theta}$, where $\mathbf{Z}$ is an n × J matrix of observable, nonstochastic test variables and $\boldsymbol{\theta}$ the corresponding set of J coefficients.

Equation (11.1) may now be rewritten as:

$$\mathbf{y} = \mathbf{X}_1\boldsymbol{\beta}_1 + \mathbf{Z}\boldsymbol{\theta} + \boldsymbol{\varepsilon} \qquad \textbf{(11.3)}$$

But what does the $\mathbf{Z}$ matrix look like? Ramsey's suggestion is to include in $\mathbf{Z}$ powers of the predicted values of the dependent variable (which are, of course, linear combinations of powers and cross-product terms of the explanatory variables). Specifically Ramsey suggests that $\mathbf{Z}$ should be powers of the vector of fitted $\mathbf{y}$ values from the regression of $\mathbf{y}$ on $\mathbf{X}_1$. One possibility, for instance, is $\mathbf{Z} = \hat{\mathbf{y}}^2$ which is the vector of squared fitted values of $\mathbf{y}$. Yet another possibility is $\mathbf{Z} = (\hat{\mathbf{y}}^2\ \hat{\mathbf{y}}^3)$ or yet again $\mathbf{Z} = (\hat{\mathbf{y}}^2\ \hat{\mathbf{y}}^3\ \hat{\mathbf{y}}^4)$ and so on. The first power is not included, since it is perfectly collinear with the $\mathbf{X}_1$ matrix. You need to specify the number of powers of the fitted values to be included in the test regression, beginning with the squared fitted value.

The above procedure is the one followed in EViews but it is not the only one possible. An alternative specification is suggested by Thursby and Schmidt (1977), who show experimentally that a useful approximation is obtained by $\mathbf{Z} = (\mathbf{X}_1^2\ \mathbf{X}_1^3\ \mathbf{X}_1^4)$. Here, $\mathbf{X}_1^p$ is the matrix of all the elements of $\mathbf{X}_1$ raised to the power p, and p is chosen so that $\boldsymbol{\varepsilon}$, is empirical white noise.

It can be shown that the OLS (maximum likelihood) estimator of $\boldsymbol{\theta}$ is:

$$\hat{\boldsymbol{\theta}} = (\mathbf{Z}'\mathbf{M}_1\mathbf{Z})^{-1}\mathbf{Z}'\mathbf{M}_1\mathbf{y}$$

where:

$$\mathbf{M}_1 = \mathbf{I} - \mathbf{X}_1(\mathbf{X}_1'\mathbf{X}_1)^{-1}\mathbf{X}_1'$$

EXHIBIT 11.1
OLS estimation of $M_t = \beta_1 + \beta_2 Y_t + u_t$

```
==============================================================
LS // Dependent Variable is IMPORTS
Date: 02/01/96   Time: 22:52
Sample: 1967 1991
Included observations: 25
==============================================================
     Variable      Coefficient Std. Error  T-Statistic   Prob.
==============================================================
        C           -3707.823   538.7572  -6.882178    0.0000
      INCOME         0.452149   0.032915   13.73681    0.0000
==============================================================
R-squared            0.891356   Mean dependent var    3556.082
Adjusted R-squared   0.886632   S.D. dependent var    1531.723
S.E. of regression   515.7336   Akaike info criter    12.56780
Sum squared resid    6117567.   Schwarz criterion     12.66531
Log likelihood      -190.5710   F-statistic           188.7000
Durbin-Watson stat   1.121388   Prob(F-statistic)     0.000000
==============================================================
```

It is easily shown that:

$$E(\hat{\boldsymbol{\theta}}) = (\mathbf{Z}'\mathbf{M}_1\mathbf{Z})^{-1}\mathbf{Z}'\mathbf{M}_1\mathbf{X}_2\boldsymbol{\beta}_2$$

which, under the null hypothesis, is equal to zero. This means that a test of significance of $\boldsymbol{\theta}$ would discriminate between the null and alternative hypotheses as we have defined them.

The mechanism for carrying out the RESET test is as follows. First, fit equation (11.2) (as if H_0 were true) and obtain the vector of OLS residuals $\hat{\mathbf{u}}$. Then fit equation (11.3) (with $\mathbf{Z}$ appropriately defined) and obtain the vector of OLS residuals $\hat{\boldsymbol{\varepsilon}}$. An F-statistic is constructed as:

$$F = \frac{(\hat{\boldsymbol{\varepsilon}}'\hat{\boldsymbol{\varepsilon}} - \hat{\mathbf{u}}'\hat{\mathbf{u}})/J}{\hat{\boldsymbol{\varepsilon}}'\hat{\boldsymbol{\varepsilon}}/[n-(k+J)]}$$

which, under the null, is distributed as $F_{J,\, n-(k+J)}$.

Illustration of the Ramsey RESET Test

Consider an import function of the form:

$$M_t = \beta_1 + \beta_2 Y_t + u_t$$

In the first step, OLS is applied to this model. The output from EViews when this is done is shown in Exhibit 11.1.

EXHIBIT 11.2
RESET test applied to $M_t = \beta_1 + \beta_2 Y_t + u_t$ using $Z = \hat{y}^2$

Ramsey RESET Test:

F-statistic	11.90623	Probability	0.002279
Log likelihood	10.81391	Probability	0.001007

Test Equation:
LS // Dependent Variable is IMPORTS
Date: 02/01/96 Time: 22:53
Sample: 1967 1991
Included observations: 25

Variable	Coefficient	Std. Error	T-Statistic	Prob.
C	-9209.192	1654.946	-5.564648	0.0000
INCOME	0.923315	0.139214	6.632363	0.0000
Fitted^2	-0.000141	4.09E-05	-3.450541	0.0023

R-squared	0.929506	Mean dependent var	3556.082
Adjusted R-squared	0.923098	S.D. dependent var	1531.723
S.E. of regression	424.7659	Akaike info criter	12.21524
Sum squared resid	3969373.	Schwarz criterion	12.36151
Log likelihood	-185.1640	F-statistic	145.0424
Durbin-Watson stat	1.469401	Prob(F-statistic)	0.000000

The output obtained from applying the test for $\mathbf{Z} = \hat{\mathbf{y}}^2$ and for $\mathbf{Z} = (\hat{\mathbf{y}}^2\ \hat{\mathbf{y}}^3\ \hat{\mathbf{y}}^4)$ is shown in Exhibit 11.2 and Exhibit 11.3, respectively.

The output is almost self-explanatory. What conclusions do you draw? If you conclude that the null hypothesis (the model is correctly specified) is convincingly rejected, you are correct. Do you have any other comments to make?

THE JARQUE–BERA TEST FOR NORMALITY

An important assumption underlying the use of OLS is that the error term of the model is normally distributed, with a mean of $\mathbf{0}$ and variance-covariance matrix $\sigma^2\mathbf{I}$. Jarque and Bera (1980) propose a procedure that tests for departures from normality. It is based on the simple idea that, if the assumption of normality is correct, then there will be no skewness or kurtosis in the distribution, since the normal distribution is fully characterized by its first- and second-order moments of mean and covariance (skewness and kurtosis are third- and fourth-order moments, respectively).

A measure of skewness is given by the formula:

EXHIBIT 11.3
RESET test applied to $M_t = \beta_1 + \beta_2 Y_t + u_t$ using $Z = (\hat{y}^2\ \hat{y}^3\ \hat{y}^4)$

```
=================================================================
Ramsey RESET Test:
=================================================================
F-statistic              6.574791    Probability           0.002849
Log likelihood           17.15582    Probability           0.000656
=================================================================
Test Equation:
LS // Dependent Variable is IMPORTS
Date: 02/01/96   Time: 23:02
Sample: 1967 1991
Included observations: 25
=================================================================
     Variable      Coefficient Std. Error  T-Statistic   Prob.
=================================================================
        C             10939.59    17168.57    0.637187     0.5312
      INCOME         -1.053945    1.736267   -0.607018     0.5507
     Fitted^2         0.001410    0.001722    0.818944     0.4225
     Fitted^3        -2.12E-07    3.21E-07   -0.662433     0.5153
     Fitted^4         9.42E-12    2.11E-11    0.446602     0.6600
=================================================================
R-squared                0.945301    Mean dependent var    3556.082
Adjusted R-squared       0.934361    S.D. dependent var    1531.723
S.E. of regression       392.4288    Akaike info criter    12.12157
Sum squared resid        3080007.    Schwarz criterion     12.36534
Log likelihood          -181.9930    F-statistic           86.40926
Durbin-Watson stat       1.844254    Prob(F-statistic)     0.000000
=================================================================
```

$$SK = \left[\frac{1}{n}\sum_{t=1}^{n} u_t^3\right] \Big/ \left[\frac{1}{n}\sum_{t=1}^{n} u_t^2\right]^{\frac{3}{2}}$$

It is centred on 0 and, when standardized by $\sqrt{n}$, has a variance of 6.

Kurtosis is measured by:

$$EK = \left[\frac{1}{n}\sum_{t=1}^{n} u_t^4\right] \Big/ \left[\frac{1}{n}\sum_{t=1}^{n} u_t^2\right]^{2} \qquad \textbf{(11.4)}$$

which, when standardized by $\sqrt{n}$, has a mean of 3 and a variance of 24.

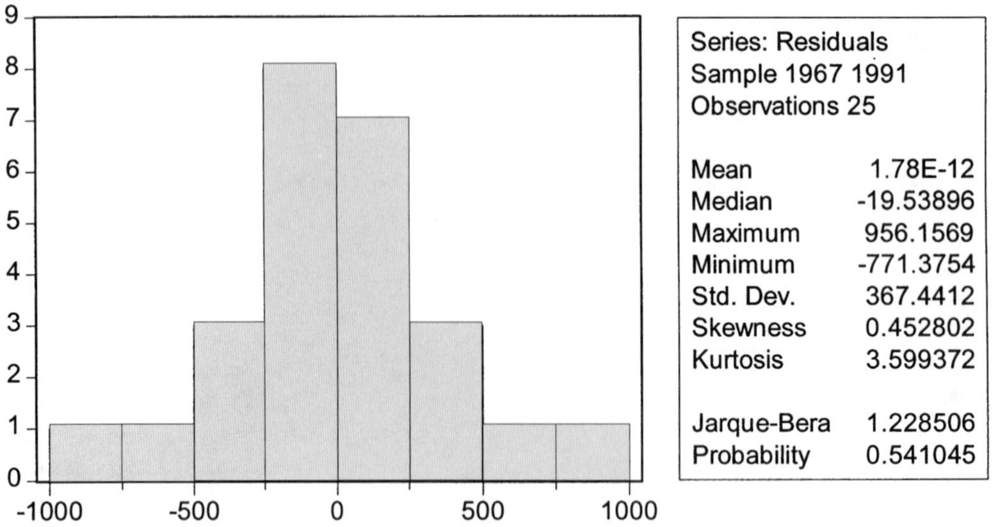

EXHIBIT 11.4
The Jarque–Bera test applied to $M_t = \beta_1 + \beta_2 Y_t + \beta_3 p_{mt}/p_{dt} + u_t$

Given those properties, it is possible to construct the Jarque–Bera test statistic, which is given by:

$$JB = \left[\frac{n}{6}SK^2 + \frac{n}{24}(EK-3)^2\right] \qquad \textbf{(11.5)}$$

Under the null hypothesis that the error term is normally distributed with moments as hypothesized:

$$JB \sim \chi_2^2$$

Illustration of the Jarque–Bera Test for Normality

Consider the import function:

$$M_t = \beta_1 + \beta_2 Y_t + \beta_3 p_{mt}/p_{dt} + u_t$$

which first appeared in chapter 1 and which was estimated by OLS there. The output obtained from the application in EViews of the Jarque–Bera test to these results is shown in Exhibit 11.4. A histogram of the residuals has the general shape of the normal distribution. The Jarque–Bera test leads to non-rejection of the null hypothesis.

THE LJUNG–BOX AND BOX–PIERCE TESTS FOR WHITE NOISE

The Ljung–Box (LB) test, due to Ljung and Box (1978), is an update of the Box–Pierce (BP) test, due to Box and Pierce (1970). The idea behind both tests is that, if the estimated model is indeed correctly specified, then the resulting residuals would be white noise. The BP and LB statistics therefore examine the regression residuals for the properties of white noise.

Let us define r_i as the *i*th-order autocorrelation of the residuals. It can be shown that asymptotically, under the null of no serial correlation of these residuals:

$$n^{1/2} r_i \sim NID(0,1)$$

The Box–Pierce statistic is defined as:

$$Q = n \sum_{i=1}^{m} r_i^2 \quad \textbf{(11.7)}$$

and is therefore asymptotically distributed as $\chi^2(m)$ under the null hypothesis.

It has been noted, however, that this Q-statistic has poor small sample properties, and a better small sample statistic is given by the related Ljung–Box statistic, defined as:

$$Q* = n(n+2) \sum_{i=1}^{m} (n-i)^{-1} r_i^2 \quad \textbf{(11.8)}$$

which is also asymptotically distributed as $\chi^2(m)$ under the null hypothesis of no serial correlation.

Illustration of the Ljung–Box Test

The output obtained from applying the Ljung–Box procedure to the import function shown above is presented in Exhibit 11.5. On the left appears a graph of the autocorrelations (or correlogram) which shows the plot of r_i against i for up to 12 lags, as well as the 95% confidence band for the r_i values. The second graph is of the partial autocorrelations (a concept we will study later on in this course). The Q*-statistic based on autocorrelations up to order 12 are displayed here under the column headed "Q-Stat" (the user may choose a shorter or longer series). The first column of numeric values shows the value of "m" on which the Q*-statistic is calculated. The second column (the one headed AC) shows the values of the autocorrelations r_i for i ranging from 1 to 12. The third column (which does not interest us here) shows the value of the partial autocorrelations.

The p-values associated with the Q*-statistic are shown in the last column. They seem, quite convincingly, not to lead to rejection of the null (although at lag 5 there seems to be a slight aberration from this general conclusion).

We have, up to this point, met only the AR(1) form of serial correlation. As we will very soon come to see, however, this is not the only form that exists. The autocorrelations and partial autocorrelations are an important tool in detecting both the presence and the form of serial correlation. What the Q- and Q*-statistics really allow us to do is to test the hypothesis that the first m autocorrelations are purely random.

EXHIBIT 11.5

Ljung–Box test applied to $M_t = \beta_1 + \beta_2 Y_t + \beta_3 p_{mt}/p_{dt} + u_t$

```
=========================================================================
Autocorrelation        Partial Correlation        AC      PAC    Q-Stat  Prob

   .  |* .    |           .  |* .    |    1    0.159    0.159   0.7086  0.400
   . **|  .   |           ***|  .    |    2   -0.302   -0.336   3.3843  0.184
   .  |  .    |           .  |* .    |    3    0.029    0.169   3.4101  0.333
   . *|  .    |           .**|  .    |    4   -0.100   -0.294   3.7311  0.444
   ***|  .    |           .**|  .    |    5   -0.406   -0.311   9.2910  0.098
   .  |  .    |           .  |  .    |    6   -0.033    0.009   9.3301  0.156
   .  |**.    |           .  |  .    |    7    0.205   -0.045   10.906  0.143
   .  |* .    |           .  |* .    |    8    0.118    0.140   11.456  0.177
   .  |* .    |           .  |  .    |    9    0.111    0.039   11.975  0.215
   .  |  .    |           . *|  .    |   10    0.011   -0.137   11.980  0.286
   . *|  .    |           .  |  .    |   11   -0.119   -0.028   12.658  0.316
   . *|  .    |           . *|  .    |   12   -0.108   -0.063   13.262  0.350
=========================================================================
```

THE WHITE TEST FOR HETEROSCEDASTICITY

In chapter 4, we considered tests for heteroscedasticity. Here we consider another, due to White (1980). The mechanism for applying the test is as follows: OLS (maximum likelihood) is first applied to:

$$\hat{u}_t^2 = \delta_0 + \delta_1 Z_{1t} + \ldots + \delta_p Z_{pt} + v_t$$

where the Zs are p fixed and known values. Asymptotically, under the null hypothesis of homoscedasticity:

$$nR_w^2 \sim \chi^2(p)$$

where R_w^2 is the classic coefficient of determination from the above regression.

How are the Zs determined? Consider the model:

$$y_t = \beta_0 + \beta_1 x_{1t} + \ldots + \beta_k x_{kt} + u_t$$

where there exist (k + 1) variables. Our "test" equation would be:

$$\hat{u}_t^2 = \delta_0 + \delta_1 x_{1t} + \ldots + \delta_k x_{kt} + \delta_{k+1} x_{1t}^2 + \delta_{k+2} x_{2t}^2 + \ldots + \delta_{2k-1} x_{kt}^2 + v_t$$

that is, the Zs include the explanatory variables from the initial model, as well as their values squared.

Illustration of the White Heteroscedasticity Test

The output obtained from applying the White heteroscedasticity test to the import function shown above is presented in Exhibit 11.6. The output shows that the squared

EXHIBIT 11.6
The White test applied to $M_t = \beta_1 + \beta_2 Y_t + \beta_3 p_{mt}/p_{dt} + u_t$

White Heteroscedasticity Test:

F-statistic	1.025257	Probability	0.418374
Obs*R-squared	4.253997	Probability	0.372721

Test Equation:
LS // Dependent Variable is RESID^2
Date: 02/03/96 Time: 17:58
Sample: 1967 1991
Included observations: 25

Variable	Coefficient	Std. Error	T-Statistic	Prob.
C	372804.5	2049836.	0.181870	0.8575
INCOME	-42.27877	254.5493	-0.166093	0.8698
INCOME^2	0.001553	0.007050	0.220351	0.8278
RATIO	169504.9	918819.5	0.184481	0.8555
RATIO^2	-75567.52	275712.1	-0.274081	0.7868

R-squared	0.170160	Mean dependent var	129630.1
Adjusted R-squared	0.004192	S.D. dependent var	213279.1
S.E. of regression	212831.6	Akaike info criter	24.71337
Sum squared resid	9.06E+11	Schwarz criterion	24.95714
Log likelihood	-339.3906	F-statistic	1.025257
Durbin-Watson stat	2.625591	Prob(F-statistic)	0.418374

residuals of the original fit (RESID^2) are regressed on "INCOME" and "RATIO" as well as on their squared values. The statistic of interest to us is shown in the line which starts "Obs*R-squared". The null of homoscedasticity cannot be rejected given the high p-value (0.372721).

THE BREUSCH–GODFREY TEST FOR SERIAL CORRELATION

This LM test is an alternative to the Durbin–Watson (DW) and Durbin tests, which we met in chapters 4 and 5, respectively. The test considered here is based on the work of Breusch (1978) and Godfrey (1978) and, theoretically, possesses some major advantages over the ones we have already encountered.

Recall that the alternative hypothesis in the DW test and the Durbin h-test is that u_t follows a *first-order autoregressive AR(1) scheme* defined as:

$$u_t = \rho u_{t-1} + \varepsilon_t$$

where ε_t is a white noise process. The null hypothesis is that u_t is white noise (equivalent to $\rho = 0$).

This is, however, a very restrictive form of autocorrelation. The error terms could, for example, follow an AR(2) process, defined as:

$$u_t = \phi_1 u_{t-1} + \phi_2 u_{t-2} + \varepsilon_t$$

In general, the error terms could follow an autoregressive process of any order p. Such an AR(p) process is defined as:

$$u_t = \phi_1 u_{t-1} + \phi_2 u_{t-2} + \ldots + \phi_p u_{t-p} + \varepsilon_t$$

The error terms are also not constrained to follow autoregressive processes. They may also follow a moving average (MA) process. A moving average process of order 1, or MA(1), is defined as:

$$u_t = \varepsilon_t + \theta \varepsilon_{t-1}$$

while an MA(2) is defined as:

$$u_t = \varepsilon_t + \theta_1 \varepsilon_{t-1} + \theta_2 \varepsilon_{t-2}$$

In general, an MA(q) is defined as:

$$u_t = \varepsilon_t + \theta_1 \varepsilon_{t-1} + \ldots + \theta_q \varepsilon_{t-q}$$

where ε_t is again a white noise process.

Unlike the DW and Durbin tests which can detect serial correlation of an AR(1) form only, the Breusch–Godfrey procedure tests for autocorrelation of an AR(p) or MA(q) form.[1] It also remains valid in the presence of lagged endogenous variables among the regressors.

The testing procedure is as follows. Run OLS on the general linear regression model and obtain the vector of OLS residuals $\hat{\mathbf{u}}$. Consider the matrix:

$$\underset{(n,p)}{\hat{\mathbf{u}}_p} = \begin{bmatrix} 0 & 0 & \cdots & \cdots & 0 \\ \hat{u}_1 & 0 & \cdots & \cdots & 0 \\ \hat{u}_2 & \hat{u}_1 & \ddots & & 0 \\ \vdots & \vdots & & \ddots & \vdots \\ \hat{u}_{n-1} & \hat{u}_{n-2} & \cdots & \cdots & \hat{u}_{n-p} \end{bmatrix}$$

The statistic:

$$l = \frac{\hat{\mathbf{u}}'\hat{\mathbf{u}}_p\left[\hat{\mathbf{u}}_p'\hat{\mathbf{u}}_p - \hat{\mathbf{u}}_p'\mathbf{X}(\mathbf{X}'\mathbf{X})^{-1}\mathbf{X}'\hat{\mathbf{u}}_p\right]\hat{\mathbf{u}}_p'\hat{\mathbf{u}}}{\hat{\sigma}^2}$$

[1] Note, however, that in practice, rejection of the presence of serial correlation of an AR(1) form implies the rejection of the presence of serial correlation of an AR form of any higher order.

is asymptotically distributed as $\chi^2(p)$ under the null hypothesis of the absence of serial correlation.

The fundamental limitation of this test is that, although it tests for serial correlation of both AR(p) and MA(q) forms, it cannot distinguish between them. Hence, if serial correlation is found by this testing procedure, the researcher will have some difficulty in correcting for it due to ignorance about its exact form. This is in direct contrast to the DW and Durbin tests, which detect serial correlation of the AR(1) variety. This is considered by some to be a marked advantage of the DW and Durbin tests over the Breusch–Godfrey test. The counterargument to this, however, is that the existence of serial correlation of *any* form is indicative of a misspecified model, on the grounds that the residuals of a correctly specified model would be a white noise process. As such, the onus is on the investigator to alter the content of the signal, rather than correcting the noise. Evidence as given by the Breusch–Godfrey test that the residuals are *not* white noise, therefore, is enough – the particular *form* of the complication becomes of very little importance.

Illustration of the Breusch–Godfrey Test for Serial Correlation

The output obtained from applying the Breusch–Godfrey test for serial correlation to the import function shown above is presented in Exhibit 11.7. The statistic of interest to us is shown in the line which starts "Obs*R-squared". The null of no serial correlation cannot be rejected except at levels of significance higher than 16%.

THE CHOW TEST FOR STRUCTURAL BREAKS

When observations are made on time series covering a relatively long period of time, it seems difficult to accept the notion of the *constancy* of the parameter vector over time as is required by the general linear regression model. To some extent, we have already alluded to this problem when dealing with dummy variables: we impose *structural shifts* in both slope and intercept terms over time. But strictly speaking, we should test for these changes. Chow (1960) proposes such a test.

A typical equation in the general linear regression model would look like:

$$y_t = \beta_1 x_{1t} + \beta_2 x_{2t} + \ldots + \beta_k x_{kt} + u_t \quad t = 1, 2, \ldots, n$$

In some respects, the implicit assumption of the parameter constancy over time being made here is a restriction imposed by us on the model. Suppose that at some point in time, say $t > n_1$, there occurs a once and for all shift in parameter values, or a *structural break*, so the model really ought to be defined for two distinct subperiods. For the first period, it might be:

$$y_t = \beta_1^1 x_{1t} + \beta_2^1 x_{2t} + \ldots + \beta_k^1 x_{kt} + u_t \quad t = 1, 2, \ldots n_1 \qquad \textbf{(11.9)}$$

while for the second it might be:

$$y_t = \beta_1^2 x_{1t} + \beta_2^2 x_{2t} + \ldots + \beta_k^2 x_{kt} + u_t \quad t = n_1 + 1, n_2 + 2, \ldots, n \qquad \textbf{(11.10)}$$

EXHIBIT 11.7

The Breusch–Godfrey test applied to $M_t = \beta_1 + \beta_2 Y_t + \beta_3 p_{mt}/p_{dt} + u_t$

Breusch-Godfrey Serial Correlation LM Test:

F-statistic	1.691986	Probability	0.209468
Obs*R-squared	3.617832	Probability	0.163832

Test Equation:
LS // Dependent Variable is RESID
Date: 09/29/02 Time: 13:30

Variable	Coefficient	Std. Error	T-Statistic	Prob.
C	-91.01137	678.2426	-0.134187	0.8946
INCOME	0.004822	0.029005	0.166239	0.8696
RATIO	11.98213	151.3081	0.079190	0.9377
RESID(-1)	0.205677	0.210360	0.977738	0.3399
RESID(-2)	-0.371147	0.222441	-1.668513	0.1108

R-squared	0.144713	Mean dependent var	7.37E-13
Adjusted R-squared	-0.026344	S.D. dependent var	367.4661
S.E. of regression	372.2749	Akaike info criter	12.01612
Sum squared resid	2771773.	Schwarz criterion	12.25990
Log likelihood	-180.6750	F-statistic	0.845993
Durbin-Watson stat	1.881817	Prob(F-statistic)	0.512595

Equations (11.9) and (11.10) may be rewritten in more compact form, respectively, as:

$$\mathbf{y}_1 = \mathbf{X}_1\boldsymbol{\beta}_1 + \mathbf{u}_1$$
$$\mathbf{y}_2 = \mathbf{X}_2\boldsymbol{\beta}_2 + \mathbf{u}_2$$

where $\mathbf{X}_1$ and $\mathbf{X}_2$ represent the same variables but different observations, as do $\mathbf{y}_1$ and $\mathbf{y}_2$. This system represents the unrestricted form of the model and, provided that $n_1 \geq k$ and $n_2 \geq k$, then we should really run two separate regressions to obtain:

$$\hat{\boldsymbol{\beta}}_1 = (\mathbf{X}_1'\mathbf{X}_1)^{-1}\mathbf{X}_1'\mathbf{y}_1$$
$$\hat{\boldsymbol{\beta}}_2 = (\mathbf{X}_2'\mathbf{X}_2)^{-1}\mathbf{X}_2'\mathbf{y}_2$$

Note that this unrestricted model could also be set up as follows:

$$\begin{bmatrix}\mathbf{y}_1\\ \mathbf{y}_2\end{bmatrix} = \begin{bmatrix}\mathbf{X}_1 & 0\\ 0 & \mathbf{X}_2\end{bmatrix}\begin{bmatrix}\boldsymbol{\beta}_1\\ \boldsymbol{\beta}_2\end{bmatrix} + \begin{bmatrix}\mathbf{u}_1\\ \mathbf{u}_2\end{bmatrix} \qquad \textbf{(11.11)}$$

or in a form similar to the general linear regression model of chapter 2:

$$\mathbf{y} = \mathbf{X}*\boldsymbol{\beta}* + \mathbf{u} \tag{11.12}$$

which is a model containing 2k coefficients. OLS/maximum likelihood estimation of this equation yields:

$$\hat{\boldsymbol{\beta}}* = \begin{bmatrix} \hat{\boldsymbol{\beta}}_1 \\ \hat{\boldsymbol{\beta}}_2 \end{bmatrix} = \left(\mathbf{X}*'\mathbf{X}*\right)^{-1}\mathbf{X}*'\mathbf{y}$$

$$= \begin{bmatrix} \mathbf{X}_1'\mathbf{X}_1 & 0 \\ 0 & \mathbf{X}_2'\mathbf{X}_2 \end{bmatrix}^{-1} \begin{bmatrix} \mathbf{X}_1' & 0 \\ 0 & \mathbf{X}_2' \end{bmatrix} \begin{bmatrix} \mathbf{y}_1 \\ \mathbf{y}_2 \end{bmatrix}$$

$$= \begin{bmatrix} \left(\mathbf{X}_1'\mathbf{X}_1\right)^{-1}\mathbf{X}_1'\mathbf{y}_1 \\ \left(\mathbf{X}_2'\mathbf{X}_2\right)^{-1}\mathbf{X}_2'\mathbf{y}_2 \end{bmatrix}$$

which is the very same result obtained from fitting the two subsystems separately.

The standard linear regression model introduced in chapter 1 is this time the restricted model or the null hypothesis. To account for the two distinct subperiods under consideration, however, it would have to be rewritten as follows:

$$\begin{bmatrix} \mathbf{y}_1 \\ \mathbf{y}_2 \end{bmatrix} = \begin{bmatrix} \mathbf{X}_1 \\ \mathbf{X}_2 \end{bmatrix} \boldsymbol{\beta} + \mathbf{u} \tag{11.13}$$

This is equivalent to equation (11.11) with the restriction that $\boldsymbol{\beta}_1 = \boldsymbol{\beta}_2$ (= $\boldsymbol{\beta}$) which is our null hypothesis. This hypothesis can be rewritten as $\boldsymbol{\beta}_1 - \boldsymbol{\beta}_2 = \mathbf{0}$ and defining:

$$\mathbf{R} = (\mathbf{I} - \mathbf{I})$$

it becomes, in the manner of equation (10.1) of the previous chapter, $\mathbf{R}\boldsymbol{\beta}* = \mathbf{r}$, where $\mathbf{r} = \mathbf{0}$. The alternative hypothesis, of course, is $\boldsymbol{\beta}_1 \neq \boldsymbol{\beta}_2$, or $\mathbf{R}\boldsymbol{\beta}* \neq \mathbf{r}$. An LR statistic identical in form to equation (10.2) can therefore be constructed which is distributed as χ^2_{n-k} under the null hypothesis. Defining $\hat{\mathbf{u}}_c$ as the OLS residuals of equation (11.13), the restricted model, and $\hat{\mathbf{u}}$ as the OLS residuals of equation (11.12), the restricted model, the F-statistic equivalent to equation (10.3) is:

$$F_{CHOW} = \frac{\hat{\mathbf{u}}_c'\hat{\mathbf{u}}_c - \hat{\mathbf{u}}'\hat{\mathbf{u}}}{\hat{\mathbf{u}}'\hat{\mathbf{u}}} \frac{n-2k}{k} \tag{11.14}$$

which is distributed as $F_{k,\, n-2k}$ under the null.

Illustration of the Chow Test for Structural Breaks

The researcher must decide at what point the hypothesized break takes place. In the case of the import function we have been using, it is hypothesized that it takes place in 1974 and the corresponding output is shown in Exhibit 11.8. The null hypothesis clearly cannot be rejected given the very high p-value.

EXHIBIT 11.8
The Chow test for structural breaks applied to $M_t = \beta_1 + \beta_2 Y_t + \beta_3 p_{mt}/p_{dt} + u_t$

```
==================================================================
Chow Breakpoint Test: 1974
==================================================================
F-statistic          0.040667     Probability           0.988711
Log likelihood       0.160016     Probability           0.983770
==================================================================
```

EXERCISES

1. Using data provided in Appendix 1.2 of chapter 1, fit the two models:

$$M_t = \beta_1 + \beta_2 Y_t + \beta_3 p_{mt} + \beta_4 p_{dt} + u_t$$

$$C_t = \beta_1 + \beta_2 Y_t + \beta_3 C_{t-1} + \beta_4 C_{t-2} + \beta_5 Y_{t-1} + \beta_6 Y_{t-2} + u_t$$

Then carry out the following tests:
a) The Chow test for structural breaks (use the year 1976 as the break point).
b) Ramsey's RESET test.
c) The Jarque–Bera test for normality.
d) The Ljung–Box test.
e) The White test for heteroscedasticity.
f) The Breusch–Godfrey test for serial correlation.

CHAPTER 12

Stationarity and Unit Roots

THE CONCEPT OF STATIONARITY

This chapter represents something of a turning point. It introduces some very important concepts which are at the heart of modern econometric theory and practice and which will be used extensively in the rest of this book. We begin by introducing the concept of stationarity. What does this mean? Look at the time plot of private consumption shown in Exhibit 12.1.

The private consumption variable is an example of nonstationary time series. As a matter of fact, most economic series are nonstationary. But what does this mean? What is there about this series that tells us that it is nonstationary? If you plot a typical economic time series against time, you will notice that it grows or declines in a fairly systematic manner. The notion of a mean in a context like this is quite meaningless, since the mean of the series is clearly changing with time. Most economic time series are nonstationary in the sense that they do not fluctuate around some fixed mean. We notice that private consumption increases in value for most of the period. There is then a continuous decline which seems to disappear towards the end of the period when values are increasing once again.

Now look at Exhibit 12.2, which is an example of a stationary time series. Notice how it fluctuates around a fixed mean, with a tendency to return quickly to this mean whenever there is movement away from it. The series in Exhibit 12.2 is the plot of the *first difference* in private consumption. For any variable x_t, the first difference is defined as:

$$\Delta x_t = x_t - x_{t-1}$$

This is another feature of many economic time series: a nonstationary series becomes a stationary series after *first differencing*. Such a series is said to be integrated of order 1 and written I(1). A stationary series is integrated of order 0 and written I(0). So here, C_{pt} is I(1) while ΔC_{pt} is I(0). Other series (as we shall see) require two differencings before stationarity is attained. They are said to be integrated of order 2 or I(2).

Let us become a bit more formal. Let us first of all consider a series z_t which is stationary or I(0). The strict definition of stationarity requires the probability density function associated with the series to be unaffected by displacement over time. Practically, however, this definition is unduly restrictive and, in most applied work, it is the concept of "weak" or "second-order" stationarity that is employed. This requires that the moments of first and second order (mean, variances and covariances) be independent of time, i.e.:

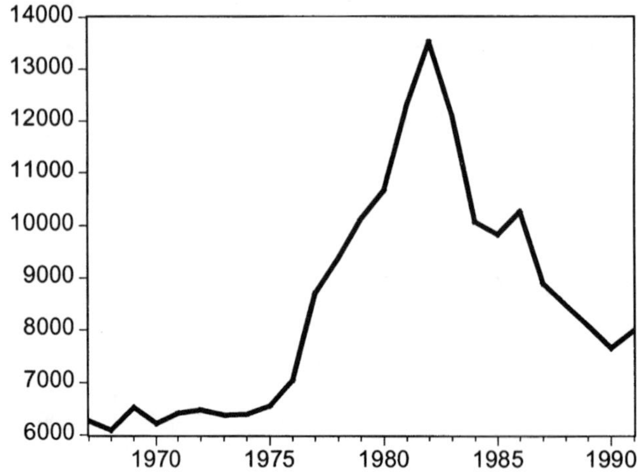

EXHIBIT 12.1
Time plot of private consumption, 1967–1991

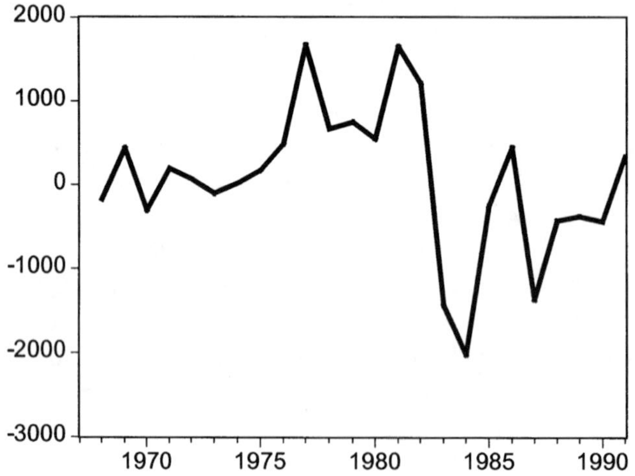

EXHIBIT 12.2
Time plot of a stationary time series

$$E(z_t) = \mu$$

$$var(z_t) = E(z_t - \mu)^2 = \gamma_0$$

$$covar(z_t, z_{t-k}) = E[(z_t - \mu)(z_{t-k} - \mu)] = \gamma_k, k = 1, 2, \ldots$$

γ_k is usually defined as the autocovariance function of order k. For many purposes, the autocorrelation function of order k defined by:

$$\rho_k = \frac{\gamma_k}{\gamma_0}, k = 1, 2, \ldots$$

is more useful than the autocovariance and it is this concept that will be more frequently employed in this text. Strict stationarity, of course, implies weak stationarity but the converse is not true, except in cases such as the normal distribution where the distribution is fully characterized by moments of first and second order.

Let us consider an example of a stationary series and look at some of its characteristics. Suppose z_t were an AR(1) process, which we met for the first time in chapter 4. It is defined by:

$$z_t = \phi z_{t-1} + \varepsilon_t, |\phi| < 1 \tag{12.1}$$

where ε is a white noise process. It is easily established that:

$$\mu = 0$$

$$\gamma_k = \phi^k \sigma_\varepsilon^2 \left(\frac{1}{1-\phi^2} \right), k = 0,1,2,\ldots$$

and:

$$\rho_k = \phi^k$$

This is clearly an example of a (weakly) stationary series, since the moments of first and second order do not depend on time. It is important to note, however, that the stationarity property depends crucially on the assumption that $|\phi| < 1$. In the case where $|\phi| \geq 1$, it can be shown that the moments of first and second order are not time independent and so the process is not stationary. Some intuitive justification for this is obtained if we expand equation (12.1) following the procedure in chapter 4, to yield:

$$z_t = \varepsilon_t + \phi \varepsilon_{t-1} + \phi^2 \varepsilon_{t-2} + \phi^3 \varepsilon_{t-3} + \ldots + \phi^s \varepsilon_{t-s} + \ldots = \sum_{i=0}^{\infty} \phi^i \varepsilon_{t-i}$$

This shows z as a moving average process of infinite order and, clearly, z would not converge unless $|\phi| < 1$. In fact it would explode in the case of $|\phi| > 1$.

Let us look at this illustration in a slightly different way. Define the "lag operator" L by:

$$Lz_t = z_{t-1}$$

It follows from this definition that $Lz_{t-1} = z_{t-2}$ and since $Lz_{t-1} = L(Lz_t)$, the convention is adopted to write $L^2 z_t = z_{t-2}$. By similar argument, we obtain:

$$L^k z_t = z_{t-k}$$

Making use of the lag operator L, equation (12.1) may be rewritten as:

$$z_t = \phi L z_t + \varepsilon_t$$

or as:

$$z_t - \phi L z_t = \varepsilon_t$$

or yet again as:

$$(1 - \phi L) z_t = \varepsilon_t \qquad \textbf{(12.2)}$$

It can be shown that the condition for stationarity of the series z_t is that the root of the equation:

$$(1 - \phi L) = 0 \qquad \textbf{(12.3)}$$

is greater than one or, as mathematicians sometimes prefer to say, that the root lies outside the unit circle. Solving equation (12.3) for L yields $L^* = 1/\phi$. For stationarity, L^* must lie outside the unit circle, which is the same as the requirement that $|\phi| < 1$. In the case where $|\phi| = 1$ the root of equation (12.3) is actually equal to one – hence the name "unit root", a term that is synonymous with "nonstationarity in the mean".

UNIT ROOTS: DEFINITION

In this section we propose to develop a more formal definition of unit roots while, in the following section, we concentrate on formal tests for unit roots.

Consider a stationary series, z_t, obtained by first differencing a nonstationary series x_t, i.e.:

$$z_t = \Delta x_t = x_t - x_{t-1}$$

The series x_t is said to contain one unit root. It is I(1) and z_t, which contains no unit roots, is I(0). Some justification may be given for use of the term. We may clearly rewrite z_t as:

$$z_t = x_t - L x_t = (1 - L) x_t$$

The root of the equation $(1 - L) = 0$ is clearly $L = 1$ (hence the term "unit root").

Suppose, now, that the stationary z was obtained, not after one, but two differencings, i.e.:

$$z_t = \Delta(\Delta x_t) = \Delta x_t - \Delta x_{t-1} = \Delta^2 x_t = (1 - L)^2 x_t$$

In this case, the equation $(1 - L)^2 = 0$ yields two roots, each one having the value of unity. In the most general case, a series may admit d unit roots where d is a positive integer. In this case:

$$z_t = \Delta^d x_t = (1 - L)^d x_t$$

However, in practice, d hardly ever exceeds 2.

LOOKING FOR UNIT ROOTS: AN INFORMAL APPROACH

We have already seen how inspection of a time plot may suggest that a series is nonstationary in the mean, in which case it admits at least one unit root. Inspection of the empirical correlograms is also another useful way to detect the presence of unit roots. Why is this so? Simply because the empirical autocorrelation function (ACF) of nonstationary series exhibits high positive values that decay at a very slow rate while that of stationary series either displays low values or values that decay (almost) exponentially. Look at Exhibits 12.3 and 12.4, which show, among other things, the estimated autocorrelations of C_{pt} (nonstationary series) and of ΔC_{pt} (stationary series).

Notice the slow decline of the ACF in Exhibit 12.3. It starts with the very high value of 0.898, then goes to 0.727, then 0.570 and so on. In Exhibit 12.4, on the other hand, the values of the ACF are very low. Moreover, they fluctuate between positive and negative values. This is a stationary process. The one unit root has been eliminated by first differencing.

FORMAL TESTING FOR UNIT ROOTS

The main emphasis of this section will be the Dickey–Fuller (DF) tests for the detection of unit roots. Other tests, such as the Phillips–Perron tests, will not be considered here. The DF tests are not very powerful and it is advisable to complement them by some of the informal procedures discussed in the previous section. Our discussion of the DF tests lays emphasis on the mechanisms of the tests rather than on formal justifications. The latter may be found in Fuller (1976) and Dickey and Fuller (1979, 1981). Very readable expositions can be found in Holden and Perman (1994), Holden and Thompson (1992) and Dickey, Bell and Miller (1986). What follows draws heavily on these works.

The DF tests involve the use of standard regression models and the use of t- and F-statistics derived from them. However, it is important to note up front that, because of the presence of nonstationary variables, the distributions of these statistics are nonstandard (i.e. they are *not* the Student and Fischer–Snedecor distributions) and are derived by simulation methods. Critical values of the t-statistics appear on page 373 of Fuller (1976) but these values have been criticized by MacKinnon (1991) on the grounds that they are based on too few simulations (10,000 at most) and he himself offers values based on more (at least 25,000). MacKinnon's values are preferable and are used in most standard econometric packages, including EViews. As for the F-statistics, critical values are given in Dickey and Fuller (1981). In this

EXHIBIT 12.3
ACF (and PACF) of C_{pt}

```
=================================================================
Autocorrelation   Partial Correlation  AC      PAC    Q-Stat  Prob

     .  |*******|       .  |*******| 1    0.898   0.898  22.680  0.000
     .  |******  |      ***|   .    | 2    0.727  -0.411  38.186  0.000
     .  |****    |       .  |*  .    | 3    0.570   0.111  48.151  0.000
     .  |***     |      ***|   .    | 4    0.395  -0.324  53.174  0.000
     .  |*  .    |      .  *|   .    | 5    0.191  -0.174  54.406  0.000
     .  |   .    |      .  *|   .    | 6   -0.016  -0.168  54.415  0.000
    .**|    .    |       .  |   .    | 7   -0.191  -0.031  55.789  0.000
    .**|    .    |       .  |   .    | 8   -0.314   0.050  59.698  0.000
    ***|    .    |       .  |   .    | 9   -0.391   0.002  66.132  0.000
    ***|    .    |       .  |   .    | 10  -0.437  -0.036  74.722  0.000
    ***|    .    |       .  |   .    | 11  -0.440   0.049  84.040  0.000
    ***|    .    |      .**|   .    | 12  -0.421  -0.200  93.249  0.000
=================================================================
```

EXHIBIT 12.4
ACF (and PACF) of ΔC_{pt}

```
=================================================================
Autocorrelation   Partial Correlation  AC      PAC    Q-Stat  Prob

     .  |***     |       .  |***     | 1    0.404   0.404  4.4341  0.035
     .  |   .    |      .**|   .    | 2   -0.031  -0.232  4.4611  0.107
     .  |*  .    |       .  |**.    | 3    0.075   0.232  4.6268  0.201
     .  |**.     |       .  |*  .    | 4    0.215   0.093  6.0746  0.194
     .  |   .    |      .  *|   .    | 5    0.048  -0.101  6.1499  0.292
    .**|    .    |      .**|   .    | 6   -0.245  -0.235  8.2260  0.222
    ***|    .    |      .**|   .    | 7   -0.347  -0.227  12.637  0.081
    .**|    .    |      .  *|   .    | 8   -0.238  -0.129  14.845  0.062
    .  *|   .    |       .  |   .    | 9   -0.122  -0.018  15.466  0.079
    .  *|   .    |       .  |   .    | 10  -0.120   0.024  16.105  0.097
    .  *|   .    |       .  |*  .    | 11  -0.107   0.074  16.655  0.118
    .  *|   .    |       .  |   .    | 12  -0.073  -0.040  16.932  0.152
=================================================================
```

book, we concentrate only on the use of the t-statistics while pointing out the serious limitations in so doing.

The DF tests are conducted within the context of three distinct types of generating processes of a series x:

$$x_t = \rho x_{t-1} + u_t \tag{12.7}$$

$$x_t = \alpha + \rho x_{t-1} + u_t \tag{12.8}$$

$$x_t = \alpha + \beta t + \rho x_{t-1} + u_t \tag{12.9}$$

The three processes defined above differ according to whether:

- The mean of the series is zero, as in equation (12.7)
- The mean is non-zero (we say that the process has a drift), as in equation (12.8)
- The mean is non-zero *and* a time trend is included, as in equation (12.9)

The competing hypotheses for the DF tests are:

$$H_0: \rho = 1$$
$$H_1: \rho < 1$$

Under the null hypothesis (when $\rho = 1$), the random variable x is said to be a random walk. This concept plays a very important role in the unit root and cointegration literature and we will meet it over and over again. The EViews package provides an automatic routine for carrying out this test when each of equations (12.7) to (12.9) is the estimated equation. But there is a major pitfall in using this routine: when equation (12.8) is the estimated equation, the test on ρ assumes that $\alpha = 0$ and when equation (12.9) is the estimated equation it is assumed that $\alpha = \beta = 0$. In other words, whatever the estimating equation, the underlying data generating process is assumed to be equation (12.7). Unless there is some very definite procedure for establishing the hypothesized values for α and β, the choice of any one of the test equations will be a matter of guesswork or, at best, based on some subjective procedure like the examination of time plots. We will return to this problem later in this chapter but, for the moment, let us ignore it.

OLS may be applied directly to any of these equations and the corresponding t-statistic calculated as:

$$T = \frac{\hat{\rho} - 1}{SE(\hat{\rho})}$$

This t-statistic is then compared to the critical values of the nonstandard distributions proposed by Dickey and Fuller and refined by MacKinnon. But it is usually more practical to modify the test equation as follows (using equation (12.7) as an illustration):

$$x_t - x_{t-1} = \rho x_{t-1} - x_{t-1} + u_t = (\rho - 1) x_{t-1} + u_t$$

or:

$$\Delta x_t = \phi x_{t-1} + u_t \qquad \textbf{(12.10)}$$

where $\phi = \rho - 1$ (similar transformations can be done for equations (12.8) and (12.9)). The null and alternative hypotheses now become:

$$H_0: \phi = 0$$
$$H_1: \phi < 0$$

The great convenience here is that the t-statistic is calculated directly by EViews and other econometric packages as:

$$T = \frac{\hat{\phi}}{SE(\hat{\phi})}$$

There is yet another problem associated with testing the stated hypothesis on the basis of equations (12.7) to (12.9): the DF tests require that the u_t be a white noise (non-serially correlated) process. However, a simple modification of the testing procedure in the case where u_t is a stationary process (but not white noise) has been proposed. Using equation (12.7) as the starting point (equation (12.8) or (12.9) can be similarly modified), the following test equation is derived:

$$\Delta x_t = \phi x_{t-1} + \delta_1 \Delta x_{t-1} + \delta_2 \Delta x_{t-2} + \ldots + \delta_r \Delta x_{t-r} + \upsilon_t \quad \textbf{(12.11)}$$

where r is chosen so that υ is empirical white noise. The test statistic, as well as the critical values of the test, remains as before. When used like this, the test is called the *augmented Dickey–Fuller (ADF) test.* Of course, in practice the DF test is a special case of the ADF test with r = 0.

Once again, there is a problem in using the "canned" EViews procedure since we are asked to give a value for r without knowing whether or not the resulting "error" is white noise. A widely used alternative is to choose the value of r that minimizes the *Akaike information criterion* (AIC) or the *Schwarz Bayesian criterion* (SBC) defined by:

$$AIC = n^* \log(\text{residual sum of squares of equation } (12.11)) + 2k$$

$$SBC = n^* \log(\text{residual sum of squares of equation } (12.11)) + k \log n^*$$

where k is the number of parameters estimated and n* is the number of usable observations (usually not equal to the sample size). The value of n* must be the same for all models being compared. The models must therefore have been estimated over the same sample period. Ideally, both AIC and SBC must be as small as possible (note that they can take on negative values). This is *not* an ideal procedure but it is very simple to apply in practice.

We wish to apply the DF testing procedure to the imports variable, M_t. We use equation (12.9), which incorporates both the drift and trend terms and fit the test equation (12.11) for r = 4, 3, 2, 1 and 0. The lowest AIC and SBC values were obtained for r = 0. Exhibit 12.5 illustrates the output from applying the relevant EViews procedure to the Imports variable for the full sample period.

The ADF test statistic is calculated as –0.909. The MacKinnon critical values are also clearly shown. The conclusion is obvious: the null hypothesis (that the series admits a unit root) cannot be rejected at conventional levels. Even at the 10% significance level, the critical value is –3.2418 and the test statistic is a much larger value than this. We conclude therefore that there is one unit root.

EXHIBIT 12.5
The EViews unit root procedure applied to M_t
(Test equation: $\Delta M_t = \alpha + \beta t + \phi M_{t-1} + u_t$)

```
==============================================================
ADF Test Statistic   -0.909557     1%  Critical Value*    -4.3942
                                   5%  Critical Value     -3.6118
                                   10% Critical Value     -3.2418
*MacKinnon critical values for rejection of hypothesis of a
unit root.

Augmented Dickey-Fuller Test Equation
Dependent Variable: D(IMPORTS)
Method: Least Squares
Date: 04/14/01   Time: 17:37
Sample(adjusted): 1968 1991
Included observations: 24 after adjusting endpoints
==============================================================
     Variable      Coefficient Std. Error  T-Statistic   Prob.
==============================================================
      IMPORTS(-1)    -0.102847   0.113074  -0.909557    0.3734
        C             516.6543   279.3921   1.849209    0.0786
      @TREND(1967)   -2.482169   24.95005  -0.099486    0.9217
==============================================================
R-squared              0.101386   Mean dependent var    122.2604
Adjusted R-squared     0.015803   S.D. dependent var    547.3778
S.E. of regression     543.0354   Akaike info criter    15.54869
Sum squared resid      6192636.   Schwarz criterion     15.69595
Log likelihood        -183.5843   F-statistic           1.184657
Durbin-Watson stat     1.892172   Prob(F-statistic)     0.325477
==============================================================
```

The test equation is also shown. If we examine the test equation, we see that $\hat{\phi}$ is calculated as –0.1028 and the corresponding t-statistic as –0.9095 (which we know already). It is interesting to note the p-value corresponding to this t-statistic. Its value is 0.3734 *but* that result is based on the standard distribution, which is not applicable here.[1] The AIC and SBC values are also clearly seen.

The canned procedure in EViews is very convenient but it is also intellectually unsatisfactory. First, there is the matter of the verification of the values of α and β, and then there is the question as to whether or not the error term in the estimated test equations is white noise. A more rigorous approach involving seven steps has been outlined in Holden and Perman (1994) which helps answer these questions more satisfactorily and which makes extensive use of the "F"-statistics defined in Dickey and Fuller (1981). However, this approach can become quite cumbersome in practice, especially in systems involving several variables.

The foregoing procedure is valid when we suspect that there is only one unit root. It is helpful because the vast majority of economic time series admit exactly one unit root. Many, however, do contain two unit roots. We must therefore have a

[1] The p-value of 0.3734 is also based on a two-tailed test. The one-tailed test equivalent is half this value.

EXHIBIT 12.6
Dickey–Pantula test for two unit roots in M_t
(Test equation: $\Delta^2 M_t = \alpha + \delta_1 \Delta M_{t-1} + u_t$)

```
==============================================================
ADF Test Statistic  -4.312325    1%  Critical Value*   -3.7497
                                 5%  Critical Value    -2.9969
                                 10% Critical Value    -2.6381
*MacKinnon critical values for rejection of hypothesis of a
unit root.

Augmented Dickey-Fuller Test Equation
Dependent Variable: D(IMPORTS,2)
Method: Least Squares
Date: 04/14/01   Time: 18:05
Sample(adjusted): 1969 1991
Included observations: 23 after adjusting endpoints
==============================================================
     Variable      Coefficient Std. Error  T-Statistic   Prob.
==============================================================
   D(IMPORTS(-1))    -0.947533   0.219727  -4.312325    0.0003
         C            120.7451   121.5180   0.993640    0.3317
==============================================================
R-squared             0.469645   Mean dependent var   18.98217
Adjusted R-squared    0.444390   S.D. dependent var   766.9594
S.E. of regression    571.6856   Akaike info criter   15.61800
Sum squared resid     6863314.   Schwarz criterion    15.71674
Log likelihood       -177.6070   F-statistic          18.59614
Durbin-Watson stat    1.971379   Prob(F-statistic)    0.000308
==============================================================
```

satisfactory procedure for determining whether there are two unit roots, or even more. Since in most practical situations we will never encounter cases involving more than two unit roots, we will limit our discussion to the case of two roots.

Dickey and Pantula (1987) propose that, if two unit roots are suspected, we should use the equation:

$$\Delta^2 x_t = \alpha + \delta_1 \Delta x_{t-1} + \upsilon_t \quad \textbf{(12.12)}$$

and use the corresponding t-statistics to determine whether or not δ_1 is significant. If the null that $\delta_1 = 0$ cannot be rejected, then we will conclude that the process admits two unit roots. If the null is rejected, then we have to determine whether there is one unit root by employing the test equation:

$$\Delta^2 x_t = \alpha + \delta_1 \Delta x_{t-1} + \delta_2 x_{t-1} + \upsilon_t \quad \textbf{(12.13)}$$

The null hypothesis of one unit root is rejected if both δ_1 and δ_2 are statistically different from zero. If x_t is stationary (the alternative hypothesis), then both coefficients are

EXHIBIT 12.7
Dickey–Pantula test for one unit root in M_t
(Test equation: $\Delta^2 M_t = \alpha + \delta_1 \Delta M_{t-1} + \delta_2 M_{t-1} + u_t$)

```
==============================================================
Dependent Variable: D(IMPORTS,2)
Method: Least Squares
Date: 09/27/01   Time: 10:49
Sample(adjusted): 1969 1991
Included observations: 23 after adjusting endpoints
==============================================================
     Variable      Coefficient Std. Error  T-Statistic   Prob.
==============================================================
        C            590.9878   304.3153    1.942025    0.0664
  D(IMPORTS(-1))    -0.938185   0.210954   -4.447339    0.0002
    IMPORTS(-1)     -0.129619   0.077478   -1.672982    0.1099
==============================================================
R-squared             0.534753  Mean dependent var    18.98217
Adjusted R-squared    0.488229  S.D. dependent var    766.9594
S.E. of regression    548.6688  Akaike info criter    15.57397
Sum squared resid     6020749.  Schwarz criterion     15.72208
Log likelihood       -176.1007  F-statistic           11.49398
Durbin-Watson stat    1.994713  Prob(F-statistic)     0.000475
==============================================================
```

significantly negative. We may therefore use the corresponding t-statistics to test the nullity of the coefficients, δ_1 and δ_2.

Let us test to see whether M_t admits two unit roots using the Dickey–Pantula procedure. Based on equation (12.12), we must use the following test equation:

$$\Delta^2 M_t = \alpha + \delta_1 \Delta M_{t-1} + u_t$$

You will notice that this very same equation would be used if we were looking for one unit root in ΔM_t. Exhibit 12.6 illustrates the output from applying the relevant EViews procedure to ΔM_t.

Now, the ADF test statistic of –4.312 leads to outright rejection of the null. The conclusion? M_t does *not* have two unit roots. The next step is to determine whether it has one unit root (or none at all). The test equation is:

$$\Delta^2 M_t = \alpha + \delta_1 \Delta M_{t-1} + \delta_2 M_{t-1} + u_t$$

This time, we cannot use the canned EViews routine. Instead, we must use the standard routines for OLS, with which we are very familiar by now. These results are shown in Exhibit 12.7.

The t-statistic for δ_1 is –4.48, which is significant, but for δ_2 it is –1.67, which is not significant (the critical values used are shown in Exhibit 12.6). We conclude that the null hypothesis (of one unit root) cannot be rejected.

EXHIBIT 12.8
Dickey–Pantula test for two unit roots in p_{dt}
(Test equation: $\Delta^2 p_{dt} = \alpha + \delta_1 \Delta p_{dt-1} + u_t$)

```
    Augmented Dickey-Fuller Unit Root Test on D(D_PRICE)
=============================================================
ADF Test Statistic -1.872680    1%   Critical Value*    -3.7497
                                5%   Critical Value     -2.9969
                                10%  Critical Value     -2.6381
=============================================================
*MacKinnon critical values for rejection of hypothesis of a
unit root.
```

For completeness, we close this chapter with an illustration of the determination of an I(2) variable: it is the domestic price variable (p_d) which, in the EViews output of Exhibit 12.8, appears as D_PRICE. Once again, the desired output from EViews may be obtained by applying the canned procedure to Δp_{dt}. We have not reported the output associated with the corresponding test equation. The null hypothesis cannot be rejected: this means that p_d admits two unit roots.

EXERCISES

1. Explain the following:
   a) Strict stationarity
   b) Second-order (covariance) stationarity
   c) A series is integrated of order d.
2. Examine the time series plots and ACFs of the series M, Y, p_m and p_d which appear in Appendix 1.2 of chapter 1. Comment on the stationarity of these series. Do the same for the first and second differences of these series.
3. Conduct appropriate tests on the series M, Y, p_m and p_d and determine the number of unit roots found in each case.

CHAPTER 13

An Introduction to ARIMA Modelling

INTRODUCTION

A major reason behind the construction and estimation of econometric models is forecasting. As economists, we know the importance of forecasting to the process of rational decision making. We may consider a forecast to be a prediction of the future value of one or more economic variables. It is in fact an *estimation* of that value. The first thing to understand is that such forecasts need not be determined by analytical methods. The small businessman who knows his firm and market well may be able to correctly interpret relevant signals and so make reasonably good forecasts. As economic activity becomes increasingly intricate and complex, however, such educated guesses may become more and more difficult to make. It becomes necessary, then, to formalize the problem by means of a model and so take into account some of the more pertinent features of the problem at hand.

In the early days of the discipline, the *structural econometric models* considered so far in this book had very limited success in forecasting the future values of variables. There may be some very good reasons for this. In the first place, economic theory may give very little indication about the form of this causal structure, in particular the short-run dynamics. Second, data on some of the variables may not be available, either because they are imprecisely defined or it is simply not possible to measure them. Even if we overcome these problems, there remains the third problem that, in such models, the variables whose future values are of interest to us are specified as some function of various (unknown) explanatory variables. Having estimated the unknown parameters, it is necessary to obtain predicted values of the unknown explanatory variables before a forecast of the dependent variable can be made. This, as we know from our study of earlier chapters, is easier said than done. Nevertheless, these problems do not negate our need for knowledge of the future direction of the variable of interest.

Economists and others looked towards other kinds of models and in particular to *time-series models*. It has long occurred to decision makers that a study of the present and past behaviour of a variable should give an indication as to how it will behave in the future. This is the basis of time-series models, such as ARIMA models, which are the subject of this chapter, and vector autoregression (VAR) models, which will be considered in the next chapter.

ARIMA MODELS

Autoregressive Processes of Order p AR(p)

We met this process in chapter 11. In chapter 12, we studied the AR(1) process in some detail. This process is defined by:

$$z_t = \phi z_{t-1} + \varepsilon_t$$

Stationarity required that the root of the polynomial equation:

$$(1 - \phi L) = 0$$

lie outside the unit circle. This is equivalent to the requirement that $|\phi| < 1$. The special case of the AR(1) where $\phi = 1$ is known in the literature as a "random walk". This plays a very important role in the unit root and cointegration analysis.

The AR(1) process is but one way to model a time series. Let us generalize the model. Consider a stationary time series z_t which may or may not have been derived after one or more differencings of some nonstationary series x_t. The series z_t is a *p*th-order autoregressive process, or AR(p), if it can be written as:

$$z_t = \phi_1 z_{t-1} + \phi_2 z_{t-2} + \ldots + \phi_p z_{t-p} + \varepsilon_t \quad \textbf{(13.1)}$$

The current observation of z_t is postulated to be generated by a weighted average of past observations going back p periods, together with a random disturbance in the current period. Using the lag operator, this can be written as:

$$\left(1 - \phi_1 L - \phi_2 L^2 - \ldots - \phi_p L^p\right) z_t = \varepsilon_t$$

It can be shown that the condition for stationarity is that all p roots of the polynomial equation:

$$\phi(L) = 1 - \phi_1 L - \phi_2 L^2 - \ldots - \phi_p L^p = 0$$

lie outside the unit circle.

We saw that, if z_t is an AR(1) process, then:

$$\rho_k = \phi^k$$

This property tells us that, for an autoregressive process of order 1, the autocorrelation function never vanishes, i.e. its value never actually becomes zero although it may get quite close to this limiting value. This property (nonvanishing autocorrelations) of the AR(1) process extends to autoregressive processes of all orders and it can be used to help us identify an autoregressive process by an inspection of the autocorrelation function (ACF) or correlogram. We will return to this point below.

Moving Average Processes of Order q MA(q)

We remember from chapter 11 that a moving average process of order q is written as:

$$z_t = \varepsilon_t - \theta_1 \varepsilon_{t-1} - \theta_2 \varepsilon_{t-2} - \ldots - \theta_q \varepsilon_{t-q} \qquad \textbf{(13.2)}$$

which suggests that each observation z_t is generated by a weighted average of random disturbances going back q periods.

Using the lag operator, this process may be written as:

$$z_t = \left(1 - \theta_1 L - \theta_2 L^2 - \ldots - \theta_q L^q\right)\varepsilon_t$$

Because an MA(q) process is, by definition, an average of q stationary white noise terms, it follows that every moving average process is stationary.

Let us now, for illustrative purposes, consider a moving average process of order 1, defined as:

$$z_t = \varepsilon_t - \theta \varepsilon_{t-1}$$

We wish to determine its autocorrelation of order 1, ρ_1. The autocovariance of order 1, γ_1, is calculated as:

$$\begin{aligned}
\gamma_1 &= E\left(z_t z_{t-1}\right) \\
&= E\left[\left(\varepsilon_t - \theta \varepsilon_{t-1}\right)\left(\varepsilon_{t-1} - \theta \varepsilon_{t-2}\right)\right] \\
&= E\left(\varepsilon_t \varepsilon_{t-1}\right) - \theta E\left(\varepsilon_t \varepsilon_{t-2}\right) - \theta E\left(\varepsilon_{t-1}^2\right) + \theta^2 E\left(\varepsilon_{t-1} \varepsilon_{t-2}\right) \\
&= -\theta \sigma_\varepsilon^2
\end{aligned}$$

and the variance, γ_0, is calculated as:

$$\begin{aligned}
\gamma_0 &= E\left(z_t^2\right) \\
&= E\left(\varepsilon_t - \theta \varepsilon_{t-1}\right)^2 \\
&= E\left(\varepsilon_t^2 - 2\theta \varepsilon_t \varepsilon_{t-1} + \theta^2 \varepsilon_{t-1}^2\right) \\
&= \left(1 + \theta^2\right)\sigma_\varepsilon^2
\end{aligned}$$

Therefore:

$$\rho_1 = \frac{\gamma_1}{\gamma_0} = -\frac{\theta}{1 + \theta^2}$$

We may similarly calculate the autocorrelation of order 2:

$$\begin{aligned}\gamma_2 &= E(z_t z_{t-2}) \\ &= E[(\varepsilon_t - \theta\varepsilon_{t-1})(\varepsilon_{t-2} - \theta\varepsilon_{t-3})] \\ &= 0\end{aligned}$$

It follows that:

$$\rho_2 = \frac{\gamma_2}{\gamma_0} = 0$$

It is easily established that, for the MA(1) process:

$$\rho_k = 0, k > 1$$

In fact, it is also easily established that, for the general MA(q) process:

$$\begin{aligned}\rho_k &\neq 0, k \leq q \\ \rho_k &= 0, k > q\end{aligned}$$

It is important to summarize what has been established so far. The ACF of an autoregressive process never vanishes: it never takes the value zero. This is true for all AR(p) processes. On the other hand, the ACF of order 1 of an MA(1) is non-zero while ACFs of higher order are zero. More generally, ACFs of order 1, 2, …, q of an MA(q) process are non-zero while ACFs of higher order vanish. This important result helps us to distinguish pure autoregressive processes from pure moving average processes. If it is a moving average process, the ACF will also tell us the order of that process.

This is a very important result, but it is of limited use for, although the correlogram can indicate the order of a moving average process, it is unable to guide us as to the *order* of an autoregressive process. Furthermore, a time series with mixed properties cannot be correctly modelled on the basis of the correlogram alone. More than this, we may actually be misled into modelling the time series as a pure autoregressive or moving average process if the correlogram exhibits one of the above properties. For these reasons, it is usual to consider the ACF function and the corresponding correlogram in conjunction with the partial autocorrelation function (PACF). We will return to this in a while.

Autoregressive Moving Average Processes of Order p, q ARMA(p, q)

Our previous encounters have been with time series that were, or at least were assumed to be, purely autoregressive or moving average processes. It is frequently the case, however, that a time series has qualities of both types of processes. Clearly, the more appropriate thing to do here would be to model the time series as a *combination* of both autoregressive and moving average components, rather than purely one or the other. Hence, the logical extension of the above two models is the ARMA process. The ARMA(1, 1) process is defined as:

$$z_t - \phi_1 z_{t-1} = \varepsilon_t - \theta_1 \varepsilon_{t-1}$$

More generally, the ARMA(p,q) process is defined as:

$$z_t = \phi_1 z_{t-1} - \phi_2 z_{t-2} - \ldots - \phi_p z_{t-p} = \varepsilon_t - \theta_1 \varepsilon_{t-1} - \theta_2 \varepsilon_{t-2} - \ldots - \theta_q \varepsilon_{t-q} \qquad \textbf{(13.3)}$$

Using this lag operator, equation (13.3) may be rewritten as:

$$\phi(L) z_t = \theta(L) \varepsilon_t$$

where $\phi(L) = 1 - \phi_1 L - \phi_2 L^2 - \ldots - \phi_p L^p$ and $\theta(L) = 1 - \theta_1 L - \theta_2 L^2 - \ldots - \theta_q L^q$. The stationarity of an ARMA process depends entirely on its autoregressive component, and requires that the roots of $\phi(L) = 0$ lie outside of the unit circle. When modelling a time series as an ARMA process, it is desirable also that the roots of $\theta(L) = 0$ lie outside of the unit circle. This is what is known as the *invertibility* condition that is often discussed in relation to moving average processes, and becomes relevant in the actual forecasting exercise.

In the case of the mixed ARMA(p,q) process, it can be shown that the ACF shares the characteristics of the autoregressive processes, i.e. the ACF will not vanish. Examination of the ACF of a series, therefore, will not allow us to distinguish between a pure autoregressive process and a mixed ARMA process.

Autoregressive Integrated Moving Average Processes of Order p, d, q ARIMA(p, d, q)

Suppose that, while the stochastic process z_t in equation (13.3) above was a stationary series, it represented, not an original series, but a *differenced* series, such as:

$$z_t = \Delta^d x_t = (1 - L)^d x_t$$

In this case, equation (13.3) may be rewritten as:

$$\phi(L) \Delta^d x_t = \phi(L)(1 - L)^d x_t = \theta(L) \varepsilon_t \qquad \textbf{(13.4)}$$

If, after differencing the series x_t d times to produce the stationary series z_t, we can model z_t as an ARMA(p,q) process, then we can say that x_t is an *autoregressive integrated moving average process of order (p,d,q)*, or simply an ARIMA(p,d,q).

In most cases of nonseasonal economic time series encountered, $d \leq 2$. In the vast majority of cases, $d = 1$.

In previous chapters we have seen appearing in some of the EViews output values referred to as partial autocorrelations. We also mentioned above that it was a possible means of helping us distinguish between a pure autoregressive and a pure moving average process. We now turn to a study of this concept.

THE PARTIAL AUTOCORRELATION FUNCTION (PACF)

In this book, we shall not go into any formal derivation of the PACF. We shall simply define the partial autocorrelation coefficient of order j as:

$$\phi_{jj} = \frac{|\mathbf{R}_j^*|}{|\mathbf{R}_j|}, j = 1, 2, \ldots$$

where:

$$\mathbf{R}_j = \begin{bmatrix} 1 & \rho_1 & \rho_2 & \cdots & \rho_{j-1} \\ \rho_1 & 1 & \rho_1 & \cdots & \rho_{j-2} \\ \vdots & \vdots & \ddots & & \vdots \\ \vdots & \vdots & & \ddots & \vdots \\ \rho_{j-1} & \rho_{j-2} & \cdots & \cdots & 1 \end{bmatrix}$$

and:

$$\mathbf{R}_j^* = \begin{bmatrix} 1 & \rho_1 & \rho_2 & \cdots & \rho_1 \\ \rho_1 & 1 & \rho_1 & \cdots & \rho_2 \\ \vdots & \vdots & \ddots & & \vdots \\ \vdots & \vdots & & \ddots & \vdots \\ \rho_{j-1} & \rho_{j-2} & \cdots & \cdots & \rho_j \end{bmatrix}$$

Consider, as an illustration, the theoretical partial autocorrelation of an AR(1) process. In this case, $|\mathbf{R}_1^*| = \rho_1$ and $|\mathbf{R}_1| = 1$. Clearly the partial autocorrelation coefficient of order 1 is:

$$\phi_{11} = \frac{\rho_1}{1} = \rho_1$$

The autocorrelation of order 1 and the partial autocorrelation of order 1 are equal in the AR(1) case. It can be shown that, whatever the process:

$$\phi_{11} = \rho_1$$

Consider, now, the partial autocorrelation of order 2 of the AR(1) process:

$$\phi_{22} = \frac{|\mathbf{R}_2^*|}{|\mathbf{R}_2|} = \frac{\begin{bmatrix} 1 & \rho_1 \\ \rho_1 & \rho_2 \end{bmatrix}}{\begin{bmatrix} 1 & \rho_1 \\ \rho_1 & 1 \end{bmatrix}} = 0$$

This is equal to zero because the expression in the numerator is equal to zero. The value of the determinant in the numerator is equal to $(\rho_2 - \rho_1^2)$. Recall that, in the AR(1) case):

$$\rho_k = \phi^k, k = 0,1,2,\ldots$$

So $\rho_2 = \phi^2$ and $(\rho_1)^2 = (\phi)^2$. So $(\rho_2 - \rho_1^2) = (\phi^2 - \phi^2) = 0$.

It can be shown that, for the AR(1) process, all partial autocorrelations of order higher than one are equal to zero:

$$\phi_{kk} = 0, k > 1$$

In the case of an AR(2) process, it can be shown that:

$$\phi_{11} \neq 0, \phi_{22} \neq 0$$

$$\phi_{kk} = 0, k > 2$$

An interesting pattern is emerging here. In the AR(1) case, partial autocorrelations of order higher than one are equal to zero. In the AR(2) case, partial autocorrelations of order higher than two are equal to zero. It can be shown that, in the more general AR(p) case, partial autocorrelations of order higher than p are equal to zero. More concisely, for the AR(p):

$$\phi_{kk} \neq 0, k \leq p$$
$$\phi_{kk} = 0, k > p$$

What about a moving average process? We saw in chapter 4 that an AR(1) process can be represented as a moving average process of infinite order and it is just as easy to show that the more general AR(p) may be written as a MA(∞). Furthermore, the MA(q) process can be represented as an AR(∞) process.[1] Clearly, this means that the PACF of an MA(1) process, and in fact the PACF of a moving average process

[1] More generally, we can say that any autoregressive process can be represented as a moving average process of infinite order, and vice versa. The principle of parsimony suggests that we work with the one of smaller order.

EXHIBIT 13.1
ACF and PACF properties of autoregressive and moving average processes

	AR(p)	MA(q)
ACF	$\rho_k \neq 0, \forall k$	$\rho_k \neq 0, k \leq q$ $\rho_k = 0, k > q$
PACF	$\phi_{kk} \neq 0, k \leq p$ $\phi_{kk} = 0, k > p$	$\phi_{kk} \neq 0, \forall k$

of any order, will decay slowly and should never vanish. In other words, for an MA(q) process:

$$\phi_{kk} \neq 0, \forall k$$

Our findings to this point may be summarized in Exhibit 13.1.

By considering both the ACF and PACF, we can therefore distinguish between an AR(p) and an MA(q) process. In the case of the mixed ARMA(p,q) process, the characteristics of both the autoregressive and moving average processes will be shared, i.e. both the ACF and PACF will not vanish.

These properties can be used to identify a given process. In practice, it is usually the case that, for nonseasonal data, $p + q \leq 2$. In other words, we normally will consider only the following possible alternatives: AR(1), AR(2), MA(1), MA(2), or ARMA(1,1). In Appendix 13.1 we show typical theoretical ACFs and PACFs of stationary ARMA processes.

ESTIMATING THE AUTOCORRELATION AND PARTIAL AUTOCORRELATION FUNCTIONS

In order that the ACF and PACF be useful in practice, we must find appropriate estimators of the autocorrelation and partial autocorrelation coefficients and establish their sampling distributions.

Estimation of the Mean

For a stationary time series z_t, a natural candidate for the estimator of the mean would be:

$$\bar{z} = \frac{z_1 + z_2 + \ldots + z_n}{n}$$

It is important to note that the series $z_1, z_2, \ldots, z_n$ is not a random sample in the classic sense, since the elements of the series are not drawn independently of each other. Rather, they represent the generating mechanism known as the stochastic process which determines *one* element in the random sample. The classic properties of the sample estimator in the case of a random sample (unbiasedness and efficiency, for instance) are not automatically verified when the estimator $\bar{z}$ is calculated on the basis of a time series. It can be shown, however, that under conditions collectively referred to as *ergodicity*, $\bar{z}$ is a consistent estimator of μ. These conditions are usually verified for economic time series.

Estimation of the Autocovariance of Order k

It seems natural to estimate the autocovariance of order k by:

$$\hat{\gamma}_k = \frac{\sum_{t=1}^{n-k}(z_t - \bar{z})(z_{t-k} - \bar{z})}{n} \quad k = 0,1,2,\ldots$$

Of course:

$$\hat{\gamma}_0 = \frac{\sum_{t=1}^{n}(z_t - \bar{z})^2}{n}$$

defines the estimated variance.

Estimation of the Autocorrelation of Order k

The autocorrelation of order k is quite naturally estimated as:

$$\hat{\rho}_k = \frac{\hat{\gamma}_k}{\hat{\gamma}_0}$$

It can be shown that, under conditions of ergodicity, $\hat{\rho}_k$ is a consistent estimator of ρ_k.

Estimation of the Partial Autocorrelation of Order j

Once the ρ_j are estimated, we can estimate the elements of $\mathbf{R}_j$ and $\mathbf{R}_j^*$, and so obtain an estimate of the partial autocorrelation coefficients:

$$\hat{\phi}_{jj} = \frac{|\hat{\mathbf{R}}_j^*|}{|\hat{\mathbf{R}}_j|}, j = 1,2,\ldots$$

It can be shown that, under conditions of ergodicity, $\hat{\phi}_{jj}$ is a consistent estimator of ϕ_{jj}.

Sampling Distributions of $\hat{\rho}_k$ and $\hat{\phi}_{jj}$

Asymptotically:

$$\frac{\hat{\rho}_j - \rho_j}{SE(\hat{\rho}_j)} \sim N(0,1)$$

and:

$$\frac{\hat{\phi}_{jj} - \phi_{jj}}{SE\left(\hat{\phi}_{jj}\right)} \sim N(0,1)$$

where:

$$SE\left(\hat{\rho}_j\right) = \frac{1}{\sqrt{n}}\left[1 + \sum_{i=1}^{j} \hat{\rho}_i^2\right]^{\frac{1}{2}}$$

(known in the literature as Bartlett's formula), and:

$$SE\left(\hat{\phi}_{jj}\right) = \frac{1}{\sqrt{n}}$$

(known in the literature as Quenouille's formula). We can use these results to test empirically the orders of the ACF and PACF and so determine the order of the underlying process.

THE BOX–JENKINS ITERATIVE CYCLE

Pure time-series modelling involves trying to fit a time series into the form of an ARIMA(p,d,q) model. Box and Jenkins (1976) suggest an iterative three-step approach for obtaining an appropriate model, which is then used for forecasting future values. This procedure is summarized in Exhibit 13.2.

At the *identification* stage, a tentative ARIMA model is specified which may approximate the time series under analysis. Once the magnitudes of p, d and q have been tentatively identified, the next stage is the *estimation* of the parameters of the model. We then move on to the stage of *diagnostic checking*, where the appropriateness of the model is judged on the basis of certain criteria. If the selected model is unsatisfactory on these counts, then we return to the identification stage and the cycle begins again. It is only when an acceptable model specification is obtained that the forecasting exercise begins.

Identification

ARIMA models are characterized by three parameters p, d and q where:

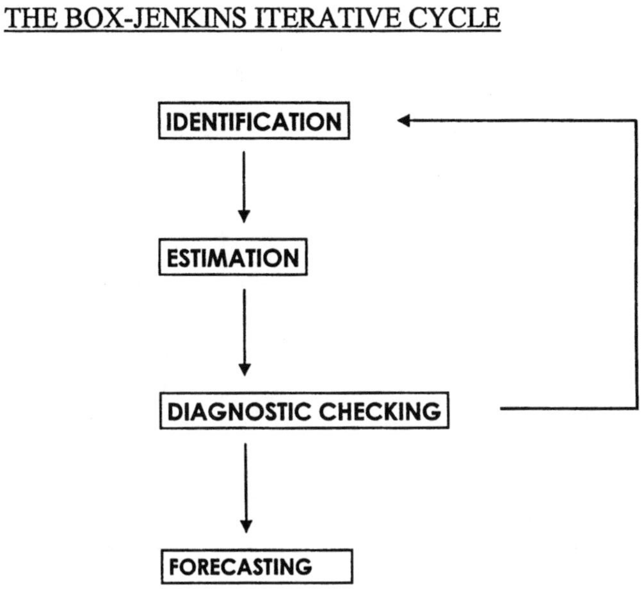

EXHIBIT 13.2
The Box–Jenkins iterative cycle

- p represents the order of the stationary AR component
- q represents the order of the invertible MA component
- d represents the order of integration of the time series

The first step in the Box–Jenkins cycle is to identify these three parameters. Determination of p and q through inspection and analysis of the ACF and PACF (as discussed above) is only possible if the series is stationary since, strictly speaking, these are not defined for a nonstationary series. The very first step, therefore, is the determination of d, the order of integration of the series. If the series is stationary (d = 0), then we can proceed to establish p and q using the techniques discussed above. If, however, the series is nonstationary, then we must difference it as required to obtain a stationary process, and then determine the values of p and q for the *differenced* series.

How do we determine d? We have already studied how to do this in chapter 12. There, we looked at the use of the Dickey–Fuller (DF) tests. We indicated then that these tests are quite weak and should always be complemented by the less formal procedures such as inspection of the plots of the time series to detect any "wandering" behaviour typical of nonstationary time series, as well as inspection of the correlograms. Why the latter? Simply because the ACF of nonstationary series has high positive values which decay at a very slow rate while that of stationary series either displays low values or values which decay (almost) exponentially. We used both the DF tests and the less formal procedures to establish that the private consumption series, C_{pt},was a nonstationary series and that ΔC_{pt} was a stationary series. In this case, d = 1: the series C_{pt} admits one unit root.

EXHIBIT 13.3
ACF and PACF of ΔC_{pt}

```
==============================================================
Sample: 1967 1991
Included observations: 24

Autocorrelation       Partial Correlation        AC      PAC     Q-Stat   Prob

    .  |***     |          .  |***     |    1    0.404   0.404   4.4341  0.035
    .  |   .    |          .**|   .    |    2   -0.031  -0.232   4.4611  0.107
    .  |*  .    |          .  |**.     |    3    0.075   0.232   4.6268  0.201
    .  |** .    |          .  |*  .    |    4    0.215   0.093   6.0746  0.194
    .  |   .    |          . *|   .    |    5    0.048  -0.101   6.1499  0.292
    .**|   .    |          .**|   .    |    6   -0.245  -0.235   8.2260  0.222
    ***|   .    |          .**|   .    |    7   -0.347  -0.227   12.637  0.081
    .**|   .    |          . *|   .    |    8   -0.238  -0.129   14.845  0.062
    . *|   .    |          .  |   .    |    9   -0.122  -0.018   15.466  0.079
    . *|   .    |          .  |   .    |   10   -0.120   0.024   16.105  0.097
    . *|   .    |          .  |*  .    |   11   -0.107   0.074   16.655  0.118
    . *|   .    |          .  |   .    |   12   -0.073  -0.040   16.932  0.152
==============================================================
```

What we have to learn to do now is determine the values of p and q for a given series. In the following section, we illustrate how this may be done using the private consumption series.

Illustrating the Identification of p and q

Once we have identified the order of integration, d, of a series, we must then identify the values of p and q. We have already "proven" that the private consumption series, C_{pt}, is integrated of order 1. Exhibit 13.3 shows the ACF and PACF of the stationary series ΔC_{pt}.

There is some evidence that we have a mixed process: both the ACF and the PACF do not appear to vanish. However, it is only the autocorrelation and partial autocorrelation of order 1 that are significant at the 5% level. Technically, therefore, all the other autocorrelations and partial autocorrelations are zero, at least at the 5% significance level. We can determine this by direct inspection of the plots, which show the 95% confidence bands constructed using Bartlett's formula (in the case of the ACF) and Quenouille's formula (in the case of the PACF).[2] It is not a foregone conclusion, therefore, that we have an ARMA(p,q) process.

We may consider other significance levels. However, the EViews output does not allow detailed analysis of the ACFs and PACFs, largely because the standard errors (based on Bartlett's and Quenouille's formulae) are not shown. The 95% confidence bands are shown and these can be used for testing at the 5% significance level. But we may be satisfied sometimes with significance at other levels (like 10%) which are not available here. However, it is easy to calculate values using the Bartlett's and Quenouille's formulae with nothing more than a hand-held calculator. For instance, let us test to see if the partial autocorrelation of third order is significantly different from 0 at the 10% level of significance. Using Quenouille's formula, we know that:

[2] The autocorrelation of order 7 appears to be significant but this may be an aberration.

$$SE\left(\hat{\phi}_{33}\right) = \frac{1}{\sqrt{24}}$$

since there are 24 observations. The relevant t-statistic is therefore:

$$T = \frac{0.232}{\frac{1}{\sqrt{24}}} = 0.232 \times \sqrt{24} = 1.136$$

The 10% critical value for this statistic is 1.645. The null hypothesis that the third partial autocorrelation is zero cannot be rejected even at the 10% level.

The truth is that when we are working with real live series, especially short series like this one, there is always a certain amount of ambiguity about the true underlying generating process. Fortunately, today, computing power is readily available and relatively cheap as well. This allows us to test for a range of possible specifications and choose the one that fits the data best. Recently, Koreisha and Pukkila (1998) proposed an elaborate data search procedure for determining the best fit. This procedure is a computer intensive alternative to the Box–Jenkins identification–estimation–diagnostic checking cycle and may result in the examination of hundreds of alternatives.

Let us nevertheless proceed on the assumption that we have identified ΔC_{pt} as a stationary ARMA(p,q) process. More specifically, we will hypothesize it as an ARMA(1,1). This means that C_{pt} is identified as an ARIMA(1,1,1).

Estimation and Diagnostic Checking

These two phases are intimately linked, since the diagnostic checking is based on the results of the estimation exercise. Consider the ARIMA(p,d,q) model represented in equation (13.4). Having identified p, d and q, we need to estimate ϕ_1, ϕ_2, …, ϕ_p, θ_1, θ_2, …, θ_q, and σ^2. Fundamentally, a least squares criterion is employed which seeks to minimize the "conditional sum of squares" defined by:

$$S\left(\phi, \theta, \sigma^2\right) = \sum_{t=1}^{n} \varepsilon_t^2$$

Derivation of the estimators and analysis of their properties is beyond the scope of this book. See Pankratz (1983).

Let us now consider the diagnostic checking phase. Look again at equation (13.4) and rewrite it as:

$$\theta^{-1}(L)\phi(L)\Delta^d x_t = \varphi(L)x_t = \varepsilon_t \qquad \textbf{(13.5)}$$

where $\varphi(L) = \theta^{-1}(L)\ \phi(L)\Delta^d$. We may imagine that $\varphi(L)$ is a filter that converts the observed series x_t into a white noise process ε_t and, if the parameters p, d and q are properly identified, then we should expect that the residuals resulting from the estimation exercise would be empirical white noise. An immediate and obvious test of model adequacy would therefore be one that tests whether these residuals form a white noise process. A procedure capable of doing just this involves the use of the Ljung–Box (Q) statistic, which we met in the previous chapter.

Passing the white noise test is *the* fundamental requirement of an ARIMA model. Diagnostic checking, however, usually involves much more than this. In addition to the application of the Ljung–Box test, the following points should be taken into account in the diagnostic checking exercise:

1. The estimated coefficients must be significant.
2. It is not unusual to find that competing specifications of the same model pass the white noise test. What do we do then? Two well-known criteria are the Akaike information criterion (AIC) and the Schwarz Bayesian criterion (SBC), which we already met in chapter 12. These are defined as:
   $AIC = n^* \log(\text{residual sum of squares}) + 2k$
   $SBC = n^* \log(\text{residual sum of squares}) + k \log n^*$
   where k is the number of parameters estimated and n^* is the number of usable observations (usually not equal to the sample size). The model with the smaller AIC/SBC values is retained.
3. There is also the question of the near nonstationarity and near invertibility of systems. For instance, we may estimate the ϕ coefficient in an AR(1) with a value that is very close to unity (the nonstationarity frontier). Similarly, the θ coefficient in an MA(1) model may be estimated with a value close to unity (the invertibility frontier). The forecasts obtained from such models may be very unreliable, notwithstanding the good fits we may obtain at the estimation stage. We should therefore choose alternative specifications to models having coefficient values too cose to the nonstationarity and invertibility frontiers.
4. We may also wish to look at the plot of the series of the residuals as well as the ACF plot which accompanies the Q statistic in the EViews output. Furthermore, it does not seem unreasonable to require that the fitted values of the series obtained from the estimation exercise should closely correspond to the observed values over the sample period. A rough-and-ready way to establish this is by examination of the time plots of the actual and fitted values of the time series.
5. It is frequently stated that the ultimate diagnostic check on an ARIMA model is its usefulness in forecasting outside of the sample period which, of course, requires a comparison between actual and forecasted values. When we make our forecasts, however, we do not have available the actual values (why then should we bother to make a forecast!). But a useful compromise might be to estimate the model with less data than are available, say from $t = 1$ to $t = n - p$ rather than to $t = n$. We can then use the model to predict the p known values $x_{n-(p+1)}, x_{n-(p+2)}, \ldots, x_n$. This procedure is known as *ex post forecasting* and has a lot of intuitive appeal. However, it does suffer from the obvious drawback of the loss of p degrees of freedom at the identification and estimation stages, which can matter a lot when the series is already quite short (as is the case with the series C_{pt}).

EXHIBIT 13.4
Fit of $\Delta C_{pt} = \alpha + \phi\Delta C_{pt-1} + \varepsilon_t + \theta\varepsilon_{t-1}$

```
=================================================================
Sample(adjusted): 1969 1991
Included observations: 23 after adjusting endpoints
Convergence achieved after 52 iterations
Backcast: 1968
=================================================================
     Variable      Coefficient Std. Error  T-Statistic   Prob.
=================================================================
         C            92.46158   231.5311   0.399348    0.6939
       AR(1)         -0.379206   0.193968  -1.954995    0.0647
       MA(1)          0.989949   0.000274   3618.319    0.0000
=================================================================
R-squared             0.327648   Mean dependent var   83.12000
Adjusted R-squared    0.260412   S.D. dependent var   894.0977
S.E. of regression    768.9176   Akaike info criter   16.24895
Sum squared resid     11824685   Schwarz criterion    16.39706
Log likelihood       -183.8630   F-statistic          4.873154
Durbin-Watson stat    1.773321   Prob(F-statistic)    0.018879
=================================================================
```

Illustration of the Estimation and Diagnostic Checking Phases

Identification of C_{pt} as an ARMA(1,1) in the first difference is the first stage of the Box–Jenkins three-step procedure and, in this section, we fit the model:

$$\Delta C_{pt} = \alpha + \phi\Delta C_{pt-1} + \varepsilon_t - \theta\varepsilon_{t-1}$$

You will notice that a constant term has been included, although there has been no such inclusion to date. The presence or absence of this term in the ARIMA model has no effect on the general conclusions drawn so far and it was left out largely for the algebraic simplicity that it afforded. But a constant term in the model is a real possibility and we must determine, using the usual statistical criteria, whether or not its inclusion is warranted. If one is present in any ARIMA model, it must be estimated (and used in the forecasting exercise as well).

The results of the estimation exercise are shown in Exhibit 13.4. Here, the estimated values of ϕ, θ and α are, respectively, –0.379, 0.990 and 92.5. There are two immediate stumbling blocks to retaining this equation, even before we carry out the acid test for white noise residuals. In the first place, the constant is not significant. Second, the value of the moving average coefficient is dangerously close to the invertibility frontier (which is unity). This high value may be a result of a high correlation between the autoregressive and moving average coefficients (something like a multicollinearity problem in the ARIMA model). Let us see what happens when we drop the constant term. Exhibit 13.5 shows the results obtained.

Once again, the MA coefficient is way too high. We simply cannot retain the ARMA specification, with or without the constant term. What do we do?

EXHIBIT 13.5
Fit of $\Delta C_{pt} = \phi\Delta C_{pt-1} + \varepsilon_t + \theta\varepsilon_{t-1}$

Sample: 1969 1991
Included observations: 23
Convergence achieved after 11 iterations
Backcast: 1968

Variable	Coefficient	Std. Error	T-Statistic	Prob.
AR(1)	-0.368735	0.187121	-1.970568	0.0621
MA(1)	0.983301	0.032298	30.44449	0.0000

R-squared	0.320816	Mean dependent var	83.12000
Adjusted R-squared	0.288474	S.D. dependent var	894.0977
S.E. of regression	754.1893	Akaike info criter	16.17211
Sum squared resid	11944833	Schwarz criterion	16.27084
Log likelihood	-183.9792	F-statistic	9.919459
Durbin-Watson stat	1.795967	Prob(F-statistic)	0.004837

EXHIBIT 13.6
Fit of $\Delta C_{pt} = \phi\Delta C_{pt-1} + \varepsilon_t$

Sample: 1969 1991
Included observations: 23
Convergence achieved after 2 iterations

Variable	Coefficient	Std. Error	T-Statistic	Prob.
AR(1)	0.410691	0.194926	2.106913	0.0468

R-squared	0.160380	Mean dependent var	83.12000
Adjusted R-squared	0.160380	S.D. dependent var	894.0977
S.E. of regression	819.2687	Akaike info criter	16.29721
Sum squared resid	14766426	Schwarz criterion	16.34658
Log likelihood	-186.4179	Durbin-Watson stat	1.761673

If we go back to the identification stage, we may wish to consider two other possibilities: an MA(1) specification and an AR(2) specification (with or without constant term). We looked at the AR(2) specification and found that the AR(2) term was not significant. We eventually fitted an AR(1) model, without the constant. The results obtained are displayed in Exhibit 13.6.

This model represents a very real possibility. Its estimated coefficient is reasonably far from the nonstationarity frontier and it is significant at the 5% level. Let us compare it with the MA(1) case (no constant), using the same sample period. These results are shown in Exhibit 13.7.

EXHIBIT 13.7
Fit of $\Delta C_{pt} = \varepsilon_t + \theta\varepsilon_{t-1}$

```
==============================================================
(Sample period: 1969-1991)
Sample: 1969 1991
Included observations: 23
Convergence achieved after 3 iterations
Backcast: 1968
==============================================================
     Variable      Coefficient Std. Error  T-Statistic   Prob.
==============================================================
       MA(1)          0.621502   0.159673    3.892335    0.0008
==============================================================
R-squared             0.259133   Mean dependent var   83.12000
Adjusted R-squared    0.259133   S.D. dependent var   894.0977
S.E. of regression    769.5823   Akaike info criter   16.17208
Sum squared resid     13029654   Schwarz criterion    16.22145
Log likelihood       -184.9789   Durbin-Watson stat   2.042447
==============================================================
```

EXHIBIT 13.8
ACF of residuals of fit of $\Delta C_{pt} = \varepsilon_t + \theta\varepsilon_{t-1}$

```
==============================================================
(Sample period: 1968-1991)
Sample(adjusted): 1968 1991
Included observations: 24 after adjusting endpoints
Convergence achieved after 4 iterations
Backcast: 1967
==============================================================
     Variable      Coefficient Std. Error  T-Statistic   Prob.
==============================================================
       MA(1)          0.589606   0.162324    3.632268    0.0014
==============================================================
R-squared             0.240212   Mean dependent var   72.52667
Adjusted R-squared    0.240212   S.D. dependent var   875.9835
S.E. of regression    763.5579   Akaike info criter   16.15463
Sum squared resid     13409477   Schwarz criterion    16.20371
Log likelihood       -192.8555   Durbin-Watson stat   2.025438
==============================================================
```

This model too is acceptable for similar reasons. It is also marginally preferable on the basis of the AIC/SBC criteria. This is the one we will retain here, provided that its residuals pass the Ljung–Box test for white noise. The EViews ARIMA routine automatically generates the estimated residuals and the fitted values of the variable. These can be stored for further use, including for the diagnostic checks discussed in the previous section. We will retain and test the residuals for the MA(1) specification estimated over the entire sample (1968 to 1991). The estimation results for this model are shown in Exhibit 13.8.

EXHIBIT 13.9

ACF of residuals of fit of $\Delta C_{pt} = \varepsilon_t + \theta\varepsilon_{t-1}$

```
=====================================================================
Sample: 1968 1991
Included observations: 24

Q-statistic probabilities adjusted for 1 ARMA term(s)

Autocorrelation      Partial Correlation       AC       PAC     Q-Stat   Prob

    .  |  .    |         .  |  .    |    1   -0.022   -0.022   0.0132
    .  |  .    |         .  |  .    |    2   -0.026   -0.026   0.0318   0.858
    .  |  .    |         .  |  .    |    3   -0.011   -0.013   0.0357   0.982
    .  |** .   |         .  |** .   |    4    0.211    0.210   1.4183   0.701
    .  |  .    |         .  |  .    |    5   -0.001    0.008   1.4183   0.841
    . *|  .    |         . *|  .    |    6   -0.146   -0.142   2.1531   0.828
    .**|  .    |         .**|  .    |    7   -0.215   -0.231   3.8443   0.698
    . *|  .    |         .**|  .    |    8   -0.153   -0.243   4.7629   0.689
    .  |  .    |         . *|  .    |    9   -0.016   -0.059   4.7734   0.781
    . *|  .    |         .  |  .    |   10   -0.086   -0.037   5.1030   0.825
    .  |  .    |         .  |* .    |   11   -0.021    0.091   5.1238   0.883
    .  |  .    |         .  |  .    |   12   -0.054    0.032   5.2731   0.917
=====================================================================
```

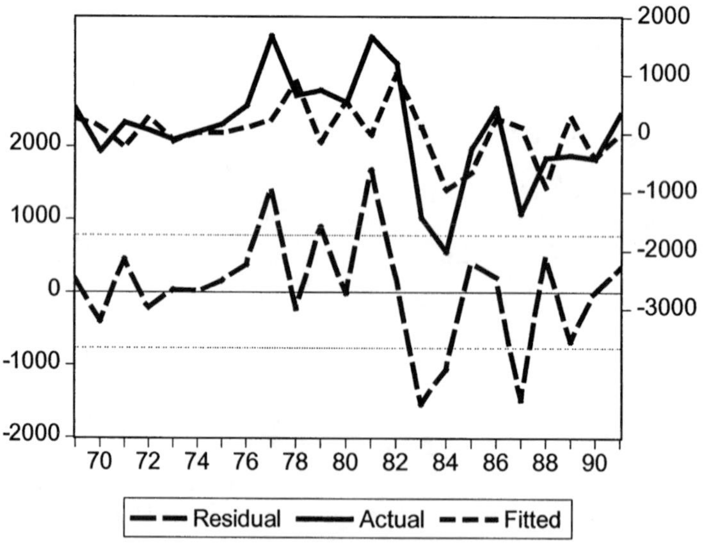

EXHIBIT 13.10

Time-series plots of actual, fitted and residual values for equation $\Delta C_{pt} = \varepsilon_t - \theta\varepsilon_{t-1}$

Exhibit 13.9 shows the ACF and accompanying Q (Ljung–Box) statistics of the residuals obtained from the estimation exercise displayed in Exhibit 13.8 and stored under the name "resid". On the basis of the Ljung–Box statistic, there is no evidence for the rejection of the null that the series is white noise (the lowest p-value is around 70%). The estimated model in Exhibit 13.8 is therefore very acceptable, moreso as the θ coefficient is highly significant (p-value of 0.0014). Exhibit 13.10 shows the time-series plot of the actual, fitted and residuals of the equation. This exhibit

EXHIBIT 13.11
Observed values of private consumption expenditure (C_{pt}) 1992–1994 and forecast errors (constant 1985 prices)

Year	C_{pt}^{*}	% Error
1992	7437.7	10.4
1993	7228.4	13.6
1994	7664.0	7.5

* Source: Central Statistical Office of Trinidad and Tobago

strengthens the case for the retention of the chosen model. We can now move on to the forecasting exercise.

Forecasting

The forecasting exercise involves using the model estimated on the basis of the sample $x_1, x_2, \ldots, x_n$ to predict the as yet unobserved (future) values $x_{n+1}, x_{n+2}, \ldots, x_{n+m}$ (m is called the *forecasting horizon*). Forecasting in the Box–Jenkins framework is based upon a mean square error (MSE) criterion but formal derivation and justification for these forecasts are beyond the scope of this book. The interested reader is instead referred to Granger and Newbold (1986), chapter 5, or Anderson (1977) for a more formal discussion. We do, however, underscore one important point: the forecasts become less and less reliable the longer the forecast horizon.

Illustration of the Forecasting Phase

Although this phase is the ultimate reason for all the previous phases, it is the most mechanical phase of all. It is simply a question of extrapolating into the future based on predetermined formulae (such as those referred to in the previous section). We did this for the series C_{pt} and obtained the value of 8213.6 for 1992 onwards. Observed values of C_{pt} provided by the Central Statistical Office of Trinidad and Tobago for the period 1992 to 1994 and the corresponding forecast errors based on our forecasts (shown as a percentage of the observed values) are shown in Exhibit 13.11. There is room for improvement but the forecasts obtained are clearly not unreasonable.

SEASONAL MODELS

Special problems arise when the data used contain seasonal components. This occurs in particular when the data are quarterly or monthly. We will illustrate the various problems associated with the identification of a seasonal model by working though an example using the famous airline data of Box and Jenkins (1976). We will also introduce the concept of seasonal *additive* and *multiplicative* models. The other stages of the Box–Jenkins cycle are exactly as they have been described for nonseasonal models.

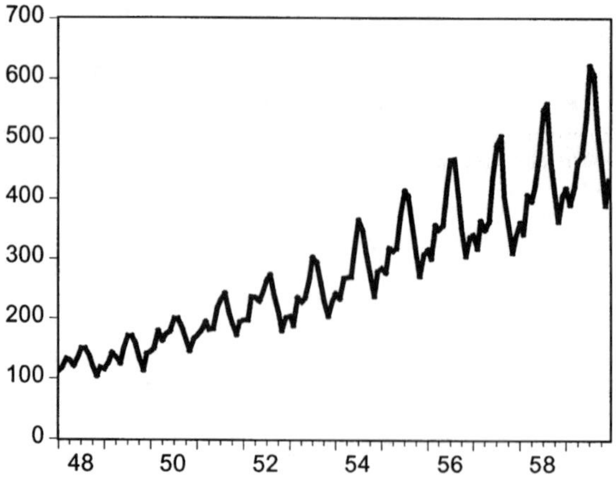

EXHIBIT 13.12
Passenger miles (000s) flown from January 1948 to December 1959

So far in this book, we have been looking at annual data only. Seasonality is not a problem with this kind of data. Now take a look at the time-series plot in Exhibit 13.12. It shows monthly data on passenger miles flown from January 1948 to December 1959.

This is, of course, a plot of the famous airline data of Box and Jenkins (1976). There are several features about this plot that are worthy of note. In the first place, it is clearly nonstationary in the mean (in that it does not fluctuate about some fixed mean). There is also clear evidence of *seasonality* in the data: notwithstanding the obvious upward trend in the data, every year there is a similar pattern of month-to-month fluctuations. We have studied how to handle nonstationary data but, up to now, we have not been bothered by seasonal patterns. For modelling purposes, it would be clearly unwise to ignore this phenomenon.

There is yet another novelty in the airline data that we have not considered up to now: the variation is increasing with time and, when this happens, we say that the series is nonstationary in the variance (as opposed to being nonstationary in the mean). We will treat this first because it is the simplest problem to deal with. Exhibit 13.13 shows the plot of the logarithm of the series is fairly similar. The logarithmic transformation transforms a series that is not stationary in the variance to one that is. From now on we will be treating the logarithmically transformed airline data series and not the original raw data. We will denote this series as x_t.

The transformed series may now be stationary in the variance but it is still clearly nonstationary in the mean and still displays the seasonal patterns alluded to above. Exhibit 13.14 shows the plot of the ACF up to order 48 (4 years). The slow decline in the ACF observed is typical of a nonstationary series. But there is an added feature. Look at the values of the ACF at the points of the *seasonal lags* (12, 24, 36, 48): they are clearly quite high. In fact, in the case being considered, they dominate the values in their neighbourhood. There is a clear seasonal pattern contributing to the nonstationary behaviour and repeating itself every 12 months. In such a series, we may expect to obtain stationarity if we *seasonally difference* the series. What does this mean? In the case of a monthly data series x_t, a seasonal difference of order 1 is defined by:

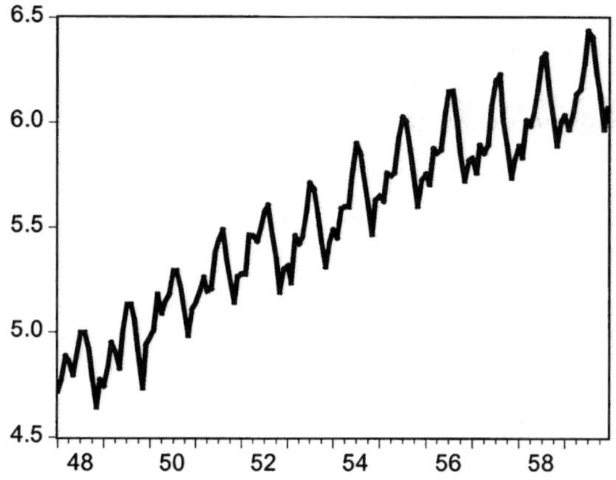

EXHIBIT 13.13
Passenger miles (000s) flown from January 1948 to December 1959 (logs)

$$z_t = \Delta_{12} x_t = x_t - x_{t-12} = \left(1 - L^{12}\right) x_t$$

In general for periodicity of order s (s = 4 for quarterly data, s = 12 for monthly data and so on):

$$z_t = \Delta_s x_t = x_t - x_{t-s} = \left(1 - L^s\right) x_t$$

Exhibit 13.15 shows the ACF for the seasonally differenced series (this time we display only the first 36). The seasonal effect seems to have been overcome. If we had not accomplished this with one seasonal differencing, then we could effect a seasonal differencing of order 2. Indeed there is no reason why we should not envisage seasonal differencing up to order D. In this most general case, the derived series z_t is defined by:

$$z_t = \left(1 - L^{12}\right)^D x_t$$

The ACF shown in Exhibit 13.15 is still typical of a nonstationary series, since the ACF is still high and slowly declining. What does this mean? We must clearly difference the series in the usual way (i.e. in addition to the seasonal differencing). In this case the new series is defined as:

$$\Delta z_t = \Delta\left(1 - L^{12}\right)^D x_t = (1 - L)\left(1 - L^{12}\right)^D x_t$$

The ACF of the series resulting from standard differencing as well as seasonal differencing is shown in Exhibit 13.16. The ACF plot shows clearly that this is a stationary series. To confirm this, look at Exhibit 13.17, which displays the results of the DF test

EXHIBIT 13.14
ACF of passenger miles (logarithms) series

```
==============================================================================
Sample: 1948:01 1959:12
Included observations: 144

Autocorrelation        Partial Correlation      AC      PAC     Q-Stat    Prob

       .|*******|         .|*******|   1      0.954   0.954   133.72    0.000
       .|*******|        *|.       |   2      0.899  -0.118   253.36    0.000
       .|*******|         .|.      |   3      0.851   0.054   361.29    0.000
       .|******  |        .|.      |   4      0.808   0.024   459.44    0.000
       .|******  |        .|*      |   5      0.779   0.116   551.20    0.000
       .|******  |        .|.      |   6      0.756   0.044   638.37    0.000
       .|******  |        .|.      |   7      0.738   0.038   721.86    0.000
       .|******  |        .|*      |   8      0.727   0.100   803.60    0.000
       .|******  |        .|**     |   9      0.734   0.204   887.42    0.000
       .|******  |        .|.      |  10      0.744   0.064   974.33    0.000
       .|******  |        .|*      |  11      0.758   0.106   1065.2    0.000
       .|******  |        .|.      |  12      0.762  -0.042   1157.6    0.000
       .|******  |     ****|.      |  13      0.717  -0.485   1240.0    0.000
       .|*****   |        .|.      |  14      0.663  -0.034   1311.1    0.000
       .|*****   |        .|.      |  15      0.618   0.042   1373.4    0.000
       .|****    |        .|.      |  16      0.576  -0.044   1428.0    0.000
       .|****    |        .|.      |  17      0.544   0.028   1476.9    0.000
       .|****    |        .|.      |  18      0.519   0.037   1521.9    0.000
       .|****    |        .|.      |  19      0.501   0.042   1564.1    0.000
       .|****    |        .|.      |  20      0.490   0.014   1604.9    0.000
       .|****    |        .|*      |  21      0.498   0.073   1647.3    0.000
       .|****    |        .|.      |  22      0.506  -0.033   1691.5    0.000
       .|****    |        .|.      |  23      0.517   0.061   1737.9    0.000
       .|****    |        .|.      |  24      0.520   0.031   1785.3    0.000
       .|****    |       **|.      |  25      0.484  -0.194   1826.6    0.000
       .|***     |        .|.      |  26      0.437  -0.035   1860.7    0.000
       .|***     |        .|.      |  27      0.400   0.036   1889.5    0.000
       .|***     |        .|.      |  28      0.364  -0.035   1913.5    0.000
       .|***     |        .|.      |  29      0.337   0.044   1934.3    0.000
       .|**      |        .|.      |  30      0.315  -0.045   1952.6    0.000
       .|**      |        .|.      |  31      0.297  -0.003   1969.0    0.000
       .|**      |        .|.      |  32      0.289   0.034   1984.6    0.000
       .|**      |        .|.      |  33      0.295  -0.020   2001.1    0.000
       .|**      |        .|.      |  34      0.305   0.028   2018.8    0.000
       .|**      |        .|.      |  35      0.315   0.029   2038.0    0.000
       .|**      |        .|.      |  36      0.319  -0.004   2057.8    0.000
       .|**      |        *|.      |  37      0.286  -0.132   2073.9    0.000
       .|**      |        .|.      |  38      0.245  -0.003   2085.8    0.000
       .|**      |        .|.      |  39      0.211  -0.025   2094.8    0.000
       .|*       |        *|.      |  40      0.175  -0.059   2101.0    0.000
       .|*       |        .|.      |  41      0.146   0.006   2105.3    0.000
       .|*       |        .|.      |  42      0.125   0.038   2108.5    0.000
       .|*       |        .|.      |  43      0.106  -0.032   2110.9    0.000
       .|*       |        .|.      |  44      0.099   0.031   2112.9    0.000
       .|*       |        .|.      |  45      0.104  -0.049   2115.2    0.000
       .|*       |        .|.      |  46      0.111   0.011   2117.9    0.000
       .|*       |        .|.      |  47      0.120   0.029   2121.0    0.000
       .|*       |        .|.      |  48      0.125  -0.006   2124.4    0.000
==============================================================================
```

EXHIBIT 13.15
ACF of seasonally differenced passenger miles (logarithms) series

```
==========================================================================
Sample: 1948:01 1959:12
Included observations: 132

Autocorrelation          Partial Correlation      AC      PAC     Q-Stat    Prob

      .|******  |            .|******  |   1    0.714   0.714   68.774   0.000
      .|*****   |            .|**      |   2    0.623   0.232   121.60   0.000
      .|****    |            .|.       |   3    0.480  -0.057   153.24   0.000
      .|***     |            .|*       |   4    0.441   0.105   180.15   0.000
      .|***     |            .|.       |   5    0.387   0.045   200.97   0.000
      .|**      |            .|.       |   6    0.319  -0.056   215.25   0.000
      .|**      |            *|.       |   7    0.242  -0.059   223.52   0.000
      .|*       |            .|.       |   8    0.194   0.007   228.89   0.000
      .|*       |            .|.       |   9    0.153  -0.006   232.24   0.000
      .|.       |           **|.       |  10   -0.006  -0.294   232.25   0.000
      *|.       |            *|.       |  11   -0.115  -0.155   234.18   0.000
     **|.       |            *|.       |  12   -0.243  -0.141   242.88   0.000
      *|.       |            .|**      |  13   -0.143   0.295   245.93   0.000
      *|.       |            .|.       |  14   -0.141   0.062   248.90   0.000
      *|.       |            .|.       |  15   -0.099   0.046   250.38   0.000
      *|.       |            .|.       |  16   -0.146  -0.041   253.63   0.000
      *|.       |            .|*       |  17   -0.096   0.125   255.06   0.000
      *|.       |            *|.       |  18   -0.111  -0.059   256.97   0.000
      *|.       |            *|.       |  19   -0.141  -0.149   260.07   0.000
      *|.       |            .|.       |  20   -0.158  -0.019   264.01   0.000
      *|.       |            .|*       |  21   -0.114   0.123   266.07   0.000
      *|.       |            *|.       |  22   -0.084  -0.182   267.20   0.000
      .|.       |            .|.       |  23    0.001   0.063   267.20   0.000
      .|.       |           **|.       |  24   -0.052  -0.192   267.65   0.000
      *|.       |            .|.       |  25   -0.103   0.027   269.40   0.000
      *|.       |            .|.       |  26   -0.094   0.028   270.87   0.000
      *|.       |            .|.       |  27   -0.128  -0.033   273.64   0.000
      *|.       |            *|.       |  28   -0.145  -0.109   277.22   0.000
      *|.       |            .|.       |  29   -0.187   0.036   283.26   0.000
     **|.       |            *|.       |  30   -0.196  -0.111   289.92   0.000
     **|.       |            .|.       |  31   -0.190  -0.038   296.23   0.000
      *|.       |            .|.       |  32   -0.146   0.049   299.99   0.000
     **|.       |            .|.       |  33   -0.224  -0.019   308.95   0.000
     **|.       |            *|.       |  34   -0.226  -0.058   318.19   0.000
     **|.       |            .|.       |  35   -0.267  -0.010   331.19   0.000
     **|.       |            *|.       |  36   -0.223  -0.069   340.36   0.000
==========================================================================
```

applied to the same series (equation (12.7) used with two lags in the ADF equation). This is a convincing rejection of the null.

What does examination of the ACF and PACF reveal? The first spikes of the ACF and the PACF (these are always equal) are clearly significant. Beyond this, the evidence is not clear and certainly does not pronounce in favour of a pure autoregressive or moving average process. For this reason, we may wish to suggest a mixed process. But what is the order of this process? To help us along, look at the "seasonal" spikes (values at 12, 24 and 36). Both the ACF and PACF display a relatively large spike at 12 (they are even higher than the first spike). At spikes 24 and 36, the ACF

EXHIBIT 13.16

ACF of passenger miles (logarithms) series with standard and seasonal differencing

```
==================================================================
Sample: 1948:01 1959:12
Included observations: 131

Autocorrelation       Partial Correlation       AC      PAC     Q-Stat    Prob

    ***|.     |          ***|.     |  1   -0.341  -0.341   15.596   0.000
      .|*     |            .|.     |  2    0.105  -0.013   17.086   0.000
     **|.     |           **|.     |  3   -0.202  -0.193   22.648   0.000
      .|.     |            *|.     |  4    0.021  -0.125   22.710   0.000
      .|.     |            .|.     |  5    0.056   0.033   23.139   0.000
      .|.     |            .|.     |  6    0.031   0.035   23.271   0.001
      .|.     |            *|.     |  7   -0.056  -0.060   23.705   0.001
      .|.     |            .|.     |  8   -0.001  -0.020   23.705   0.003
      .|*     |            .|**    |  9    0.176   0.226   28.147   0.001
      *|.     |            .|.     | 10   -0.076   0.043   28.987   0.001
      .|.     |            .|.     | 11    0.064   0.047   29.589   0.002
    ***|.     |          ***|.     | 12   -0.387  -0.339   51.473   0.000
      .|*     |            *|.     | 13    0.152  -0.109   54.866   0.000
      *|.     |            *|.     | 14   -0.058  -0.077   55.361   0.000
      .|*     |            .|.     | 15    0.150  -0.022   58.720   0.000
      *|.     |            *|.     | 16   -0.139  -0.140   61.645   0.000
      .|*     |            .|.     | 17    0.070   0.026   62.404   0.000
      .|.     |            .|*     | 18    0.016   0.115   62.442   0.000
      .|.     |            .|.     | 19   -0.011  -0.013   62.460   0.000
      *|.     |            *|.     | 20   -0.117  -0.167   64.598   0.000
      .|.     |            .|*     | 21    0.039   0.132   64.834   0.000
      *|.     |            *|.     | 22   -0.091  -0.072   66.168   0.000
      .|**    |            .|*     | 23    0.223   0.143   74.210   0.000
      .|.     |            *|.     | 24   -0.018  -0.067   74.265   0.000
      *|.     |            *|.     | 25   -0.100  -0.103   75.918   0.000
      .|.     |            .|.     | 26    0.049  -0.010   76.310   0.000
      .|.     |            .|.     | 27   -0.030   0.044   76.463   0.000
      .|.     |            *|.     | 28    0.047  -0.090   76.839   0.000
      .|.     |            .|.     | 29   -0.018   0.047   76.894   0.000
      .|.     |            .|.     | 30   -0.051  -0.005   77.344   0.000
      .|.     |            *|.     | 31   -0.054  -0.096   77.848   0.000
      .|*     |            .|.     | 32    0.196  -0.015   84.590   0.000
      *|.     |            .|.     | 33   -0.122   0.012   87.254   0.000
      .|*     |            .|.     | 34    0.078  -0.019   88.340   0.000
      *|.     |            .|.     | 35   -0.152   0.023   92.558   0.000
      .|.     |            *|.     | 36   -0.010  -0.165   92.577   0.000
==================================================================
```

EXHIBIT 13.17

DF test applied to passenger miles (logarithms) series with standard and seasonal differencing

```
==================================================================
ADF Test Statistic    -16.04147   1%  Critical Value*     -3.4831
                                  5%  Critical Value      -2.8844
                                  10% Critical Value      -2.5788
*MacKinnon critical values for rejection of hypothesis of a
unit root.
==================================================================
```

EXHIBIT 13.18

Results for fitting model $\Delta z_t = \alpha + \phi_1 \Delta z_{t-1} + \phi_{12} \Delta z_{t-12} + \varepsilon_t + \theta_1 \varepsilon_{t-1} + \ldots + \theta_{12} \varepsilon_{t-12}$

```
==============================================================
Sample(adjusted): 1950:02 1959:12
Included observations: 119 after adjusting endpoints
Convergence achieved after 22 iterations
Backcast: 1981:02 1982:01
==============================================================
     Variable      Coefficient Std. Error  T-Statistic   Prob.
==============================================================
        C            -0.000606  0.002451    -0.247457  0.8050
      AR(1)          -0.015127  0.087675    -0.172541  0.8633
     AR(12)          -0.715937  0.062360    -11.48075  0.0000
      MA(1)          -0.323345  0.086924    -3.719872  0.0003
     MA(12)           0.609903  0.000563     1082.872  0.0000
==============================================================
R-squared              0.348409   Mean dependent var  -0.001406
Adjusted R-squared     0.325547   S.D. dependent var   0.046303
S.E. of regression     0.038026   Akaike info criter  -3.659986
Sum squared resid      0.164841   Schwarz criterion   -3.543216
Log likelihood         222.7691   F-statistic          15.23913
Durbin-Watson stat     2.183975   Prob(F-statistic)    0.000000
==============================================================
```

appears to be zero while the PACF, though not zero, is quite small. Some evidence seems to be emerging for a mixed process of the form:

$$\Delta z_t = \alpha + \phi_1 \Delta z_{t-1} + \phi_{12} \Delta z_{t-12} + \varepsilon_t + \theta_1 \varepsilon_{t-1} + \ldots + \theta_{12} \varepsilon_{t-12}$$

where:

$$\Delta z_t = \Delta \Delta_{12} x_t = \Delta(x_t - x_{t-12}) = (1-L)(1-L^{12}) x_t$$

and x_t is the variable representing passenger miles (logs). The lags at 12 are introduced to account for possible "seasonal" moving average and autoregressive components. This is an example of an *additive ARIMA model. A priori*, there seems to be stronger evidence for the inclusion of the seasonal moving average term rather than the seasonal autoregressive term. But this is only marginally so. Let us fit this model and test its goodness of fit. These results are shown in Exhibit 13.18. The constant and AR(1) terms are not significant. This is confirmed by a joint test of their significance which yields the results shown in Exhibit 13.19.

The null that the restricted model is true cannot be rejected. So we fit the model:

$$\Delta z_t = \phi_{12} \Delta z_{t-12} + \varepsilon_t + \theta_1 \varepsilon_{t-1} + \ldots + \theta_{12} \varepsilon_{t}.$$

The corresponding results are shown in Exhibit 13.20.

EXHIBIT 13.19

Testing coefficient restrictions in the model $\Delta z_t = \alpha + \phi_1 \Delta z_{t-1} + \phi_{12} \Delta z_{t-12} + \varepsilon_t + \theta_1 \varepsilon_{t-1} + \ldots + \theta_{12} \varepsilon_{t-12}$

```
=================================================================
Redundant Variables:  C AR(1)

F-statistic            0.200108          Probability  0.818929
Log likelihood ratio   0.417039          Probability  0.811785
=================================================================
```

EXHIBIT 13.20

Results for fitting model $\Delta z_t = \phi_{12} \Delta z_{t-12} + \varepsilon_t + \theta_1 \varepsilon_{t-1} + \ldots + \theta_{12} \varepsilon_{t-12}$

```
=================================================================
Sample: 1950:02 1959:12
Included observations: 119
Convergence achieved after 10 iterations
Backcast: 1981:02 1982:01
=================================================================
     Variable      Coefficient Std. Error  T-Statistic   Prob.
=================================================================
       AR(12)       -0.712124   0.058160  -12.24423    0.0000
        MA(1)       -0.345863   0.063952  -5.408162    0.0000
       MA(12)        0.590861   0.000594   993.8797    0.0000
=================================================================
R-squared             0.346122   Mean dependent var   -0.001406
Adjusted R-squared    0.334848   S.D. dependent var    0.046303
S.E. of regression    0.037763   Akaike info criter   -3.690094
Sum squared resid     0.165420   Schwarz criterion    -3.620033
Log likelihood        222.5606   F-statistic           30.70156
Durbin-Watson stat    2.171162   Prob(F-statistic)     0.000000
=================================================================
```

Both the AIC and the SBC criteria pronounce in favour of this form of the model. However, the model fails the white noise test as is shown in Exhibit 13.21. The Q-statistics are not unambiguous in pronouncing in favour of the white noise hypothesis.

You may remember that we had expressed some reservations about the autoregressive component in this model. It would seem that our fears have been allayed, since the AR(12) coefficient is very significant. It is still possible, however, that a model *not* containing this term will be better. We fitted this model and indeed it performed better than the previous one on the basis of the AIC and SBC criteria. But it too failed the white noise test for its residuals. What do we do?

Box and Jenkins (1976) propose a multiplicative model, which is the principal innovation of their work. In the case of the model with moving average coefficients only, this would be represented as:

$$\Delta z_t = \left(1 - \Theta_{12} L^{12}\right)\left(1 - \theta_1 L\right)\varepsilon_t$$

EXHIBIT 13.21
ACF and Q-statistics for model $\Delta z_t = \phi_{12}\Delta z_{t-12} + \varepsilon_t + \theta_1\varepsilon_{t-1} + \ldots + \theta_{12}\varepsilon_{t-12}$

```
==============================================================
Q-statistic probabilities adjusted for 3 ARMA term(s)

Autocorrelation        Partial Correlation      AC      PAC    Q-Stat   Prob

      *|.      |          *|.      |  1  -0.091  -0.091  0.9997
      .|.      |          .|.      |  2   0.021   0.013  1.0544
      *|.      |          *|.      |  3  -0.140  -0.138  3.4770
      .|.      |          *|.      |  4  -0.053  -0.080  3.8307  0.050
      .|*      |          .|*      |  5   0.114   0.108  5.4776  0.065
      .|*      |          .|*      |  6   0.069   0.075  6.0852  0.108
      *|.      |          *|.      |  7  -0.072  -0.084  6.7455  0.150
      .|.      |          .|.      |  8  -0.043  -0.035  6.9828  0.222
      .|*      |          .|**     |  9   0.162   0.206  10.435  0.107
      *|.      |          *|.      | 10  -0.072  -0.070  11.129  0.133
      .|.      |          .|.      | 11   0.034  -0.034  11.284  0.186
      *|.      |          *|.      | 12  -0.175  -0.118  15.406  0.080
      *|.      |          *|.      | 13  -0.129  -0.140  17.669  0.061
      .|.      |          *|.      | 14  -0.026  -0.106  17.764  0.087
      .|*      |          .|.      | 15   0.073   0.017  18.497  0.101
      *|.      |          *|.      | 16  -0.085  -0.110  19.513  0.108
      .|.      |          .|.      | 17   0.017  -0.011  19.553  0.145
      .|.      |          .|.      | 18  -0.018   0.022  19.600  0.188
      *|.      |          .|.      | 19  -0.059  -0.048  20.107  0.215
      *|.      |          *|.      | 20  -0.081  -0.166  21.065  0.223
      .|*      |          .|*      | 21   0.087   0.147  22.184  0.224
      *|.      |          *|.      | 22  -0.113  -0.077  24.073  0.193
      .|*      |          .|.      | 23   0.140   0.064  27.006  0.135
     **|.      |         **|.      | 24  -0.219  -0.269  34.301  0.034
      .|.      |          .|.      | 25  -0.018  -0.035  34.349  0.045
      .|*      |          .|.      | 26   0.086   0.024  35.505  0.046
      .|.      |          .|.      | 27   0.009  -0.040  35.519  0.061
      *|.      |          *|.      | 28  -0.058  -0.179  36.045  0.071
      .|.      |          .|*      | 29   0.013   0.080  36.071  0.090
      .|.      |          .|.      | 30   0.002  -0.007  36.072  0.114
      *|.      |          *|.      | 31  -0.077  -0.141  37.044  0.118
      .|*      |          .|.      | 32   0.175   0.003  42.110  0.055
      *|.      |          .|.      | 33  -0.149   0.004  45.843  0.032
      .|.      |          *|.      | 34   0.037  -0.078  46.070  0.040
      .|.      |          .|.      | 35  -0.007  -0.025  46.078  0.051
      .|.      |          .|.      | 36   0.043  -0.053  46.394  0.061
==============================================================
```

or:

$$\Delta z_t = \left(1 - \theta_1 L - \Theta_{12} L^{12} + \theta_1 \Theta_{12} L^{13}\right)\varepsilon_t$$

or yet again:

$$\Delta z_t = \varepsilon_t - \theta_1 \varepsilon_{t-1} - \Theta_{12}\varepsilon_{t-12} + \theta_1 \Theta_{12}\varepsilon_{t-13}$$

EXHIBIT 13.22

Estimation phase of multiplicative model $(1 - L)(1 - L^{12})x_t = (1 - \Theta_{12}L^{12})(1-\theta_1 L)\varepsilon_t$

```
==============================================================
Sample(adjusted): 1949:02 1959:12
Included observations: 131 after adjusting endpoints
Convergence achieved after 6 iterations
Backcast: 1980:01 1981:01
==============================================================
     Variable        Coefficient Std. Error  T-Statistic   Prob.
==============================================================
       MA(1)          -0.377159   0.080438   -4.688826    0.0000
      SMA(12)         -0.623284   0.070243   -8.873266    0.0000
==============================================================
R-squared              0.364021   Mean dependent var    0.000291
Adjusted R-squared     0.359091   S.D. dependent var    0.045848
S.E. of regression     0.036705   Akaike info criter   -3.756676
Sum squared resid      0.173793   Schwarz criterion    -3.712780
Log likelihood         248.0623   F-statistic           73.83696
Durbin-Watson stat     1.959576   Prob(F-statistic)     0.000000
==============================================================
```

Remember that:

$$\Delta z_t = \Delta\left(1 - L^{12}\right)^D x_t = (1 - L)\left(1 - L^{12}\right)^D x_t$$

The equation therefore becomes:

$$(1 - L)\left(1 - L^{12}\right)^D x_t = \varepsilon_t - \theta_1 \varepsilon_{t-1} - \Theta_{12}\varepsilon_{t-12} + \theta_1 \Theta_{12}\varepsilon_{t-13}$$

Notice that we use notation that clearly distinguishes between the seasonal and non-seasonal moving average coefficients. Routines are available in EViews for estimating θ_1 and Θ_{12} directly. Let us do so now and evaluate the resulting model. The estimation results are shown in Exhibit 13.22.

The estimated parameters have appropriate sizes and are very significant (very low p-values). The estimated model is:

$$(1 - L)\left(1 - L^{12}\right)x_t = \left(1 - 0.623L^{12}\right)(1 - 0.377L)\varepsilon_t$$

The acid test, of course, is whether the resulting residuals form a white noise process. Exhibit 13.23 shows the ACF of the residuals and the corresponding Box–Ljung statistics.

The Q-statistics show that this is clearly a white noise process, which indicates that the model as identified is appropriate. As an exercise, plot the actual and fitted values and comment.

EXHIBIT 13.23
ACF of residuals of the multiplicative model (and Box–Ljung statistics)

Sample: 1949:02 1959:12
Included observations: 131
Q-statistic probabilities adjusted for 2 ARMA term(s)

Autocorrelation	Partial Correlation		AC	PAC	Q-Stat	Prob
.|.	.|.	1	0.016	0.016	0.0323	
.|.	.|.	2	0.011	0.011	0.0501	
*|.	*|.	3	-0.123	-0.123	2.1019	0.147
*|.	*|.	4	-0.138	-0.136	4.7081	0.095
.|.	.|*	5	0.060	0.068	5.2086	0.157
.|*	.|.	6	0.071	0.061	5.9027	0.207
*|.	*|.	7	-0.071	-0.113	6.6183	0.251
.|.	.|.	8	-0.040	-0.048	6.8462	0.335
.|*	.|*	9	0.106	0.155	8.4465	0.295
*|.	*|.	10	-0.078	-0.093	9.3331	0.315
.|.	.|.	11	0.046	-0.011	9.6395	0.380
.|.	.|.	12	-0.008	0.032	9.6490	0.472
.|.	.|*	13	0.043	0.084	9.9186	0.538
.|.	.|.	14	0.031	-0.018	10.066	0.610
.|.	.|.	15	0.050	0.042	10.449	0.657
*|.	*|.	16	-0.150	-0.111	13.836	0.462
.|.	.|.	17	0.028	0.049	13.960	0.529
.|.	.|.	18	0.008	0.005	13.971	0.601
*|.	*|.	19	-0.104	-0.128	15.657	0.548
*|.	*|.	20	-0.108	-0.164	17.480	0.490
.|.	.|.	21	-0.028	0.039	17.606	0.549
.|.	.|.	22	-0.029	-0.041	17.742	0.604
.|**	.|*	23	0.229	0.154	26.211	0.199
.|.	.|.	24	0.037	-0.017	26.435	0.233
.|.	.|.	25	-0.018	0.049	26.487	0.278
.|.	.|*	26	0.060	0.073	27.093	0.300
.|.	.|.	27	-0.042	0.006	27.393	0.337
.|.	*|.	28	-0.052	-0.097	27.853	0.366
.|.	.|.	29	-0.054	-0.035	28.351	0.393
*|.	.|.	30	-0.073	-0.046	29.265	0.399
.|.	.|.	31	-0.051	-0.040	29.711	0.429
.|*	.|.	32	0.116	0.019	32.086	0.364
*|.	*|.	33	-0.126	-0.093	34.902	0.288
.|.	.|.	34	-0.001	-0.007	34.902	0.332
.|.	*|.	35	-0.050	-0.058	35.357	0.357
.|.	*|.	36	-0.017	-0.067	35.408	0.402

Above, we derived a special case of a *multiplicative ARIMA(p, d, q) (P, D, Q) model* where p = 0, d = 1, q = 1, P = 0, D = 1 and Q = 1. Consider some other possibilities:

$$(1-L)(1-L^{12})(1-\phi L)(1-\Phi_{12}L^{12})x_t = \varepsilon_t$$

This is a case of P = 1, D = 1, Q = 0, p = 1, d = 1 and q = 0. And what about:

$$(1-L)(1-L^{12})(1-\phi L)(1-\Phi_{12}L^{12})x_t = (1-\Phi_{12}L^{12})(1-\theta L)\varepsilon_t$$

This is clearly a case where P = D = Q = p = d = q = 1.

For a series of periodicity s, the models shown above would be modified by changing "12" into s.

EXERCISES

1. What is an ARIMA(p,d,q) model? What is the Box–Jenkins iterative cycle?
2. What steps might have been taken to arrive at the following conclusions about observed time series (a), (b) and (c)?
   a) It is an ARIMA(2,1,0).
   b) It is an ARIMA(0,2,1).
   c) It is an ARIMA(1,1,1).
3. The following time-series data are supplied in an EXCEL file WT_DATA.XLS:

SERIESA	Daily data on flower sales
SERIESB	Annual data on rainfall
SERIESC	Daily data on stock prices
SERIESD	Quarterly data on unemployment
SERIESE	Annual data on sunspot numbers
SERIESF	Daily data on composite stock price index
AIRLINE	Box–Jenkins airline data

SIMUL1, SIMUL2, SIMUL3, SIMUL4: Simulated data

Carry out a full Box–Jenkins type analysis (identification–estimation–diagnostic checking) on each of the above series and forecast each one three periods ahead.

APPENDIX 13.1

Possible Theoretical
ACF for an AR(p)
PACF for an MA(q)
ACF, PACF for an ARMA(p,q)

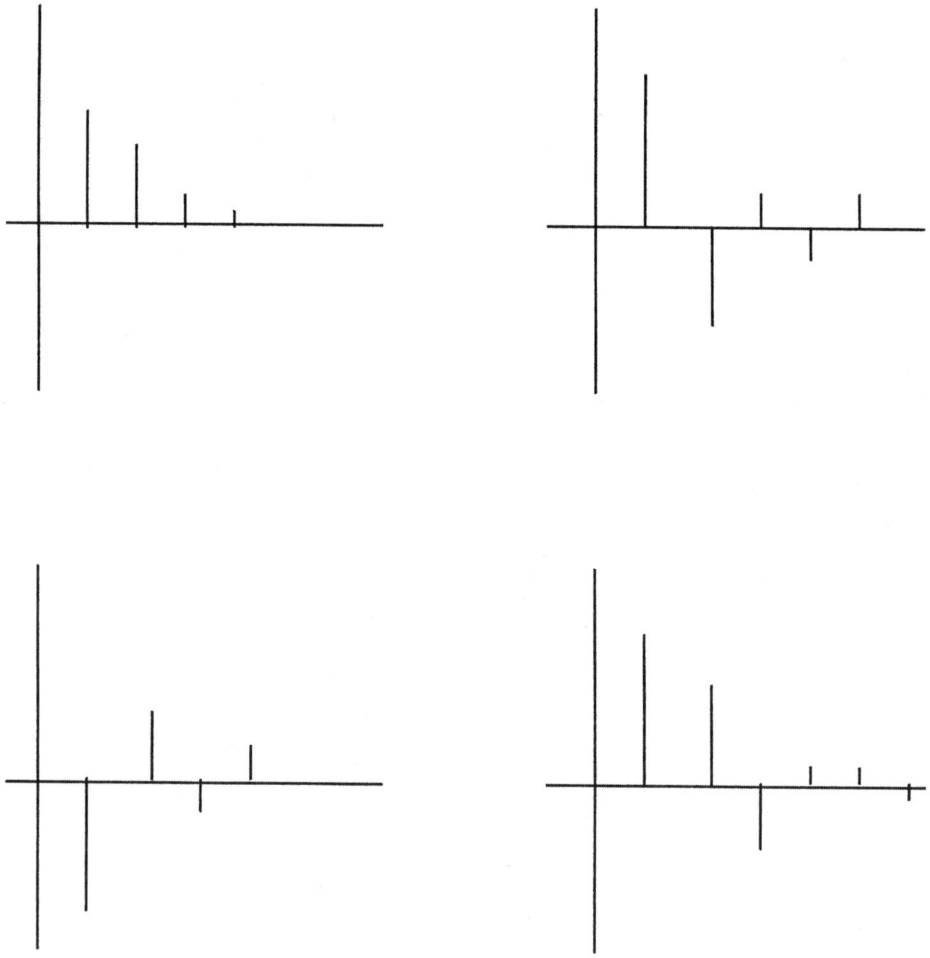

Possible Theoretical
ACF for an MA(1)
PACF for an AR(1)

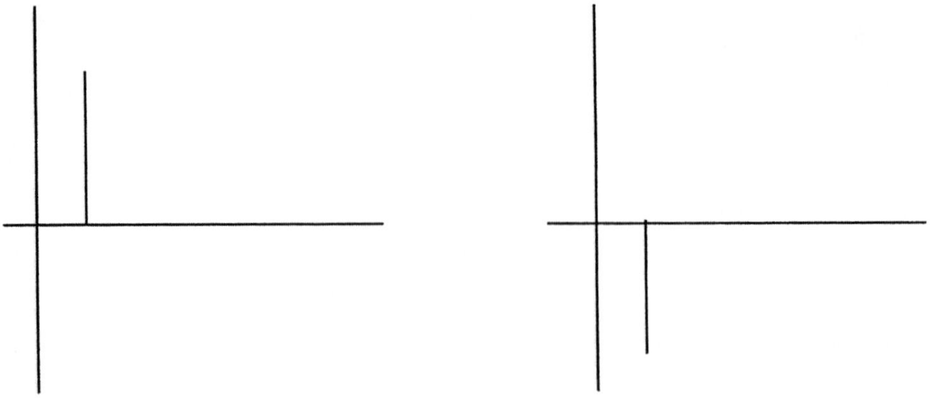

Possible Theoretical
ACF for an MA(2)
PACF for an AR(2)

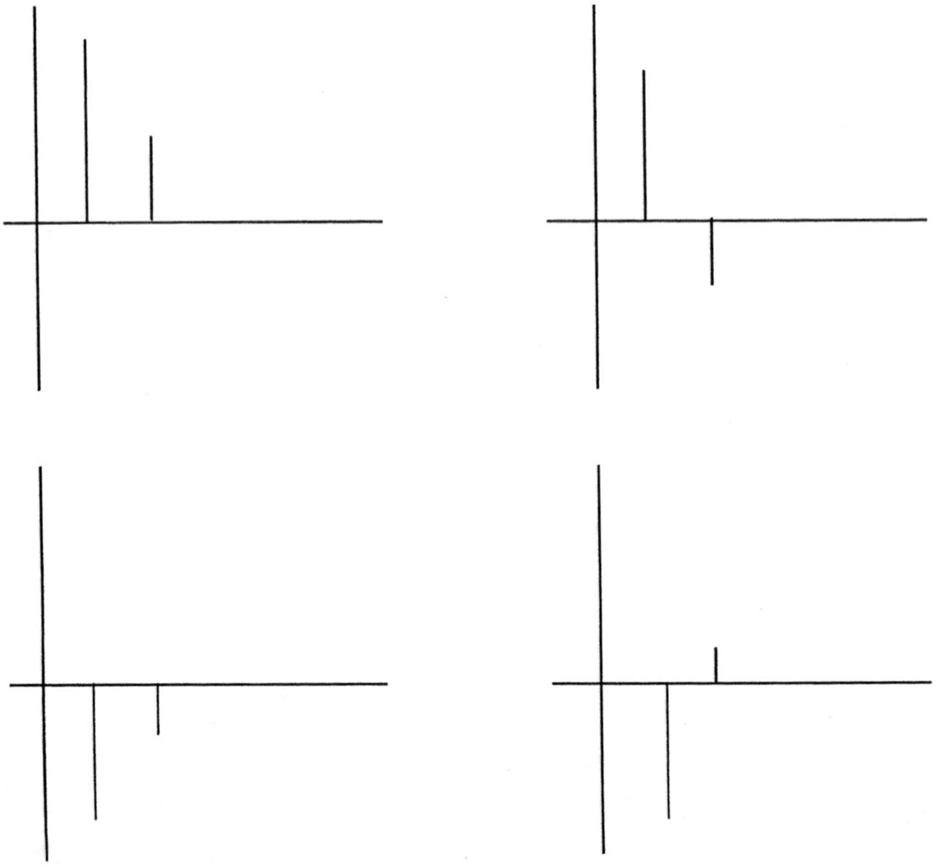

CHAPTER 14

Vector Autoregression (VAR) Modelling with Some Applications

INTRODUCTION

In this chapter, we introduce the concept of vector autoregression (VAR) modelling. We will also consider its application to policy making, forecasting and causality analysis. In the following chapter, we will see how it is applied to cointegration analysis.

Let us begin the discussion by looking at the following simple form of the import function:

$$M_t = \beta Y_t + e_t$$

The specification of a model like this is an example of *structural form* (SF) modelling, which dominated our early study of econometrics (see, in particular, chapters 1 to 8). In this case, M is endogenous while Y is exogenous (with the implicit assumption that Y *causes* M and not vice versa). A more elaborate example of an SF model is to be found summarized in equations (7.1) to (7.4) in chapter 7:

$$C_{pt} = g_{11} + b_{14} Y_t + g_{12} C_{pt-1} + u_{1t} \tag{7.1}$$

$$M_t = g_{21} + b_{24} Y_t + g_{23} \frac{p_{mt}}{p_{dt}} + u_{2t} \tag{7.2}$$

$$I_t = g_{31} + g_{34} Y_{t-1} + g_{35} D_t + u_{3t} \tag{7.3}$$

$$Y_t = C_{pt} + C_{gt} + I_t + X_t - M_t \tag{7.4}$$

where another important feature of SF modelling is immediately evident, namely the imposition of *zero-type* restrictions on each equation; for example, the variable I is not found in equation (7.1). Both the endogenous-exogenous dichotomy and the zero-type restrictions are determined largely on the basis of economic theory although it is quite possible for zero-type restrictions to be arbitrarily imposed in order to assure the identifiability of the system.

VECTOR AUTOREGRESSION MODELS

Some well-known econometricians have challenged the basic underpinnings of structural models. Liu (1960) was probably the first to do so in an articulate manner when he challenged the constancy of the parameters over time. Lucas (1976) provided what is perhaps the best-known critique of such models: policies being evaluated will eventually result in action by economic agents tending to counter the intended effects of such policies. Decisions and forecasts based on them are therefore flawed.

In a seminal article, Sims (1980) followed up on these criticisms and challenged the usefulness of the "incredible" theoretical restrictions imposed on SF models. He instead proposed an approach to modelling based on the following three tenets which form the basis of VAR models:

1. There is no *a priori* endogenous-exogenous dichotomy in the system
2. There are no zero-type restrictions
3. There is no strict underlying economic theory on which the model is based

The last tenet has been the reason behind the naming of the VAR approach to modelling as *atheoretical econometrics*. See Cooley and LeRoy (1985). Modern VAR analysis is not totally faithful to these tenets and, in particular, takes into account the endogenous-exogenous dichotomy, albeit in a limited way. See Giannini (1992).

Let us illustrate a traditional VAR by presenting a VAR alternative to the simple import function introduced at the beginning of the chapter. This alternative is displayed in equations (14.1) and (14.2) below:

$$M_t = a_1 M_{t-1} + a_2 M_{t-2} + b_1 Y_{t-1} + b_2 Y_{t-2} + \varepsilon_{1t} \qquad \textbf{(14.1)}$$

$$Y_t = c_1 M_{t-1} + c_2 M_{t-2} + d_1 Y_{t-1} + d_2 Y_{t-2} + \varepsilon_{2t} \qquad \textbf{(14.2)}$$

where ε_1 and ε_2 are correlated white noise processes. You will notice that the current value of each variable of interest is "regressed" on all the variables in the system (here, only two) lagged a certain number of times (here only two lags). In matrix notation, this system can be written as:

$$\begin{bmatrix} M_t \\ Y_t \end{bmatrix} = \begin{bmatrix} a_1 & b_1 \\ c_1 & d_1 \end{bmatrix} \begin{bmatrix} M_{t-1} \\ Y_{t-1} \end{bmatrix} + \begin{bmatrix} a_2 & b_2 \\ c_2 & d_2 \end{bmatrix} \begin{bmatrix} M_{t-2} \\ Y_{t-2} \end{bmatrix} + \begin{bmatrix} \varepsilon_{1t} \\ \varepsilon_{2t} \end{bmatrix}$$

or more succinctly as:

$$\mathbf{x}_t = \mathbf{\Pi}_1 \mathbf{x}_{t-1} + \mathbf{\Pi}_2 \mathbf{x}_{t-2} + \boldsymbol{\varepsilon}_t \qquad \textbf{(14.3)}$$

where:

$$\mathbf{x}_t = \begin{bmatrix} M_t \\ Y_t \end{bmatrix}, \mathbf{\Pi}_j = \begin{bmatrix} a_j & b_j \\ c_j & d_j \end{bmatrix}, j = 1,2$$

and:

$$\boldsymbol{\varepsilon}_t = \begin{bmatrix} \varepsilon_{1t} \\ \varepsilon_{2t} \end{bmatrix}, \ \text{cov}\left(\boldsymbol{\varepsilon}_t\right) = \boldsymbol{\Omega}$$

The elements of $\boldsymbol{\varepsilon}_t$ are correlated with each other but are uncorrelated with their own lagged values and with $\mathbf{x}_{t-i}$, i = 1, 2, …, k. The correlations are captured in $\boldsymbol{\Omega}$.

A more general formulation of the two-variable VAR model might be:

$$M_t = a_1 M_{t-1} + a_2 M_{t-2} + \ldots + a_p M_{t-p} + b_1 Y_{t-1} + b_2 Y_{t-2} + \ldots + b_q Y_{t-q} + \varepsilon_{1t} \quad \textbf{(14.4)}$$

$$Y_t = c_1 M_{t-1} + c_2 M_{t-2} + \ldots + c_r M_{t-r} + d_1 Y_{t-1} + d_2 Y_{t-2} + \ldots + d_s Y_{t-s} + \varepsilon_{2t} \quad \textbf{(14.5)}$$

This formulation also introduces the possibility of different lag lengths although in practice the same length is employed.

There is some resemblance between the VAR formulation shown so far and the reduced form of a structural econometric model and, in fact, it constitutes an unrestricted reduced form of a structural model in the case where there are no exogenous variables. See chapter 7.

Equation (14.3) lends itself to generalization in two directions. In the first place it allows for the inclusion of more than two variables if we imagine the **x** vector is of dimension p × 1, p = 2, 3, … . A second generalization involves the incorporation of a lag of order k, k = 1, 2, … . The more general form of the model may be written as:

$$\mathbf{x}_t = \boldsymbol{\Pi}_1 \mathbf{x}_{t-1} + \boldsymbol{\Pi}_2 \mathbf{x}_{t-2} + \ldots + \boldsymbol{\Pi}_n \mathbf{x}_{t-k} + \boldsymbol{\varepsilon}_t$$

where $\mathbf{x}_t$ is a vector of p variables, $\boldsymbol{\Pi}_1$, $\boldsymbol{\Pi}_2$, ..., and $\boldsymbol{\Pi}_k$ are (p × p) matrices of coefficients to be estimated, and $\boldsymbol{\varepsilon}_t$ is a vector of innovations with mean zero and covariance matrix $\boldsymbol{\Omega}$.

There is a possible third generalization which will only receive partial coverage in this book. It concerns the generalization resulting from the introduction of purely "exogenous" and other deterministic elements into the VAR model. These include items such as a constant term, a deterministic trend, dummy variables and other variables like the price ratio p_{mt}/p_{dt} which appears in the SF model above. This is the most general form of the VAR which, in *standard form*, may be written as:

$$\mathbf{x}_t = \boldsymbol{\mu}_0 + \boldsymbol{\mu}_1 t + \boldsymbol{\psi}\mathbf{d}_t + \boldsymbol{\Theta}\mathbf{f}_t + \boldsymbol{\Pi}_1 \mathbf{x}_{t-1} + \boldsymbol{\Pi}_2 \mathbf{x}_{t-2} + \ldots + \boldsymbol{\Pi}_n \mathbf{x}_{t-k} + \mathbf{B}_0 \mathbf{z}_t + \mathbf{B}_1 \mathbf{z}_{t-1}$$
$$+ \ldots + \mathbf{B}_k \mathbf{z}_{t-k} + \boldsymbol{\varepsilon}_t$$

where:

- $\mathbf{B}_j$, j = 0, 2, …, k are p × K matrices of fixed coefficients
- $\mathbf{z}_t$ is a (K × 1) vector of exogenous variables
- $\boldsymbol{\mu}_0$ is the (G × 1) constant term vector
- $\boldsymbol{\mu}_1$ is a (G × 1) vector of fixed coefficients

- t is the trend variable (used also as the time subscript)
- $\mathbf{d}_t$ is a (k × 1) vector of "intervention" dummies
- $\mathbf{f}_t$ is a (s × 1) vector of seasonal dummies (s + 1 is the number of "seasons")
- $\boldsymbol{\Psi}$ is a (G × k) matrix of fixed coefficients
- $\boldsymbol{\Theta}$ is a (G × s) matrix of fixed coefficients

This very general form of the VAR model has become standard in modern VAR analysis. See Giannini (1992). A special case of this, which we will use in chapter 15, is the following:

$$M_t = m_{01} + m_{11}t + a_{11}M_{t-1} + a_{12}M_{t-2} + b_{11}Y_{t-1} + b_{12}Y_{t-2} + f_{11}\left(p_{mt}/p_{dt}\right)_{-1} + f_{12}\left(p_{mt}/p_{dt}\right)_{-2} + \varepsilon_{1t}$$

$$Y_t = m_{02} + m_{12}t + a_{21}M_{t-1} + a_{22}M_{t-2} + b_{21}Y_{t-1} + b_{22}Y_{t-2} + f_{21}\left(p_{mt}/p_{dt}\right)_{-1} + f_{22}\left(p_{mt}/p_{dt}\right)_{-2} + \varepsilon_{2t}$$

$$\left(p_{mt}/p_{dt}\right) = m_{03} + m_{13}t + a_{31}M_{t-1} + a_{32}M_{t-2} + b_{31}Y_{t-1} + b_{32}Y_{t-2} + f_{31}\left(p_{mt}/p_{dt}\right)_{-1} + f_{32}\left(p_{mt}/p_{dt}\right)_{-2} + \varepsilon_{2t}$$

This includes three endogenous variables (M_t, Y_t and p_{mt}/p_{dt}) as well as two deterministic terms: a constant and a trend term.

ILLUSTRATION OF VECTOR AUTOREGRESSION ESTIMATION USING EVIEWS

EViews requires three types of information before it can estimate a VAR. First you must specify the lag interval (nearest and farthest lag) to be included for the endogenous variables, then the list of endogenous variables, and finally (optionally) any exogenous variables (including a constant term).

In the example given above, imports and income are endogenous variables, lags 1 through 2 are included in the estimation, and no exogenous variables are included. EViews allows you to specify flexible lag structures on the endogenous variables. Exhibit 14.1 shows the output from EViews applied to equations (14.1) to (14.2).

The coefficient values shown in Exhibit 14.1 are similar to reduced form coefficients and therefore without great interest in their own right. Evaluation is done through an analysis of *impulse response functions* and *forecast error variance decompositions*, which together make up what is termed *innovations accounting*.

EVALUATION OF VECTOR AUTOREGRESSION MODELS

The estimated coefficients of a standard form VAR model are difficult to interpret from an economic point of view and indeed you should never attempt to do that. We

EXHIBIT 14.1

Estimated VAR system:

$$M_t = a_1 M_{t-1} + a_2 M_{t-2} + b_1 Y_{t-1} + b_2 Y_{t-2} + \varepsilon_{1t}$$
$$Y_t = c_1 M_{t-1} + c_2 M_{t-2} + d_1 Y_{t-1} + d_2 Y_{t-2} + \varepsilon_{2t}$$

```
Vector Autoregression Estimates
========================================
Sample(adjusted): 1969 1991
 Included observations: 23 after adjusting endpoints
 Standard errors & t-statistics in parentheses
========================================
                    INCOME      IMPORTS
========================================
   INCOME(-1)       1.533452    0.190049
                   (0.20350)   (0.12482)
                   (7.53536)   (1.52261)

   INCOME(-2)      -0.490096   -0.121025
                   (0.22140)   (0.13580)
                  (-2.21361)  (-0.89122)

  IMPORTS(-1)      -0.019177    0.718785
                   (0.37682)   (0.23112)
                  (-0.05089)   (3.10995)

  IMPORTS(-2)      -0.157611    0.004760
                   (0.35448)   (0.21742)
                  (-0.44463)   (0.02189)
========================================
 R-squared          0.932780    0.887961
 Adj. R-squared     0.922167    0.870270
 Sum sq. resids     13138812    4942835.
 S.E. equation      831.5747    510.0482
 Log likelihood    -185.0748   -173.8321
 Akaike AIC         16.44129    15.46366
 Schwarz SC         16.63877    15.66114
 Mean dependent     16481.83    3762.002
 S.D. dependent     2980.701    1416.092
========================================
 Determinant Residual Covaria 1.17E+11
 Log Likelihood              -358.3715
 Akaike Information Criteria  31.85839
 Schwarz Criteria             32.25335
========================================
```

mentioned above that a VAR resembles the reduced form of a structural model where there are no exogenous variables. Let us follow up on this idea to arrive at a model whose coefficients *would* make good economic sense.

Consider the model:

$$M_t = A_1 M_{t-1} + A_2 M_{t-2} + B_0 Y_t + B_1 Y_{t-1} + B_2 Y_{t-2} + e_{1t}$$

$$Y_t = C_0 M_t + C_1 M_{t-1} + C_2 M_{t-2} + D_1 Y_{t-1} + D_2 Y_{t-2} + e_{2t}$$

This is an example of a *structural* VAR. It differs from the standard form VAR by the presence of contemporaneous values of all the variables in each equation and by the fact that the disturbances, e_1 and e_2, are uncorrelated. One consequence of this addition is that there is now the equivalence of a simultaneous bias and the coefficients of the model cannot be estimated by OLS.

If this model is expressed in its reduced form, it will appear in the form of equations (14.1) and (14.2). As an exercise, derive the reduced form from the structural form. Show in particular that the disturbances in the reduced form are $\varepsilon_{1t} = (e_{1t} + B_0 e_{2t})$ and $\varepsilon_{2t} = (C_0 e_{1t} + e_{2t})$. Clearly the disturbances of the reduced (standard) form are correlated even though those of the structural form are not.

The coefficients of the structural form, however, remain unidentifiable unless *a priori* restrictions are imposed on the structural form. A very popular approach is to apply the Choleski decomposition. An illustration of this procedure in the current context is to set $C_0 = 0$. This in effect converts the structural VAR into a recursive system: we can solve for Y_t which feeds forward into the solution of M_t. One interesting consequence of the decomposition is its implication for *impulse response functions* and *variance decompositions*, which help us to evaluate the model as well as to formulate policy prescriptions.

The Impulse Response Function

An impulse response function traces the response of an endogenous variable to a change in one of the innovations. Consider the structural VAR above. A change in e_{2t} will immediately change the value of Y_t (income). It will also change all future values of imports and income through the dynamic structure of the system. An impulse response function describes the response of an endogenous variable to a unit change in one of the innovations.

The ambiguity in interpreting impulse response functions arises from the fact that the errors in the standard form are not uncorrelated. When the errors are correlated they have a common component which cannot be identified with any specific variable. The *Choleski decomposition* is a somewhat arbitrary method of dealing with this problem and it attributes all of the effect of any common component to the variable that is first in the ordering of the recursive VAR system. In our example, the common component of ε_{1t} and ε_{2t} is totally attributed to ε_{2t}, because it precedes ε_{1t} in the solution of the model. Changing the order of the equations can dramatically change the impulse responses and care should be given to interpreting the impulse response functions. The weaker the correlation between the innovations the less the

EXHIBIT 14.2 (A)
Impulse response function for model (5) to (6): response to income innovation

Effect of One S.D. INCOME Innovation

Period	INCOME	IMPORTS
1	755.8126	98.87104
	(111.438)	(95.5574)
2	1157.106	214.7084
	(217.155)	(111.351)
3	1384.245	283.2347
	(339.834)	(125.680)
4	1516.307	327.6429
	(445.237)	(131.460)
5	1595.846	357.4980
	(526.998)	(134.735)
6	1645.521	378.3023
	(588.889)	(139.075)
7	1677.609	393.2128
	(636.262)	(145.177)
8	1698.903	404.1155
	(673.600)	(152.498)
9	1713.272	412.1868
	(704.178)	(160.285)
10	1722.997	418.1939
	(730.289)	(167.987)

Ordering: INCOME IMPORTS

ordering matters. In EViews you are always required to order the VAR in order to determine the nature and extent of the responses.

The tabular version of the impulse response function display, based on a once-and-for-all shock[1] to the income innovations, is shown in Exhibit 14.2(A) for our two-variable VAR and for 10 periods.

What does this output tell us? Note first that the ordering is income followed by imports. The income innovation, which has been "shocked" by an increase of $755.81 million (equivalent to one standard deviation), causes income, in the first round, to increase by this very amount. The immediate effect on imports is to increase these by $98.9 million. By round 2 (one period ahead), income has now increased by $1157.11 million, relative to the case of "no shock", as a result of the exogenous shock to income. Imports have increased by $214.7 million. All this seems quite reasonable given our understanding of the relationship between income and imports.

[1] The size of the shock is equal to one standard deviation of the income varible. This is the default in EViews.

EXHIBIT 14.2 (B)
Impulse response function for model (5) to (6): response to imports innovation

Effect of One S.D. IMPORTS Innovation

Period	INCOME	IMPORTS
1	0.000000	452.9132
	(0.00000)	(66.7784)
2	-8.685536	325.5473
	(155.124)	(106.564)
3	-90.94593	234.5039
	(245.856)	(98.2581)
4	-191.0113	153.8746
	(331.784)	(107.739)
5	-288.2456	86.42424
	(414.457)	(117.633)
6	-374.3064	31.18924
	(490.691)	(126.767)
7	-446.9323	-13.42196
	(558.430)	(135.423)
8	-506.5613	-49.13775
	(617.119)	(143.952)
9	-554.6897	-77.56500
	(667.078)	(152.474)
10	-593.0940	-100.0983
	(709.030)	(160.904)

Ordering: INCOME IMPORTS

Let us now examine the response of the system to a shock in the imports innovations shown in Exhibit 14.2 (B). In this case we see clearly that all the initial shock to the imports innovation is absorbed by the imports variable only but by the second round (since imports affect income with a lag) income falls by $8.68 million. Try yourself to say what happens after.

EViews will also show the two sets of results (shown above) in the alternative form shown in Exhibit 14.3 (A). These results combine in a different way the results already shown in Exhibits 14.2 (A) and 14.2 (B). The top half of the table shows the response of income to a shock to the income innovations (first column) *and* the shock to the imports innovations (second column). The lower half of the table shows the response of imports to a shock to the income innovations (first column) *and* the shock to the imports innovations (second column).

The ordering used in Exhibit 14.3 (A) is income–imports, which is what theory comes closest to suggesting. What if we reverse the order of the VAR? Look at Exhibit 14.3 (B). What does this output tell us? Take the effects of the shocks on imports, shown in the bottom half of the table (the upper half of Exhibit 14.3 (B) shows the effect on income of the innovation shocks). The imports innovation, which

EXHIBIT 14.3 (A)
Impulse response function for model (5) to (6): response to income and imports innovations

Impulse Response to One S.D. Innovations

Response of INCOME:

Period	INCOME	IMPORTS
1	755.8126	0.000000
	(111.438)	(0.00000)
2	1157.106	-8.685536
	(217.155)	(155.124)
3	1384.245	-90.94593
	(339.834)	(245.856)
4	1516.307	-191.0113
	(445.237)	(331.784)
5	1595.846	-288.2456
	(526.998)	(414.457)
6	1645.521	-374.3064
	(588.889)	(490.691)
7	1677.609	-446.9323
	(636.262)	(558.430)
8	1698.903	-506.5613
	(673.600)	(617.119)
9	1713.272	-554.6897
	(704.178)	(667.078)
10	1722.997	-593.0940
	(730.289)	(709.030)

Response of IMPORTS:

Period	INCOME	IMPORTS
1	98.87104	452.9132
	(95.5574)	(66.7784)
2	214.7084	325.5473
	(111.351)	(106.564)
3	283.2347	234.5039
	(125.680)	(98.2581)
4	327.6429	153.8746
	(131.460)	(107.739)
5	357.4980	86.42424
	(134.735)	(117.633)
6	378.3023	31.18924
	(139.075)	(126.767)
7	393.2128	-13.42196
	(145.177)	(135.423)
8	404.1155	-49.13775
	(152.498)	(143.952)
9	412.1868	-77.56500
	(160.285)	(152.474)
10	418.1939	-100.0983
	(167.987)	(160.904)

Ordering: INCOME IMPORTS

EXHIBIT 14.3 (B)
Impulse response function for model (5) to (6)
(with order of equations reversed)

```
Impulse Response to One S.D. Innovations
==================================
 Response of INCOME:
 Period     INCOME      IMPORTS
==================================
   1       738.4226     161.1978
          (108.874)    (155.795)
   2       1132.335     238.2989
          (215.702)    (283.612)
   3       1371.792     206.3748
          (332.634)    (383.073)
   4       1522.158     136.7776
          (433.419)    (468.632)
   5       1620.605     58.74455
          (513.617)    (544.312)
   6       1687.492    -14.74162
          (576.278)    (610.893)
   7       1734.331    -78.85290
          (625.671)    (668.806)
   8       1767.853    -132.5683
          (665.468)    (718.645)
   9       1792.156    -176.5248
          (698.448)    (761.116)
  10       1809.847    -211.9715
          (726.650)    (796.961)
==================================
 Response of IMPORTS:
 Period INCOME     IMPORTS
==================================
   1       0.000000     463.5794
          (0.00000)    (68.3511)
   2       140.3364     363.8495
          (86.2886)    (112.061)
   3       226.7036     289.5159
          (109.135)    (115.686)
   4       287.2864     220.2130
          (121.995)    (128.707)
   5       330.8402     160.6820
          (129.874)    (139.850)
   6       362.9463     111.1550
          (136.811)    (149.598)
   7       387.0282     70.75028
          (144.115)    (158.591)
   8       405.2975     38.18156
          (151.877)    (167.177)
   9       419.2460     12.12980
          (159.796)    (175.458)
  10       429.9207    -8.603849
          (167.561)    (183.394)
==================================
 Ordering: IMPORTS INCOME
==================================
```

has been "shocked" by an increase of \$463.57 million (equivalent to one standard deviation), causes imports, in the first round, to increase by this very amount. But the income innovation has no effect on imports in this round. By round 2 (one period ahead), imports have increased by \$363.8 million relative to the "base" period as a result of the exogenous shock to imports and by \$140.3 million as a result of the income shock (and so on).

The question then arises: are these responses (both in sign and magnitude) reasonable? Would an increase in imports result in increasing income, as is shown in the lower half of Exhibit 14.3 (B)? This seems to run counter to all reasonable expectations and should then give rise to some doubts about the validity of this ordering.

Variance Decomposition

The variance decomposition of a VAR gives information about the relative importance of each of the random innovations in the explanation of each variable in the system. This is done through an analysis of the forecast error of each variable. Let us elaborate on this by explaining the output in Exhibit 14.4, which shows the variance decomposition of income and imports.

The top half of Exhibit 14.4 shows the variance decomposition of income following a shock to the income innovations of TT\$ 755.8 million. Given the ordering income-imports, the entire change in income in the first round (100%) resulting from the shock to the income innovations is due to this initial shock. This shock to the income innovations also causes an immediate change in the imports variable, but the resulting change in imports has no effect itself on income at this point, since current imports has no effect on current income. The import variable only has an effect on income in round two, when it accounts for a negligible 0.003% of the change in income, with income still accounting for the lion's share of 99.996% of its own variation. For the entire 10-year period considered here, the effect of imports on income, following the initial shock to the income innovation, is negligible, never getting larger than 6%.

Now look at the lower half of Exhibit 14.4, which traces the variation of income and imports due to an initial shock of TT\$463.6 million to the imports variable. Because of the ordering income-imports, this shock has an immediate effect on imports but current income also has an effect on current imports. In round one, the import shock accounts for 95.4% of the variation in the import variable, while income accounts for the rest of the variation. The round one change in imports has an impact on income in round two and this in turn has an impact on imports in round two. This time, income accounts for 15% of the variation in imports and imports itself for 85% of its own variation. The influence of income on imports increases round after round and by the end of the 10-year period it is accounting for 74% of the total variation in imports. Imports accounts for only 26% of its own variation by this time, notwithstanding the fact that the initial push came from the imports variable and it accounted then for over 95% of the initial variation in imports.

As with the impulse response functions, the above conclusions depend crucially on the ordering of the variables.

EXHIBIT 14.4
Variance decomposition of income and imports

Variance Decomposition

Variance Decomposition of INCOME:

Period	S.E.	INCOME	IMPORTS
1	755.8126	100.0000	0.000000
2	1382.108	99.99605	0.003949
3	1958.220	99.78234	0.217664
4	2484.009	99.27342	0.726576
5	2966.498	98.54641	1.453589
6	3412.910	97.69897	2.301028
7	3829.109	96.80965	3.190347
8	4219.592	95.93161	4.068393
9	4587.803	95.09664	4.903360
10	4936.437	94.32127	5.678730

Variance Decomposition of IMPORTS:

Period	S.E.	INCOME	IMPORTS
1	463.5794	4.548728	95.45127
2	605.7942	15.22540	84.77460
3	708.6611	27.10015	72.89985
4	795.7561	38.44540	61.55460
5	876.6423	48.30851	51.69149
6	955.2943	56.36332	43.63668
7	1033.143	62.67481	37.32519
8	1110.454	67.49534	32.50466
9	1187.022	71.12651	28.87349
10	1262.508	73.84740	26.15260

Ordering: INCOME IMPORTS

FORECASTING WITH VECTOR AUTOREGRESSION MODELS

VAR models have proven successful for forecasting systems of interrelated time-series variables. Structural econometric models (SEMs), you may remember, are frequently used for forecasting. In chapter 12, it was pointed out that one of the major attractions of forecasting with ARIMA models (as opposed to using SEMs) was that there was no need to forecast the exogenous variables as a prelude to obtaining forecasts of the variable(s) of interest. The same advantage applies to VAR models that do not include exogenous variables so that if, for instance, we wanted to forecast the 1992 import value, it is easily obtained as:

$$M^{f}_{1992} = 0.719M_{1991} + 0.005M_{1990} + 0.190Y_{1991} - 0.121Y_{1990}$$

EXHIBIT 14.5
Example of EViews program for forecasting using VAR estimation in Exhibit 14.1

```
=============================================================
ASSIGN @ALL F

IMPORTS = 0.71878519*IMPORTS(-1) + 0.0047602133*IMPORTS(-2) +
0.19004896*INCOME(-1) - 0.12102464*INCOME(-2)

INCOME = - 0.019177043*IMPORTS(-1) - 0.15761087*IMPORTS(-2) +
1.5334516*INCOME(-1) - 0.49009603*INCOME(-2)
=============================================================
```

while the corresponding forecast for the income value is:

$$Y^f_{1992} = -0.019M_{1991} - 0.158M_{1990} + 1.53Y_{1991} - 0.490Y_{1990}$$

You will notice that all the right-hand-side values on which the calculation of the forecast is based are known at the time of the operation. To forecast 1993 values, the following formulae are applied:

$$M^f_{1993} = 0.719M^f_{1992} + 0.005M_{1991} + 0.190Y^f_{1992} - 0.121Y_{1991}$$

$$Y^f_{1993} = -0.019M^f_{1992} - 0.158M_{1991} + 1.53Y^f_{1992} - 0.490Y_{1991}$$

You will notice that the forecasted values for 1992 are used. To forecast values for 1994 and onwards, similar recursive formulae are applied so that at any point in time the right-hand-side variables are either known or are the (best) forecasts. In general, unbiased forecasts of the elements of the vector $\mathbf{X}^f_{n+h}$, where n is the sample size on which estimation is based and h is the forecast horizon, are obtained by the recursive formula:

$$\mathbf{X}^f_{n+h} = \mathbf{\Pi}_1\mathbf{X}^f_{n+h-1} + \mathbf{\Pi}_2\mathbf{X}^f_{n+h-2}$$

where $\mathbf{X}^f_{n+h-i} = \mathbf{X}_{n+h-i}$ if $h \leq i$. Otherwise, it is the forecasted value.

Illustration of Forecasting with Vector Autoregression Models

Exhibit 14.5 shows an example of a program, based on estimation of equations (14.1) and (14.2), that may be set up in EViews in order to obtain forecasts. In order to forecast to 1993, make sure that the "Range" of the sample period is extended up to 1993. The "Solve" command in EViews (choose the "static solution" option) then calculates the forecasted values.

Of course, it is a simple enough matter to calculate these values using a pocket calculator. Using the forecasting formulae shown above, we can calculate the 1992 forecasts as:

$$M^{f}_{1992} = 0.719(4108.5) + 0.005(3644.4) + 0.190(16636.8) - 0.121(16134.4) = 4179.6$$

$$Y^{f}_{1992} = -0.019(4108.5) - 0.158(3644.4) + 1.53(16636.8) - 0.490(16134.4) = 16951.1$$

Calculate the 1993 forecasts as an exercise.

In larger models, however, or models with longer lags, use of a pocket calculator can become very cumbersome. EViews would provide the forecasts and you ought to rely on these.

VECTOR AUTOREGRESSION MODELLING AND CAUSALITY TESTING

Consider equation (14.1). Taken on its own, this equation is identical in form to an ADL model. In the spirit of general-to-specific modelling usually associated with ADLs, we may wish to ask a question like the following: are the β coefficients (β_1 and β_2) significantly different from zero? If they are not, then in the interest of parsimony (and efficiency) we should eliminate the lagged Y values from these equations and explain M_t only in terms of its own past values. In this case, we would say that Y does not cause M (in the sense that it does not help to explain or predict it better). On the other hand, if the β coefficients turn out to be jointly significant, then the conclusion would be that Y causes M.

The concept of causation in science is quite complex and is still the subject of passionate debate. It is essentially a philosophical rather than an empirical issue, with theories ranging from an extreme "everything causes everything", to denying the existence of any causation whatsoever. However, it is not our place here to enter into the debate. Given that philosophical definitions have important influences on statistical counterparts, the need for an operational and testable definition of causality becomes clear. This concept of causation or *causality* was first introduced into the econometric literature by Granger (1969) and as a consequence is often referred to as *Granger causality*.[2] It can be described in the following way:

> x is a Granger cause of y (denoted as $x \rightarrow y$) if present y can be predicted with better accuracy by using *past* values of x rather than by not doing so, other information being identical. (Charemza and Deadman, 1997, p.165)

In simple English, if knowledge of past x allows us to predict y more accurately than knowledge of y alone, then x causes y. This definition can be extended to that of *instantaneous causation* (denoted $x \Rightarrow y$) which exists if present y can be better predicted by using *present and past* values of x, other information being identical.

The concepts of Granger causality and Granger instantaneous causality may be defined in a more formal way. Let U_t be the set of all present and past information existing at time t (not restricted to knowledge of x and y) and let X_t be the set of all present and past information on a variable x existing at time t, that is, $X_t = \{x_1, x_2, \ldots, x_t\}$. Let y_t be the current value of a variable y and $\tilde{y}_t$ be an unbiased prediction of y_t.

[2] In what follows, we will take the terms "causality" and "Granger causality" to mean the same thing.

Granger causality

$$\text{if } MSE(\tilde{y}_t | U_{t-1}) < MSE(\tilde{y}_t | U_{t-1} \setminus X_{t-1}), \text{ then } x \rightarrow y$$

Granger instantaneous causality

$$\text{if } MSE(\tilde{y}_t U_t \setminus y_t) < MSE(\tilde{y}_t U_{t-1} \setminus X_t, y_t) \text{ then } x \Rightarrow y$$

The causality defined so far is *unidirectional*, but it is also possible that y can cause x in the same manner. If y → x and x → y, then we have *feedback causality.*

In the above definitions, there is the use of the vague notion of "all information" (U_t). Since the set of all information is not well defined, it is up to the researcher to decide which available information is to be used and which is to be ignored. The set of "all information" then becomes the set of "all relevant information", with the decision of what information is to be considered "relevant" being an arbitrary one. We can assume that the set of all relevant information is that which is included in an econometric model, allowing for the inclusion of some irrelevant information, which will be inevitable prior to estimation and testing. In the light of the previous discussions, a general unrestricted VAR model fits the bill perfectly, with the problem of testing whether x → y reducing simply to the question of whether x can be eliminated from that part of a VAR model that describes y. The tests for causality that we shall now consider (as well as many other tests that can be found in the extensive literature on the subject) are based on this general principle.

TESTING FOR CAUSALITY

Direct Granger Tests

If we believe that x causes y, then it seems quite natural to expect that the regression:

$$y_t = \sum_{j=1}^{k} \alpha_j y_{t-j} + \sum_{j=1}^{k} \beta_j x_{t-j} + u_t \, [\qquad \textbf{(14.6)}$$

will have significantly more explanatory power than the regression:

$$y_t = \sum_{j=1}^{k} \alpha_j y_{t-j} + u_t \qquad \textbf{(14.7)}$$

This appears to be a classic case of an "unrestricted" versus a "restricted" model as was discussed in previous chapters, with the restrictions imposed on equation (14.7) being that $\beta_j = 0, j = 1, 2, \ldots, k$. A natural statistic that can be used to establish causality would therefore be:

EXHIBIT 14.6

Testing Granger causality between imports and income

Pairwise Granger Causality Tests

Sample: 1967 1991

Lags: 2

Null Hypothesis:	Obs	F-Statistic	Probability
INCOME does not Granger Cause IMPORTS	23	3.96833	0.03734
IMPORTS does not Granger Cause INCOME		0.90966	0.42039

$$Q = \frac{(SSE_c - SSE_u)/k}{SSE_u/n - 2k}$$

where SSE_u is the sum of squared errors associated with equation 14.6 (the unconstrained form of the model) and SSE_c is the sum of squared errors associated with equation 14.7 (the constrained form of the model) and:

k = the number of constraints (equal to the number of lags)
n = the number of observations

Under the null hypothesis that equation (14.7) is the true model, this statistic is asymptotically distributed as $\chi^2/k(k)$, and can be approximated by $F_{k,n-2k}$.

This most natural testing procedure is often identified in the literature as a *direct Granger test*. Other direct Granger tests have been proposed based on the Wald, likelihood ratio and Lagrange multiplier principles. The following are considered in Geweke et al. (1981):

$$Q_W = \frac{n(SSE_c - SSE_u)}{SSE_u}$$

$$Q_{LR} = \frac{n(SSE_e - SSE_u)}{SSE_c}$$

$$Q_{LM} = n \ln \frac{SSE_c}{SSE_u}$$

These are all asymptotically distributed as χ_k^2 under the null hypothesis. Note, however, that these are all large sample tests, and small sample use may not be reliable.

Given the definitions of our null and alternative hypotheses in equations (14.6) and (14.7), these tests are all for *non-instantaneous* causality. It would seem natural to extend to the instantaneous case by writing the alternative hypothesis or the restricted model of equation (14.6) as:

$$y_t = \sum_{j=1}^{k} \alpha_j y_{t-j} + \sum_{j=0}^{k} \beta_j x_{t-j} + u_t$$

and adapting the test as required. There are, however, "identification" problems involved in using this equation. See Pierce and Haugh (1977), who show that it is impossible to determine a unique direction of causality if instantaneous causality exists.

Illustration of Direct Granger Tests

Exhibit 14.6 shows the output obtained from EViews when testing for causality between imports (M_t) and income (Y_t). The clear conclusion is that there is unidirectional causality from income to imports.

The Sims Test

The notion that the future cannot "cause" the present is one of the most straightforward features of the contemporary concept of causality, and is what was used by Sims (1972) to develop this second causality test. Consider the following VAR system:

$$a(L)y_t + b(L)x_t = \varepsilon_t$$
$$c(L)y_t + d(L)x_t = u_t$$

where a(L), b(L), c(L) and d(L) are polynomials in L of appropriate order. This can be written more succinctly as:

$$\begin{bmatrix} a(L) & b(L) \\ c(L) & d(L) \end{bmatrix} \begin{bmatrix} y_t \\ x_t \end{bmatrix} = \begin{bmatrix} \varepsilon_t \\ u_t \end{bmatrix} \quad \textbf{(14.8)}$$

Clearly, if x is not causing y, then b(L) = 0, and if y is not causing x, then c(L) = 0. We can rewrite equation (14.8) as:

$$\begin{bmatrix} y_t \\ x_t \end{bmatrix} = \begin{bmatrix} a(L) & b(L) \\ c(L) & d(L) \end{bmatrix}^{-1} \begin{bmatrix} \varepsilon_t \\ u_t \end{bmatrix} = \begin{bmatrix} \alpha(L) & \beta(L) \\ \phi(L) & \psi(L) \end{bmatrix} \begin{bmatrix} \varepsilon_t \\ u_t \end{bmatrix} \quad \textbf{(14.9)}$$

This is what is known as the "Wold decomposition" which here explains time series x_t and y_t in terms of an infinite linear combination of white noise processes. If x does not Granger cause y, then $\beta(L) = 0$, and if y does not Granger cause x, $\phi(L) = 0$.

Let us consider the possibility that x does not Granger cause y as our null hypothesis. The system of equation (14.9) then becomes (in equation form):

$$y_t = \alpha(L)\varepsilon_t \quad \textbf{(14.10)}$$

$$x_t = \phi(L)\varepsilon_t + \psi(L)u_t \quad \textbf{(14.11)}$$

Under the null hypothesis, therefore, we can substitute for $\varepsilon_t = \alpha^{-1}(L)\, y_t$ from equation (14.10) into equation (14.11), to obtain:

$$\begin{aligned} x_t &= \phi(L)\alpha^{-1}(L)y_t + \psi(L)u_t \\ &= \sum_{i=-\infty}^{+\infty} \theta_i\, y_{t-i} + \psi(Y)u_t \end{aligned} \quad \textbf{(14.12)}$$

Note the negative lower summation limit of equation (14.12), which means that it contains future (as well as past) values of y. Evidently, if the coefficients of the leading y values are all zeros, then we would have a typical VAR equation for x_t. But what if the hypothesis that $\theta_{-1} = \theta_{-2} = \ldots = \theta_{-(i-1)} = 0$ *cannot* be rejected? Since the future cannot cause the present, then future y values cannot cause the current x. Indeed, a necessary condition for x not to cause y is that the leading y terms in equation (14.12) have zero coefficients. Thus, the logical conclusion of finding non-zero coefficients on leading y terms is that x Granger causes y. The technique for computing the Wald, likelihood ratio and Lagrange multiplier statistics is analogous to that described for the Granger test, with the unrestricted and restricted forms defined as:

$$x_t = \sum_{i=-n}^{m} \theta_i\, y_{t-i} + \omega_t \quad \text{(unrestricted form)}$$

$$x_t = \sum_{i=0}^{m} \theta_i\, y_{t-i} + \omega_t \quad \text{(restricted form)}$$

It is difficult to say which of these two sets of tests (direct Granger and Sims) is better. Geweke et al. (1981) show experimentally that direct Granger tests are superior. They are certainly more intuitively appealing and easier to carry out. We also cannot deny the fact that the Sims test is more costly in terms of degrees of freedom, since we have more parameters to estimate (with some of them associated with leading variables!). Nevertheless, because of the different philosophical backgrounds of the tests, it is advisable to consider them as complements to, rather than substitutes for, one another. EViews only provides for the direct Granger tests.

EXERCISES

1. Discuss the following in some detail:
   a) VAR models
   b) Granger causality
   c) Causality tests
2. Using the data provided in Appendix 1.2, Chapter 1:
   a) Estimate a VAR involving M, Y and p_m/p_d (the ratio of foreign to domestic prices). Analyse the impulse response to a shock to Y and carry out a variance decomposition analysis.
   b) Test for Granger causality between M and Y.

APPENDIX 14.1

Critical values for DF and ADF tests for unit roots

No.	No Constant, No Trend in test equation			Constant, No Trend in test equation			Constant and Trend in test equation		
of Obs	1%	5%	10%	1%	5%	10%	1%	5%	10%
19	–2.697	–1.960	–1.625	–3.830	–3.029	–2.655	–4.535	–3.675	–3.276
20	–2.689	–1.959	–1.625	–3.807	–3.020	–2.650	–4.500	–3.659	–3.268
21	–2.682	–1.958	–1.624	–3.786	–3.011	–2.646	–4.469	–3.645	–3.260
22	–2.676	–1.957	–1.624	–3.767	–3.004	–2.642	–4.441	–3.633	–3.253
23	–2.670	–1.957	–1.623	–3.750	–2.997	–2.638	–4.417	–3.622	–3.247
24	–2.665	–1.956	–1.623	–3.734	–2.991	–2.635	–4.394	–3.612	–3.242
25	–2.660	–1.955	–1.623	–3.720	–2.985	–2.632	–4.374	–3.603	–3.237
26	–2.656	–1.955	–1.623	–3.708	–2.980	–2.629	–4.355	–3.594	–3.232
27	–2.652	–1.954	–1.622	–3.696	–2.975	–2.627	–4.338	–3.587	–3.228
28	–2.649	–1.954	–1.622	–3.685	–2.971	–2.624	–4.323	–3.580	–3.224
29	–2.645	–1.953	–1.622	–3.675	–2.966	–2.622	–4.308	–3.573	–3.220
30	–2.642	–1.953	–1.622	–3.666	–2.963	–2.620	–4.295	–3.567	–3.217
31	–2.639	–1.952	–1.621	–3.658	–2.959	–2.618	–4.283	–3.561	–3.214

CHAPTER 15

Cointegration

INTRODUCTION

This is an important chapter, which introduces a concept that has radically altered the discipline of econometrics. To begin the discussion, let us consider the following very simple form of the import function, which we also considered in the previous chapter:

$$M_t = \beta Y_t + e_t \quad \textbf{(15.1)}$$

Now take a look at the time plots of both variables shown in Exhibit 15.1 (drawn to two separate scales). Both these series are clearly nonstationary. In chapter 12, we said that a series was integrated of order 1, and written I(1), if it became stationary after first differencing. It is then said to have one unit root.

Strictly speaking, estimation and hypothesis testing based on OLS is justified only if the two variables involved are I(0). Since both M_t and Y_t are I(1), a fairly reasonable expectation is that any linear combination of these two variables, such as e_t, would also be I(1). This violates the basic assumptions for OLS estimation and if we insist on applying OLS, we are likely to establish nothing more than *spurious correlation*, i.e. a correlation that does not establish any *causal* relationship between the two variables. See Granger and Newbold (1974).

A tempting solution to this apparent problem is to fit the regression using the first differences of both variables. But in a seminal paper, Davidson, Hendry, Srba and Yeo (1978) argue that such an approach would ignore valuable information about the "long run". They propose instead an approach that blends the two and incorporates the short run dynamics implied by the first differences as well as the static or long run relationship between the undifferenced values which enter the relationship as an "error correction mechanism" (ECM).

In yet another seminal paper, Engle and Granger (1987) show that the solution proposed by Davidson et al. (1978) is possible if and only if the variables involved in the relationship are *cointegrated*. Before we develop a formal definition of cointegration, let us get an intuitive feel for this important concept, which has revolutionized the way in which econometricians approach the estimation problem.

Look once again at the plots in Exhibit 15.1. Notwithstanding the fact that both variables appear to be nonstationary, an examination of the plots tends to suggest that they do not diverge systematically over time. This, in turn, suggests that the error term e_t has a constant mean (of zero), a constant variance and so on, in which

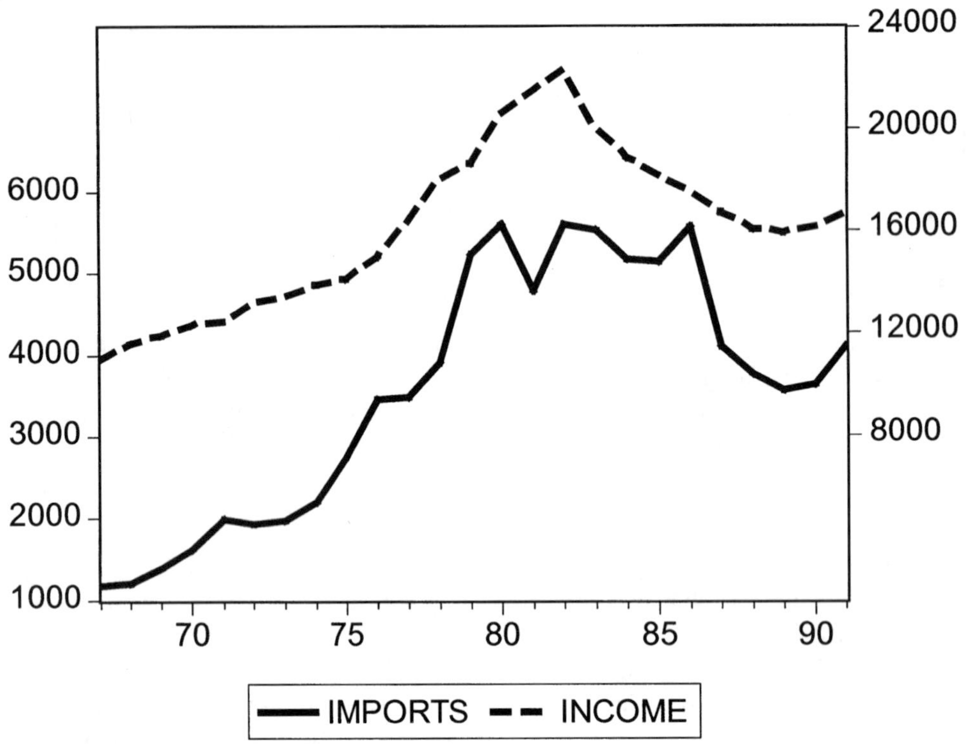

EXHIBIT 15.1
Time plots of imports and income

case e_t might be I(0). Put another way, although M_t and Y_t increase or decrease systematically over time, the linear combination of the two variables represented by:

$$e_t = M_t - \beta Y_t \qquad \textbf{(15.2)}$$

does not and in fact appears to vary around a fixed mean (zero in this case). When this happens, M_t and Y_t are said to be *cointegrated*. This simply means that they tend to move together in the long run and equation (15.2) has the simple intuitive economic interpretation of being the long-run or equilibrium relationship so that M will return to the value βY in the long run. Naturally, e_t can be interpreted as an equilibrium error at a given point in time. As we will see, when two (or more) variables are cointegrated, OLS regression involving variables that are not I(0) is still possible.

It is quite another matter if the two (or more) variables in a regression are not cointegrated. For instance, consider the regression:

$$M_t = \beta p_{dt} + e_t \qquad \textbf{(15.3)}$$

Compare the plots of imports (M) and domestic prices (p_d) shown in Exhibit 15.2. The paths of the two variables seem to have nothing in common and we can therefore expect that the error term in this case would not be I(0). In this case the two variables are not cointegrated.

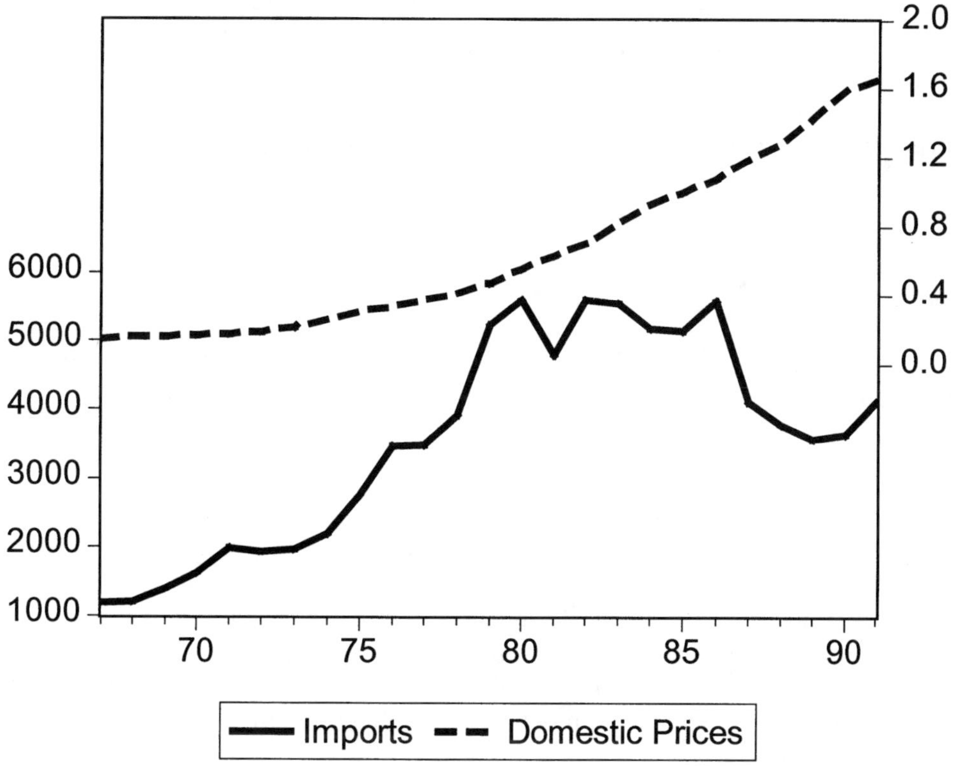

EXHIBIT 15.2
Time plots of imports and domestic prices variables

The process of eyeballing the data, such as was done above, is useful in getting a feel for the existence of cointegration between variables but should not be used as proof of this existence. To do this, we will use the more formal tests which are developed below.

THE VECTOR ERROR CORRECTION MODEL (VECM)

We will begin the discussion using a very simple model. Consider the two-variable VAR system we introduced in chapter 14:

$$M_t = a_1 M_{t-1} + a_2 M_{t-2} + b_1 Y_{t-1} + b_2 Y_{t-2} + \varepsilon_{1t}$$

$$Y_t = c_1 M_{t-1} + c_2 M_{t-2} + d_1 Y_{t-1} + d_2 Y_{t-2} + \varepsilon_{2t}$$

In matrix notation, this may be represented as:

$$\mathbf{x}_t = \mathbf{\Pi}_1 \mathbf{x}_{t-1} + \mathbf{\Pi}_2 \mathbf{x}_{t-2} + \boldsymbol{\varepsilon}_t$$

where:

$$\mathbf{x}_t = \begin{bmatrix} M_t \\ Y_t \end{bmatrix}, \mathbf{\Pi}_j = \begin{bmatrix} a_j & b_j \\ c_j & d_j \end{bmatrix}, j = 1,2 \text{ and } \boldsymbol{\varepsilon}_t = \begin{bmatrix} \varepsilon_{1t} \\ \varepsilon_{2t} \end{bmatrix}$$

It is easy to show that this VAR system may be rewritten as:

$$\Delta\mathbf{x}_t = \mathbf{\Gamma}_1 \Delta\mathbf{x}_{t-1} + \mathbf{\Gamma}\mathbf{x}_{t-1} + \boldsymbol{\varepsilon}_t \quad \textbf{(15.4)}$$

where:

$$\mathbf{\Gamma}_1 = -\mathbf{\Pi}_2$$

and:

$$\mathbf{\Gamma} = \left(-\mathbf{I} + \mathbf{\Pi}_1 + \mathbf{\Pi}_2\right)$$

This form of the model is frequently referred to as a vector error correction model (VECM). It is a VAR in first differences with $\mathbf{x}_{t-1}$ as an "exogenous" variable. The term $\mathbf{\Gamma}\mathbf{x}_{t-1}$ is the error correction term (we will understand this more clearly soon), which is at the heart of the cointegration problem. There are three cases to consider and they relate to the rank of $\mathbf{\Gamma}$:

1. The rank of $\mathbf{\Gamma}$ is equal to 0. This can only occur if $\mathbf{\Gamma}$ is the null matrix so that equation (15.4) reduces to:

   $$\Delta\mathbf{x}_t = \mathbf{\Gamma}_1 \Delta\mathbf{x}_{t-1} + \boldsymbol{\varepsilon}_t$$

   which is a VAR in first difference. Since $\mathbf{x}_t$ is I(1), $\Delta\mathbf{x}_t$ is I(0) and there is no cointegration.
2. The rank of $\mathbf{\Gamma}$ is equal to 2 (the number of variables in the system). This is possible only if $\mathbf{x}_t$ is a vector of I(0) variables, which contradicts the original assumption that they are I(1). In this case, $\Delta\mathbf{x}_t$ is over-differenced and the correct model would be in levels rather than in differences.
3. The rank of $\mathbf{\Gamma}$ is equal to 1. In this case, there exists a factorization of $\mathbf{\Gamma}$ such that

   $$\mathbf{\Gamma} = \boldsymbol{\alpha}\boldsymbol{\beta}'$$

   where $\boldsymbol{\alpha}$ and $\boldsymbol{\beta}$ are both (2, 1) matrices. In this case, equation (15.4) may be rewritten as:

   $$\Delta\mathbf{x}_t = \mathbf{\Gamma}_1 \Delta\mathbf{x}_{t-1} + \boldsymbol{\alpha}\boldsymbol{\beta}'\mathbf{x}_{t-1} + \boldsymbol{\varepsilon}_t \quad \textbf{(15.5)}$$

$\boldsymbol{\beta}$ is the cointegrating vector which has the property that $\boldsymbol{\beta}'\mathbf{x}_t$ is I(0) (i.e. the elements of the vector $\mathbf{x}_t$ are cointegrated) and $\boldsymbol{\alpha}$ is the matrix of adjustment parameters. There is an element of arbitrariness about both the vectors, $\boldsymbol{\alpha}$ and $\boldsymbol{\beta}$, in that we can replace $\boldsymbol{\beta}$ by $\boldsymbol{\beta}\mathbf{B}$, as long as $\mathbf{B}$ is a nonsingular matrix of size (r, r), and $\boldsymbol{\alpha}$ by $\boldsymbol{\alpha}(\mathbf{B}')^{-1}$ and leave the matrix multiplying $\mathbf{x}_{t-1}$ in equation (15.5) unchanged. This means that the parameters of the two matrices, $\boldsymbol{\alpha}$ and $\boldsymbol{\beta}$, are not identified. Identification is obtained through normalization of $\boldsymbol{\beta}$, which is always arbitrary. This amounts to choosing a matrix $\mathbf{B}$ to attain the normalization required. Let us illustrate these points using our model.

A possible ECM formulation of this model might be:

$$\Delta M_t = \gamma_{11}\Delta M_{t-1} + \gamma_{12}\Delta Y_{t-1} - \alpha_1\left(\beta_1 M_{t-1} + \beta_2 Y_{t-1}\right) + \varepsilon_{1t}$$

$$\Delta Y_t = \gamma_{21}\Delta M_{t-1} + \gamma_{22}\Delta Y_{t-1} - \alpha_2\left(\beta_1 M_{t-1} + \beta_2 Y_{t-1}\right) + \varepsilon_{1t}$$

When normalized, it may look like:

$$\Delta M_t = \gamma_{11}\Delta M_{t-1} + \gamma_{12}\Delta Y_{t-1} - \alpha *_1\left(M_{t-1} - \beta Y_{t-1}\right) + \varepsilon_{1t} \qquad \textbf{(15.6)}$$

$$\Delta Y_t = \gamma_{21}\Delta M_{t-1} + \gamma_{22}\Delta Y_{t-1} - \alpha *_2\left(M_{t-1} - \beta Y_{t-1}\right) + \varepsilon_{2t} \qquad \textbf{(15.7)}$$

where $\alpha_{*1} = -\ \alpha_1\beta_1$, $\alpha_{*2} = -\ \alpha_2\beta_1$ and $\beta = -(\beta_2/\beta_1)$. A formulation such as that in equations (15.6) and (15.7) has a simple yet interesting economic interpretation: it presupposes that some variable M has an equilibrium path defined by:

$$M_t = \beta Y_t$$

and, at any point in time t, there are deviations from the long run path equal to e_t. Adjustments are made from one period to the next with the speed of adjustment equal to α_{*1} and α_{*2}. This was the idea behind the consumption function of the United Kingdom by Davidson et al. (1978).

We have already seen that, if M_t and Y_t are I(1) while e_t is I(0), then M and Y are cointegrated. Furthermore, equations (15.6) and (15.7) contain only I(0) variables. It was shown by Engle and Granger (1987) that if M and Y are cointegrated as indicated, then there exists an error correction such as the one appearing in equation (15.5). What is more, the converse is true: if an error correction formulation such as equation (15.5) can be found, then M and Y are cointegrated. This is the famous *Granger representation theorem*. An important implication of the theorem is that at least one of the adjustment coefficients (α_{*1} and α_{*2}) must be non-zero.

There are two distinct problems associated with a model like equation (15.5). In the first place we must establish that the variables in question (here M and Y) are cointegrated and, second, we must establish a procedure for estimating the parameters of the model. In what follows, we shall concentrate on two of these procedures that will allow us to do both these things: the one proposed by Engle and Granger (1987) and the other proposed by Johansen (1988).

THE ENGLE–GRANGER (EG) TWO-STEP PROCEDURE

This procedure, first proposed in the seminal article by Engle and Granger (1987), enjoyed widespread popularity in the 1990s. Its greatest appeal is its simplicity and indeed nontechnical applied economists find it much easier to understand than its competitors. However, it suffers from some serious shortcomings, which we shall allude to below.

Step 1 of the EG procedure has two facets to it: in the first place, it involves a preliminary test for the cointegratability of the variables M and Y and then, following from this, the error correction term is estimated. The preliminary test for cointegratability of the variables is based on the application of OLS to the equation $M_t = \beta Y_t + e_t$ (which Engle and Granger call the cointegrating equation) and the consequent application of unit root tests on the OLS residuals:

$$\hat{e}_t = M_t - \hat{\beta} Y_t \tag{15.8}$$

where $\hat{\beta}$ is the OLS estimator of β. The mechanism of the unit root tests described in the previous chapter is applicable here (the DF and ADF tests) and, in this instance, the null and alternative hypotheses are:

H_0: The variables are not cointegrated (i.e. the OLS residuals admit a unit root)
H_1: The variables are cointegrated (i.e. the OLS residuals do not admit a unit root)

However, Engle and Granger also suggest the use of the cointegrating regression Durbin–Watson (CRDW) statistic. This statistic is identical in appearance to the standard Durbin–Watson statistic that we met in chapter 4 but it is applied in a somewhat different way here. In the presence of spurious correlation (i.e. the absence of cointegratability), the CRDW statistic tends to zero. However, the ADF test is shown by Engle and Granger to be more powerful than the CRDW test. If cointegratability is established, the error correction term is estimated by equation (15.8).

Step 2 of the EG makes use of the estimated error correction term defined to formulate a model such as:

$$\Delta M_t = \gamma_{11} \Delta M_{t-1} + \gamma_{12} \Delta Y_{t-1} + \alpha_1 \left(M_{t-1} - \hat{\beta} Y_{t-1} \right) + \varepsilon_{1t} \tag{15.9}$$

$$\Delta Y_t = \gamma_{21} \Delta M_{t-1} + \gamma_{22} \Delta Y_{t-1} + \alpha_2 \left(M_{t-1} - \hat{\beta} Y_{t-1} \right) + \varepsilon_{2t} \tag{15.10}$$

or, given that $\hat{e}_t = M_t - \hat{\beta} Y_t$:

$$\Delta M_t = \gamma_{11} \Delta M_{t-1} + \gamma_{12} \Delta Y_{t-1} + \alpha_1 \hat{e}_{t-1} + \varepsilon_{1t} \tag{15.11}$$

EXHIBIT 15.3
OLS fit of $M_t = \beta Y_t + e_t$

```
==============================================================
Dependent Variable: IMPORTS
Method: Least Squares
Sample: 1967 1991
Included observations: 25
==============================================================
     Variable     Coefficient Std. Error  T-Statistic    Prob.
==============================================================
      INCOME         0.229811   0.010790    21.29823    0.0000
==============================================================
R-squared              0.667623   Mean dependent var    3556.082
Adjusted R-squared     0.667623   S.D. dependent var    1531.723
S.E. of regression     883.0718   Akaike info criter    16.44387
Sum squared resid      18715578   Schwarz criterion     16.49262
Log likelihood        -204.5483   Durbin-Watson stat    0.318164
==============================================================
```

$$\Delta Y_t = \gamma_{21}\Delta M_{t-1} + \gamma_{22}\Delta Y_{t-1} + \alpha_2 \hat{e}_{t-1} + \varepsilon_{2t} \quad \textbf{(15.12)}$$

The coefficients γ_{11}, γ_{12}, γ_{21}, γ_{22}, α_1 and α_2 are then estimated by OLS. The model is acceptable if at least one of the α coefficients is significant and economically meaningful and if ε_t is a stationary process.

Illustration of the Engle–Granger Two-Step Procedure[1]

For this illustration, we consider the import function:

$$M_t = \beta Y_t + e_t$$

This is the "cointegrating regression" to be tested.

Step 1 of the EG two-step procedure requires that we fit the cointegrating regression (by OLS) and test the residuals for unit roots (we have already established that M and Y are I(1)). If the residuals are stationary, then we must reject the null of no cointegration. If they are nonstationary (the null hypothesis), then they do not cointegrate. Exhibit 15.3 displays the results of the OLS regression.

A crude test for cointegratability may be one based on the CRDW statistic, here approximately 0.32. The critical values for the test given by Engle and Granger (1987) are reproduced in Appendix 15.1. They show that the null of no cointegration is just barely rejected at the10% level (critical value 0.32). Selected results obtained from the application of the more formal ADF tests to the residuals (saved under the label RES_C) are shown in Exhibit 15.4. The fitted test equation has an intercept but no trend.

[1] The reader should also refer to the very simple illustration in Engle and Granger (1987).

EXHIBIT 15.4
Testing for cointegratability

```
==============================================================
ADF Test Statistic  -1.753580    1%    Critical Value*   -3.7343
                                 5%    Critical Value    -2.9907
                                 10%   Critical Value    -2.6348
*MacKinnon critical values for rejection of hypothesis of a
unit root.
==============================================================
```

A word of caution is necessary here. Great care should be exercised in using the "canned" routine in EViews since the critical values shown above are not applicable to the OLS residuals obtained from the fit shown in Exhibit 15.3. Appropriate critical values are shown in Appendix 15.1 under the heading "Two Variable Case" with no trend in the test equation. They are calculated on the basis of a formula given by MacKinnon (1991). For 24 observations, the critical values at the 1%, 5% and 10% significance levels are read as:

1%	5%	10%
–4.391	–3.602	–3.226

As you can see, these values are "further to the left" than the values shown in Exhibit 15.4 and which in fact are identical to those shown for the unit root tests in Appendix 12.1. Our calculated value of –1.75 cannot reject the null of "no cointegration". Evidence for the cointegration appears tenuous and will have to depend a lot on the CRDW statistic, and the latter is not convincing.

Suppose we were to reject the null hypothesis of "no cointegration" based on the evidence of the CRDW statistic. The next step in the EG procedure is to estimate the short-run dynamics in an equation system such as equations (15.11) and (15.12) above, with:

$$\hat{e}_{t-1} = M_{t-1} - 0.2298Y_{t-1}$$

The results are shown in Exhibit 15.5.[2]

α_1 is estimated as –0.265. It has correctly signed and it is significant at about 6%. This is enough to confirm that M and Y are cointegrated and that the ECM form estimated here is a valid representation of the model. α_2 is estimated as –0.171 but it is not significant. A test of the residuals of these equations verifies that they are white noise. This is further evidence of the cointegratability of M and Y.

[2] We show the results obtained from the application of OLS to each equation. However, since the system is really a VAR with an added "exogenous" term (the error correction term), we may estimate it as such in EViews. Try it and see that you will get the same results.

EXHIBIT 15.5 (A)

OLS fit of $\Delta M_t = \gamma_{11}\Delta M_{t-1} + \gamma_{12}\Delta Y_{t-1} + \alpha_1 \hat{e}_{t-1} + \varepsilon_{1t}$

Dependent Variable: D(IMPORTS)
Method: Least Squares
Sample(adjusted): 1969 1991
Included observations: 23 after adjusting endpoints

Variable	Coefficient	Std. Error	T-Statistic	Prob.
D(IMPORTS(-1))	0.010164	0.214925	0.047291	0.9628
D(INCOME(-1))	0.141856	0.132359	1.071752	0.2966
RES_C(-1)	-0.265201	0.135528	-1.956797	0.0645

R-squared	0.256055	Mean dependent var	126.3800
Adjusted R-squared	0.181661	S.D. dependent var	559.2994
S.E. of regression	505.9540	Akaike info criter	15.41188
Sum squared resid	5119790.	Schwarz criterion	15.55998
Log likelihood	-174.2366	F-statistic	3.441858
Durbin-Watson stat	2.107495	Prob(F-statistic)	0.051929

EXHIBIT 15.5 (B)

OLS fit of $\Delta Y_t = \gamma_{21}\Delta M_{t-1} + \gamma_{22}\Delta Y_{t-1} + \alpha_2 \hat{e}_{t-1} + \varepsilon_{2t}$

Dependent Variable: D(INCOME)
Method: Least Squares
Sample(adjusted): 1969 1991
Included observations: 23 after adjusting endpoints

Variable	Coefficient	Std. Error	T-Statistic	Prob.
D(IMPORTS(-1))	0.165008	0.344870	0.478465	0.6375
D(INCOME(-1))	0.500450	0.212384	2.356343	0.0288
RES_C(-1)	-0.171198	0.217469	-0.787228	0.4404

R-squared	0.341743	Mean dependent var	220.6522
Adjusted R-squared	0.275917	S.D. dependent var	954.0802
S.E. of regression	811.8562	Akaike info criter	16.35763
Sum squared resid	13182208	Schwarz criterion	16.50574
Log likelihood	-185.1128	F-statistic	5.191626
Durbin-Watson stat	2.215414	Prob(F-statistic)	0.015274

Strengths and Weaknesses of the Engle–Granger Two-Step Procedure

The EG two-step procedure is very attractive to the applied economist largely because of its apparent simplicity. It separates the estimation of the long run parameter(s) from those of the short run and requires, in each instance, the use of standard OLS methods. This means, in particular, that no specialist programming skills are required. But what theoretical justifications can be advanced for the use of OLS at each stage and are there any serious theoretical shortcomings in so doing?

Let us look first of all at the estimation of the parameter(s) of the cointegrating regression (step 1). Stock (1987) shows that OLS estimation of the long run parameter(s) is consistent and highly efficient. Indeed, the estimator is *super consistent* in the sense that it converges even more quickly than the OLS estimator in the standard case (i.e. where the variables are I(0)). Stock also shows that the consistency property does not require the absence of correlation between the explanatory variable(s) and the error term, unlike consistency results in the classical regression context.

However, as Banerjee et al. (1986) show, in small samples, bias is likely to be considerable. In the two variable case that we are considering here, this bias is negatively correlated with the R^2 statistic of the cointegrating regression (although this result does not carry over to the multivariate case, which we will consider below). Little trust, therefore, should be placed in results obtained when R^2 differs appreciably from unity. In addition to this, Phillips and Ouliaris (1990) show that the asymptotic distribution of the OLS estimator of the parameter(s) of the cointegrating regression is highly dependent on "nuisance" parameters. Similarly, the standard t- and F-statistics based on this estimator have very complicated asymptotic distributions so it is not possible to make inferences by the use of standard test statistics.

Turning now to OLS estimation of the short run parameters (step 2), the picture is a little bit more encouraging. First, this estimator is not only consistent but is efficient asymptotically as if obtained using the true value of the long run parameter (rather than its OLS estimate obtained in step 1). Finally, the standard t- and F-statistics can be used to make inferences about the parameter estimates.

Let us now consider the normalization. If e_t is I(0) while M_t and Y_t are I(1), then the (2, 1) vector $\boldsymbol{\beta}$ represents the linear combination of the two I(1) variables, which "transforms" these variables into an I(0) variable. Clearly, if $\boldsymbol{\beta}$ is a "cointegrating vector" in the sense that $\boldsymbol{\beta}'\mathbf{x}_t$ is stationary, then, for any scalar $\lambda \neq 0$, $\lambda\boldsymbol{\beta}'$ is also a cointegrating vector since $\lambda\boldsymbol{\beta}'\mathbf{x}_t$ is also stationary. However, this vector, if it exists, is unique provided that one of the variables is normalized to be 1, as is the case for M. Consider, for instance, replacing β by $(\beta + \lambda)$. This would yield:

$$e_t = M_t - \beta Y_t - \lambda Y_t$$

We know, by assumption, that $(M_t - \beta Y_t)$ is I(0) and that λY_t is I(1), in which case e_t must be I(1), which contradicts the original assumption unless $\lambda = 0$.

However, the question still arises: on which variable is the normalization to be carried out? This question is never satisfactorily answered and, in the end, it must be arbitrarily imposed. Implicit in this imposition is the economist's *a priori* view about the exogenous-endogenous dichotomy typical of traditional econometrics, which we met in the early chapters of this book. The test for cointegration is asymptotically invariant to the normalization but, as Dickey et al. (1991) have shown, the test results may be very sensitive to the normalization in small samples.

Let us now consider the problems arising when there are more than two variables in the system. Up to now, we have considered the very special case of a two-variable model. Cointegration would indeed be very limited in scope if it could only deal with cases of relationships between only two variables for, as we already know, more than two variables can be related in an economic sense. Indeed, the general linear regression model that we met in chapter 2 is based on this assumption and if cointegration is to be an improvement on this it would have to contend with the *multivariate* case, and not simply the *bivariate* one that has occupied our attention up to now.

Consider a (p, 1) vector of I(1) variables $\mathbf{x}_t$ and consider the following vector autoregressive (VAR) representation of it:

$$\mathbf{x}_t = \mathbf{\Pi}_1\mathbf{x}_{t-1} + \mathbf{\Pi}_2\mathbf{x}_{t-2} + \ldots + \mathbf{\Pi}_k\mathbf{x}_{t-k} + \boldsymbol{\varepsilon}_t \qquad \textbf{(15.13)}$$

where the $\mathbf{\Pi}$s are (p, p) matrices. This VAR form can be shown to be equivalent to the following:

$$\Delta\mathbf{x}_t = \mathbf{\Gamma}_1\Delta\mathbf{x}_{t-1} + \mathbf{\Gamma}_2\Delta\mathbf{x}_{t-2} + \ldots + \mathbf{\Gamma}_{k-1}\Delta\mathbf{x}_{t-k+1} + \mathbf{\Gamma}\mathbf{x}_{t-1} + \boldsymbol{\varepsilon}_t \qquad \textbf{(15.14)}$$

where:

$$\mathbf{\Gamma}_i = -\left(\mathbf{\Pi}_{i+1} + \mathbf{\Pi}_{i+2} + \ldots + \mathbf{\Pi}_k\right) \quad i = 1, 2, \ldots, k$$

and:

$$\mathbf{\Gamma} = \left(-\mathbf{I} + \mathbf{\Pi}_1 + \mathbf{\Pi}_2 + \ldots + \mathbf{\Pi}_k\right)$$

Cointegration this time is synonymous with the case where the rank of $\mathbf{\Gamma}$ is r, $0 < r < p$. In other words, we must now allow for the possibility of up to (p – 1) cointegrating vectors. If r = 0, the variables are not cointegrated and equation (15.14) is a VAR in first differences. If r = p, we are in the stationary case, in which case equation (15.13), which is in levels, should be used to estimate the coefficient values. For $0 < r < p$, there exists a representation of $\mathbf{\Gamma}$ such that:

$$\mathbf{\Gamma} = \boldsymbol{\alpha}\boldsymbol{\beta}' \qquad \textbf{(15.15)}$$

where $\boldsymbol{\alpha}$ and $\boldsymbol{\beta}$ are both (p, r) matrices.

Consider, for instance, the introduction of a new variable, p_{mt}/p_{dt} (the relative price) so that we now have three variables: M_t, Y_t and p_{mt}/p_{dt}. The EG two-step procedure has been used widely in the literature to establish the cointegratability of three or more variables (see Hall, 1986). However, there are certain limitations in applying it to such cases. In the first place, and most importantly, there may now be more than one cointegrating vector. In fact, in the three-variable case there may exist another cointegrating vector that is linearly independent of the first. There may be two (at most) long run relationships linking the three variables.

This possibility of more than one cointegrating vector highlights the most fundamental weakness in the EG two-step procedure, since underlying it is the assumption that there is only *one* cointegrating vector (which means that it is not possible to test for the number of cointegrating vectors in a multivariate system). Clearly, an economist would want to know if there are more than one "equilibrium" relationship among a set of variables. If OLS is used to estimate one static cointegrating regression equation, it will not yield consistent estimators if there are in fact more than one cointegrating vector. Furthermore, the ECM formulation in step 2 of this procedure will be misspecified if all equilibrium conditions are not taken into account.

In the more general case of p variables and r cointegrating vectors ($r \le p - 1$), the matrices $\boldsymbol{\alpha}$ and $\boldsymbol{\beta}$ are (p, r) and are full column rank. They will look like:

$$\boldsymbol{\alpha} = \begin{bmatrix} \alpha_{11} & \alpha_{12} & \cdots & \alpha_{1r} \\ \alpha_{21} & \alpha_{22} & \cdots & \alpha_{2r} \\ \vdots & \vdots & \cdots & \vdots \\ \alpha_{p1} & \alpha_{p2} & \cdots & \alpha_{pr} \end{bmatrix}, \boldsymbol{\beta} = \begin{bmatrix} \beta_{11} & \beta_{12} & \cdots & \beta_{1r} \\ \beta_{21} & \beta_{22} & \cdots & \beta_{2r} \\ \vdots & \vdots & \cdots & \vdots \\ \beta_{p1} & \beta_{p2} & \cdots & \beta_{pr} \end{bmatrix}$$

The r columns of $\boldsymbol{\beta}$ (or, equivalently, the r rows of $\boldsymbol{\beta}'$) are the r non-normalized cointegrating vectors.

It is important to understand that, when there are r cointegrating vectors, there are automatically r error correction terms in the system as a whole and all of these terms appear in each of the p equations in equation (15.14). For example, in the first equation, which explains Δx_{1t} (first element of $\Delta\mathbf{x}$), $\boldsymbol{\alpha\beta}'\mathbf{x}_{t-1}$ will contribute:

$$\boldsymbol{\alpha}_{11}\left(\boldsymbol{\beta}_1'\mathbf{x}_{t-1}\right)+\boldsymbol{\alpha}_{12}\left(\boldsymbol{\beta}_2'\mathbf{x}_{t-1}\right)+\ldots+\boldsymbol{\alpha}_{1r}\left(\boldsymbol{\beta}_r'\mathbf{x}_{t-1}\right)$$

to the explanation of Δx_{1t}. Leaving out any of these r terms is tantamount to a misspecification.

THE JOHANSEN PROCEDURE

We have noted the many (theoretical) shortcomings of the EG two-step procedure when there are more than two variables in the system. A theoretically more satisfying approach, though not as intuitively appealing to the applied economist, is the maximum likelihood method of Johansen (1988). This approach can be used for two purposes: (1) determining the maximum number of cointegrating vectors and (2) obtaining maximum likelihood estimators of the cointegrating matrix ($\boldsymbol{\beta}$) and adjustment parameters ($\boldsymbol{\alpha}$). The Johansen procedure is based on the factorization shown in equation (15.15) and produces maximum likelihood estimators of $\boldsymbol{\alpha}$ and $\boldsymbol{\beta}$ for a given value of r (which is obtained through a testing sequence to be described below). Once $\boldsymbol{\alpha}$ and $\boldsymbol{\beta}$ are estimated, OLS may be applied to each of the following p equations to obtain consistent estimators of the "short run" parameters $\boldsymbol{\Gamma}_1, \boldsymbol{\Gamma}_2, \ldots, \boldsymbol{\Gamma}_{k-1}$:

$$\left(\Delta\mathbf{x}_t - \hat{\boldsymbol{\Gamma}}\mathbf{x}_{t-1}\right) = \boldsymbol{\Gamma}_1\Delta\mathbf{x}_{t-1} + \boldsymbol{\Gamma}_2\Delta\mathbf{x}_{t-2} + \ldots + \boldsymbol{\Gamma}_{k-1}\Delta\mathbf{x}_{t-k+1} + \boldsymbol{\varepsilon}_t$$

where $\hat{\boldsymbol{\Gamma}} = \hat{\boldsymbol{\alpha}}\hat{\boldsymbol{\beta}}$ (the ^ over $\boldsymbol{\alpha}$ and $\boldsymbol{\beta}$ indicates that they are the Johansen maximum likelihood estimators). EViews employs a slight modification of this approach: it applies OLS in turn to each of the equations in the system:

$$\Delta\mathbf{x}_t = \boldsymbol{\Gamma}_1\Delta\mathbf{x}_{t-1} + \boldsymbol{\Gamma}_2\Delta\mathbf{x}_{t-2} + \ldots + \boldsymbol{\Gamma}_{k-1}\Delta\mathbf{x}_{t-k+1} + \boldsymbol{\alpha}\left(\hat{\boldsymbol{\beta}}\mathbf{x}_{t-1}\right) + \boldsymbol{\varepsilon}_t$$

to obtain consistent estimators of $\boldsymbol{\Gamma}_i$, i = 1, 2, …, (k – 1) and $\boldsymbol{\alpha}$, which is similar to the second step of the EG two-step procedure. As in that case, we may make use of the fact that this is a VAR in first differences with the addition of an "exogenous" term $\hat{\boldsymbol{\beta}}\mathbf{x}_{t-1}$ (the error correction term).

Estimation of α and β

The likelihood function of equation (15.14) is proportional to:

$$L\left(\boldsymbol{\alpha}, \boldsymbol{\beta}, \boldsymbol{\Delta}; \boldsymbol{\Gamma}_1, \ldots, \boldsymbol{\Gamma}_{k-1}\right) = |\boldsymbol{\Omega}|^{-T/2} \exp\left\{-\frac{1}{2}\sum \boldsymbol{\varepsilon}_t' \boldsymbol{\Omega}^{-1} \boldsymbol{\varepsilon}_t\right\}$$

where T is the number of observations and $\boldsymbol{\Omega}$ is the covariance matrix of $\boldsymbol{\varepsilon}_t$.

Step 1(a)
Regress $\Delta\mathbf{x}_t$ on $\Delta\mathbf{x}_{t-1}$, $\Delta\mathbf{x}_{t-2}$, …, $\Delta\mathbf{x}_{t-k+1}$ (p separate regressions). Construct the vectors of residuals $\underset{(p,1)}{\mathbf{R}_{0t}}$, t = 1, 2, …,T.

Step 1(b)
Regress $\mathbf{x}_{t-k}$ on $\Delta\mathbf{x}_{t-1}$, $\Delta\mathbf{x}_{t-2}$, …, $\Delta\mathbf{x}_{t-k+1}$. Construct a series of residual vectors $\mathbf{R}_{kt}$, t = 1, 2, …, T, based on these regressions.

Step 2
Compute the four p × p matrices:

$$\mathbf{S}_{ij} = \frac{1}{T}\sum_{t=1}^{n} \mathbf{R}_{it}\mathbf{R}_{jt}' \quad i, j = 0, k$$

Step 3

Solve the following polynomial equation in λ:

$$\left|\lambda\mathbf{S}_{kk} - \mathbf{S}_{k0}\mathbf{S}_{00}^{-1}\mathbf{S}_{0k}\right| = 0$$

that is, find the roots (eigenvalues) of the polynomial equation in λ (this is a nonstandard form of the eigenvalue problem). Obtain $\hat{\lambda}_1, \hat{\lambda}_2, \ldots, \hat{\lambda}_p$ (going from the largest to the smallest) and associated eigenvectors $\hat{\mathbf{v}}_1, \hat{\mathbf{v}}_2, \ldots, \hat{\mathbf{v}}_p$, obtained such that the eigenvectors are normalized using:

$$\hat{\mathbf{V}}'\mathbf{S}_{kk}\hat{\mathbf{V}} = \mathbf{I}$$

where:

$$\hat{\mathbf{V}} = \left(\hat{\mathbf{v}}_1, \hat{\mathbf{v}}_2, \ldots, \hat{\mathbf{v}}_p\right)$$

If $\boldsymbol{\beta}$ is of rank $0 < r \leq p - 1$, then the first r eigenvectors are the cointegrating vectors, i.e. the maximum likelihood estimator of $\boldsymbol{\beta}$ is:

$$\hat{\boldsymbol{\beta}} = \left(\hat{\mathbf{v}}_1, \hat{\mathbf{v}}_2, \ldots, \hat{\mathbf{v}}_r\right)$$

The maximum likelihood estimator of $\boldsymbol{\alpha}$ is derived from this as:

$$\hat{\boldsymbol{\alpha}} = \mathbf{S}_{0k}\hat{\boldsymbol{\beta}}$$

Testing for the Cointegrating Rank r

If $\boldsymbol{\beta}$ is of rank r, clearly:

$$\lambda_{r+1} = \lambda_{r+2} = \ldots = \lambda_p = 0$$

where λ_i is the "population" parameter associated with $\hat{\lambda}_i$. If $\lambda_1 = 0$, then $r = 0$ (there are no cointegrating vectors). If $\lambda_2 = 0$, and $\lambda_1 \neq 0$, then $r = 1$ (there is one cointegrating vector) and so on. We therefore wish to test:

$$H_0: \lambda_i = 0$$

$$H_1: \lambda_i \neq 0$$

for $i = r + 1, r + 2, \ldots, p$. Johansen proposes a test based on the trace statistic, computed as:

$$\text{Trace} = -T\sum_{i=r+1}^{p} \ln\left(1 - \hat{\lambda}_i\right)$$

He also proposes a second test (weaker than the first) based on the "maximum eigenvalue" statistic:

$$LR_{max} = -T\ln\left(1 - \hat{\lambda}_1\right)$$

where $\hat{\lambda}_i$ is the largest eigenvalue. Johansen (1988) establishes the distribution of these two statistics under the null that r is the cointegrating rank and Osterwald–Lenum (1992) calculates critical values for them at various levels of significance by simulation methods. However, only the 1% and 5% critical values are available in EViews.

Whichever of the trace or the maximum eigenvalue statistics is used, the test to determine the cointegrating rank proceeds as follows. In the first instance, we discriminate between the following two alternatives:

$$H_0{:}r = 0$$
$$H_1{:}r \geq 1$$

If the null is rejected, the following two alternatives are then considered:

$$H_0{:}r = 1$$
$$H_1{:}r \geq 2$$

If the null hypothesis is not rejected (but r = 0 is rejected) then r = 1. If the null is rejected, then we move on to:

$$H_0{:}r = 2$$
$$H_1{:}r \geq 3$$

and so on.

Illustration of the Johansen Procedure

In this section, the Johansen procedure will be applied to the three variables, M_t, Y_t and p_{mt}/p_{dt} which appear in the import function introduced in chapter 1. The underlying VAR system used is:

$$\begin{aligned} M_t &= m_{01} + m_{11}t + a_{11}M_{t-1} + a_{12}M_{t-2} + b_{11}Y_{t-1} + b_{12}Y_{t-2} + f_{11}(p_{mt}/p_{dt})_{-1} \\ &\quad + f_{12}(p_{mt}/p_{dt})_{-2} + \varepsilon_{1t} \end{aligned}$$

$$\begin{aligned} Y_t &= m_{02} + m_{12}t + a_{21}M_{t-1} + a_{22}M_{t-2} + b_{21}Y_{t-1} + b_{22}Y_{t-2} + + f_{21}(p_{mt}/p_{dt})_{-1} \\ &\quad + f_{22}(p_{mt}/p_{dt})_{-2} + \varepsilon_{2t} \end{aligned}$$

$$\begin{aligned} (p_{mt}/p_{dt}) &= m_{03} + m_{13}t + a_{31}M_{t-1} + a_{32}M_{t-2} + b_{31}Y_{t-1} + b_{32}Y_{t-2} + \\ &\quad + f_{31}(p_{mt}/p_{dt})_{-1} + f_{32}(p_{mt}/p_{dt})_{-2} + \varepsilon_{2t} \end{aligned}$$

You will notice that, in addition to the introduction of the relative price ratio, we have also introduced two deterministic elements into the system: a constant and a trend term t. You may recall that this system was introduced in the previous chapter. The more general form of a system like this one, in matrix notation, is:

$$\mathbf{x}_t = \boldsymbol{\mu}_0 + \boldsymbol{\mu}_1 t + \boldsymbol{\Pi}_1\mathbf{x}_{t-1} + \boldsymbol{\Pi}_2\mathbf{x}_{t-2} + \ldots + \boldsymbol{\Pi}_k\mathbf{x}_{t-k} + \boldsymbol{\varepsilon}_t \qquad \textbf{(15.16)}$$

As an exercise, determine the terms of the various vectors and matrices for the specific case that we are considering here so that the system appears as in equation (15.16).

Now consider the following decompositions:

$$\boldsymbol{\mu}_0 = \boldsymbol{\alpha\mu}_{01} + \boldsymbol{\alpha}_\perp \boldsymbol{\mu}_{02}$$

$$\boldsymbol{\mu}_1 = \boldsymbol{\alpha\mu}_{11} + \boldsymbol{\alpha}_\perp \boldsymbol{\mu}_{12}$$

where $\boldsymbol{\alpha}_\perp$ is a $p \times (p - r)$ matrix of full rank, orthogonal to $\boldsymbol{\alpha}$. It can be shown that equation (15.16) may be rewritten as:

$$\Delta\mathbf{x}_t = \boldsymbol{\alpha}_\perp \boldsymbol{\mu}_{02} + \boldsymbol{\alpha}_\perp \boldsymbol{\mu}_{12} t + \boldsymbol{\Gamma}_1 \Delta\mathbf{x}_{t-1} + \boldsymbol{\Gamma}_2 \Delta\mathbf{x}_{t-2} + \ldots + \boldsymbol{\Gamma}_{k-1} \Delta\mathbf{x}_{t-k+1} + \boldsymbol{\alpha} \begin{pmatrix} \boldsymbol{\beta} \\ \boldsymbol{\mu}_{01} \\ \boldsymbol{\mu}_{11} \end{pmatrix} \tilde{\mathbf{z}}_{t-1} + \boldsymbol{\varepsilon}_t \quad \textbf{(15.17)}$$

where $\tilde{\mathbf{z}}_t = (\mathbf{x}'_t, 1, t)$.

This may appear foreboding but it is in fact very simple. Suppose in the model that we are using for the illustration, we obtain only one cointegrating equation. The cointegration equation may appear as (normalization assumed):

$$e_t = \left(M_t + \beta_1 Y_t + \beta_2\, p_{mt}/p_{dt} + c_{01} + c_{11} t\right)$$

A possible specific form of system (15.17) may be:

$$\begin{aligned}
\Delta M_t &= v_{01} + v_{11}t + \gamma_{11}\Delta M_{t-1} + \gamma_{12}\Delta Y_{t-1} + \gamma_{13}\Delta(p_{mt}/p_{dt})_{-1} + \alpha_1 e_{t-1} + \varepsilon_{1t} \\
\Delta Y_t &= v_{02} + v_{12}t + \gamma_{21}\Delta M_{t-1} + \gamma_{22}\Delta Y_{t-1} + \gamma_{23}\Delta(p_{mt}/p_{dt})_{-1} + \alpha_2 e_{t-1} + \varepsilon_{2t} \\
\Delta(p_{mt}/p_{dt}) &= v_{03} + v_{13}t + \gamma_{31}\Delta M_{t-1} + \gamma_{32}\Delta Y_{t-1} + \gamma_{33}\Delta(p_{mt}/p_{dt})_{-1} + \alpha_3 e_{t-1} + \varepsilon_{3t}
\end{aligned}$$

Constant and trend terms appear not only in the VAR but also in the cointegrating equation. Try and write out the vectors and matrices that will make this system appear as equation (15.17).

Five assumptions are possible in the case where constant and trend terms are being used (they are all available in EViews):

1. $\boldsymbol{\mu}_1 = \mathbf{0}$ and $\boldsymbol{\mu}_2 = \mathbf{0}$. There is no deterministic trend in the data, with no intercept or trend in the cointegrating equation (CE) or test VAR (this is the case we have been using so far but, in practice, it is perhaps the most unlikely).
2. $\boldsymbol{\mu}_2 = \mathbf{0}$, $\boldsymbol{\mu}_{11} = \mathbf{0}$, $\boldsymbol{\mu}_{01}$ unrestricted. There is no deterministic trend in the data, but there is an intercept (no trend) in the CE (and no intercept in the VAR).
3. $\boldsymbol{\mu}_2 = \mathbf{0}$, $\boldsymbol{\mu}_{11}$ and $\boldsymbol{\mu}_{01}$ unrestricted. There is a linear deterministic trend in the data, as well as an intercept (but no trend) in the CE and test VAR.

4. $\boldsymbol{\mu}_{12} = \mathbf{0}$, $\boldsymbol{\mu}_{11}$, $\boldsymbol{\mu}_{01}$ and $\boldsymbol{\mu}_{02}$ unrestricted. This allows for a linear deterministic trend in the data, an intercept and trend in the CE but no trend in the VAR.
5. $\boldsymbol{\mu}_{12}$, $\boldsymbol{\mu}_{11}$, $\boldsymbol{\mu}_{01}$ and $\boldsymbol{\mu}_{02}$ unrestricted. This allows for a quadratic deterministic trend in the data, an intercept and trend in CE and a linear trend in the VAR (you must have proper justification of quadratic trend if you want to use this case).

Osterwald–Lenum (1992) gives critical values for these five cases at various significance levels. The 1% and 5% values are available in EViews.

The first step is to establish whether the variables are cointegrated and, indeed, whether there may be more than one cointegrating vector (a maximum of two is possible here). We use assumption 2 (no deterministic trend in the data, intercept in the CE) and an underlying VAR with two lags. The results are displayed in Exhibit 15.6.

The first thing to do is to test the null of $r = 0$ against the alternative $r \geq 1$. Unfortunately, the 10% critical value is not shown by EViews but it can be found in Osterwald–Lenum (1992), Table 1*. For the test based on the trace statistic, it is 32 so that the null is rejected at this level, since the trace statistic is calculated as 34.74. In the case of the maximum eigenvalue statistic, the critical value is 19.77 so that the null cannot be rejected, since the maximum eigenvalue statistic is calculated as 18.88. Let us accept the result based on the trace statistic that, at the 10% level of significance, there is at least one cointegrating vector.

The next step is to test the null of $r = 1$ against the alternative of $r \geq 2$. Here, the null cannot be rejected using either the trace statistic (the 10% critical value is 17.85 while the calculated value is 15.85) or the maximum eigenvalue statistic (the 10% critical value is 13.75 while the calculated value is 11.55), and so we conclude that there is exactly one cointegrating vector.

The normalized cointegrating vector is estimated as (including the constant term):

$$\hat{\beta}' = (1 \quad -0.4066 \quad 464.01 \quad 2065.87)$$

The corresponding cointegrating regression deduced from normalization in EViews is (the constant term is included):

$$e_t = M_t - 0.4066Y_t + 464.01p_{mt}/p_{dt} + 2065.87$$

where the right-hand side of this equation is in the form $\hat{\boldsymbol{\beta}}'\mathbf{x}_t$. For purposes of comparison with OLS, it is perhaps better to write this result in the following more conventional format:

$$M_t = -2065.87 + 0.4066Y_t - 464.01p_{mt}/p_{dt} + e_t$$

This is somewhat different from the OLS result (which would have been the cointegrating vector obtained by application of the EG two-step procedure) although the difference is not dramatic.[3]

[3] The direct OLS estimation of this equation is: $M_t = -1188.64 + 0.378\,Y_t - 688.7\,p_{mt}/p_{dt}$.

EXHIBIT 15.6
Johansen Cointegration Test on M_t, Y_t and p_{mt}/p_{dt}

```
                        Johansen Cointegration Test
=====================================================================
Sample(adjusted): 1969 1991
Included observations: 23 after adjusting endpoints
Trend assumption: No deterministic trend (restricted constant)
Series: IMPORTS INCOME RATIO
Lags interval (in first differences): 1 to 1

Unrestricted Cointegration Rank Test

Hypothesized                   Trace      5 Percent     1 Percent
No. of CE(s)  Eigenvalue     Statistic  Critical ValuCritical Value
=====================================================================
    None        0.559910      34.73371      34.91         41.07
  At most 1     0.394761      15.85584      19.96         24.60
  At most 2     0.170765      4.306792       9.24         12.97
=====================================================================
 *(**) denotes rejection of the hypothesis at the 5%(1%) level
 Trace test indicates no cointegration at both 5% and 1% levels

=====================================================================
Hypothesized                 Max-Eigen    5 Percent     1 Percent
No. of CE(s)  Eigenvalue     Statistic  Critical ValuCritical Value
=====================================================================
    None        0.559910      18.87787      22.00         26.81
  At most 1     0.394761      11.54905      15.67         20.20
  At most 2     0.170765      4.306792       9.24         12.97
=====================================================================
 *(**) denotes rejection of the hypothesis at the 5%(1%) level
 Max-
eigenvalue test indicates no cointegration at both 5% and 1% levels

 Unrestricted Cointegrating Coefficients (normalized by b'*S11*b=I):
=====================================================================
   IMPORTS       INCOME        RATIO          C
   0.003415    -0.001389     1.584668     7.055307
  -0.000632    -3.61E-05    -1.619548     5.061472
  -1.13E-05     0.000237    -0.509962    -3.379694
=====================================================================

 Unrestricted Adjustment Coefficients (alpha):
=====================================================================
 D(IMPORTS)    -271.1813     102.1383    -70.91229
  D(INCOME)     257.6051     239.8087    -198.7632
  D(RATIO)      0.067624     0.094435     0.024198
=====================================================================

 1 Cointegrating Equation(sLog likelihood -336.1931
```

EXHIBIT 15.6 (continued)
Johansen Cointegration Test on M_t, Y_t and p_{mt}/p_{dt}

```
=====================================================================
Normalized cointegrating coefficients (std.err. in parentheses)
   IMPORTS       INCOME          RATIO           C
   1.000000     -0.406650      464.0084      2065.872
                (0.02450)     (151.874)     (615.301)

Adjustment coefficients (std.err. in parentheses)
 D(IMPORTS)     -0.926131
                (0.26416)
  D(INCOME)      0.879765
                (0.51329)
  D(RATIO)       0.000231
                (0.00013)
=====================================================================

2 Cointegrating Equation(sLog likelihood -330.4185
=====================================================================
Normalized cointegrating coefficients (std.err. in parentheses)
   IMPORTS       INCOME          RATIO           C
   1.000000      0.000000      2303.680     -6766.759
                              (796.257)     (1554.81)
   0.000000      1.000000      4523.972     -21720.49
                              (1974.87)     (3856.23)

Adjustment coefficients (std.err. in parentheses)
 D(IMPORTS)     -0.990699      0.372925
                (0.25603)     (0.10241)
  D(INCOME)      0.728167     -0.366410
                (0.48578)     (0.19431)
  D(RATIO)       0.000171     -9.73E-05
                (0.00011)     (4.6E-05)
=====================================================================
```

We turn now to the estimation of the ECM model which, in this case, contains three equations. This can be done directly in EViews. The results obtained are shown in Exhibit 15.7.

At the top of Exhibit 15.7 the (normalized) cointegrating vector (which also appears in Exhibit 15.6) is displayed and, below, the ECMs involving ΔM_t, ΔY_t and $\Delta p_{mt}/p_{dt}$ as "dependent" variables are shown. On the right-hand side of each equation appears the cointegrating regression (CointEq1) and the coefficient attached to it is the "adjustment parameter". Here the adjustment coefficient associated with the ΔM_t equation is negative (–0.926131) and it is also significant (t-statistic = 3.50592). This is sufficient to reject any "no cointegration" hypothesis. The other two adjustment factors are not significant at the 5% level but are close to being significant at the 10% level. Can you give a possible economic interpretation of these results?

EXHIBIT 15.7
Estimation of the (Vector) ECM model using M_t, Y_t and p_{mt}/p_{dt}: EViews output

```
            Vector Error Correction Estimates
=====================================================
 Vector Error Correction Estimates
 Sample(adjusted): 1969 1991
 Included observations: 23 after adjusting endpoints
 Standard errors in ( ) & t-statistics in [ ]
=====================================================
Cointegrating Eq:  CointEq1
=====================================================
  IMPORTS(-1)      1.000000

   INCOME(-1)     -0.406650
                   (0.02450)
                  [-16.5986]

   RATIO(-1)       464.0084
                   (151.874)
                  [ 3.05521]

        C          2065.872
                   (615.301)
                  [ 3.35750]
=====================================================
Error Correction:D(IMPORTS)  D(INCOME)     D(RATIO)
=====================================================
    CointEq1      -0.926131    0.879765     0.000231
                   (0.26416)   (0.51329)    (0.00013)
                  [-3.50592]  [ 1.71398]   [ 1.71290]

 D(IMPORTS(-1))    0.143153   -0.568999    -0.000167
                   (0.20941)   (0.40690)    (0.00011)
                  [ 0.68361]  [-1.39839]   [-1.55891]

 D(INCOME(-1))     0.161389    0.987717     7.62E-05
                   (0.12235)   (0.23774)    (6.2E-05)
                  [ 1.31908]  [ 4.15470]   [ 1.21984]

  D(RATIO(-1))    -1381.890   -2160.797    -0.025090
                   (476.167)   (925.231)    (0.24304)
                  [-2.90211]  [-2.33541]   [-0.10323]
=====================================================
```

EXHIBIT 15.7 (continued)
Estimation of the (Vector) ECM model using M_t, Y_t and p_{mt}/p_{dt}:
EViews output

R-squared	0.620087	0.507071	0.018084
Adj. R-squared	0.560101	0.429240	-0.136955
Sum sq. resids	2614543.	9871357.	0.681120
S.E. equation	370.9549	720.7948	0.189337
F-statistic	10.33714	6.515033	0.116643
Log likelihood	-166.5083	-181.7866	7.838787
Akaike AIC	14.82681	16.15536	-0.333808
Schwarz SC	15.02429	16.35283	-0.136330
Mean dependent	126.3800	220.6522	-0.071203
S.D. dependent	559.2994	954.0802	0.177567

Determinant Residual Covaria	1.77E+09
Log Likelihood	-336.1931
Log Likelihood (d.f. adjuste	-342.7845
Akaike Information Criteria	31.19865
Schwarz Criteria	31.98856

COINTEGRATION AND CAUSALITY

In chapter 14, we used the following equation to test for Granger causality:

$$y_t = \sum_{j=1}^{k} \alpha_j y_{t-j} + \sum_{j=1}^{k} \beta_j x_{t-j} + u_t$$

You should know by now that the OLS fit of this equation is valid if either y and x are both I(0) or they are cointegrated. It would therefore seem necessary to test for cointegration between the two variables as a prelude to causality testing.[4] If y and x are both I(1) and they are cointegrated, then estimation of the coefficients of equation (14.6) is a valid exercise. On the other hand, if they are not cointegrated, then the test for causality must be based on equations involving the use of first differences. In other words, instead of equations (14.6) and (14.7) of chapter 14, we would use:

$$\Delta y_t = \sum_{j=1}^{k} \alpha_j \Delta y_{t-j} + \sum_{j=1}^{k} \beta_j \Delta x_{t-j} + u_t \qquad \textbf{(15.18)}$$

$$\Delta y_t = \sum_{j=1}^{k} \alpha_j \Delta y_{t-j} + u_t \qquad \textbf{(15.19)}$$

[4] Mosconi and Giannini (1992) establish a framework for the simultaneous determination of cointegration and causality that results in a substantial gain in the efficiency of the estimators.

A frequent error that appears in the literature is the use of equations (15.18) and (15.19) with no regard as to whether y and x are cointegrated. If they are, then the Granger representation theorem makes it quite clear that equation (15.18) is mis-specified, since it does not contain an error correction term (see MacDonald and Kearney, 1987).

EXERCISES

1. Explain the term "cointegration".
2. Use the Engle–Granger two-step procedure to determine whether the following pairs of variables (see Appendix 1.2, chapter 1) are cointegrated:
   a) X and Y
   b) M and Y
   c) C_p and Y
   d) M and p_m
3. Use the Engle–Granger two-step procedure and the Johansen procedure to establish whether the following *four* variables admit cointegrating relationships:

$$M, Y, p_m, p_d$$

   Compare the results obtained following the two procedures.

APPENDIX 15.1: CRITICAL VALUES FOR ADF TESTS OF COINTEGRATABILITY

(constant term included in test equations)

Two-Variable Case

No. of	No Trend in test equation			Trend in test equation		
Obs	1%	5%	10%	1%	5%	10%
19	–4.538	–3.677	–3.276	–5.238	–4.318	–3.886
20	–4.502	–3.659	–3.264	–5.188	–4.290	–3.866
21	–4.470	–3.642	–3.253	–5.143	–4.264	–3.848
22	–4.441	–3.627	–3.243	–5.103	–4.240	–3.832
23	–4.415	–3.614	–3.234	–5.066	–4.219	–3.817
24	–4.391	–3.602	–3.226	–5.033	–4.200	–3.803
25	–4.370	–3.591	–3.218	–5.002	–4.182	–3.790
26	–4.350	–3.580	–3.211	–4.974	–4.166	–3.779
27	–4.331	–3.571	–3.205	–4.949	–4.150	–3.768
28	–4.315	–3.562	–3.199	–4.925	–4.137	–3.758
29	–4.299	–3.554	–3.193	–4.903	–4.124	–3.749
30	–4.285	–3.547	–3.188	–4.882	–4.112	–3.740
31	–4.271	–3.540	–3.183	–4.863	–4.100	–3.732

Three-Variable Case

No. of	No Trend in test equation			Trend in test equation		
Obs	1%	5%	10%	1%	5%	10%
19	–5.152	–4.220	–3.788	–5.778	–4.789	–4.331
20	–5.104	–4.194	–3.771	–5.716	–4.753	–4.306
21	–5.060	–4.171	–3.755	–5.660	–4.722	–4.283
22	–5.021	–4.150	–3.741	–5.610	–4.693	–4.262
23	–4.985	–4.131	–3.728	–5.565	–4.667	–4.243
24	–4.953	–4.114	–3.717	–5.524	–4.643	–4.226
25	–4.924	–4.098	–3.706	–5.486	–4.621	–4.210
26	–4.897	–4.084	–3.696	–5.452	–4.601	–4.195
27	–4.872	–4.071	–3.687	–5.420	–4.583	–4.181
28	–4.850	–4.058	–3.678	–5.391	–4.565	–4.169
29	–4.829	–4.047	–3.670	–5.364	–4.550	–4.157
30	–4.809	–4.036	–3.663	–5.339	–4.535	–4.146
31	–4.791	–4.026	–3.656	–5.315	–4.521	–4.136

Four-Variable Case

No. of	No Trend in test equation			Trend in test equation		
Obs	1%	5%	10%	1%	5%	10%
19	–5.718	–4.725	–4.252	–6.293	–5.247	–5.032
20	–5.657	–4.691	–4.229	–6.220	–5.203	–5.000
21	–5.602	–4.661	–4.208	–6.155	–5.164	–4.971
22	–5.553	–4.633	–4.189	–6.096	–5.129	–4.945
23	–5.509	–4.608	–4.171	–6.043	–5.097	–4.922
24	–5.468	–4.585	–4.156	–5.994	–5.068	–4.900
25	–5.432	–4.564	–4.141	–5.950	–5.041	–4.880
26	–5.398	–4.545	–4.128	–5.909	–5.016	–4.861
27	–5.367	–4.528	–4.115	–5.872	–4.993	–4.844
28	–5.339	–4.511	–4.104	–5.837	–4.972	–4.829
29	–5.312	–4.496	–4.093	–5.805	–4.953	–4.814
30	–5.288	–4.482	–4.083	–5.775	–4.934	–4.801
31	–5.265	–4.469	–4.074	–5.748	–4.918	–4.788

Five-Variable Case

No. of	No Trend in test equation			Trend in test equation		
Obs	1%	5%	10%	1%	5%	10%
19	–6.227	–5.195	–4.708	–6.787	–5.679	–5.169
20	–6.159	–5.153	–4.678	–6.704	–5.628	–5.132
21	–6.098	–5.116	–4.652	–6.629	–5.583	–5.098
22	–6.042	–5.082	–4.628	–6.561	–5.542	–5.067
23	–5.992	–5.052	–4.606	–6.500	–5.505	–5.039
24	–5.946	–5.024	–4.585	–6.444	–5.470	–5.013
25	–5.904	–4.998	–4.567	–6.393	–5.439	–4.990
26	–5.865	–4.974	–4.550	–6.346	–5.410	–4.968
27	–5.830	–4.953	–4.534	–6.303	–5.384	–4.948
28	–5.797	–4.933	–4.520	–6.263	–5.359	–4.930
29	–5.766	–4.914	–4.506	–6.226	–5.336	–4.912
30	–5.738	–4.897	–4.493	–6.192	–5.315	–4.896
31	–5.712	–4.881	–4.482	–6.160	–5.295	–4.881

Critical values for CRDW test for cointegratability

Significance Levels		
1%	5%	10%
0.511	0.386	0.322

Appendices

Statistical Tables

APPENDIX I
Standard Normal Distribution

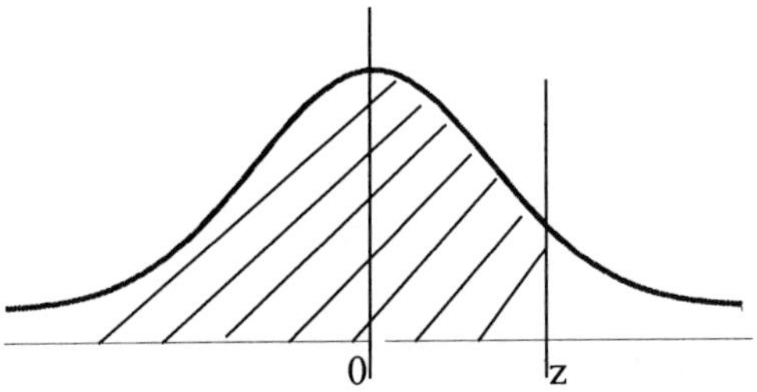

z	0	0.01	0.02	0.03	0.04	0.05	0.06	0.07	0.08	0.09
0	0.5000	0.5040	0.5080	0.5120	0.5160	0.5199	0.5239	0.5279	0.5319	0.5359
0.1	0.5398	0.5438	0.5478	0.5517	0.5557	0.5596	0.5636	0.5675	0.5714	0.5753
0.2	0.5793	0.5832	0.5871	0.5910	0.5948	0.5987	0.6026	0.6064	0.6103	0.6141
0.3	0.6179	0.6217	0.6255	0.6293	0.6331	0.6368	0.6406	0.6443	0.6480	0.6517
0.4	0.6554	0.6591	0.6628	0.6664	0.6700	0.6736	0.6772	0.6808	0.6844	0.6879
0.5	0.6915	0.6950	0.6985	0.7019	0.7054	0.7088	0.7123	0.7157	0.7190	0.7224
0.6	0.7257	0.7291	0.7324	0.7357	0.7389	0.7422	0.7454	0.7486	0.7517	0.7549
0.7	0.7580	0.7611	0.7642	0.7673	0.7704	0.7734	0.7764	0.7794	0.7823	0.7852
0.8	0.7881	0.7910	0.7939	0.7967	0.7995	0.8023	0.8051	0.8079	0.8106	0.8133
0.9	0.8159	0.8186	0.8212	0.8238	0.8264	0.8289	0.8315	0.8340	0.8365	0.8389
1	0.8413	0.8438	0.8461	0.8485	0.8508	0.8531	0.8554	0.8577	0.8599	0.8621
1.1	0.8643	0.8665	0.8686	0.8708	0.8729	0.8749	0.8770	0.8790	0.8810	0.8830
1.2	0.8849	0.8869	0.8888	0.8907	0.8925	0.8944	0.8962	0.8980	0.8997	0.9015
1.3	0.9032	0.9049	0.9066	0.9082	0.9099	0.9115	0.9131	0.9147	0.9162	0.9177
1.4	0.9192	0.9207	0.9222	0.9236	0.9251	0.9265	0.9279	0.9292	0.9306	0.9319
1.5	0.9332	0.9345	0.9357	0.9370	0.9382	0.9394	0.9406	0.9418	0.9429	0.9441
1.6	0.9452	0.9463	0.9474	0.9484	0.9495	0.9505	0.9515	0.9525	0.9535	0.9545
1.7	0.9554	0.9564	0.9573	0.9582	0.9591	0.9599	0.9608	0.9616	0.9625	0.9633
1.8	0.9641	0.9649	0.9656	0.9664	0.9671	0.9678	0.9686	0.9693	0.9699	0.9706
1.9	0.9713	0.9719	0.9726	0.9732	0.9738	0.9744	0.9750	0.9756	0.9761	0.9767
2	0.9773	0.9778	0.9783	0.9788	0.9793	0.9798	0.9803	0.9808	0.9812	0.9817
2.1	0.9821	0.9826	0.9830	0.9834	0.9838	0.9842	0.9846	0.9850	0.9854	0.9857
2.2	0.9861	0.9864	0.9868	0.9871	0.9875	0.9878	0.9881	0.9884	0.9887	0.9890
2.3	0.9893	0.9896	0.9898	0.9901	0.9904	0.9906	0.9909	0.9911	0.9913	0.9916
2.4	0.9918	0.9920	0.9922	0.9925	0.9927	0.9929	0.9931	0.9932	0.9934	0.9936
2.5	0.9938	0.9940	0.9941	0.9943	0.9945	0.9946	0.9948	0.9949	0.9951	0.9952
2.6	0.9953	0.9955	0.9956	0.9957	0.9959	0.9960	0.9961	0.9962	0.9963	0.9964
2.7	0.9965	0.9966	0.9967	0.9968	0.9969	0.9970	0.9971	0.9972	0.9973	0.9974
2.8	0.9974	0.9975	0.9976	0.9977	0.9977	0.9978	0.9979	0.9979	0.9980	0.9981
2.9	0.9981	0.9982	0.9983	0.9983	0.9984	0.9984	0.9985	0.9985	0.9986	0.9986
3	0.9987	0.9987	0.9987	0.9988	0.9988	0.9989	0.9989	0.9989	0.9990	0.9990
3.1	0.9990	0.9991	0.9991	0.9991	0.9992	0.9992	0.9992	0.9992	0.9993	0.9993

This table displays the values of $Pr(Z \leq z)$.

E.G. $Pr(Z \leq 1.29) = 0.90$.

APPENDIX 2
The *t* Distribution

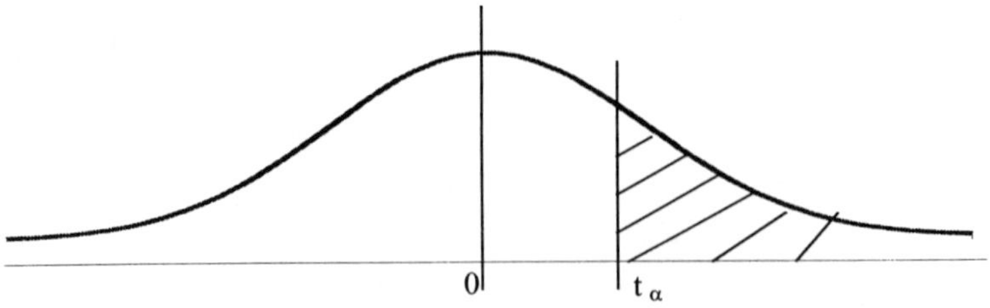

Degrees of Freedom	P = 0.10	0.05	0.025	0.010	0.005
1	3.0777	6.3138	12.7062	31.8205	63.6567
2	1.8856	2.9200	4.3027	6.9646	9.9248
3	1.6377	2.3534	3.1825	4.5407	5.8409
4	1.5332	2.1319	2.7765	3.7470	4.6041
5	1.4759	2.0151	2.5706	3.3649	4.0321
6	1.4398	1.9432	2.4469	3.1427	3.7074
7	1.4149	1.8946	2.3646	2.9980	3.4995
8	1.3968	1.8596	2.3060	2.8965	3.3554
9	1.3830	1.8331	2.2622	2.8214	3.2498
10	1.3722	1.8125	2.2281	2.7638	3.1693
11	1.3634	1.7959	2.2010	2.7181	3.1058
12	1.3562	1.7823	2.1788	2.6810	3.0545
13	1.3502	1.7709	2.1604	2.6503	3.0123
14	1.3450	1.7613	2.1448	2.6245	2.9768
15	1.3406	1.7531	2.1315	2.6025	2.9467
16	1.3368	1.7459	2.1199	2.5835	2.9208
17	1.3334	1.7396	2.1098	2.5669	2.8982
18	1.3304	1.7341	2.1009	2.5524	2.8784
19	1.3277	1.7291	2.0930	2.5395	2.8609
20	1.3253	1.7247	2.0860	2.5280	2.8453
21	1.3232	1.7207	2.0796	2.5177	2.8314
22	1.3212	1.7171	2.0739	2.5083	2.8188
23	1.3195	1.7139	2.0687	2.4999	2.8073
24	1.3178	1.7109	2.0639	2.4922	2.7969
25	1.3164	1.7081	2.0595	2.4851	2.7874
26	1.3150	1.7056	2.0555	2.4786	2.7787
27	1.3137	1.7033	2.0518	2.4727	2.7707
28	1.3125	1.7011	2.0484	2.4671	2.7633
29	1.3114	1.6991	2.0452	2.4620	2.7564
30	1.3104	1.6973	2.0423	2.4573	2.7500
40	1.3031	1.6839	2.0211	2.4233	2.7045
50	1.2987	1.6759	2.0086	2.4033	2.6778
60	1.2958	1.6707	2.0003	2.3901	2.6603
∞	1.29	1.65	1.96	2.33	2.57

This table displays the values of t_α for given $p = \Pr(T \geq t_\alpha)$, where α is the number of degrees of freedom.

E.G. For $p = 0.05$ and $\alpha = 20$, $t_\alpha = 1.7247$.

APPENDIX 3
The Chi-Square Distribution

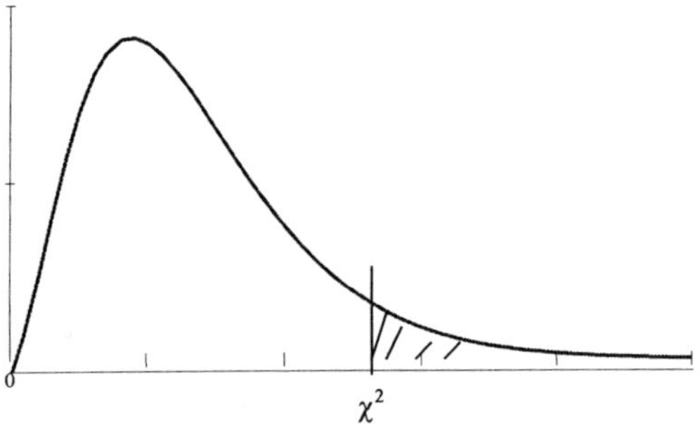

Degrees of Freedom	0.995	0.99	0.975	0.95	0.05	0.025	0.01	0.005
1	0.00004	0.00016	0.00098	0.00393	3.84146	5.02389	6.6349	7.87944
2	0.01	0.0201	0.0506	0.1026	5.9915	7.3778	9.2103	10.5966
3	0.0717	0.1148	0.2158	0.3518	7.8147	9.3484	11.3449	12.8382
4	0.207	0.2971	0.4844	0.7107	9.4877	11.1433	13.2767	14.8603
5	0.4117	0.5543	0.8312	1.1455	11.0705	12.8325	15.0863	16.7496
6	0.6757	0.8721	1.2373	1.6354	12.5916	14.4494	16.8119	18.5476
7	0.9893	1.239	1.6899	2.1673	14.0671	16.0128	18.4753	20.2777
8	1.3444	1.6465	2.1797	2.7326	15.5073	17.5345	20.0902	21.955
9	1.7349	2.0879	2.7004	3.3251	16.919	19.0228	21.666	23.5894
10	2.1559	2.5582	3.247	3.9403	18.307	20.4832	23.2093	25.1882
11	2.6032	3.0535	3.8157	4.5748	19.6751	21.92	24.725	26.7568
12	3.0738	3.5706	4.4038	5.226	21.0261	23.3367	26.217	28.2995
13	3.565	4.1069	5.0088	5.8919	22.362	24.7356	27.6882	29.8195
14	4.0747	4.6604	5.6287	6.5706	23.6848	26.1189	29.1412	31.3193
15	4.6009	5.2293	6.2621	7.2609	24.9958	27.4884	30.5779	32.8013
16	5.1422	5.8122	6.9077	7.9616	26.2962	28.8454	31.9999	34.2672
17	5.6972	6.4078	7.5642	8.6718	27.5871	30.191	33.4087	35.7185
18	6.2648	7.0149	8.2307	9.3905	28.8693	31.5264	34.8053	37.1565
19	6.844	7.6327	8.9065	10.117	30.1435	32.8523	36.1909	38.5823
20	7.4338	8.2604	9.5908	10.8508	31.4104	34.1696	37.5662	39.9968
21	8.0337	8.8972	10.2829	11.5913	32.6706	35.4789	38.9322	41.4011
22	8.6427	9.5425	10.9823	12.338	33.9244	36.7807	40.2894	42.7957
23	9.2604	10.1957	11.6886	13.0905	35.1725	38.0756	41.6384	44.1813
24	9.8862	10.8564	12.4012	13.8484	36.415	39.3641	42.9798	45.5585
25	10.5197	11.524	13.1197	14.6114	37.6525	40.6465	44.3141	46.9279
26	11.1602	12.1981	13.8439	15.3792	38.8851	41.9232	45.6417	48.2899
27	11.8076	12.8785	14.5734	16.1514	40.1133	43.1945	46.9629	49.6449
28	12.4613	13.5647	15.3079	16.9279	41.3371	44.4608	48.2782	50.9934
29	13.1211	14.2565	16.0471	17.7084	42.557	45.7223	49.5879	52.3356
30	13.7867	14.9535	16.7908	18.4927	43.773	46.9792	50.8922	53.672
40	20.7065	22.1643	24.433	26.5093	55.7585	59.3417	63.6907	66.766
60	35.5345	37.4849	40.4817	43.188	79.0819	83.2977	88.3794	91.9517
120	83.852	86.923	91.573	95.705	146.567	152.211	158.95	163.648

This table displays the values of χ^2 for given p = Pr ($C \geq \chi^2$) for number of degrees of freedom (DF) stated. E.G. For p =0.05 and DF = 20, χ^2 = 31.41.

APPENDIX 4
The F Distribution

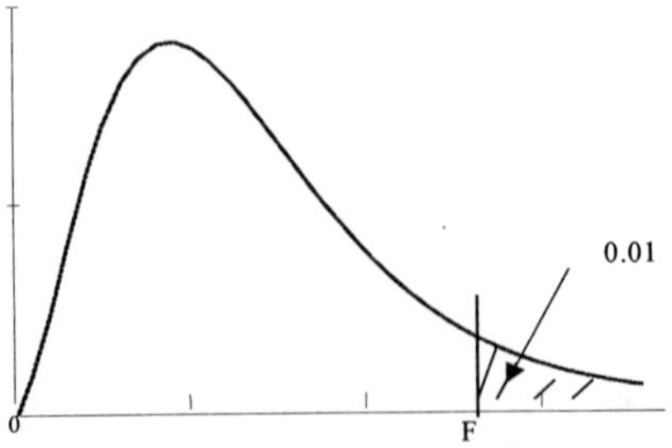

Degrees of Freedom for the Numerator

Degrees of Freedom for the Denominator	1	2	3	4	5	6	7	8	9
1	4052.18	4999.5	5403.35	5624.58	5763.65	5858.99	5928.36	5981.07	6022.47
2	98.5025	99	99.1662	99.2494	99.2993	99.3326	99.3564	99.3742	99.3881
3	34.1162	30.8165	29.4567	28.7099	28.2371	27.9107	27.6717	27.4892	27.3452
4	21.1977	18	16.6944	15.977	15.5219	15.2069	14.9758	14.7989	14.6591
5	16.2582	13.2739	12.06	11.3919	10.967	10.6723	10.4555	10.2893	10.1578
6	13.745	10.9248	9.77954	9.1483	8.7459	8.46613	8.26	8.10165	7.97612
7	12.2464	9.54658	8.45129	7.84665	7.46044	7.1914	6.99283	6.84005	6.71875
8	11.2586	8.64911	7.59099	7.00608	6.63183	6.37068	6.17762	6.02887	5.91062
9	10.5614	8.02152	6.99192	6.42209	6.05694	5.80177	5.61287	5.46712	5.35113
10	10.0443	7.55943	6.55231	5.99434	5.63633	5.38581	5.20012	5.05669	4.94242
11	9.64603	7.20571	6.21673	5.6683	5.31601	5.06921	4.88607	4.74447	4.63154
12	9.33021	6.92661	5.95254	5.41195	5.06434	4.82057	4.6395	4.49937	4.38751
13	9.07381	6.70096	5.73938	5.20533	4.86162	4.62036	4.441	4.30206	4.19108
14	8.86159	6.51488	5.56389	5.03538	4.69496	4.45582	4.27788	4.13995	4.02968
15	8.68312	6.35887	5.41696	4.89321	4.55561	4.31827	4.14155	4.00445	3.89479
16	8.53097	6.22624	5.29221	4.77258	4.43742	4.20163	4.02595	3.88957	3.78042
17	8.39974	6.11211	5.185	4.66897	4.33594	4.10151	3.92672	3.79096	3.68224
18	8.28542	6.0129	5.09189	4.57904	4.24788	4.01464	3.84064	3.70542	3.59707
19	8.18495	5.92588	5.01029	4.50026	4.17077	3.93857	3.76527	3.63052	3.5225
20	8.09596	5.84893	4.93819	4.43069	4.10268	3.87143	3.69874	3.56441	3.45668
21	8.0166	5.78042	4.87405	4.36882	4.04214	3.81173	3.63959	3.50563	3.39815
22	7.94539	5.71902	4.81661	4.31343	3.98796	3.7583	3.58666	3.45303	3.34577
23	7.88113	5.6637	4.76488	4.26357	3.93919	3.71022	3.53902	3.40569	3.29863
24	7.82287	5.61359	4.71805	4.21845	3.89507	3.66672	3.49593	3.36287	3.25599
25	7.7698	5.568	4.67546	4.17742	3.85496	3.62717	3.45675	3.32394	3.21722
30	7.56248	5.39035	4.50974	4.01788	3.69902	3.47348	3.3045	3.17262	3.06652
40	7.3141	5.17851	4.31257	3.82829	3.51384	3.29101	3.12376	2.99298	2.88756
60	7.07711	4.97743	4.12589	3.64905	3.33888	3.11867	2.95305	2.82328	2.71845
120	6.85089	4.78651	3.9491	3.47953	3.17355	2.95585	2.79176	2.66291	2.55857

Areas in the Right Tail under the F Distribution Curve = 0.01.

APPENDIX 4 (continued)
The F Distribution

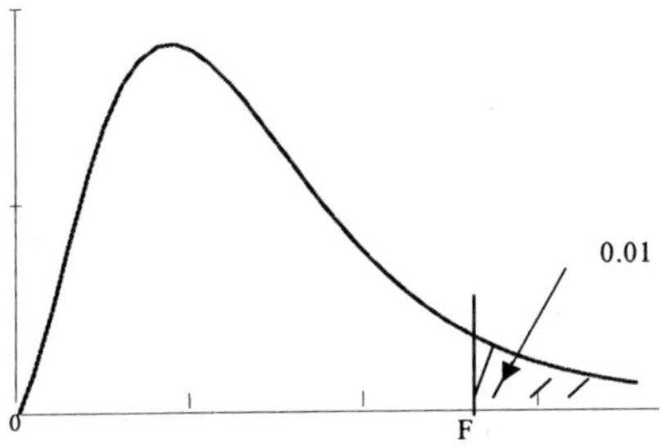

Degrees of Freedom for the Numerator (columns); Degrees of Freedom for the Denominator (rows)

	10	12	15	20	24	30	40	60	120
1	6055.85	6106.32	6157.28	6208.73	6234.63	6260.65	6286.78	6313.03	6339.39
2	99.3992	99.4159	99.4325	99.4492	99.4575	99.4658	99.4742	99.4825	99.4908
3	27.2287	27.0518	26.8722	26.6898	26.5975	26.5045	26.4108	26.3164	26.2211
4	14.5459	14.3736	14.1982	14.0196	13.9291	13.8377	13.7454	13.6522	13.5581
5	10.051	9.88828	9.72222	9.55265	9.46647	9.37933	9.29119	9.20201	9.11177
6	7.87412	7.71833	7.55899	7.39583	7.31272	7.22853	7.14322	7.05674	6.96902
7	6.62006	6.46909	6.31433	6.15544	6.07432	5.99201	5.90845	5.82357	5.73729
8	5.81429	5.66672	5.51512	5.35909	5.27926	5.19813	5.11561	5.03162	4.94605
9	5.25654	5.11143	4.96208	4.808	4.729	4.64858	4.56665	4.48309	4.39777
10	4.84915	4.70587	4.55814	4.40539	4.32693	4.24693	4.16529	4.08186	3.99648
11	4.53928	4.3974	4.25087	4.09905	4.02091	3.94113	3.85957	3.77607	3.69044
12	4.29605	4.15526	4.00962	3.85843	3.78049	3.70079	3.61918	3.53547	3.44944
13	4.10027	3.96033	3.81537	3.66461	3.58675	3.50704	3.42529	3.34129	3.25476
14	3.9394	3.80014	3.6557	3.50522	3.42739	3.3476	3.26564	3.18127	3.09419
15	3.80494	3.66624	3.52219	3.37189	3.29403	3.21411	3.13191	3.04713	2.95945
16	3.69093	3.55269	3.40895	3.25874	3.18081	3.10073	3.01825	2.93305	2.84474
17	3.59307	3.4552	3.31169	3.16152	3.0835	3.00324	2.92046	2.83481	2.74585
18	3.50816	3.37061	3.22729	3.0771	2.99897	2.91852	2.83542	2.74931	2.6597
19	3.43382	3.29653	3.15334	3.00311	2.92487	2.8442	2.76079	2.67421	2.58394
20	3.36819	3.23112	3.08804	2.93774	2.85936	2.77848	2.69475	2.60771	2.51678
21	3.30983	3.17295	3.02995	2.87956	2.80105	2.71995	2.6359	2.54839	2.45681
22	3.25761	3.12089	2.97795	2.82745	2.7488	2.66749	2.58311	2.49515	2.40292
23	3.2106	3.07402	2.93112	2.7805	2.70172	2.62019	2.5355	2.44708	2.35421
24	3.16807	3.03161	2.88873	2.738	2.65907	2.57733	2.49232	2.40346	2.30996
25	3.12941	2.99306	2.85019	2.69932	2.62026	2.53831	2.45299	2.36369	2.26956
30	2.97909	2.8431	2.70018	2.54866	2.46892	2.38597	2.29921	2.20785	2.11076
40	2.80055	2.66483	2.52162	2.36888	2.288	2.20338	2.11423	2.01941	1.91719
60	2.63175	2.49612	2.3523	2.19781	2.11536	2.02848	1.93602	1.83626	1.72632
120	2.47208	2.3363	2.1915	2.03459	1.95002	1.86001	1.76285	1.65569	1.53299

Areas in the Right Tail under the F Distribution Curve = 0.01.

APPENDIX 4 (continued)
The F Distribution

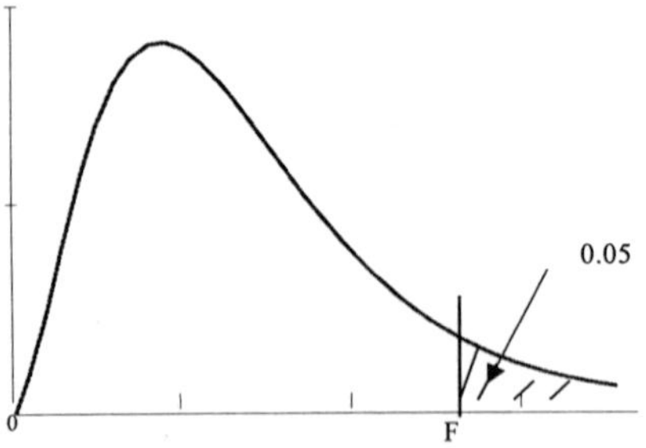

Degrees of Freedom for the Numerator

Degrees of Freedom for the Denominator	1	2	3	4	5	6	7	8	9
1	161.45	199.5	215.71	224.58	230.16	233.99	236.77	238.88	240.54
2	18.5128	19	19.1643	19.2468	19.2964	19.3295	19.3532	19.371	19.3848
3	10.128	9.5521	9.2766	9.1172	9.0135	8.9406	8.8867	8.8452	8.8123
4	7.7086	6.9443	6.5914	6.3882	6.2561	6.1631	6.0942	6.041	5.9988
5	6.6079	5.7861	5.4095	5.1922	5.0503	4.9503	4.8759	4.8183	4.7725
6	5.9874	5.1433	4.75706	4.53368	4.38737	4.28387	4.20666	4.1468	4.09902
7	5.5914	4.73741	4.34683	4.12031	3.97152	3.86597	3.78704	3.72573	3.67667
8	5.3177	4.45897	4.06618	3.83785	3.6875	3.58058	3.50046	3.4381	3.38813
9	5.1174	4.25649	3.86255	3.63309	3.48166	3.37375	3.29275	3.22958	3.17889
10	4.9646	4.10282	3.70826	3.47805	3.32583	3.21717	3.13546	3.07166	3.02038
11	4.84434	3.9823	3.58743	3.35669	3.20387	3.09461	3.01233	2.94799	2.89622
12	4.74723	3.88529	3.49029	3.25917	3.10588	2.99612	2.91336	2.84857	2.79638
13	4.66719	3.80557	3.41053	3.17912	3.02544	2.91527	2.8321	2.76691	2.71436
14	4.60011	3.73889	3.34389	3.11225	2.95825	2.84773	2.7642	2.69867	2.64579
15	4.54308	3.68232	3.28738	3.05557	2.90129	2.79046	2.70663	2.6408	2.58763
16	4.494	3.63372	3.23887	3.00692	2.85241	2.74131	2.6572	2.5911	2.53767
17	4.45132	3.59153	3.19678	2.96471	2.81	2.69866	2.6143	2.54796	2.49429
18	4.41387	3.55456	3.15991	2.92774	2.77285	2.6613	2.57672	2.51016	2.45628
19	4.38075	3.52189	3.12735	2.89511	2.74006	2.62832	2.54353	2.47677	2.4227
20	4.35124	3.49283	3.09839	2.86608	2.71089	2.59898	2.51401	2.44706	2.39281
21	4.32479	3.4668	3.07247	2.8401	2.68478	2.57271	2.48758	2.42046	2.36605
22	4.30095	3.44336	3.04912	2.81671	2.66127	2.54906	2.46377	2.3965	2.34194
23	4.27934	3.42213	3.028	2.79554	2.64	2.52766	2.44223	2.37481	2.32011
24	4.25968	3.40283	3.00879	2.77629	2.62065	2.50819	2.42263	2.35508	2.30024
25	4.2417	3.38519	2.99124	2.75871	2.60299	2.49041	2.40473	2.33706	2.2821
30	4.17088	3.31583	2.92228	2.68963	2.53355	2.42052	2.33434	2.26616	2.2107
40	4.08475	3.23173	2.83875	2.60597	2.44947	2.33585	2.24902	2.18017	2.12403
60	4.00119	3.15041	2.75808	2.52522	2.36827	2.25405	2.16654	2.09697	2.0401
120	3.92012	3.07178	2.68017	2.44724	2.28985	2.17501	2.08677	2.01643	1.95876

Areas in the Right Tail under the F Distribution Curve = 0.05.

APPENDIX 4 (continued)
The F Distribution

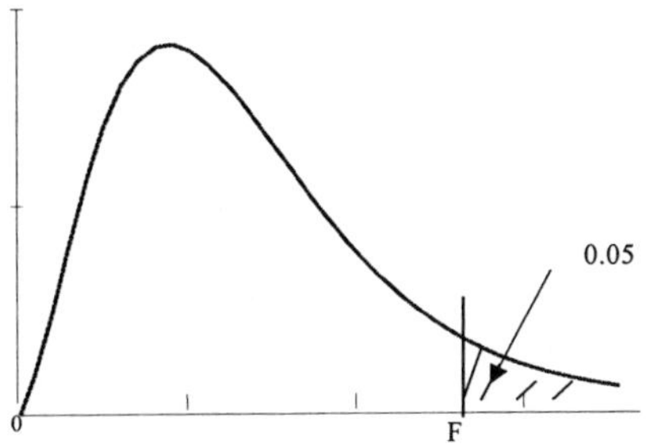

Degrees of Freedom for the Denominator	Degrees of Freedom for the Numerator								
	10	12	15	20	24	30	40	60	120
1	241.88	243.91	245.95	248.01	249.05	250.1	251.14	252.2	253.25
2	19.3959	19.4125	19.4291	19.4458	19.4541	19.4624	19.4707	19.4791	19.4874
3	8.7855	8.7446	8.7029	8.6602	8.6385	8.6166	8.5944	8.572	8.5494
4	5.9644	5.9117	5.8578	5.8025	5.7744	5.7459	5.717	5.6877	5.6581
5	4.7351	4.6777	4.61876	4.55813	4.52715	4.49571	4.46379	4.43138	4.39845
6	4.05996	3.99994	3.93806	3.87419	3.84146	3.80816	3.77429	3.7398	3.70467
7	3.63652	3.57468	3.51074	3.44452	3.41049	3.37581	3.34043	3.30432	3.26745
8	3.34716	3.28394	3.21841	3.15032	3.11524	3.07941	3.04278	3.0053	2.96692
9	3.13728	3.07295	3.0061	2.93646	2.90047	2.86365	2.82593	2.78725	2.74752
10	2.97824	2.91298	2.84502	2.77402	2.73725	2.69955	2.66086	2.62108	2.58012
11	2.85362	2.78757	2.71864	2.64645	2.60897	2.57049	2.53091	2.49012	2.44802
12	2.75339	2.68664	2.61685	2.54359	2.50548	2.46628	2.42588	2.38417	2.34099
13	2.67102	2.60366	2.53311	2.45888	2.4202	2.38033	2.33918	2.2966	2.25241
14	2.60216	2.53424	2.463	2.3879	2.34868	2.30821	2.26635	2.22295	2.17781
15	2.54372	2.47531	2.40345	2.32754	2.28783	2.24679	2.20428	2.16011	2.11406
16	2.49351	2.42466	2.35222	2.27557	2.23541	2.19384	2.15071	2.10581	2.0589
17	2.44992	2.38065	2.30769	2.23035	2.18977	2.14771	2.104	2.05841	2.01066
18	2.4117	2.34207	2.26862	2.19065	2.14966	2.10714	2.06289	2.01664	1.9681
19	2.37793	2.30795	2.23406	2.1555	2.11414	2.07119	2.02641	1.97954	1.93024
20	2.34788	2.27758	2.20327	2.12416	2.08245	2.03909	1.99382	1.94636	1.89632
21	2.32095	2.25036	2.17567	2.09603	2.054	2.01025	1.96452	1.91649	1.86574
22	2.2967	2.22583	2.15078	2.07066	2.02832	1.9842	1.93802	1.88945	1.83802
23	2.27473	2.20361	2.12822	2.04764	2.00501	1.96054	1.91394	1.86484	1.81276
24	2.25474	2.18338	2.10767	2.02666	1.98376	1.93896	1.89195	1.84236	1.78964
25	2.23647	2.16489	2.08889	2.00747	1.96431	1.91919	1.8718	1.82173	1.7684
30	2.16458	2.09206	2.0148	1.93165	1.88736	1.84087	1.79179	1.73957	1.68345
40	2.07725	2.00346	1.92446	1.83886	1.79294	1.74443	1.6928	1.63725	1.57661
60	1.99259	1.9174	1.83644	1.74798	1.70012	1.64914	1.59427	1.53431	1.46727
120	1.91046	1.8337	1.7505	1.65868	1.60844	1.55434	1.4952	1.42901	1.35189

Areas in the Right Tail under the F Distribution Curve = 0.05.

APPENDIX 4 (continued)
The F Distribution

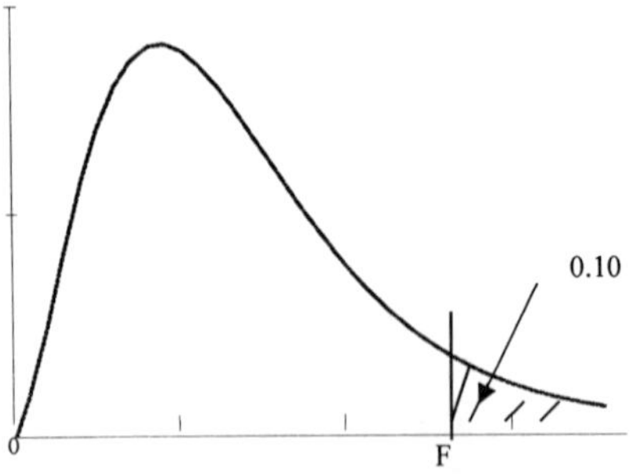

Degrees of Freedom for the Denominator	Degrees of Freedom for the Numerator								
	1	2	3	4	5	6	7	8	9
1	39.86	49.5	53.59	55.83	57.24	58.2	58.91	59.44	59.86
2	8.5263	9	9.1618	9.2434	9.2926	9.3255	9.3491	9.3668	9.3805
3	5.5383	5.4624	5.3908	5.3426	5.3092	5.2847	5.2662	5.2517	5.24
4	4.5448	4.3246	4.1909	4.1072	4.0506	4.0097	3.979	3.9549	3.9357
5	4.0604	3.7797	3.6195	3.5202	3.453	3.4045	3.3679	3.3393	3.3163
6	3.7759	3.4633	3.28876	3.18076	3.10751	3.05455	3.01446	2.98304	2.95774
7	3.5894	3.25744	3.07407	2.96053	2.88334	2.82739	2.78493	2.75158	2.72468
8	3.4579	3.11312	2.9238	2.80643	2.72645	2.66833	2.62413	2.58935	2.56124
9	3.3603	3.00645	2.81286	2.69268	2.61061	2.55086	2.50531	2.46941	2.44034
10	3.285	2.92447	2.72767	2.60534	2.52164	2.46058	2.41397	2.37715	2.34731
11	3.2252	2.85951	2.66023	2.53619	2.45118	2.38907	2.34157	2.304	2.2735
12	3.17655	2.8068	2.60552	2.4801	2.39402	2.33102	2.28278	2.24457	2.21352
13	3.13621	2.76317	2.56027	2.43371	2.34672	2.28298	2.2341	2.19535	2.16382
14	3.10221	2.72647	2.52222	2.39469	2.30694	2.24256	2.19313	2.1539	2.12195
15	3.07319	2.69517	2.48979	2.36143	2.27302	2.20808	2.15818	2.11853	2.08621
16	3.04811	2.66817	2.46181	2.33274	2.24376	2.17833	2.128	2.08798	2.05533
17	3.02623	2.64464	2.43743	2.30775	2.21825	2.15239	2.10169	2.06134	2.02839
18	3.00698	2.62395	2.41601	2.28577	2.19583	2.12958	2.07854	2.03789	2.00467
19	2.9899	2.60561	2.39702	2.2663	2.17596	2.10936	2.05802	2.0171	1.98364
20	2.97465	2.58925	2.38009	2.24893	2.15823	2.09132	2.0397	1.99853	1.96485
21	2.96096	2.57457	2.36489	2.23334	2.14231	2.07512	2.02325	1.98186	1.94797
22	2.94858	2.56131	2.35117	2.21927	2.12794	2.0605	2.0084	1.9668	1.93273
23	2.93736	2.54929	2.33873	2.20651	2.11491	2.04723	1.99492	1.95312	1.91888
24	2.92712	2.53833	2.32739	2.19488	2.10303	2.03513	1.98263	1.94066	1.90625
25	2.91774	2.52831	2.31702	2.18424	2.09216	2.02406	1.97138	1.92925	1.89469
30	2.88069	2.48872	2.27607	2.14223	2.04925	1.98033	1.92692	1.88412	1.84896
40	2.83535	2.44037	2.22609	2.09095	1.99682	1.92688	1.87252	1.82886	1.7929
60	2.79107	2.39325	2.17741	2.04099	1.94571	1.87472	1.81939	1.77483	1.73802
120	2.74781	2.34734	2.12999	1.9923	1.89587	1.82381	1.76748	1.72196	1.68425

Areas in the Right Tail under the F Distribution Curve = 0.10.

APPENDIX 4 (continued)
The F Distribution

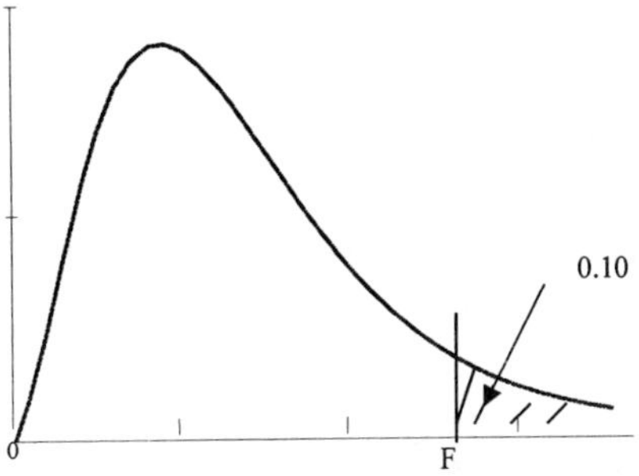

Degrees of Freedom for the Numerator

Degrees of Freedom for the Denominator	10	12	15	20	24	30	40	60	120
1	60.19	60.71	61.22	61.74	62	62.26	62.53	62.79	63.06
2	9.3916	9.4081	9.4247	9.4413	9.4496	9.4579	9.4662	9.4746	9.4829
3	5.2304	5.2156	5.2003	5.1845	5.1764	5.1681	5.1597	5.1512	5.1425
4	3.9199	3.8955	3.8704	3.8443	3.831	3.8174	3.8036	3.7896	3.7753
5	3.2974	3.26824	3.23801	3.20665	3.19052	3.17408	3.15732	3.14023	3.12279
6	2.93693	2.90472	2.87122	2.83634	2.81834	2.79996	2.78117	2.76195	2.74229
7	2.70251	2.66811	2.63223	2.59473	2.57533	2.55546	2.5351	2.51422	2.49279
8	2.53804	2.50196	2.46422	2.42464	2.4041	2.38302	2.36136	2.3391	2.31618
9	2.41632	2.37888	2.33962	2.29832	2.27683	2.25472	2.23196	2.20849	2.18427
10	2.3226	2.28405	2.24351	2.20074	2.17843	2.15543	2.13169	2.10716	2.08176
11	2.24823	2.20873	2.16709	2.12305	2.10001	2.07621	2.05161	2.02612	1.99965
12	2.18776	2.14744	2.10485	2.05968	2.03599	2.01149	1.9861	1.95973	1.93228
13	2.13763	2.09659	2.05316	2.00698	1.98272	1.95757	1.93147	1.90429	1.87591
14	2.0954	2.05371	2.00953	1.96245	1.93766	1.91193	1.88516	1.85723	1.828
15	2.05932	2.01707	1.97222	1.92431	1.89904	1.87277	1.84539	1.81676	1.78672
16	2.02815	1.98539	1.93992	1.89127	1.86556	1.83879	1.81084	1.78156	1.75075
17	2.00094	1.95772	1.91169	1.86236	1.83624	1.80901	1.78053	1.75063	1.71909
18	1.97698	1.93334	1.88681	1.83685	1.81035	1.78269	1.75371	1.72322	1.69099
19	1.95573	1.9117	1.86471	1.81416	1.78731	1.75924	1.72979	1.69876	1.66587
20	1.93674	1.89236	1.84494	1.79384	1.76667	1.73822	1.70833	1.67678	1.64326
21	1.91967	1.87497	1.82715	1.77555	1.74807	1.71927	1.68896	1.65691	1.62278
22	1.90425	1.85925	1.81106	1.75899	1.73122	1.70208	1.67138	1.63885	1.60415
23	1.89025	1.84497	1.79643	1.74392	1.71588	1.68643	1.65535	1.62237	1.58711
24	1.87748	1.83194	1.78308	1.73015	1.70185	1.6721	1.64067	1.60726	1.57146
25	1.86578	1.82	1.77083	1.71752	1.68898	1.65895	1.62718	1.59335	1.55703
30	1.81949	1.7727	1.72227	1.66731	1.63774	1.60648	1.57323	1.53757	1.49891
40	1.76269	1.71456	1.66241	1.60515	1.57411	1.54108	1.50562	1.46716	1.42476
60	1.70701	1.65743	1.60337	1.54349	1.51072	1.47554	1.43734	1.3952	1.34757
120	1.65238	1.6012	1.545	1.48207	1.44723	1.40938	1.3676	1.32034	1.26457

Areas in the Right Tail under the F Distribution Curve = 0.10.

APPENDIX 5A

Durbin–Watson Statistic: 1% Significance points of *dL* and *dU*

	k′ = 1		*k′ = 2*		*k′ = 3*		*k′ = 4*		*k′ = 5*	
n	*dL*	*dU*	*dL*	*dU*	*dL*	*dU*	*dL*	*dU*	*dL*	*dU*
6	0.390	1.142	—	—	—	—	—	—	—	—
7	0.435	1.036	0.294	1.676	—	—	—	—	—	—
8	0.497	1.003	0.345	1.489	0.229	2.102	—	—	—	—
9	0.554	0.998	0.408	1.389	0.279	1.875	0.183	2.433	—	—
10	0.604	1.001	0.466	1.333	0.340	1.733	0.230	2.193	0.150	2.690
11	0.653	1.010	0.519	1.297	0.396	1.640	0.286	2.030	0.193	2.453
12	0.697	1.023	0.569	1.274	0.449	1.575	0.339	1.913	0.244	2.280
13	0.738	1.038	0.616	1.261	0.499	1.526	0.391	1.826	0.294	2.150
14	0.776	1.054	0.660	1.254	0.547	1.490	0.441	1.757	0.343	2.049
15	0.811	1.070	0.700	1.252	0.591	1.464	0.488	1.704	0.391	1.967
16	0.844	1.086	0.737	1.252	0.633	1.446	0.532	1.663	0.437	1.900
17	0.874	1.102	0.772	1.255	0.672	1.432	0.574	1.630	0.480	1.847
18	0.902	1.118	0.805	1.259	0.708	1.422	0.613	1.604	0.522	1.803
19	0.928	1.132	0.835	1.265	0.742	1.415	0.650	1.584	0.561	1.767
20	0.952	1.147	0.863	1.271	0.773	1.411	0.685	1.567	0.598	1.737
21	0.975	1.161	0.890	1.277	0.803	1.408	0.718	1.554	0.633	1.712
22	0.997	1.174	0.914	1.284	0.831	1.407	0.748	1.543	0.667	1.691
23	1.018	1.187	0.938	1.291	0.858	1.407	0.777	1.534	0.698	1.673
24	1.037	1.199	0.960	1.298	0.882	1.407	0.805	1.528	0.728	1.658
25	1.055	1.211	0.981	1.305	0.906	1.409	0.831	1.523	0.756	1.645
26	1.072	1.222	1.001	1.312	0.928	1.411	0.855	1.518	0.783	1.635
27	1.089	1.233	1.019	1.319	0.949	1.413	0.878	1.515	0.808	1.626
28	1.104	1.244	1.037	1.325	0.969	1.415	0.900	1.513	0.832	1.618
29	1.119	1.254	1.054	1.332	0.988	1.418	0.921	1.512	0.855	1.611
30	1.133	1.263	1.070	1.339	1.006	1.421	0.941	1.511	0.877	1.606
31	1.147	1.273	1.085	1.345	1.023	1.425	0.960	1.510	0.897	1.601
32	1.160	1.282	1.100	1.352	1.040	1.428	0.979	1.510	0.917	1.597
33	1.172	1.291	1.114	1.358	1.055	1.432	0.996	1.510	0.936	1.594
34	1.184	1.299	1.128	1.364	1.070	1.435	1.012	1.511	0.954	1.591
35	1.195	1.307	1.140	1.370	1.085	1.439	1.028	1.512	0.971	1.589
36	1.206	1.315	1.153	1.376	1.098	1.442	1.043	1.513	0.988	1.588
37	1.217	1.323	1.165	1.382	1.112	1.446	1.058	1.514	1.004	1.586
38	1.227	1.330	1.176	1.388	1.124	1.449	1.072	1.515	1.019	1.585
39	1.237	1.337	1.187	1.393	1.137	1.453	1.085	1.517	1.034	1.584
40	1.246	1.344	1.198	1.398	1.148	1.457	1.098	1.518	1.048	1.584
45	1.288	1.376	1.245	1.423	1.201	1.474	1.156	1.528	1.111	1.584
50	1.324	1.403	1.285	1.446	1.245	1.491	1.205	1.538	1.164	1.587
55	1.356	1.427	1.320	1.466	1.284	1.506	1.247	1.548	1.209	1.592
60	1.383	1.449	1.350	1.484	1.317	1.520	1.283	1.558	1.249	1.598
65	1.407	1.468	1.377	1.500	1.346	1.534	1.315	1.568	1.283	1.604
70	1.429	1.485	1.400	1.515	1.372	1.546	1.343	1.578	1.313	1.611
75	1.448	1.501	1.422	1.529	1.395	1.557	1.368	1.587	1.340	1.617
80	1.466	1.515	1.441	1.541	1.416	1.568	1.390	1.595	1.364	1.624
85	1.482	1.528	1.458	1.553	1.435	1.578	1.411	1.603	1.386	1.630
90	1.496	1.540	1.474	1.563	1.452	1.587	1.429	1.611	1.406	1.636
95	1.510	1.552	1.489	1.573	1.468	1.596	1.446	1.618	1.425	1.642
100	1.522	1.562	1.503	1.583	1.482	1.604	1.462	1.625	1.441	1.647
150	1.611	1.637	1.598	1.651	1.584	1.665	1.571	1.679	1.557	1.693
200	1.664	1.684	1.653	1.693	1.643	1.704	1.633	1.715	1.623	1.725

Note: k′ is the number of regressors excluding the intercept.

Source: N.E. Savin and K.J. White (1977), "The Durbin–Watson Test for Serial Correlation with Extreme Sample Sizes or Many Regressors", *Econometrica*, 45, pp. 1992–1995. Reproduced with the permission of the Econometric Society.

APPENDIX 5A (continued)

Durbin–Watson Statistic: 1% Significance points of *dL* and *dU*

k′ = 6		*k′ = 7*		*k′ = 8*		*k′ = 9*		*k′ = 10*	
dL	***dU***	***dL***	***dU***	***dL***	***dU***	***dL***	***dU***	***dL***	***dU***
—	—	—	—	—	—	—	—	—	—
—	—	—	—	—	—	—	—	—	—
—	—	—	—	—	—	—	—	—	—
—	—	—	—	—	—	—	—	—	—
—	—	—	—	—	—	—	—	—	—
0.124	2.892	—	—	—	—	—	—	—	—
0.164	2.665	0.105	3.053	—	—	—	—	—	—
0.211	2.490	0.140	2.838	0.090	3.182	—	—	—	—
0.257	2.354	0.183	2.667	0.122	2.981	0.078	3.287	—	—
0.303	2.244	0.226	2.530	0.161	2.817	0.107	3.101	0.068	3.374
0.349	2.153	0.269	2.416	0.200	2.681	0.142	2.944	0.094	3.201
0.393	2.078	0.313	2.319	0.241	2.566	0.179	2.811	0.127	3.053
0.435	2.015	0.355	2.238	0.282	2.467	0.216	2.697	0.160	2.925
0.476	1.963	0.396	2.169	0.322	2.381	0.255	2.597	0.196	2.813
0.515	1.918	0.436	2.110	0.362	2.308	0.294	2.510	0.232	2.714
0.552	1.881	0.474	2.059	0.400	2.244	0.331	2.434	0.268	2.625
0.587	1.849	0.510	2.015	0.437	2.188	0.368	2.367	0.304	2.548
0.620	1.821	0.545	1.977	0.473	2.140	0.404	2.308	0.340	2.479
0.652	1.797	0.578	1.944	0.507	2.097	0.439	2.255	0.375	2.417
0.682	1.766	0.610	1.915	0.540	2.059	0.473	2.209	0.409	2.362
0.711	1.759	0.640	1.889	0.572	2.026	0.505	2.168	0.441	2.313
0.738	1.743	0.669	1.867	0.602	1.997	0.536	2.131	0.473	2.269
0.764	1.729	0.696	1.847	0.630	1.970	0.566	2.098	0.504	2.229
0.788	1.718	0.723	1.830	0.658	1.947	0.595	2.068	0.533	2.193
0.812	1.707	0.748	1.814	0.684	1.925	0.622	2.041	0.562	2.160
0.834	1.698	0.772	1.800	0.710	1.906	0.649	2.017	0.589	2.131
0.856	1.690	0.794	1.788	0.734	1.889	0.674	1.995	0.615	2.104
0.876	1.683	0.816	1.776	0.757	1.874	0.698	1.975	0.641	2.080
0.896	1.677	0.837	1.766	0.779	1.860	0.722	1.957	0.665	2.057
0.914	1.671	0.857	1.757	0.800	1.847	0.744	1.940	0.689	2.037
0.932	1.666	0.877	1.749	0.821	1.836	0.766	1.925	0.711	2.018
0.950	1.662	0.895	1.742	0.841	1.825	0.787	1.911	0.733	2.001
0.966	1.658	0.913	1.735	0.860	1.816	0.807	1.899	0.754	1.985
0.982	1.655	0.930	1.729	0.878	1.807	0.826	1.887	0.774	1.970
0.997	1.652	0.946	1.724	0.895	1.799	0.844	1.876	0.789	1.956
1.065	1.643	1.019	1.704	0.974	1.768	0.927	1.834	0.881	1.902
1.123	1.639	1.081	1.692	1.039	1.748	0.997	1.805	0.955	1.864
1.172	1.638	1.134	1.685	1.095	1.734	1.057	1.785	1.018	1.837
1.214	1.639	1.179	1.682	1.144	1.726	1.108	1.771	1.072	1.817
1.251	1.642	1.218	1.680	1.186	1.720	1.153	1.761	1.120	1.802
1.283	1.645	1.253	1.680	1.223	1.716	1.192	1.754	1.162	1.792
1.313	1.646	1.284	1.682	1.256	1.716	1.227	1.746	1.199	1.785
1.338	1.653	1.312	1.683	1.285	1.714	1.259	1.745	1.232	1.777
1.362	1.657	1.337	1.685	1.312	1.714	1.287	1.743	1.262	1.773
1.383	1.661	1.360	1.687	1.336	1.714	1.312	1.741	1.288	1.769
1.403	1.666	1.381	1.690	1.358	1.715	1.336	1.741	1.313	1.767
1.421	1.670	1.400	1.693	1.378	1.717	1.357	1.741	1.335	1.765
1.543	1.708	1.530	1.722	1.515	1.737	1.501	1.752	1.468	1.767
1.613	1.735	1.603	1.746	1.592	1.575	1.582	1.768	1.571	1.779

Note: k′ is the number of regressors excluding the intercept.

Source: N.E. Savin and K.J. White (1977), "The Durbin–Watson Test for Serial Correlation with Extreme Sample Sizes or Many Regressors", *Econometrica*, 45, pp. 1992–1995. Reproduced with the permission of the Econometric Society.

APPENDIX 5A (continued)
Durbin–Watson Statistic: 1% Significance points of *dL* and *dU*

	k′ = 11		*k′ = 12*		*k′ = 13*		*k′ = 14*		*k′ = 15*	
n	*dL*	*dU*	*dL*	*dU*	*dL*	*dU*	*dL*	*dU*	*dL*	*dU*
16	0.060	3.446	—	—	—	—	—	—	—	—
17	0.084	3.286	0.053	3.506	—	—	—	—	—	—
18	0.113	3.146	0.075	3.358	0.047	3.557	—	—	—	—
19	0.145	3.023	0.102	3.227	0.067	3.420	0.043	3.601	—	—
20	0.178	2.914	0.131	3.109	0.092	3.297	0.061	3.474	0.038	3.639
21	0.212	2.817	0.162	3.004	0.119	3.185	0.084	3.358	0.055	3.521
22	0.246	2.729	0.194	2.909	0.148	3.084	0.109	3.252	0.077	3.412
23	0.281	2.651	0.227	2.822	0.178	2.991	0.136	3.155	0.100	3.311
24	0.315	2.580	0.260	2.744	0.209	2.906	0.165	3.065	0.125	3.218
25	0.348	2.517	0.292	2.674	0.240	2.829	0.194	2.982	0.152	3.131
26	0.381	2.460	0.324	2.610	0.272	2.758	0.224	2.906	0.180	3.050
27	0.413	2.409	0.356	2.552	0.303	2.694	0.253	2.836	0.208	2.976
28	0.444	2.363	0.387	2.499	0.333	2.635	0.283	2.772	0.237	2.907
29	0.474	2.321	0.417	2.451	0.363	2.582	0.313	2.713	0.266	2.843
30	0.503	2.283	0.447	2.407	0.393	2.533	0.342	2.659	0.294	2.785
31	0.531	2.248	0.475	2.367	0.422	2.487	0.371	2.609	0.322	2.730
32	0.558	2.216	0.503	2.330	0.450	2.446	0.399	2.563	0.350	2.680
33	0.585	2.187	0.530	2.296	0.477	2.408	0.426	2.520	0.377	2.633
34	0.610	2.160	0.556	2.266	0.503	2.373	0.452	2.481	0.404	2.590
35	0.634	2.136	0.581	2.237	0.529	2.340	0.478	2.444	0.430	2.550
36	0.658	2.113	0.605	2.210	0.554	2.310	0.504	2.410	0.455	2.512
37	0.680	2.092	0.628	2.186	0.578	2.282	0.528	2.379	0.480	2.477
38	0.702	2.073	0.651	2.164	0.601	2.256	0.552	2.350	0.504	2.445
39	0.723	2.055	0.673	2.143	0.623	2.232	0.575	2.323	0.528	2.414
40	0.744	2.039	0.694	2.123	0.645	2.210	0.597	2.297	0.551	2.386
45	0.835	1.972	0.790	2.044	0.744	2.118	0.700	2.193	0.655	2.269
50	0.913	1.925	0.871	1.987	0.829	2.051	0.787	2.116	0.746	2.182
55	0.979	1.891	0.940	1.945	0.902	2.002	0.863	2.059	0.825	2.117
60	1.037	1.865	1.001	1.914	0.965	1.964	0.929	2.015	0.893	2.067
65	1.087	1.845	1.053	1.889	1.020	1.934	0.986	1.980	0.953	2.027
70	1.131	1.831	1.099	1.870	1.068	1.911	1.037	1.953	1.005	1.995
75	1.170	1.819	1.141	1.856	1.111	1.893	1.082	1.931	1.052	1.970
80	1.205	1.810	1.777	1.844	1.150	1.878	1.122	1.913	1.094	1.949
85	1.236	1.803	1.210	1.834	1.184	1.866	1.158	1.898	1.132	1.931
90	1.264	1.798	1.240	1.827	1.215	1.856	1.191	1.886	1.166	1.917
95	1.290	1.793	1.267	1.821	1.244	1.848	1.221	1.876	1.197	1.905
100	1.314	1.790	1.292	1.816	1.270	1.841	1.248	1.868	1.225	1.895
150	1.473	1.783	1.458	1.799	1.444	1.814	1.429	1.830	1.414	1.847
200	1.561	1.791	1.550	1.801	1.539	1.813	1.528	1.824	1.518	1.836

Note: k′ is the number of regressors excluding the intercept.

Source: N.E. Savin and K.J. White (1977), "The Durbin–Watson Test for Serial Correlation with Extreme Sample Sizes or Many Regressors", *Econometrica*, 45, pp. 1992–1995. Reproduced with the permission of the Econometric Society.

APPENDIX 5A (continued)
Durbin–Watson Statistic: 1% Significance points of *dL* and *dU*

k′ = 16		*k′ = 17*		*k′ = 18*		*k′ = 19*		*k′ = 20*	
dL	*dU*	*dL*	*dU*	*dL*	*dU*	*dL*	*dU*	*dL*	*dU*
—	—	—	—	—	—	—	—	—	—
—	—	—	—	—	—	—	—	—	—
—	—	—	—	—	—	—	—	—	—
—	—	—	—	—	—	—	—	—	—
—	—	—	—	—	—	—	—	—	—
0.035	3.671	—	—	—	—	—	—	—	—
0.050	3.562	0.032	3.700	—	—	—	—	—	—
0.070	3.459	0.046	3.597	0.029	3.725	—	—	—	—
0.092	3.363	0.065	3.501	0.043	3.629	0.027	3.747	—	—
0.116	3.274	0.085	3.410	0.060	3.538	0.039	3.657	0.025	3.766
0.141	3.191	0.107	3.325	0.079	3.452	0.055	3.572	0.036	3.682
0.167	3.113	0.131	3.245	0.100	3.371	0.073	3.490	0.051	3.602
0.194	3.040	0.156	3.169	0.122	3.294	0.093	3.412	0.068	3.524
0.222	2.972	0.182	3.098	0.146	3.220	0.114	3.338	0.087	3.450
0.249	2.909	0.208	3.032	0.171	3.152	0.137	3.267	0.107	3.379
0.277	2.851	0.234	2.970	0.196	3.087	0.160	3.201	0.128	3.311
0.304	2.797	0.261	2.912	0.221	3.026	0.184	3.137	0.151	3.246
0.331	2.746	0.287	2.858	0.246	2.969	0.209	3.078	0.174	3.184
0.357	2.699	0.313	2.808	0.272	2.915	0.233	3.022	0.197	3.126
0.383	2.655	0.339	2.761	0.297	2.865	0.257	2.969	0.221	3.071
0.409	2.614	0.364	2.717	0.322	2.818	0.282	2.919	0.244	3.019
0.434	2.576	0.389	2.675	0.347	2.774	0.306	2.872	0.268	2.969
0.458	2.540	0.414	2.637	0.371	2.733	0.330	2.828	0.291	2.923
0.482	2.507	0.438	2.600	0.395	2.694	0.354	2.787	0.315	2.879
0.505	2.476	0.461	2.566	0.418	2.657	0.377	2.748	0.338	2.838
0.612	2.346	0.570	2.424	0.528	2.503	0.488	2.582	0.448	2.661
0.705	2.250	0.665	2.318	0.625	2.387	0.586	2.456	0.548	2.526
0.786	2.176	0.748	2.237	0.711	2.298	0.674	2.359	0.637	2.421
0.857	2.120	0.822	2.173	0.786	2.227	0.751	2.283	0.716	2.338
0.919	2.075	0.886	2.123	0.852	2.172	0.819	2.221	0.786	2.272
0.974	2.038	0.943	2.082	0.911	2.127	0.880	2.172	0.849	2.217
1.023	2.009	0.993	2.049	0.964	2.090	0.934	2.131	0.905	2.172
1.066	1.984	1.039	2.022	1.011	2.057	0.983	2.097	0.955	2.135
1.106	1.965	1.080	1.999	1.053	2.033	1.027	2.068	1.000	2.104
1.141	1.948	1.116	1.979	1.091	2.012	1.066	2.044	1.041	2.077
1.174	1.934	1.150	1.963	1.126	1.993	1.102	2.023	1.079	2.054
1.203	1.922	1.181	1.949	1.158	1.977	1.136	2.006	1.113	2.034
1.400	1.863	1.385	1.880	1.370	1.897	1.355	1.913	1.340	1.931
1.507	1.847	1.495	1.860	1.484	1.871	1.474	1.883	1.462	1.896

Note: k′ is the number of regressors excluding the intercept.

Source: N.E. Savin and K.J. White (1977), "The Durbin–Watson Test for Serial Correlation with Extreme Sample Sizes or Many Regressors", *Econometrica*, 45, pp. 1992–1995. Reproduced with the permission of the Econometric Society.

APPENDIX 5B

Durbin–Watson Statistic: 5% Significance points of *dL* and *dU*

	k′ = 1		*k′ = 2*		*k′ = 3*		*k′ = 4*		*k′ = 5*	
n	*dL*	*dU*	*dL*	*dU*	*dL*	*dU*	*dL*	*dU*	*dL*	*dU*
6	0.610	1.400	—	—	—	—	—	—	—	—
7	0.700	1.356	0.467	1.896	—	—	—	—	—	—
8	0.763	1.332	0.559	1.777	0.368	2.287	—	—	—	—
9	0.824	1.320	0.629	1.699	0.455	2.128	0.296	2.588	—	—
10	0.879	1.320	0.697	1.641	0.525	2.016	0.376	2.414	0.243	2.822
11	0.927	1.324	0.758	1.604	0.595	1.928	0.444	2.283	0.316	2.645
12	0.971	1.331	0.812	1.579	0.658	1.864	0.512	2.177	0.379	2.506
13	1.010	1.340	0.861	1.562	0.715	1.816	0.574	2.094	0.445	2.390
14	1.045	1.350	0.905	1.551	0.767	1.779	0.632	2.030	0.505	2.296
15	1.077	1.361	0.946	1.543	0.814	1.750	0.685	1.977	0.562	2.220
16	1.106	1.371	0.982	1.539	0.857	1.728	0.734	1.935	0.615	2.157
17	1.133	1.381	1.015	1.536	0.897	1.710	0.779	1.900	0.664	2.104
18	1.158	1.391	1.046	1.535	0.933	1.696	0.820	1.872	0.710	2.060
19	1.180	1.401	1.074	1.536	0.967	1.685	0.859	1.848	0.752	2.023
20	1.201	1.411	1.100	1.537	0.998	1.676	0.894	1.828	0.792	1.991
21	1.221	1.420	1.125	1.538	1.026	1.669	0.927	1.812	0.829	1.964
22	1.239	1.429	1.147	1.541	1.053	1.664	0.958	1.797	0.863	1.940
23	1.257	1.437	1.168	1.543	1.078	1.660	0.986	1.785	0.895	1.920
24	1.273	1.446	1.188	1.546	1.101	1.656	1.013	1.775	0.925	1.902
25	1.288	1.454	1.206	1.550	1.123	1.654	1.038	1.767	0.953	1.886
26	1.302	1.461	1.224	1.553	1.143	1.652	1.062	1.759	0.979	1.873
27	1.316	1.469	1.240	1.556	1.162	1.651	1.084	1.753	1.004	1.861
28	1.328	1.476	1.255	1.560	1.181	1.650	1.104	1.747	1.028	1.850
29	1.341	1.483	1.270	1.563	1.198	1.650	1.124	1.743	1.050	1.841
30	1.352	1.489	1.284	1.567	1.214	1.650	1.143	1.739	1.071	1.833
31	1.363	1.496	1.297	1.570	1.229	1.650	1.160	1.735	1.090	1.825
32	1.373	1.502	1.309	1.574	1.244	1.650	1.177	1.732	1.109	1.819
33	1.383	1.508	1.321	1.577	1.258	1.651	1.193	1.730	1.127	1.813
34	1.393	1.514	1.333	1.580	1.271	1.652	1.208	1.728	1.144	1.808
35	1.402	1.519	1.343	1.584	1.283	1.653	1.222	1.726	1.160	1.803
36	1.411	1.525	1.354	1.587	1.295	1.654	1.236	1.724	1.175	1.799
37	1.419	1.530	1.364	1.590	1.307	1.655	1.249	1.723	1.190	1.795
38	1.427	1.535	1.373	1.594	1.318	1.656	1.261	1.722	1.204	1.792
39	1.435	1.540	1.382	1.597	1.328	1.658	1.273	1.722	1.218	1.789
40	1.442	1.544	1.391	1.600	1.338	1.659	1.285	1.721	1.230	1.786
45	1.475	1.566	1.430	1.615	1.383	1.666	1.336	1.720	1.287	1.776
50	1.503	1.585	1.462	1.628	1.421	1.674	1.378	1.721	1.355	1.771
55	1.528	1.601	1.490	1.641	1.452	1.681	1.414	1.724	1.374	1.768
60	1.549	1.616	1.514	1.652	1.480	1.689	1.444	1.727	1.408	1.767
65	1.567	1.629	1.536	1.662	1.503	1.696	1.471	1.731	1.438	1.767
70	1.583	1.641	1.554	1.672	1.525	1.703	1.494	1.735	1.464	1.768
75	1.598	1.652	1.571	1.680	1.543	1.709	1.515	1.739	1.487	1.770
80	1.611	1.662	1.586	1.688	1.560	1.715	1.534	1.743	1.507	1.772
85	1.624	1.671	1.600	1.696	1.575	1.721	1.550	1.747	1.525	1.774
90	1.635	1.679	1.612	1.703	1.589	1.726	1.566	1.751	1.542	1.776
95	1.645	1.687	1.623	1.709	1.602	1.732	1.579	1.755	1.557	1.778
100	1.654	1.694	1.634	1.715	1.613	1.736	1.592	1.758	1.571	1.780
150	1.720	1.746	1.706	1.760	1.693	1.774	1.679	1.788	1.665	1.802
200	1.758	1.778	1.748	1.789	1.738	1.799	1.728	1.810	1.718	1.820

Note: k′ is the number of regressors excluding the intercept.

Source: N.E. Savin and K.J. White (1977), "The Durbin–Watson Test for Serial Correlation with Extreme Sample Sizes or Many Regressors", *Econometrica*, 45, pp. 1992–1995. Reproduced with the permission of the Econometric Society.

APPENDIX 5B (continued)
Durbin–Watson Statistic: 5% Significance points of *dL* and *dU*

k′ = 6		*k′ = 7*		*k′ = 8*		*k′ = 9*		*k′ = 10*	
dL	*dU*	*dL*	*dU*	*dL*	*dU*	*dL*	*dU*	*dL*	*dU*
—	—	—	—	—	—	—	—	—	—
—	—	—	—	—	—	—	—	—	—
—	—	—	—	—	—	—	—	—	—
—	—	—	—	—	—	—	—	—	—
—	—	—	—	—	—	—	—	—	—
0.203	3.005	—	—	—	—	—	—	—	—
0.268	2.832	0.171	3.149	—	—	—	—	—	—
0.328	2.692	0.230	2.985	0.147	3.266	—	—	—	—
0.389	2.572	0.286	2.848	0.200	3.111	0.127	3.360	—	—
0.447	2.472	0.343	2.727	0.251	2.979	0.175	3.216	0.111	3.438
0.502	2.388	0.398	2.624	0.304	2.860	0.222	3.090	0.155	3.304
0.554	2.318	0.451	2.537	0.356	2.757	0.272	2.975	0.198	3.184
0.603	2.257	0.502	2.461	0.407	2.667	0.321	2.873	0.244	3.073
0.649	2.206	0.459	2.396	0.456	2.589	0.369	2.783	0.290	2.974
0.692	2.162	0.595	2.339	0.502	2.521	0.416	2.704	0.336	2.885
0.732	2.124	0.637	2.290	0.547	2.460	0.461	2.633	0.380	2.806
0.769	2.090	0.677	2.246	0.588	2.407	0.504	2.571	0.424	2.734
0.804	2.061	0.715	2.208	0.628	2.360	0.545	2.514	0.465	2.670
0.837	2.035	0.751	2.174	0.666	2.318	0.584	2.464	0.506	2.613
0.868	2.012	0.784	2.144	0.702	2.280	0.621	2.419	0.544	2.560
0.897	1.992	0.816	2.117	0.735	2.246	0.657	2.379	0.581	2.513
0.925	1.974	0.845	2.093	0.767	2.216	0.691	2.342	0.616	2.470
0.951	1.958	0.874	2.071	0.798	2.188	0.723	2.309	0.650	2.431
0.975	1.944	0.900	2.052	0.826	2.164	0.753	2.278	0.682	2.396
0.998	1.931	0.926	2.034	0.854	2.141	0.782	2.251	0.712	2.363
1.020	1.920	0.950	2.018	0.879	2.120	0.810	2.226	0.741	2.333
1.041	1.909	0.972	2.004	0.904	2.102	0.836	2.203	0.769	2.306
1.061	1.900	0.994	1.991	0.927	2.085	0.861	2.181	0.795	2.281
1.080	1.891	1.015	1.979	0.950	2.069	0.885	2.162	0.821	2.257
1.097	1.884	1.034	1.967	0.971	2.054	0.908	2.144	0.845	2.236
1.114	1.877	1.053	1.957	0.991	2.041	0.930	2.127	0.868	2.216
1.131	1.870	1.071	1.948	1.011	2.029	0.951	2.112	0.891	2.198
1.146	1.864	1.088	1.939	1.029	2.017	0.970	2.098	0.912	2.180
1.161	1.859	1.104	1.932	1.047	2.007	0.990	2.085	0.932	2.164
1.175	1.854	1.120	1.924	1.064	1.997	1.008	2.072	0.945	2.149
1.238	1.835	1.189	1.895	1.139	1.958	1.089	2.002	1.038	2.088
1.291	1.822	1.246	1.875	1.201	1.930	1.156	1.986	1.110	2.044
1.334	1.814	1.294	1.861	1.253	1.909	1.212	1.959	1.170	2.010
1.372	1.808	1.335	1.850	1.298	1.894	1.260	1.939	1.222	1.984
1.404	1.805	1.370	1.843	1.336	1.882	1.301	1.923	1.266	1.964
1.433	1.802	1.401	1.837	1.369	1.873	1.337	1.910	1.305	1.948
1.458	1.801	1.428	1.834	1.399	1.867	1.369	1.901	1.339	1.935
1.480	1.801	1.453	1.831	1.425	1.861	1.397	1.893	1.369	1.925
1.500	1.801	1.474	1.829	1.448	1.857	1.422	1.886	1.396	1.916
1.518	1.801	1.494	1.827	1.469	1.854	1.445	1.881	1.420	1.909
1.535	1.802	1.512	1.827	1.489	1.852	1.465	1.877	1.442	1.903
1.550	1.803	1.528	1.826	1.506	1.850	1.484	1.874	1.462	1.898
1.651	1.817	1.637	1.832	1.622	1.847	1.608	1.862	1.594	1.877
1.707	1.831	1.697	1.841	1.686	1.852	1.675	1.863	1.665	1.874

Note: k′ is the number of regressors excluding the intercept.

Source: N.E. Savin and K.J. White (1977), "The Durbin–Watson Test for Serial Correlation with Extreme Sample Sizes or Many Regressors", *Econometrica*, 45, pp. 1992–1995. Reproduced with the permission of the Econometric Society.

APPENDIX 5B (continued)
Durbin–Watson Statistic: 5% Significance points of *dL* and *dU*

	$k' = 11$		$k' = 12$		$k' = 13$		$k' = 14$		$k' = 15$	
n	*dL*	*dU*	*dL*	*dU*	*dL*	*dU*	*dL*	*dU*	*dL*	*dU*
16	0.098	3.503	—	—	—	—	—	—	—	—
17	0.138	3.378	0.087	3.557	—	—	—	—	—	—
18	0.177	3.265	0.123	3.441	0.078	3.603	—	—	—	—
19	0.220	3.159	0.160	3.335	0.111	3.496	0.070	3.642	—	—
20	0.263	3.063	0.200	3.234	0.145	3.395	0.100	3.542	0.063	3.676
21	0.307	2.976	0.240	3.141	0.182	3.300	0.132	3.448	0.091	3.583
22	0.349	2.897	0.281	3.057	0.220	3.211	0.166	3.358	0.120	3.495
23	0.391	2.826	0.322	2.979	0.259	3.128	0.202	3.272	0.153	3.409
24	0.431	2.761	0.362	2.908	0.297	3.053	0.239	3.193	0.186	3.327
25	0.470	2.702	0.400	2.844	0.335	2.983	0.275	3.119	0.221	3.251
26	0.508	2.649	0.438	2.784	0.373	2.919	0.312	3.051	0.256	3.179
27	0.544	2.600	0.475	2.730	0.409	2.859	0.348	2.987	0.291	3.112
28	0.578	2.555	0.510	2.680	0.445	2.805	0.383	2.928	0.325	3.050
29	0.612	2.515	0.544	2.634	0.479	2.755	0.418	2.874	0.359	2.992
30	0.643	2.477	0.577	2.592	0.512	2.708	0.451	2.823	0.392	2.937
31	0.674	2.443	0.608	2.553	0.545	2.665	0.484	2.776	0.425	2.987
32	0.703	2.411	0.638	2.517	0.576	2.625	0.515	2.733	0.457	2.840
33	0.731	2.382	0.668	2.484	0.606	2.588	0.546	2.692	0.488	2.796
34	0.758	2.355	0.695	2.454	0.634	2.554	0.575	2.654	0.518	2.754
35	0.783	2.330	0.722	2.425	0.662	2.521	0.604	2.619	0.547	2.716
36	0.808	2.306	0.748	2.398	0.689	2.492	0.631	2.586	0.575	2.680
37	0.831	2.285	0.772	2.374	0.714	2.464	0.657	2.555	0.602	2.646
38	0.854	2.265	0.796	2.351	0.739	2.438	0.683	2.526	0.628	2.614
39	0.875	2.246	0.819	2.329	0.763	2.413	0.707	2.499	0.653	2.585
40	0.896	2.228	0.840	2.309	0.785	2.391	0.731	2.473	0.678	2.557
45	0.988	2.156	0.938	2.225	0.887	2.296	0.838	2.367	0.788	2.439
50	1.064	2.103	1.019	2.163	0.973	2.225	0.927	2.287	0.882	2.350
55	1.129	2.062	1.087	2.116	1.045	2.170	1.003	2.225	0.961	2.281
60	1.184	2.031	1.145	2.079	1.106	2.127	1.068	2.177	1.029	2.227
65	1.231	2.006	1.195	2.049	1.160	2.093	1.124	2.138	1.088	2.183
70	1.272	1.986	1.239	2.026	1.206	2.066	1.172	2.106	1.139	2.148
75	1.308	1.970	1.277	2.006	1.247	2.043	1.215	2.080	1.184	2.118
80	1.340	1.957	1.311	1.991	1.283	2.024	1.253	2.059	1.224	2.093
85	1.369	1.946	1.342	1.977	1.315	2.009	1.287	2.040	1.260	2.073
90	1.395	1.937	1.369	1.966	1.344	1.995	1.318	2.025	1.292	2.055
95	1.418	1.929	1.394	1.956	1.370	1.984	1.345	2.012	1.321	2.040
100	1.434	1.923	1.416	1.948	1.393	1.974	1.371	2.000	1.347	2.026
150	1.579	1.892	1.564	1.908	1.550	1.924	1.535	1.940	1.519	1.956
200	1.654	1.885	1.643	1.896	1.632	1.908	1.621	1.919	1.610	1.931

Note: k′ is the number of regressors excluding the intercept.

Source: N.E. Savin and K.J. White (1977), "The Durbin–Watson Test for Serial Correlation with Extreme Sample Sizes or Many Regressors", *Econometrica*, 45, pp. 1992–1995. Reproduced with the permission of the Econometric Society.

APPENDIX 5B (continued)
Durbin–Watson Statistic: 5% Significance points of *dL* and *dU*

k′ = 16		k′ = 17		k′ = 18		k′ = 19		k′ = 20	
dL	dU	dL	dU	dL	dU	dL	dU	dL	dU
—	—	—	—	—	—	—	—	—	—
—	—	—	—	—	—	—	—	—	—
—	—	—	—	—	—	—	—	—	—
—	—	—	—	—	—	—	—	—	—
—	—	—	—	—	—	—	—	—	—
0.058	3.705	—	—	—	—	—	—	—	—
0.083	3.619	0.052	3.731	—	—	—	—	—	—
0.110	3.535	0.076	3.650	0.048	3.753	—	—	—	—
0.141	3.454	0.101	3.572	0.070	3.678	0.044	3.773	—	—
0.172	3.376	0.130	4.494	0.094	3.604	0.065	3.702	0.041	3.790
0.205	3.303	0.160	3.420	0.120	3.531	0.087	3.632	0.060	3.724
0.238	3.233	0.191	3.349	0.149	3.460	0.112	3.563	0.081	3.658
0.271	3.168	0.222	3.283	0.178	3.392	0.138	3.495	0.104	3.592
0.305	3.107	0.254	3.219	0.208	3.327	0.166	3.431	0.129	3.528
0.337	3.050	0.286	3.160	0.238	3.266	0.195	3.368	0.156	3.465
0.370	2.996	0.317	3.103	0.269	3.208	0.224	3.309	0.183	3.406
0.401	2.946	0.349	3.050	0.299	3.153	0.253	3.252	0.211	3.348
0.432	2.899	0.379	3.000	0.329	3.100	0.283	3.198	0.239	3.293
0.462	2.854	0.409	2.954	0.359	3.051	0.312	3.147	0.267	3.240
0.492	2.813	0.439	2.910	0.388	3.005	0.340	3.099	0.295	3.190
0.520	2.774	0.467	2.868	0.417	2.961	0.369	3.053	0.323	3.142
0.548	2.738	0.495	2.829	0.445	2.920	0.397	3.009	0.351	3.097
0.575	2.703	0.522	2.792	0.472	2.880	0.424	2.968	0.378	3.054
0.600	2.671	0.549	2.757	0.499	2.843	0.451	2.929	0.404	3.013
0.626	2.641	0.575	2.724	0.525	2.808	0.477	2.892	0.430	2.974
0.740	2.512	0.692	2.586	0.644	2.659	0.598	2.733	0.553	2.807
0.836	2.414	0.792	2.479	0.747	2.544	0.703	2.610	0.660	2.675
0.919	2.338	0.877	2.396	0.836	2.454	0.795	2.512	0.754	2.571
0.990	2.278	0.951	2.330	0.913	2.382	0.874	2.434	0.836	2.487
1.052	2.229	1.016	2.276	0.980	2.323	0.944	2.371	0.908	2.419
1.105	2.189	1.072	2.232	1.038	2.275	1.005	2.318	0.971	2.362
1.153	2.156	1.121	2.195	1.090	2.235	1.058	2.275	1.027	2.315
1.195	2.129	1.165	2.165	1.136	2.201	1.106	2.238	1.076	2.275
1.232	2.105	1.205	2.139	1.177	2.172	1.149	2.206	1.121	2.241
1.266	2.085	1.240	2.116	1.213	2.148	1.187	2.179	1.160	2.211
1.296	2.068	1.271	2.097	1.247	2.126	1.222	2.156	1.197	2.186
1.324	2.053	1.301	2.080	1.277	2.108	1.253	2.135	1.229	2.164
1.504	1.972	1.489	1.989	1.474	2.006	1.458	2.023	1.443	2.040
1.599	1.943	1.588	1.955	1.576	1.967	1.565	1.979	1.554	1.991

Note: k′ is the number of regressors excluding the intercept.

Source: N.E. Savin and K.J. White (1977), "The Durbin–Watson Test for Serial Correlation with Extreme Sample Sizes or Many Regressors", *Econometrica*, 45, pp. 1992–1995. Reproduced with the permission of the Econometric Society.

References

Almon, S. (1965). "The distributed lag between capital appropriations and expenditures", *Econometrica* 33: 178–196.

Anderson, O.D. (1977). *Time Series Analysis and Forecasting: The Box–Jenkins Approach.* London: Butterworths.

Artis, M. (1988). "The 1988 budget and the MTFS", *Fiscal Studies* 9: 14–29.

Banerjee, A., J.J. Dolado, D.F. Hendry and W. Smith Gregor (1986). "Exploring equilibrium relationships in econometrics through static models: Some Monte Carlo evidence", *Oxford Bulletin of Economics and Statistics* 48: 253–277.

Box, G.E.P. and G.M. Jenkins (1976). *Time Series Analysis: Forecasting and Control*, rev. edition, San Francisco: Holden–Day.

Box, G.E.P. and D.A. Pierce (1970). "Distribution of residual autocorrelation in autoregressive integrated moving average time series models", *Journal of the American Statistical Association* 70: 70–79.

Breusch, T.S. (1978). "Testing for autocorrelation in dynamic linear models", *Australian Economic Papers* 17: 334–355.

Breusch, T.S. and A.R. Pagan (1980). "The Lagrange multiplier test and its application to model specification in econometrics", *Review of Econometric Studies* 47, 239–253.

Buse, A. (1982). "The likelihood ratio, Wald and Lagrange multiplier tests: An expository note", *American Statistician* 36: 153–157.

Charemza, W.W. and D.F. Deadman (1997). *New Directions in Econometric Practice*, 2nd edition. Edward Elgar.

Chow, G.C. (1960). "Test of equality between sets of coefficients in two linear regressions", *Econometrica* 28: 591–605.

Cooley, T. and S. LeRoy (1985). "Atheoretical macroeconomics: A critique", *Journal of Monetary Economics* 16: 283–308.

Davidson, J.H., D.H. Hendry, F. Srba and S. Yeo (1978). "Econometric modelling of the aggregate time-series relationship between consumers' expenditure and income in the United Kingdom", *Economic Journal* 88: 661–692.

Dickey, D.A. and S. Pantula (1987). "Determining the order of differencing in autoregressive processes", *Journal of Business and Economic Statistics* 15: 455–461.

Dickey, D.A. and W.A. Fuller (1979). "Distribution of the estimators for autoregressive time series with a unit root", *Journal of the American Statistical Association* 74: 427–431.

Dickey, D.A. and W.A. Fuller (1981). "Likelihood ratio statistics for autoregressive time series with a unit root", *Econometrica* 49: 1057–1072.

Dickey, D.A., W.R. Bell and R.R. Miller (1986). "Unit roots in time series models: Tests and implications", *American Statistician* 40: 12–26.

Dickey, D.A., D.W. Jansen and D.L. Thornton (1991). "A primer on cointegration with application to money and income", *Federal Reserve Bank of St. Louis Review* 73: 58–78.

Durbin, J. (1970). "Testing for serial correlation in least-squares regression when some of the regressors are lagged dependent variables", *Econometrica* 38: 410–421.

Durbin, J. and G.S. Watson (1950). "Testing for serial correlation in least squares regression. Part I", *Biometrika* 37: 409–428.

Durbin, J. and G.S. Watson (1951). "Testing for serial correlation in least squares regression. Part II", *Biometrika* 38: 159–178.

Enders, W. (1995). *Applied Econometric Time Series*. New York: John Wiley & Sons.
Engle, R.F. (1981). "Wald, likelihood ratio and Lagrange multiplier tests in econometrics", in Z. Griliches and M. Intriligator (eds.), *Handbook of Econometrics*. Amsterdam: North Holland.
Engle, R.F. and C.W.J. Granger (1987). "Co-integration and error correction: Representation, estimation, and testing", *Econometrica* 55: 251–276.
Farebrother, R.W. (1980). "The Durbin–Watson test for serial correlation when there is no intercept in the regression", *Econometrica* 48: 1553–1563.
Fuller, W.A. (1976). *Introduction to Statistical Time Series*. New York: John Wiley & Sons.
Geweke, J., R. Meese and W. Dent (1981). "Comparing alternative tests of causality in temporal systems: Analytic results and experimental evidence", *Journal of Econometrics* 21: 161–194.
Giannini, C. (1992). *Topics in Structural VAR Econometrics*. New York: Springer–Verlag.
Godfrey, L.G. (1978). "Testing against general autoregressive and moving average models when the regressors include lagged dependent variables", *Econometrica* 46: 1293–1302.
Goldfeld, S.M. and R.E. Quandt (1965). "Some tests for homoscedasticity", *Journal of the American Statistical Association* 60: 539–547.
Granger, C.W.J. (1969). "Investigating causal relations by econometric models and cross-spectral methods", *Econometrica* 37: 424–438.
Granger, C.W.J. and P. Newbold (1973). "Some comments on the evaluation of economic forecasts", *Applied Economics* 5: 35–47.
Granger, C.W.J. and P. Newbold (1974). "Spurious regressions in econometrics", *Journal of Econometrics* 2: 111–120.
Granger, C.W.J. and P. Newbold (1986). *Forecasting Economic Time Series*, 2nd edition. New York: Academic Press.
Griliches, Z. (1985). "Data and econometricans: The uneasy alliance", *American Economic Review* 52: 196–200.
Hadley, G. (1961). *Linear Algebra*. Reading, Massachusetts: Addison–Wesley.
Hall, S.G. (1986). "An application of the Granger and Engle two-step estimation procedure to United Kingdom aggregate wage data", *Oxford Bulletin of Economics and Statistics* 48: 229–239.
Hendry, D.H. (1980). "Econometrics: Alchemy or science?", *Economica* 47: 387–406.
Hendry, D.H. and G.E. Mizon (1978). "Serial correlation as a convenient simplification, not a nuisance: A comment on a study of the demand for money by the Bank of England", *Economic Journal* 88: 549–563.
Holden, D. and R. Perman (1994). "Unit roots and cointegration for the economist", chap. 3, in B. Bhaskara Rao (ed.), *Cointegration for the Applied Economist*. New York: St. Martin's Press.
Holden, K. and J. Thompson (1992). "Co-integration: An introductory survey", *British Review of Economic Issues* 14: 1–55.
Intriligator, M.D., R.G. Bodkin and C. Hsiao (1996). *Econometric Models, Techniques and Applications*, 2nd edition. Upper Saddle River, New Jersey: Simon and Schuster, Prentice Hall.
Jarque, C.M. and A.K. Bera (1980). "Efficient tests for normality, homoscedasticity and serial independence of regression residuals", *Economics Letters* 6: 255–259.
Johansen, S. (1988). "Statistical analysis of cointegration vectors," *Journal of Economic Dynamics and Control* 12: 231–254.
Johnston, J. and J. Dinardo (1997). *Econometric Methods*. New York: McGraw–Hill.
Keynes, J.M. (1939). "Professor Tinbergen's method", *Economic Journal* 49: 558–568.
Klein, L.R. and R.M. Young (1980). *An Introduction to Econometric Forecasting and Forecasting Models*. Lexington, Massachusetts: Lexington Books, D.C. Health.
Kmenta, J. (1986). *Elements of Econometrics*. London: Macmillan.
Koenker, R. (1981). "A note on studentizing a test for heteroscedasticity", *Journal of Econometrics* 17: 107–112.
Koreisha, S.G. and Pukkila, T. (1998). "A two-step approach to identifying seasonal autoregressive time series forecasting models", *International Journal of Forecasting* 14: 483–496.
Koyck, L.M. (1954). *Distributed Lags and Investment Analysis*. Amsterdam: North–Holland.
Liu, T.C. (1960). "Underidentification, structural estimation and forecasting", *Econometrica* 28: 855–865.

Ljung, G.M. and G.E.P. Box (1978). "On a measure of lack of fit in time series models", *Biometrika* 65: 297–303.

Lucas, R.E. (1976). "Economic policy evaluation: A critique", *Journal of Monetary Economics* 1 (Supplementary Series): 19–46.

MacDonald, R. and C. Kearney (1987). "On the specification of Granger-causality tests using the cointegration methodology", *Economics Letters* 25: 149–153.

MacKinnon, J.G. (1991). "Critical values for cointegration tests", chap. 13, in R.F. Engle and C.W.J. Granger (eds.), *Long Run Economic Relationships*. London: Oxford University Press.

Maddala, G.S. (1977). *Econometrics*. New York: McGraw–Hill.

Mincer, J. and V. Zarnowitz (1969). "The evaluation of economic forecasts", pp. 3–46, in J. Mincer (ed.), *Economic Forecasts and Expectations*. New York: National Bureau of Economic Research; New York: Columbia University Press.

Mizon, G.E. (1995). "A simple message for autocorrelation correctors: Don't", *Journal of Econometrics* 69: 267–288.

Morgenstern, O. (1950). *On the Accuracy of Economic Observations*. Princeton, New Jersey: Princeton University Press.

Mosconi, R. and C. Giannini (1992). "Non causality in cointegrated systems: Representation, estimation and testing", *Oxford Bulletin of Economics and Statistics* 54, no. 3: 399–417.

Osterwald–Lenum, M. (1992). "A note with quantiles of the asymptotic distribution of the maximum likelihood cointegration rank test statistics", *Oxford Bulletin of Economics and Statistics* 54: 461–472.

Pankratz, A. (1983). *Forecasting with Univariate Box Jenkins Models*. New York: John Wiley & Sons.

Phillips, P.C.B. and S. Ouliaris (1990). "Asymptotic properties of residual-based tests for cointegration", *Econometrica* 58: 165–193.

Pierce, D.A. and L.D. Haugh (1977). "Causality in temporal systems: Characterizations and a survey", *Journal of Econometrics* 5: 265–293.

Pindyck, R.S. and D.L. Rubinfeld (1998). *Econometric Models and Economic Forecasts*, 4th edition. New York: Irwin/McGraw–Hill.

Ramsey, J.B. (1969). "Test for specification errors in classical linear least squares regression analysis", *Journal of the Royal Statistical Society B*, 31: 350–371.

Savin, N.E. and K.J. White (1977). "The Durbin–Watson test for serial correlation with extreme sample sizes or many regressors", *Econometrica* 45: 1989–1996.

Sims, C.A. (1972). "Money, income and causality", *American Economic Review* 62: 540–552.

Sims, C.A. (1980). "Macroeconomics and reality", *Econometrica* 48: 1–48.

Sowey, E. (1985). "Econometrics: The quantitative approach to economics", *Economic Review* 2: 26–29.

Stock, J.H. (1987). "Asymptotic properties of least squares estimators of cointegrating vectors", *Econometrica* 55: 1035–1056.

Suits, D.B. (1962). "Forecasting and analysis with an econometric model", *American Economic Review* 52: 104–132.

Theil, H. (1966). *Applied Economic Forecasting*. Amsterdam: North–Holland.

Thursby, J.G. and P. Schmidt (1977). "Some properties of tests for specification error in a linear regression model", *Journal of the American Statistical Association* 72: 635–641.

Watson, P.K. (1987). "On the abuse of statistical criteria in the evaluation of econometric models with particular reference to the Caribbean", *Social and Economic Studies* 36, no. 3: 119–148.

Watson, P.K. and R. Clarke (1997). "A policy oriented macro econometric model of Trinidad and Tobago", pp. 265–337, in E. Edinval, A. Maurin and J.G. Montauban (eds.), *Stratégies de développement comparées dans la Caraïbe*. Paris: L'Hermès.

White, H. (1980). "A heteroscedasticity-consistent covariance matrix estimator and a direct test for heteroscedasticity", *Econometrica* 50: 1–25.

Index

H

I

J

K

L

M

N

O

P

R

S

T

U

V

W